AMERICAN BOOK COMPANY'S

PASSING THE
SOCIAL STUDIES
GRADUATION TEST
IN
GEORGIA

2nd Edition
(based on the revised, updated Quality Core Curriculum)

DEVIN PINTOZZI
BRIAN FREEL
DR. FRANK J. PINTOZZI

AMERICAN BOOK COMPANY
P O BOX 2638
WOODSTOCK, GEORGIA 30188-1383
TOLL FREE: 1 (888) 264-5877   PHONE: 770-928-2834   FAX: 770-928-7483

ACKNOWLEDGEMENTS

We gratefully acknowledge the editing and proofreading contributions of Kelly Berg, Maria Struder, and Colleen Pintozzi. We want to thank Kelly Berg for her expertise in formatting and developing the graphics for this book. We are also grateful to the editors of *National Geographic* for permission to use selections from this periodical. Finally, we acknowledge the many students and teachers whose needs and suggestions have guided us in preparing this book.

Printed in the United States of America.

09/03   07/04

TABLE OF CONTENTS

GEORGIA SOCIAL STUDIES

PREFACE

PASSING THE SOCIAL STUDIES GRADUATION TEST IN GEORGIA (2nd Edition) will help students preparing for the Social Studies Graduation Test during their junior year of high school. This book will also assist students who have failed this test and need to review concepts and skills before taking the test again.

How Is This Revised 2nd Edition Different From the 1st Edition?

This revised 2nd edition reflects the changes made in the standards and objectives of the Quality Core Curriculum in 1997 as published by the Georgia State Department of Education. These revised standards and objectives were implemented on the Georgia High School Graduation Test in the spring of 1999. **The materials in this book are based on the revised and updated objectives and content descriptions for the Social Studies Graduation Test published by the Georgia Department of Education.**

In this book, you will find: 1) General information about the test; 2) A diagnostic test; 3) Chapters that teach concepts and skills emphasized on the test; 4) Two practice tests. Answers to tests and exercises are in a separate key.

We welcome comments and suggestions about this book. Please contact the publishers at:

American Book Company
PO Box 2638
Woodstock, GA 30188-1383

Toll Free: 1 (888) 264-5877
Phone: (770) 928-2834
Fax: (770) 928-7483

Web Site: www.americanbookcompany.com

ABOUT THE AUTHORS

Dr. Frank J. Pintozzi is a Professor of Reading/ESOL at Kennesaw State University, Kennesaw, Georgia. For over 28 years, he has taught English and reading at the high school and college levels as well as in teacher preparation courses in language arts and social studies.

Devin Pintozzi is a graduate of Oglethorpe University in Atlanta where he majored in psychology and minored in history. He is a full-time writer who strives for clear and concise communication in his publications. Currently, he is a master's degree student at Georgia State University.

Brian Freel holds a B.A. degree from Amherst College in Amherst, Massachusetts and a M.A. degree from St. Mary's University in Baltimore, Maryland. He is a writer specializing in United States and world history. He has taught students at middle school, high school, and adult levels.

The Pintozzis are the authors of the first edition of *Passing the Social Studies Graduation Test in Georgia (1996)*. They have also written best-selling books and software on passing graduation exams in Alabama, Florida, Minnesota, South Carolina, and Tennessee.

PREPARING FOR THE SOCIAL STUDIES HIGH SCHOOL GRADUATION TEST IN GEORGIA

INTRODUCTION

Students who entered grade nine after July 1, 1994, must pass the **Georgia High School Graduation Test in Social Studies** to receive a secondary school diploma. This test is one of five exams now required for graduation from Georgia high schools. The other tests are Mathematics, Writing, English Language Arts, and Science.

This book will help you prepare for the **Georgia High School Graduation Test in Social Studies**. The questions and answers that follow will provide you with general information about the **Georgia High School Graduation Test in Social Studies**.

In the first section of this book, you'll take a **Social Studies Diagnostic Test** to determine your strengths and areas for improvement. In the chapters that follow, you will learn and practice social studies skills and strategies that are important in preparing for this test. The last section of **Passing the Social Studies Graduation Test in Georgia (2nd Edition)** contains two practice tests that will provide further preparation for the actual social studies test.

What Is The Georgia High School Graduation Test in Social Studies?

For the **Georgia High School Graduation Test in Social Studies,** students will answer 90 multiple-choice questions based on world history, United States history, citizenship and government, map and globe skills, and information processing.

Why Must I Pass the Georgia High School Graduation Test in Social Studies?

You are required to pass this test for several reasons. First, the state of Georgia, your future employers, and your community need an educated workforce. Secondly, knowledge of United States history, world history, and government is essential for understanding current social and political issues and for contributing to the democratic process of government on the local, state, and national levels. Thirdly, understanding the lessons of the past often offers solutions to the challenges of the present and the major concerns of the future. Finally, by demonstrating your knowledge of United States history and world history, you can show what you have learned in school and apply this knowledge to new situations and experiences.

When Do I Take the Georgia High School Graduation Test in Social Studies?

During your junior year in high school, you must take the **Georgia High School Graduation Test in Social Studies**.

How Much Time Do I Have To Take the Test?

After completing an information sheet, you will have two hours to take the test. You may also be able to request additional time.

What Happens If I Don't Pass the Test?

You may take the **Georgia High School Graduation Test in Social Studies** up to four times before the end of the twelfth grade. The first time that you take this exam is during your junior year. You will then have three more times to pass the test before you finish high school. Students may continue to take the test as many times as necessary after leaving school.

If I Fail the Social Studies Exam, Where Can I Get Help To Pass It the Next Time?

You can sign up for summer courses in your school district. The instructors in these courses will teach you how to study and prepare for the **Georgia High School Graduation Test in Social Studies.** You can also seek extra help in classes during your senior year in high school. Finally, you can work with tutors who can help you pass the graduation test.

How Is My Test Scored?

Scoring for your test is based on four areas of social studies. The percentages of your score assigned to each area are:

1)   World Studies - 18-20%
2)   United States History to 1865 - 18-20%
3)   United States History since 1865 - 18-20%
4)   Citizenship/Government - 12-14%
5)   Map and Globe Skills - 15%
6)   Information-Processing Skills -15%

SOCIAL STUDIES DIAGNOSTIC TEST

1. The Protestant Reformation in England differed from the reform movements in other countries in which of the following ways?

   A. Political rivalries mixed with religious differences caused civil war.
   B. England was divided into Catholic and Protestant sections.
   C. The Church of England retained many of the practices of the Catholic Church.
   D. The criticism of the Roman Catholic Church focused more on religious differences than political differences.

2. The French Revolution threw France and Europe into more than 10 years of turmoil. This democratic revolt had far reaching consequences. Which of the following was **not** a result of the French Revolution?

   A. encouraged legal equality of citizens
   B. strengthened the French economy
   C. provided a model for revolutions in other countries
   D. promoted nationalism throughout Europe

3. According to this theory, a nation's power is measured by its gold reserves. A country strives to export more than it imports in order to create a surplus of gold. This theory is called

   A. capitalism.   C. socialism.
   B. supply side economics.   D. mercantilism.

4. Which of the following methods does the Federal Reserve System (Fed) use to change interest rates and monetary inflation?

   I. The Fed sets the minimum percentage that investors must purchase in cash when they purchase stocks on margin.
   II. The Fed purchases and sells Treasury bills to and from banks and investors.
   III. The Fed sets the discount interest rate at which banks can borrow money from the government.
   IV. The Fed sets the minimum percentage of money that banks must keep in storage and may not lend.

   A. I and II   C. I, II, and III
   B. II, III, and IV   D. all of the above

5. The main difference between communism and fascism in the 1930s was that

   A. fascism permitted a capitalist economy while communism did not.
   B. communism adopted an expansionist philosophy while fascism did not.
   C. fascism encouraged multiple political parties while communism did not.
   D. communism wanted the king to remain in office while fascism did not.

6. San Francisco, with its beautiful bay, became a favorite area of settlement. Because the city is situated on the San Andreas Fault, it was prone to earthquakes. In 1906, a terrible earthquake leveled the city. As a result, city planners took the initiative and built all future buildings with foundations that were sunk deep into the earth to keep buildings standing when the earth buckled.

   Earthquakes are a constant threat in San Francisco because

   A. cities near a bay are susceptible to earthquakes.
   B. the city is located near the ocean.
   C. builders have tried to make their buildings earthquake proof.
   D. the city is built on the San Andreas Fault.

7. Japan is an island nation completely surrounded by water. Culturally, one would expect that

   A. Japan possesses great diversity through invasion and immigration.
   B. the Japanese people share a common culture.
   C. shipping is the main industry of the nation.
   D. the Japanese have not developed an advanced culture.

8. As settlers moved through the mainland United States, they often decided to build settlements near fast-flowing rivers and waterfalls.

   Which statement best explains why this occurred?

   A. Fast rivers and waterfalls provided a good source of power for mills.
   B. Irrigation could be increased near fast-moving rivers.
   C. Gold was often found near waterfall regions.
   D. Fishing was best around waterfalls and fast-flowing rivers.

9. Granted a charter in 1628, the Massachusetts Bay Colony became a haven for which of the following groups?

   A. colonial trading companies   C. Puritans
   B. plantation farmers   D. fishing companies

10. The conflict considered to be the beginning of the Revolutionary War is the

   A. Boston Tea Party.   C. Battle of Lexington.
   B. Boston Massacre.   D. Battle of Bunker Hill.

11. In 1812, some members of Congress wanted to go to war with Great Britain because

   A. the British were forcing United States sailors to serve in their navy.
   B. Britain refused to ship goods to the United States.
   C. Britain was trying to recapture land in the United States.
   D. the British were sinking French ships.

2

12. President Andrew Jackson believed in appointing his friends and allies to well-paying jobs in government. This approach to democracy was called

    A. federalism.
    B. the Jackson Doctrine.
    C. Majority Rules.
    D. the spoils system.

13. As part of the Compromise of 1850, the Fugitive Slave Law

    A. required states in the North to return escaped slaves to their owners in the South.
    B. allowed slaves who escaped to the North to get jobs and be paid for their work.
    C. protected fugitive slaves in the North from being returned to their owners in the South.
    D. gave slaves who escaped to the North the right to bear arms and become Union soldiers in the Civil War.

14. Which of the following helped to secure the rights of blacks during the time of Reconstruction?

    I.   Freedman's Bureau
    II. Jim Crow Laws
    III. Black Codes
    IV. Fourteenth and Fifteenth Amendments to the United States Constitution

    A. I, II, and III
    B. II, III, and IV
    C. I and IV
    D. II and III

15. Why did the United States turn to a policy of imperialism at the turn of the twentieth century?

    I.   The United States needed colonies to feed its people.
    II. The United States wanted to influence the world balance of power.
    III. The United States produced a surplus of goods that needed foreign markets.
    IV. The United States wanted to supply other countries with raw materials.

    A. I and II
    B. II and III
    C. II, III, and IV
    D. I, II, III, and IV

16. In the early twentieth century, the United States emerged as a world power by gaining formerly held Spanish territory in the Spanish-American War. To keep the Philippines from becoming independent, 4,200 United States soldiers and an estimated 220,000 Filipinos died fighting each other from 1899 to 1902.

    What problem of foreign policy does this passage address?

    A. immigration and national security
    B. economic growth and manifest destiny
    C. imperialism versus self-determination
    D. spheres of influence versus open door policy

17. In 1904, New York City constructed the first subway providing rapid travel for the public. Why was the subway an advantage over other means of public transportation?

    A. Subways did not interfere with other modes of traffic.
    B. Subway fares were higher than public carriage fares.
    C. Cities with subway systems enjoyed a rise in their property values.
    D. Dilapidated buildings could be destroyed to make room for new subway systems.

18. Harry S Truman made the decision to drop the first of two atomic bombs on Japan on August 6, 1945. This led to Japan's immediate surrender and the end of World War II. Why did President Truman decide to use the atomic bomb?

    A. Japan was gaining military victories.
    B. Thousands of American soldiers probably would have died in the invasion of the Japanese mainland.
    C. Previous bombings of Japan had been ineffective in causing damage.
    D. Atomic bombs were more inexpensive than other bombs.

19. Which of the following issues led to the development of a Cold War policy between the United States and the Soviet Union?

    A. laser technology   C. neutral zones
    B. nuclear weapons   D. peacekeeping organizations

20. Passed in 1935, the Social Security Act (SSA) was legislation that provided income and medical care for the elderly. The act also compensated unemployed workers. The money was primarily derived from the paychecks of all employees and employers.

    What was important about the passing of the Social Security Act (SSA)?

    A. The SSA provided healthcare for all working Americans.
    B. The SSA assured that no one in the United States would have to live in poverty.
    C. The SSA produced millions of new jobs in the United States economy.
    D. The SSA gave government the responsibility of providing for the elderly and the unemployed.

4

21. In 1913, an amendment to the Constitution was ratified that gave the federal government the right to tax a person's personal income and a corporation's profits. Why was this amendment considered "reform legislation"?

    A. Many other industrialized nations, such as Germany and Australia, had already created an income tax.
    B. Many people felt the income tax would help the United States become less materialistic.
    C. Many people felt that a level playing field would be created, providing social services for the poor at the expense of the rich, who had to pay higher taxes on their incomes.
    D. Writers and journalists had promoted for years the idea that all Americans wanted their income taxed.

22. Which of the following events led to the passage of the Civil Rights Act of 1964, the first major piece of civil rights legislation in the 1960s?

    A. the March on Washington
    B. the Freedom March from Selma to Montgomery
    C. the assassination of President John F. Kennedy
    D. both A and C

23. Which of the following men accepted segregation and founded the Tuskeegee Institute in Alabama?

    A. George Washington Carver   C. George Plessy
    B. W. E. B. Du Bois   D. Booker T. Washington

Use this map for questions 24 and 25.

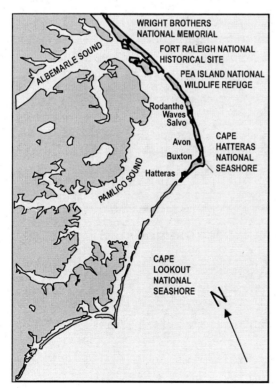

24. If someone traveled from Buxton to the Fort Raleigh National Historical Site, in what direction would he or she be traveling?

    A. northwest   C. east
    B. north   D. southeast

25. Traveling northeast from the city of Hatteras, which of the following places would someone discover?

    A. Pamlico Sound
    B. Albemarle Sound
    C. Cape Lookout National Seashore
    D. Buxton

Use the map below to answer questions 26 and 27.

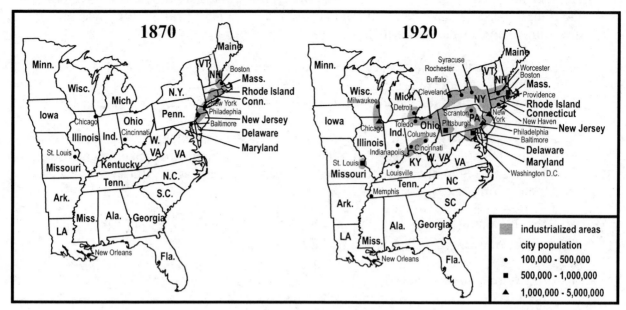

26. By comparing the maps above, one can conclude that

    A. millions of immigrants moved to the United States during this time.
    B. reconstruction promoted an agricultural economy in the South.
    C. people left the South and moved north because of the climate.
    D. the growth of industry in the North resulted in the formation of large cities.

27. What explains the fact that most of the large cities on the maps above are located near water?

    A. People like to live near the water so they settled there.
    B. Waterways provided the most economical way to transport goods.
    C. Farms in the interior of the country could not supply enough food for nearby cities.
    D. When immigrants came to the United States, they didn't want to move inland.

Use the timeline below to answer questions 28 and 29.

1492 Columbus reaches America	1513 Balboa reaches Pacific Ocean	1535 Cartier explores St. Lawrence Seaway	1539 Hernando de Soto explores the Southeast	1565 Spanish settle St. Augustine	1587 "Lost Colony" established by English at Roanoke

28. Which country was the first to establish a settlement in North America?

    A. England   C. Spain
    B. France   D. Portugal

29. In what year did an explorer cross the isthmus of Panama to reach the Pacific Ocean?

    A. 1492   C. 1535
    B. 1513   D. 1539

Read newspaper reports I - IV which describe the Reconstruction efforts of President Andrew Johnson to enforce new Constitutional Amendments during August, 1868. Then answer questions 30-31.

I.   The laws may be permanently engraved into the Constitution, but we intend to make them dead words on a printed page. – Lee Collins, *The Southern Times*

II. This is an important age for all of us in our country. Now the Negro and the white man can stand on equal footing. Each man possesses the same legal rights. – Fred Blake, *The New York Gazette*

III. Johnson's Reconstruction initiatives are now underway. Federal troops have been sent in and the South divided into federal districts to ensure that colored people retain their new rights. – Peter Holcomb, *The Nation*

IV. Reconstruction is benefiting our fellow Negroes in the South. Their new schools and free communities are being protected from Ku Klux Klan attacks. The new armies of federal troops are doing great work in the South. – John Maye, *Northern Evening Journal*

30. Which of the reports clearly demonstrate(s) fact rather than opinion?

    A.   III and IV   C.   III only
    B.   II and III   D.   I, II, and IV

31. On the basis of the information presented in the above reports, which conclusion can be drawn?

    A.   During Reconstruction, views about the rights of former slaves varied.
    B.   Northerners were oppressing Southerners during Reconstruction.
    C.   African Americans were being denied their legal rights in the North.
    D.   Fred Blake wished to prevent African Americans from using their new found rights.

32. Free speech is a right all citizens enjoy by the First Amendment. However, no citizen is allowed to use the right of free speech to threaten someone else's life or property.

Why is the right of free speech limited in this way?

    A.   The Twenty-fifth Amendment to the Constitution prohibits verbal threats.
    B.   The Constitution gives the police the right to interpret the Constitution.
    C.   The protection of the whole nation is more important than individual rights.
    D.   Rights can be exercised as long as they do not interfere with another person's rights to life or property.

33. Which of the following is an example of an implied Constitutional power of Congress?

    A.   Congress establishes committees to look into environmental legislation.
    B.   Congress declares war.
    C.   Congress decides to borrow money on United States credit.
    D.   Congress imposes a tariff on imported furniture.

Use the map below to answer questions 34 and 35.

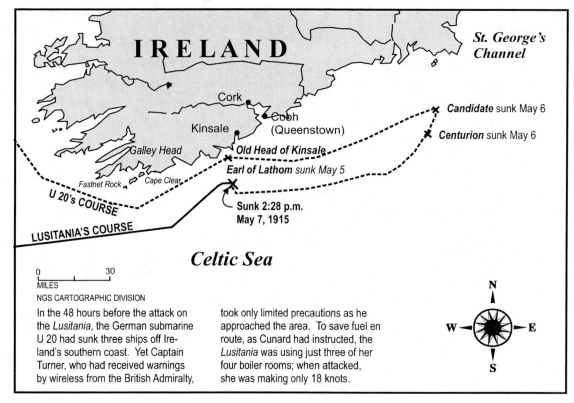

IRELAND

St. George's Channel

Cork
Cobh
(Queenstown)
Kinsale
Galley Head
Old Head of Kinsale
Earl of Lathom sunk May 5
Fastnet Rock
Cape Clear
U 20's COURSE
LUSITANIA'S COURSE
Sunk 2:28 p.m.
May 7, 1915

Candidate sunk May 6
Centurion sunk May 6

Celtic Sea

0   30
MILES
NGS CARTOGRAPHIC DIVISION

In the 48 hours before the attack on the *Lusitania*, the German submarine U 20 had sunk three ships off Ireland's southern coast. Yet Captain Turner, who had received warnings by wireless from the British Admiralty, took only limited precautions as he approached the area. To save fuel en route, as Cunard had instructed, the *Lusitania* was using just three of her four boiler rooms; when attacked, she was making only 18 knots.

N
W   E
S

34. In which direction was the *Lusitania* moving when it was sunk?

   A. west   C. north
   B. east   D. south

35. On what day was the U-20 closest to eastern Ireland?

   A. May 5, 1915   C. May 7, 1915
   B. May 6, 1915   D. May 8, 1915

36. The United States Constitution retained which of the following features from the Articles of Confederation?

   A. a national tax system
   B. Congressional control over foreign commerce
   C. a system of checks and balances
   D. a requirement that states ratify amendments

37. Under Chief Justice John Marshall, the Supreme Court ruled in *Marbury vs. Madison* (1803) that the Judiciary Act, passed by Congress, was unconstitutional. This ruling was important because it established that

   A. Congress could not pass laws.
   B. the President had the authority to appoint Supreme Court justices.
   C. the Supreme Court had the power to review any law passed by Congress.
   D. the President could not appoint federal judges.

Use the map below to answer questions 38 and 39.

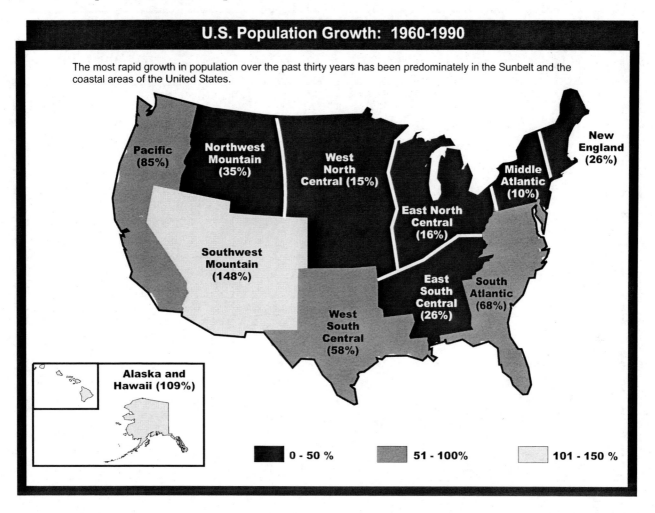

U.S. Population Growth: 1960-1990

The most rapid growth in population over the past thirty years has been predominately in the Sunbelt and the coastal areas of the United States.

Pacific (85%)
Northwest Mountain (35%)
West North Central (15%)
New England (26%)
Middle Atlantic (10%)
East North Central (16%)
Southwest Mountain (148%)
East South Central (26%)
South Atlantic (68%)
West South Central (58%)
Alaska and Hawaii (109%)

0 - 50 %   51 - 100%   101 - 150 %

38. Based on the map, what is the best summary of the population growth between 1960 and 1990?

    A. The population has migrated to the Southern and Western United States
    B. The population has grown evenly across the nation.
    C. The population in the Midwest will now grow faster than the South.
    D. The population is growing the fastest in the Pacific region.

39. Which of the following best explains why the population has grown rapidly in the South Atlantic Region?

    A. People enjoy lower tax rates in this area.
    B. Natural resources are more plentiful in this area.
    C. Many people in the United States prefer warmer, coastal climates.
    D. The water supply in the South Atlantic region is plentiful.

Use the chart below to answer questions 40-42.

	Country A	Country B
Total Population	7,193,000	123,120,000

Urban-Rural
   Urban
   Rural
	49.0%
	51.0%
		76.7%
		23.3%

Religious	Roman Catholic 92.5% Baha'i 2.6% Other 4.9%	Shinto* 89.5% Buddhist* 76.4% Christian 1.2% Other 9.3%

Life Expectancy
at Birth (years)
   Male
   Female
	50.9
	55.4
		75.9
		82.1

Age Distribution
   Under 15
   15-29
   30-44
   45-59
   60-74
   Over 74
	
	43.4%
	26.4%
	9.3%
	4.4%
	0.8 %
		
		19.0%
		21.6%
		9.2%
		9.2%
		7.7%

Percent of Population Over 25 With No Formal Schooling	48.6%	0.3%
Leading Exports (as percent of total exports):	Natural Gas 21.0% Tin 12.0% Zinc 5.7% Silver 5.6% Antimony 4.0% Coffee 2.0% Sugar 1.5% Hides 1.4%	Motor Vehicles 18.4% Machinery 10.9% Iron & Steel 5.8% Chemicals 5.3% Textiles 2.6% Vessels 1.5% Radios 0.8% Televisions 0.7%
		*Some persons practice both religions

40. Which of the following statements accurately describes Country A?

  A. Its leading exports are raw materials.
  B. It probably has a high literacy rate.
  C. It has a predominantly urban population.
  D. It will experience slow population growth.

41. Which of the following statements most accurately describes Country B?

  A. It has few medical facilities.
  B. It is industrialized.
  C. Its primary imports are manufactured goods.
  D. Its population is primarily employed in agriculture.

42. By examining the major religions, Country B is most likely

  A. Botswana   C. Ireland
  B. India   D. Japan

43. Which of the following is **not** a power of Congress?

  A. the power to pass laws
  B. the power to create and pass the federal budget
  C. the power to appoint Supreme Court Justices
  D. the power to approve presidential appointments to federal offices

44. The power to veto a bill has been given to the _____ branch. The power to impeach the President has been given to the _____ branch.

  Which of the following best fills in the blanks?

  A. executive, legislative   C. legislative, judicial
  B. executive, judicial   D. judicial, legislative

45. What are the two problems associated with continued reliance on oil as the primary energy source in the developed world?

  I.   Oil produces air pollution when it is burned.
  II. Oil is scarce throughout the world.
  III. Oil has a wide variety of uses.
  IV. The developed world is dependent on the Middle East to satisfy its consumption of oil.

  A. I and II   C. II and II
  B. II and IV   D. I and IV

EVALUATION CHART
SOCIAL STUDIES DIAGNOSTIC TEST

Directions: On the following chart, circle the question numbers that you answered incorrectly, and evaluate the results. Then turn to the appropriate topics (listed by chapters and parts), read the explanations, and complete the exercises. Review the other chapters as needed. Finally, complete the Practice Social Studies Tests at the end of the book to further prepare yourself for the **Georgia High School Graduation Test in Social Studies.**

CHAPTER 1
TRANSFORMATION IN EUROPE

RENAISSANCE

The term **Renaissance** literally means "rebirth" and refers to the great cultural developments and societal changes that began in 14th century Italy and spread to the rest of Europe in the 16th and 17th centuries.

Italy's central location in the Mediterranean region made it the crossroads for commerce between Western Europe and the **Levant** (countries of the eastern Mediterranean). Urban centers, like Florence and Venice, provided opportunities for the mingling of ideas and cultures between East and West, as well as surplus wealth to finance painters, architects, poets, and scholars.

**Doge's Palace courtyard
Renaissance Italy, Venice**

KEY FEATURES OF THE RENAISSANCE

- rise of **humanism** (focus on ancient Greek and Roman civilization and the dignity and worth of the individual)
- independence and individualism of persons and states
- decreased political and social influence of the Roman Catholic Church, though strong popular religious fervor
- decreased specialization - encouragement of upper and middle classes to be educated in various arts and sciences
- spirit of innovation, curiosity, and openness to new experiences yielded advances in the arts and sciences

Education

The intellectuals of the Renaissance believed they were beginning a new age of history. They studied the ancient Greek and Roman civilizations as models for learning and culture. They looked down on the centuries which followed the fall of the western Roman empire and considered them **barbaric** (ignorant, uncultured, primitive). Because these centuries were between the great ancient civilizations and their own time, they called them the Middle Ages or the Dark Ages (400s to 1400s). The tendency of the Renaissance to emphasize study of the **classics** (of ancient Greece or Rome) and to regard classical civilization as the model and goal of all culture is called **humanism**. Humanism came to emphasize the dignity and worth of the individual. During the Renaissance, students didn't specialize but sought to develop their individual talents in a wide variety of disciplines: from poetry and math to sword fighting and wrestling. Renaissance education encouraged development of the body and character as well as the mind, and it emphasized the duties of citizenship. In contrast, **medieval** (of the Middle Ages) education focused on the supernatural and the spiritual.

Science and Technology

The Renaissance emphasized careful observation of nature and reality. The spirit of openness to new possibilities and excitement over exploration spurred scientific inquiry. During this time, **Nicolas Copernicus** (1473-1543) put forth his theory that the Earth and other planets revolve around the sun. His idea clashed with the dominant religious and scientific view that the Earth was the center of the universe. Copernicus's idea did not become popular until it was developed later by Galileo and Isaac Newton.

Johannes Gutenberg

In 1543, the Belgian physician **Andreas Vesalius** (1514-64) published his seven volume work *On the Structure of the Human Body*. It was the most accurate and comprehensive textbook of anatomy to date because it included detailed illustrations by a talented artist, and it was based on human dissections, unlike earlier books that were based on animal dissections.

The development of the moveable metal type printing press by **Johannes Gutenberg** (1400?-1468) in 1450 exerted a powerful influence on education, religion, and politics. Printed books allowed scholars to work with identical texts and share their insights, making scholarship less individual and more collaborative. The publication of the **Gutenberg Bible** (1456) put a Latin translation of the Christian Scriptures into the hands of the **laity** (not church officials). Further, the press allowed various political and philosophical ideas to be circulated rapidly through printed pamphlets.

Politics

During the 13th and 14th centuries, the **popes** (leaders of the Roman Catholic Church) were occupied with political struggles and internal conflicts. This provided a good opportunity for the growing Italian cities to extend their influence into the surrounding countryside. At the same time, other European kingdoms were centralizing power in their own domains. These growing states saw themselves more as independent countries than as members of one Europe united by the Roman Catholic Church. They were concerned with self-preservation. *The Prince* (1513), written by **Niccoló Machiavelli** (1469-1527), shows the spirit of the Renaissance by its use of secular principles in discussing government. Machiavelli claimed that the state could use whatever means necessary to preserve itself. In other words, the end justified the means.

The Arts

While the humanist focus on Roman and Greek civilization during the Renaissance led to slavish imitation of classical art and literature, the spirit of new possibilities led to various important innovations. Interest in the arts was no longer limited to the upper classes and the church; wealthy members of the merchant class commissioned artists, also. Renaissance individuality encouraged these artists to try daring experiments in the pursuit of personal fame. Although religious themes were still very important, artistic subject matter broadened to include secular subjects of the natural and human world.

1. Literature

Dante Alighieri (1265-1321) wrote his epic poem the *Divine Comedy* (1307-1321) in Italian rather than the traditional Latin. Although the story was rooted in medieval religious thought, its powerful interest in all aspects of human life and behavior paved the way for Renaissance literature to follow. The love sonnets of **Petrarch** (1304-1374) were also written in the **vernacular** (native language of the area). They contributed to the flourishing of humanist literature in 15th century Italy.

In the 16th century, the influence of Italian Renaissance literature spread to the rest of Europe. In Spain, **Miguel de Cervantes Saavedra** produced his allegorical novel *Don Quixote* (Part I, 1605; Part II, 1615). Meanwhile, England's literature included the poetry and plays of Edmund Spenser, Christopher Marlowe, and **William Shakespeare**.

2. Music

Like other artists and intellectuals of the Renaissance, musicians showed an interest in experimentation and a desire to address the needs of secular society. Unlike other art forms, however, the innovations in music began in France, where composers developed songs involving **polyphony** (many voices and melodies moving differently at the same time). These technical innovations were used in church music, but an important trend of the Renaissance was that music gained popularity outside of the church. Men and women of the upper classes were expected to understand music, and they enjoyed singing and playing various instruments. Sometimes melodies from sacred music were used for popular entertainment.

3. Painting, Sculpture, and Architecture

The 14th century Florentine painter **Giotto** (1267-1337) is regarded as the forerunner of Renaissance painting because of his break with traditional medieval art. He based his work on observations of the real world, unlike the stylized, two-dimensional representations of earlier art. A century later, **Massacio** (1401-1428) built on Giotto's innovations by using scientific principles to paint in three dimensions.

Mona Lisa

Leonardo da Vinci (1452-1519) epitomized the Renaissance by his skill in various areas, such as sculpture, painting, architecture, science, and engineering. His varied interests resulted in many unfinished works. In fact, he never completed a sculpture nor a building project. In his fresco, *The Last Supper* (1495-1497), da Vinci revived Massacio's techniques and presented a traditional theme, Jesus Christ's last meal, in a new way. (A **fresco** is painted on fresh plaster with pigments dissolved in water.) In his *Mona Lisa* (1503-1506), he showed mastery of small transitions in color and defining forms through contrasts of light and shadow. The *Mona Lisa* is the most popular painting in the world.

Da Vinci's scientific pursuits were well ahead of his time, but he never published or even finished any books. He wrote only in his notebooks, and he wrote backwards so that his writings could only be read if held up to a mirror. He also performed dissections of human bodies and made detailed drawings of them.

In his early 20s, **Michelangelo** (1475-1564) completed one of the most famous works of art in history, the *Pietá* (1498-1500). This statue is a moving depiction of Mary holding her dead son, Jesus, across her lap. The following year he began work on his 14 foot tall marble statue *David* (1501-1504). While the statue had a basis in classical sculpture, Michelangelo added powerful emotion to formal beauty. Between 1508 and 1512, Michelangelo worked on high scaffolding to paint the ceiling of the **Sistine Chapel** in Rome, Italy. Using nine scenes from the book of Genesis in the Bible, he demonstrated his masterly understanding of human anatomy and movement in mighty images that changed the course of painting in Europe. Michalangelo's greatest architectural achievement was the dome of St. Peter's Basilica in Rome. The dome became a symbol of authority and influenced the majority

St. Peter's Basilica
Vatican City, Rome

15

of domes in the Western world, including the Capitol in Washington, DC. Considering all of these achievements, it is little wonder that the Renaissance poet Ludovico Ariosto described Michelangelo as: "Michael more than mortal, divine angel."

Raphael (1483-1520) learned from both da Vinci and Michelangelo. He painted the fresco *The School of Athens* (1509-1511) in the Vatican palace. His subjects, including Plato and Aristotle, showed the humanism of the time, and his style exhibited the principles of symmetry and perspective common in Renaissance art. In 1513, Pope Leo X commissioned Raphael as the chief architect for renovations to St. Peter's Basilica in Rome.

THE PROTESTANT REFORMATION

The Renaissance ideals encouraged people to read literature like the Bible and early writings of the church with a critical eye. Scholars did not rely on the church's Latin translation of the Bible but returned to the sources, the Greek and Hebrew manuscripts. As people studied the Bible, they wanted to reform the church by abolishing some religious practices. The **Protestant Reformation** refers to the 16th century movement that called for change in practices of the Roman Catholic Church and resulted in the development of separate churches.

Germany

On October 31, 1517, **Martin Luther** (1483-1546) displayed his **95 Theses**, a list of practices he thought the Catholic Church needed to change. The Catholic Church relied on its traditions as well as the Bible to understand God, but Luther believed that the Bible was the only source of God's truth. He also believed that a person is made right in the eyes of God only by faith and not by works, as many people of the time believed. Luther argued God's grace is freely given. It cannot be earned, but a person must accept it. He believed that God worked through people of all occupations and vocations, not just church officials.

Martin Luther

In 1546, the Holy Roman Emperor, in alliance with the Pope, waged war on the Protestant princes. The bitter conflict ended nearly ten years later with the **Peace of Augsburg** in 1555. Under this agreement, each ruler of the approximately 300 German states chose the religion for his region and enforced it on his subjects. The result was a Germany divided about one half Lutheran and one half Roman Catholic, thus ending European religious unity under the authority of the Pope.

Switzerland

Huldreich Zwingli (1484-1531) led the Protestant reform in Switzerland. The initially peaceful defiance of the Roman Catholic Church soon led to civil war and Zwingli's death. A peace agreement (1531), similar to that in Germany, divided Switzerland into Roman Catholic and Protestant sections, which remain to this day.

Geneva

In the generation after Luther and Zwingli, **John Calvin** (1509-64) was the leading Protestant reformer. Fleeing persecution in his native France, Calvin accepted an invitation from the newly independent republic of Geneva to lead its religious reform. Despite his liberal encouragement of prayer in the vernacular, education for all citizens, and democratic election of church officials, Calvin cooperated with civil authorities to enforce strict regulations on the

16

dress and behavior of Geneva's residents. Those who resisted Geneva's laws and beliefs were persecuted or expelled.

Calvin founded a university in Geneva that became famous for training pastors and teachers. He developed a clear and logical Protestant theology that spread to various countries, such as Switzerland, France, and Scotland. Today's Presbyterian church is rooted in the teachings of Calvin.

France

Initially the king of France used persecution to prevent Luther's teachings from spreading through France, but as Calvin's ideas became popular, France divided into warring factions of Catholics and Protestants. These brutal **Wars of Religion** (circa 1562-1598) tore France apart for the last half of the 16th century. The French Protestants were called **Hugenots**.

Spain

King Ferdinand V (1452-1516) and **Queen Isabella I** (1451-1504) established the Spanish Inquisition in 1478. The **Inquisition** was a group of appointed officials who had broad powers to enforce conformity to Roman Catholic beliefs and practices. In 1492, the monarchs expelled all of the Jews and Muslims from Spain. Because Ferdinand was developing Spain's political unity, and the Inquisition enforced religious uniformity, Protestantism had little opportunity to spread into Spain.

England

When **King Henry VIII** (1491-1547) of England split from Rome, he was not motivated by doctrinal differences, but by his desire for a male heir to the throne. In fact, the Pope had awarded him the title **Defender of the Faith** because of Henry's strong opposition to Luther. Henry's wife was **Catherine of Aragon** (1485-1536), the daughter of the Spanish monarchs Ferdinand and Isabella. Although Catherine bore him six children, only one girl survived infancy. Hoping for a male child, Henry wanted to divorce Catherine and marry another woman, **Anne Boleyn** (1507-1536). Henry asked the Pope to annul his first marriage, but the Pope refused. The Pope had already given Henry special permission to marry Catherine because she was the widow of his brother. Henry asked various church officials and theologians for support.

King Henry VIII

Zwingli and others supported him, but even Martin Luther supported the claim of the Pope. When Henry divorced and remarried, the Pope excommunicated him. Henry resolved the issue by convening Parliament in 1534 to declare the Church of England independent from Rome and the monarch of England as its head. The new church retained nearly all of the Roman Catholic practices. Henry punished and even executed those who opposed him, including both Lutherans and Roman Catholics remaining loyal to the Pope.

The Catholic Reformation

Although there had been earlier attempts at reforming the Roman Catholic Church, they were never widespread. The Protestant Reformation provided impetus for Catholics to pursue reform actively. In 1534, Paul III became Pope. He was a strong leader, and he called a meeting of all the Catholic bishops, known as the **Council of Trent** (1545-1563). The bishops addressed most, though not all of Luther's criticisms. In answer to Luther's **catechism** (book of Christian religious instruction), the council published its own *Roman Catechism* (1566). The conclusions of this council prevailed in the Catholic church for the next 400 years. Other leaders like **Ignatius of Loyola** (1491-1556) and **Charles Borromeo** (1538-1584) made important contributions to reform, such as establishing **seminaries** (schools to educate priests) and evangelizing the native peoples of Asia and the Americas.

REVOLUTION IN ENGLAND

From 1534 to 1688, England moved between periods of division and difficulty and periods of stability and prosperity. Matters of religion and politics put the monarchy in jeopardy resulting in division and even civil war. Despite these tragic problems, England was able to develop its commercial and military strength. In addition, the political unrest stirred democratic ideas and feelings that eventually spread across the globe.

Tudor Monarchs

Queen Mary I

Henry VIII, the second monarch of the Tudor family, eventually married a total of six women in his search for a male heir. Only one male child lived. This boy reigned as Edward VI from age 10 to age 16 when he died. Because of his youth, his advisors were able to manipulate policies according to their designs. One result was that the Church of England adopted more Protestant reforms than were allowed by Henry VIII. After Edward's death, the daughter of Henry's first wife acceded to the throne. **Mary I** (queen 1553-1558), also known as **Bloody Mary**, restored union with the Roman Catholic Church and burned nearly 300 Protestants who opposed her. She also led England into war with France when she married her cousin, Philip II of Spain (king, 1556-1598). When Mary I died in 1558, England entered a prosperous time under the strong leadership of Elizabeth I.

Elizabeth I (queen 1558-1603) cooperated with Parliament to lead the Church of England on a moderate path between Roman Catholicism and Protestant reforms. In 1588, England prevented invasion and showed its naval strength by defeating the large **Spanish Armada** (navy). Elizabeth further consolidated England's power by conquering Ireland in 1603. Elizabethan England enjoyed international respect due to economic prosperity, military strength, and the literary accomplishments of great poets such as **William Shakespeare** (1564-1616).

English Civil War (1642-1649)

Elizabeth's death marked the end of the Tudor family reign and the beginning of the Stuart monarchs. After Elizabeth's death, England was plagued by domestic conflict due to religious differences and battles between the king and parliament.

Elizabeth's successor **James I** (king 1603-1625) and his son **Charles I** (king 1625-1649) believed in the **divine right of kings**, that is, that their authority came directly from God and could not be limited by anyone. This belief in the sole authority of the monarch is called **absolutism**. Parliament, on the other hand, insisted on its own authority that the power of government comes from the people. Charles attempted to rule without Parliament for almost

11 years, but in 1640, he reconvened Parliament to help him raise money for a war against Scotland. Disagreements within Parliament led to armed conflict in 1642. Most of the House of Lords and some of the House of Commons sided with the king. They were called **Cavaliers**. Most of those who opposed the king were **Puritans** (people who wanted to "purify" the Anglican Church, making it simpler by eliminating practices not found in the Bible). They were called **Roundheads** because of their short hair.

Civil war divided the kingdom from 1642 to 1649 until **Oliver Cromwell's** (1599-1658) forces finally defeated the king and organized a new Parliament. The new Parliament executed King Charles I on January 30, 1649, abolished the monarchy and the House of Lords, and declared England a **commonwealth** or **republic** (a nation or state governed by the people).

When Cromwell died in September 1658, his son was unable to keep control of the military. In the midst of the political struggle, **Charles II** (king 1660-1685) returned from exile to replace his father as king of England. The return of the king is called the **Restoration**. Charles II gave strong support to the Anglican church, but his successor, **James II** (king 1685-1688), was Roman Catholic.

Oliver Cromwell

Glorious Revolution (1688-89)

James's eldest daughter, Mary, was married to a Protestant, William of Orange, a viceroy in the Netherlands. The opponents of James encouraged William to come to England to protect the inheritance of his wife, Mary. When William and Mary arrived in England, James's army deserted to support them. James fled England. Parliament gave William temporary control of the government. Then, it drafted a Bill of Rights listing the abuses of James and placing limits on the king's authority. When William and Mary agreed to this Bill of Rights, Parliament gave the crown to them jointly. The government was now a **limited monarchy** in which the monarch's power was limited by the authority of the people, vested in Parliament. This revolution was called "Glorious" because it succeeded, no one was killed, Parliament's power was maintained, and England became prosperous.

John Locke

In 1690, **John Locke** (1632-1704) published his *Two Treatises of Government* which attacked the theory of the divine right of kings. He proposed the following principles which influenced the leaders of the thirteen colonies in North America in their fight for independence.

1. Power to govern comes from the people.
2. The state must be bound by civil law and by what he called "natural" law.
3. People have natural rights and property rights, which the state must protect.
4. Revolution is not only a right but often an obligation.
5. Government should have a system of checks and balances including legislative, judicial, and executive branches.
6. Religious freedom is necessary.
7. Church and state must be separate.

CHAPTER 1 REVIEW

A.   Define the following names, terms, and events:

Renaissance	Michelangelo	seminaries	Cromwell
humanism	Sistine Chapel	Henry VIII	republic
Copernicus	Raphael	Defender of the Faith	Royalist
Gutenberg	Reformation	Mary I	Restoration
popes	Martin Luther	Elizabeth I	Puritans
Dante	Peace of Augsburg	William Shakespeare	Glorious Revolution
Petrarch	John Calvin	James I	limited monarchy
polyphony	vernacular	Charles I	John Locke
Giotto	Hugenots	divine right of kings	
Leonardo da Vinci	Ferdinand and Isabella	absolutism	
Mona Lisa	Inquisition	Cavaliers	
fresco	Council of Trent	Roundheads	

B.   On your own paper, write your response to each of the following:

1. List three key features of the Renaissance.
2. In what ways did Italy influence the Renaissance?
3. Contrast education in the Renaissance and education in the Middle Ages.
4. List two contributions to science and technology during the Renaissance.
5. According to Machiavelli, how should government work?
6. List and briefly describe four famous works of art created during the Renaissance.
7. Discuss four reasons why the Protestant Reformation occurred.
8. Briefly discuss the role of the following leaders in the Reformation:
    Martin Luther
    Huldreich Zwingli
    John Calvin
    Ferdinand and Isabella
    Ignatius of Loyola
    King Henry VIII
    Mary I
    Elizabeth I
9. What were three causes of the English Civil War?
10. What were two effects of the Restoration?
11. How did the English government change as a result of the Glorious Revolution?
12. List four of John Locke's principles of government.

C.   Write True if the statement is correct and False if the statement is incorrect. Be prepared to state a reason for your false answers.

1. _____   John Calvin founded a university in Geneva that became famous for training pastors and teachers.

2. _____   Michelangelo's greatest architectural achievement was painting the Sistine Chapel in Rome, Italy.

3. _____ The intellectuals of the Renaissance tried to imitate the great civilizations of the Middle Ages.

4. _____ The Glorious Revolution got its name because the English government changed without war, and Parliament's power was maintained.

5. _____ As a result of the Peace of Augsburg, Germany became united under the Roman Catholic religion.

6. _____ The Renaissance or rebirth of classical culture began in Italy.

7. _____ John Locke's principles of government influenced the thirteen colonies in their revolt against England.

8. _____ The Spanish Armada defeated the British navy and invaded England in 1588.

9. _____ The paintings of da Vinci and Raphael reflect many of the principles of Renaissance art.

10. _____ Martin Luther and John Calvin established the Presbyterian Church in Germany.

CHAPTER 2
EXPLORATION AND COLONIZATION

EXPLORATION

Marco Polo

In 1271, **Marco Polo** (1254-1324) traveled from Venice with his father and uncle for 24 years throughout Asia. His stories gave inspiration and guidance to European merchants, to the Portuguese navigators of the 15th century, and to Christopher Columbus.

Merchants

Europeans needed spices to preserve their meat. They were also enticed by the beautiful porcelain, jewels, tea, and silk that came from the East. Merchants saw that they could make a great deal of money trading with the East. However, overland routes were expensive because local rulers imposed taxes on trade moving through their land and robbers often attacked traders.

Portuguese Navigators

Prince Henry of Portugal (1394-1460) established a school for **navigation** (the science of steering ships) where he gathered Europe's leading map-makers, sailors, and shipbuilders. They also built a new and very strong sailing ship called a **caravel**. Participants in the school further developed their skills with the **astrolabe** (an instrument to determine location by using the stars) and the **compass** (a magnetized needle which points north). From this school, Prince Henry sent expeditions to the west coast of Africa and established supply bases on the Canary Islands. Portugal soon became rich from trading gold and slaves. Though he made no voyages himself, the prince is known as **Henry the Navigator** because he supported navigation.

astrolabe

caravel

Portugal continued its exploration of Africa's west coast eventually leading to **Bartolomeu Dias** (1450?-1500) sailing around the **Cape of Good Hope** (the southern tip of Africa) in February 1488. In 1498, **Vasco da Gama** (1469?-1524) sailed around Africa and became the first European to reach India by sea.

Christopher Columbus

Christopher Columbus (1451-1506) of Genoa, Italy believed that the earth was much smaller than other people thought, thus permitting a ship to reach China in a relatively short time by traveling westward from Europe. Columbus went to **King Ferdinand V** (1452-1516) and **Queen Isabella I** (1451-1504) of Spain to finance his adventure. Columbus set sail with three ships, the *Nina*, the *Pinta* and the *Santa Maria* in 1492. It took 33 days for the ships to reach land in what is now the Bahamas. Columbus thought he had reached the islands of Southeast Asia, which Europeans called the Indies. He called the people he met there "**Indians**." When he returned, Isabella and Ferdinand financed a more elaborate expedition in 1493. After three voyages, Columbus still thought he had reached Asia.

Nations Compete Over Exploration

News of Columbus's journey fascinated Europeans and increased the competition between Spain and Portugal. To settle the differences between the two Roman Catholic countries, the leader of the Catholic Church, the Pope, declared a north-south **Line of Demarcation** (1493, revised 1494) which divided the world in half, the East belonging to Portugal and the West to Spain.

VOYAGES OF COLUMBUS, DA GAMA, MAGELLAN, AND DRAKE

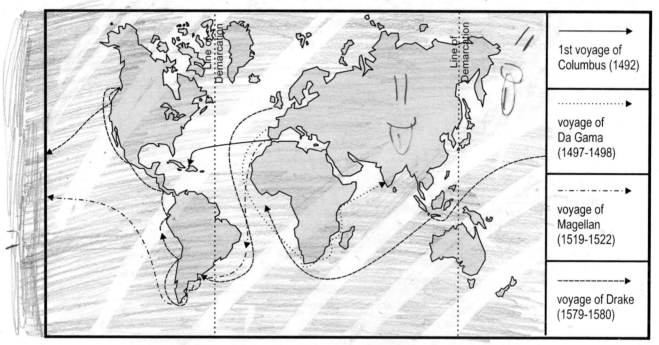

The Italian navigator, Giovanni Caboto, known as **John Cabot** (circa 1450-1499), gained sponsorship from England. On May 2, 1497, he set out with a crew of 18 on his ship, the *Matthew*. Fifty-three days later, they reached the coast of present-day Canada. Thinking he had arrived in northeast China, he claimed the land in the name of King Henry VII of England.

Sponsored by Portugal, the Italian navigator **Amerigo Vespucci** (1454-1512) set out in 1499 to explore the coast of present-day South America. A German map-maker translated the stories of Vespucci and decided to honor him by naming the new land **America**. Other map makers followed, and the name became common.

The Portuguese navigator **Ferdinand Magellan** (1480?-1521) believed he could find a waterway through South America to China. For his voyage (September 1519 to September 1522), Spain gave him five old ships and a crew made up mostly of prisoners, released only for the expedition. Struggling through shipwrecks, **mutinies** (rebellions by the sailors), and depleting food supplies, Magellan and his crew sailed around the southern tip of South America and crossed the ocean which Magellan named **Pacific** ("peaceful"). Though he died in the Philippines, Magellan's crew became the first Europeans to sail around the world, showing that Asia was farther west of Europe than people had thought, and that the world was, in fact, round.

NATIVE AMERICANS

When Europeans first set foot in the Americas, the native peoples considered them a novelty. They had not seen people with light skin. The Europeans' beards, clothes, ships, guns, and mirrors intrigued the natives. The Native Americans initially welcomed these strange visitors into their well-organized and long-established societies.

The Native Americans are probably descendants of people from Asia who crossed the Bering Strait during the Ice Age about 30,000 years ago. One way to describe the people native to the Americas is by culture area. A **culture area** is a geographical region with characteristic climate, land forms, plants, and animals. The humans who live in a certain culture area develop their tools, clothing, housing, diet, and social organizations to adapt to the environment and use its natural resources. For example, in the arctic and subarctic regions, plants cannot grow, so people eat fish and animals, use the skins for clothing, and live in small groups because resources are scarce. Even the physical traits of a people may be influenced by the environment. For example, the natives of the Andes Mountains in South America have broad chests, large hearts, and large lungs because there is less oxygen to breathe at high elevations. Descriptions of the people in the various culture areas are given in the chart on the next page.

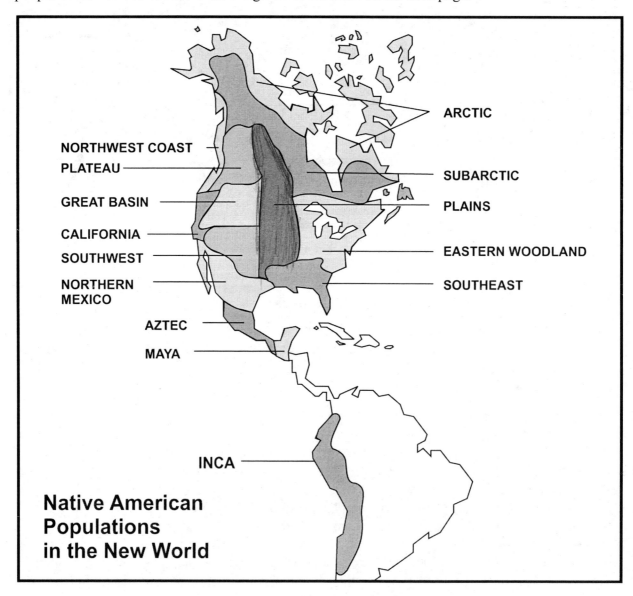

Native American Populations in the New World

NATIVE AMERICANS OF THE NEW WORLD

Group/Tribes	Area/Climate	Livelihood	Cultural Differences
Arctic - Aleut, Inuit (eskimo), Yuit	tundra	Long, dark winters - no farming, hunted seal and caribou, fished	Tents in summer, round, well-insulated, frame structures covered with skins and blocks of sod in winter, in Central Canada winter houses made of blocks of ice
Subarctic - Cree, Chippewa, Tanana, Naskapi, Beaver	tundra	Hunted moose and caribou, fished	Nomadic (moved from place to place), lived in tents or sunken round houses, used canoes in summer, sleds in winter
Northwest Pacific Coast - Nootka, Chinook, Salish	narrow habitable land between coast and mountains	Hunted sheep, goats, and elk, gathered berries, edible roots and tubers similar to potatoes, fished	Dense population lived in wooden houses 100 feet long with extended families, sometimes slaves, used iron knives, staged elaborate religious dramas in winter
California Inter-mountain/Basin - Ute, Paiute, Shoshone	pine forests in mountains, grasslands and marshes in valleys	Hunted deer, sheep, birds, fished, gathered pine nuts and wild grain	Thatched houses, little clothing in summer, advanced processing and storing of food, used shells for money
Plateau - Spokane, Nez Perce, Walla Walla	mountains covered with evergreen forests separated by grassy valleys	Ate from salmon runs, roots and tubers	Lived in sunken round houses in winter, mat houses in summer, dried salmon and roots, ran a trading center in Oregon
Southwest - Anasazi, Pueblo, Navajo, Apache	deserts or mountain valleys with pine forests	Hunted, gathered nuts, ground grain into flour, grew maize	Lived in adobe houses, irrigated their fields, learned to raise sheep and horses from Spanish
Eastern Woodlands - Illinois, Algonquin, Iroquois, Shawnee, Muskogean	temperate climate, dense forest	Hunted deer, gathered wild grain, ground seeds into flour, fished and gathered shellfish	Carved beautiful stones, mined copper in Great Lakes area, built towns on top of large mounds with temple on highest, thousands killed by epidemics
Southeast - Cherokee, Creek, Seminole, Choctaw, Chickasaw	semi-tropical, many hardwood and pine forests	Hunted deer and other wild game, gathered fruit and nuts	Burned underbrush yearly in forest to maintain high deer populations, built mounds, some had town squares
Plains - Osage, Iowa, Missouri, Omaha, Blackfoot, Kansas, Wichita, Mandan, Pawnee, Apache, Comanche, Crow, Kiowa	grasslands	Hunted buffalo, planted crops	Some lived in small nomadic bands that followed bison herds, some built teepees and farming towns along rivers, used feather headdresses and smoked pipes
Aztec	temperate climate, forests, grasslands, marshes in valley between mountain ranges	Farmers of maize and cocoa	Built aqueducts, bridges, pyramids, practiced human and animal sacrifice, used pictographic writing on leaves
Maya	dense tropical rain forest, swamps, grasslands and mountains	Farmers of maize, cotton, beans, squash, and cocoa	Built pyramids and temples, had advanced calendar, hieroglyphic writing on stone and paper, highly developed dying, spinning, and weaving of cotton
Inca	mountains down to coasts, grasslands, and deserts	Farmers of potatoes and maize, used llamas as beasts of burden	Most advanced government system for 3 to 16 million people, built temples, palaces, fortresses, stone buildings, rope suspension bridges, irrigation canals, aqueducts, used bronze, practiced human and animal sacrifice

The Native Americans of North America were a mixture of farmers and **nomads** (people who move from place to place). Where food resources were limited, people moved around in small groups in search of food. Where agriculture was possible, larger communities of hundreds or even thousands grew. Families were organized in villages, which formed alliances with nearby villages. Councils made up of representatives governed the alliances and each village. Women often held positions of authority.

In contrast, the **Aztecs, Incas,** and **Mayas** established huge empires of millions of people centered around large, complex cities. They had highly developed systems of government, roads, architecture, astronomy, writing, and art. These societies were divided into a large lower class of farmers, miners, and craft workers, a middle class of merchants and officials, and an upper class of rulers who maintained armies and a priesthood.

Each culture developed its own language, music, games, and art. Most Native Americans believed in a Supreme Being–a spiritual force that is the source of all life. They believed that all humans, plants, and animals are united in their dependence on the Supreme Being or Great Spirit. Some Europeans thought the Native Americans worshiped the sun, but the Native Americans saw the sun as one example of the power of the Supreme Being.

Europeans usually described the Native Americans as very warlike, but this was due in large part to the fact that the Native Americans were defending their homeland from the European invasion. There is evidence, however, that Native Americans fought with each other for religious reasons, for revenge, or to enlarge or defend territory. Most fought in small groups by surprise attack, though some fought in armies.

In general, the Europeans thought the Native Americans were less "civilized" than themselves, but in some ways, the Native Americans thought the same of the Europeans. To the Native Americans, the Europeans seemed ignorant of the rhythms and cycles of nature. To Europeans, nature was an obstacle, enemy, or **commodity** (something to be bought and sold). European intolerance of their beliefs and practices surprised the Native Americans, especially in regards to religion, sexual and marital arrangements, eating habits, and other customs. They also thought the Europeans were greedy in their desire for animal skins and stingy in their reluctance to share.

MOTIVES FOR COLONIZATION

Rise of Nation-States

The primary interest of the emerging nation-states in Europe was self-preservation. This led to fierce competition between the states. One way this competition was expressed was through trade. Based on the economic theory of mercantilism, trade created conflict involving rivalry for markets and exploitation of human and natural resources.

Mercantilism

Mercantilism was the dominant economic theory of the 16th, 17th, and 18th centuries in Europe. This theory assumed that the amount of wealth in the world was constant. As one country's wealth increased, some other country's wealth would decrease. This wealth was measured in gold and silver. Supporters of mercantilism thought that when a country exports more than it imports, then the debtor countries pay in gold or silver and the exporting country increases its reserves. The government regulated trade and industry in order to increase its wealth, so it could support large armies and navies and pay for wars.

According to the theory of mercantilism, the world's wealth is constant. Therefore, a country would increase its wealth by acquiring a colony. There were many motivations for Europeans to establish colonies in the "New World." Among them were the following:

Economic

- Colonies provided a good source of raw materials (such as cotton) to be manufactured into exports.
- Colonies provided a closed market for the colonizing nation's manufactured goods like clothing.
- Colonies provided opportunity for investment.
- A colonizing nation could conquer a civilization and take its riches.
- A colonizing nation could take mineral resources like silver, gold, and copper from the colony.

Strategic

- For example, a colony at the **Cape of Good Hope** (southern tip of Africa) protected the trade route to Asia.

Religious

- Roman Catholics from Spain, Portugal, and France sought converts to Catholicism.
- Some Protestants fled to the New World to escape religious persecution at home.

ROLE OF SPANISH CONQUISTADORS IN COLONIZATION

When **Hernando Cortez** (1485-1547) arrived (1519) in **Yucatan** (a peninsula on the eastern shore of present-day Mexico), the **Aztec** natives thought he was a god. Cortez encouraged this misunderstanding and imprisoned the emperor of the Aztecs, **Montezuma**. When the Aztec people rebelled against the harsh rule of the Spanish, war broke out. Though the Aztec warriors fought bravely, they were no match for the Spanish weapons. By 1521, after several battles, Cortez conquered the great Aztec empire.

Cortez meets Montezuma, King of the Aztec Empire.

In much the same way, from 1532 to 1536, **Francisco Pizzaro** (1476?-1541) ruthlessly conquered the great **Inca** empire in present-day Peru. He first charmed the Incan emperor, **Atahualpa**, and then imprisoned him, demanding a ransom of a room full of gold. When the Incas delivered the gold, the Spaniards executed Atahualpa and conquered the Incas.

The **Mayas** of Central America resisted the Spanish for decades, but the Spaniards eventually conquered them.

The bold **conquistadors** (Spanish conquerors) overtook the Native American empires for the following reasons:

- The Spanish had better weapons. For example, they could use guns and cannons against Native American bows, arrows, and spears.
- The Aztecs and Incas had never seen fair-skinned people or horses, so they were frightened.
- The native peoples thought the Spanish were gods fulfilling the prophecies of their religion.
- Lacking immunity to European diseases, entire native populations succumbed to measles and small pox.

Other Spanish explorers claimed many parts of North America for Spain. In 1513, **Juan Ponce de León** (1460-1521) explored Florida, looking for the Fountain of Youth. This mission ended in failure, but it provided valuable information that aided later Spanish conquests in Florida. **St. Augustine**, a settlement on the Florida coast, was the first European city in North America. Founded by the Spanish in 1565, it was vital to maintaining control of Florida and the Spanish trade from Mexico.

Illustration of Juan Ponce de León searching for the Fountain of Youth

COLUMBIAN EXCHANGE AND ITS OUTCOMES

After the historic voyage of Christopher Columbus, the **cultural diffusion** of the Western Hemisphere began to mix with European cultures. This mixture of cultures, called the **Columbian Exchange**, yielded the following effects:

- Europeans brought tea, sugar, and coffee to the Americas.
- Native Americans introduced tobacco, potatoes, corn, tomatoes, and chocolate to Europe.
- Europeans brought over animals, such as horses and cattle, and plants that were not native to the New World.
- The Europeans and Native Americans exchanged words from their languages.
- Europeans disrupted or destroyed Native American societies. In some cases, European diseases killed 80 percent of a Native American population. Those who survived were often forced to labor for European colonizers or were forced to flee their homeland.

NATIONS COMPETE FOR COLONIES

Spain was the first European nation to arrive in the Americas. The riches it gained from the "New World" inspired envy among other nations. Except for Portugal, Spain's political and financial power prevented other nations from colonizing for almost a century. When Spain's power declined, the Netherlands, France, and England all entered the competition for colonies.

Spain

After the Spanish conquests of the Aztecs (1521) and Incas (1536), gold and silver flowed in from the American colonies, adding to Spain's wealth, prestige, and power. After the king of Portugal died in 1580, the king of Spain, **Philip II** (1527-1598), claimed the throne, united Portugal and Spain, and acquired Portugal's many overseas possessions in Asia, Africa, and Brazil. Spain had created the most far-reaching empire in the world.

In 1588, England defeated the **Spanish Armada** (navy), severely damaging Spain's navy and signaling the decline of the Spanish empire. By Philip's death in 1598, Spain's power was declining, its economy was struggling to finance its many wars, and, by the 1640s, Spain began to deplete the gold and silver mines in the Americas. Portugal regained independence in 1640.

SPANISH AND PORTUGUESE CLAIMS IN THE 1500s

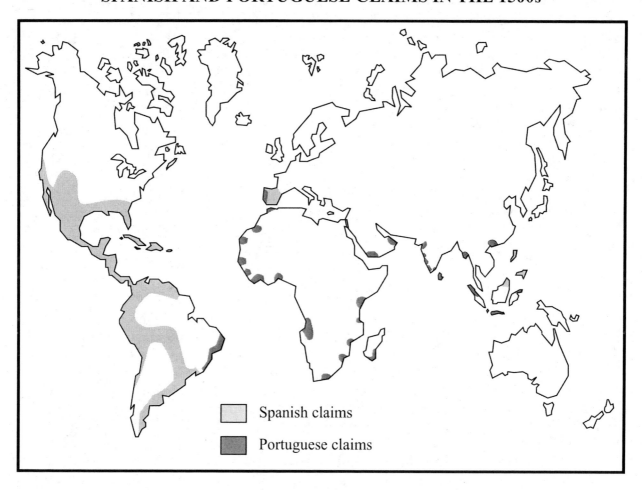

Spanish claims

Portuguese claims

The Netherlands

Once freed from Spanish domination, the Netherlands became the leading sea and commercial power in Europe. In 1602, the Dutch Parliament granted a charter to the **Dutch East India Company** giving it exclusive rights to trade in the East. (A **charter** is a government document which defines the rights and privileges of a company.) The charters for trading companies of this time included the right to take control of foreign lands and to govern them by establishing legislation, courts, and police, issuing money, waging war, and making treaties.

The Dutch exploration of the New World began in 1609 when the Englishman **Henry Hudson** (died 1611) looked for a **Northwest Passage** (a waterway to Asia through North America). Seventeen years later, Dutch settlers bought the island of Manhattan from the local Native Americans. Soon, the Dutch had a thriving colony called **New Netherland**, based out of the port city of New Amsterdam, later named New York. In 1664, England conquered this Dutch colony.

France

France commissioned the Italian navigator **Givovani da Verrazano** (c. 1480-1527) to search for a route to Asia. In 1524, Verrazano reached present-day North Carolina and followed the coastline north to Nova Scotia. Although he failed to find a route to Asia, he made France's first claims for land in the Americas.

France resumed its search for a Northwest Passage to Asia, sending **Samuel de Champlain** (1567?-1635) in 1603. The trading post he established in 1608, later became the great city of Quebec. From this base, he hoped to move westward to the Pacific and find a route to Asia. He is considered the father of **New France** (the name of France's colony in North America).

Samuel de Champlain

Robert Cavelier, Sieur de la Salle (1643-1687), explored the length of the Mississippi to its mouth. There he claimed for France all the land drained by the Mississippi River and named it **Louisiana** in honor of Louis XIV, king of France. The city of **New Orleans** was established in 1718.

Though the fur trade in New France was profitable, many more French settled on the islands of the Caribbean to profit from the trade in sugar. By the close of the 17th century, the French colony of **Saint-Domingue** (present-day Haiti) was the wealthiest colony in the Americas, exporting more wealth than all 13 British North American colonies combined.

England

At first, England was content to raid Spanish ships and colonies. The most successful of the English raiders was **Sir Francis Drake** (1540-1596). On one pirating run (1579-80), Drake led the first English crew to sail around the world.

Sir Walter Raleigh (1554-1618) sponsored a settlement in a warmer climate, on Roanoke Island off the coast of present-day North Carolina. He called the region **Virginia** in honor of the unmarried Elizabeth I, who was called the Virgin Queen. This settlement became the **Lost Colony** because its settlers disappeared.

Sir Walter Raleigh

Raleigh's business partners formed a **joint-stock company** (a private company that sells shares to investors) called the Virginia Company and obtained a charter to establish a colony in America. In May 1607, new settlers established **Jamestown**, named in honor of King James. After years of hardship, this became the first successful English colony in the Americas.

Another group of the investors sponsored colonies in New England. In 1620, a group of **Puritans** left England to escape religious persecution and settled in present-day Massachusetts. They established the **Plymouth Colony**.

EFFECTS OF COLONIZATION ON NATIVE AMERICANS

The **Spanish** founded what may be called "colonies of exploitation." In other words, Spain established political control and organized the colonies to export wealth from the people and the land. The Spaniards conquered the great Inca and Aztec civilizations and stole their wealth. They took mineral resources from silver mines and used natives, and later Africans, as slaves to farm crops for sale in Europe.

The main interest of the **French** in North America was trading animal furs. The Native Americans were important to the French because they supplied animal pelts from beaver, otter, muskrat, and mink. The Native Americans were valuable trading partners, so the French saw no need to try to conquer them. The French tended to see the **indigenous** (native) peoples as equals, and they accepted intermarriage. The Native Americans were also valuable to the French as allies in wars against the British.

The **English** colonies may be called "colonies of settlement" where settlers tried to establish English society in the New World. The English wanted control of more and more land, thus displacing great numbers of Native Americans. The English viewed Native Americans as an obstacle to progress and a nuisance.

COLONIZATION'S ECONOMIC IMPACT ON EUROPE

1. Large amounts of silver and gold came to Spain. This wealth
   - financed wars,
   - devalued money, causing inflation, and
   - made other countries envious.
     - Drake pirated Spanish ships.
     - Portugal dominated Eastern trade.
     - Rivalry between countries increased competition in trade for colonies.

2. Much silver went to China. (China's manufactured goods like porcelain and silk were superior, so Europe had little to offer in trade except precious metals.)

3. Furs, tobacco, and chocolate from the New World became valuable commodities in Europe.

CHAPTER 2 REVIEW

A. Define the following names, terms, and events:

Marco Polo	Isabella	Montezuma	Hudson
navigation	Line of Demarcation	Pizzaro	Northwest Passage
caravel	Amerigo Vespucci	Atahualpa	Verrazano
astrolabe	Magellan	Ponce de León	Champlain
compass	culture area	St. Augustine	de la Salle
Henry the Navigator	nomads	Phillip II	Francis Drake
Cape of Good Hope	commodity	Columbian Exchange	Walter Raleigh
Columbus	mercantilism	Spanish Armada	Lost Colony
Ferdinand	Cortez	charter	

B. On your own paper, write your response to each of the following:

1. List five factors that led Europeans to explore the New World.
2. How did Marco Polo's story influence European merchants and navigators?
3. Why was Prince Henry of Portugal interested in starting a school for navigators?
4. Give two reasons why Magellan's voyage was important.
5. Briefly describe the main characteristics of the following Native American groups: Arctic, Southeast, Aztec, Inca.
6. List an advantage and a disadvantage of mercantilism.
7. Briefly discuss three reasons that European nations acquired colonies.
8. Give three reasons why Spain was able to conquer the Native American empires.
9. List three effects of the Columbian Exchange.
10. How did Spain's many wars contribute to its decline?
11. What strategy did the Netherlands use to become a leading trading power in Europe?
12. List three French contributions to the exploration of North America.
13. What was the significance of the following early English settlements in North America? Roanoke Island, Lost Colony, Jamestown, Plymouth Colony
14. Discuss two effects of the following European colonizers on Native Americans: Spain, France, England.
15. List three examples of the economic impact of colonization on Europe.

C. Write True if the statement is correct and False if the statement is incorrect. Be prepared to state a reason for your false answers.

1. _____ Jamestown was named after King James I of England.

2. _____ In search of the Seven Cities of Gold, Amerigo Vespucci explored areas of present-day Georgia, Alabama, and Mississippi.

3. _____ A key factor in the exploration of the New World was the high unemployment in Europe.

4. _____ The Native Americans are probably descendants of people from South America who crossed Central America during the last Ice Age.

5. _____ In the theory of mercantilism, the amount of wealth is constant, so as one country's wealth increases, another country's wealth decreases.

6. _____ When Columbus reached the Bahamas on his first voyage, he believed he had reached a new world.

7. _____ The Aztecs, Incas, and the Mayas established huge empires of millions of people centered around large, complex cities.

8. _____ Traveling for 24 years throughout Asia, Marco Polo returned to Venice and wrote stories about his journeys that inspired European merchants and explorers.

9. _____ The French in North America persecuted Native Americans and harmed the wildlife habitat of fur-bearing animals.

10. _____ Prince Henry of Portugal taught his navigators to sail their ships near the west coast of North America to trade gold and slaves.

11. _____ The Cherokees are Native Americans who lived in the Southeastern part of the United States, hunting game and gathering fruits and nuts.

12. _____ Some settlers came to the New World to seek religious freedom.

13. _____ Conquistadors were Spanish missionaries who brought Christianity to the Native Americans.

14. _____ Samuel de Champlain founded the city of Quebec and is known as the father of New France, the French colony in North America.

15. _____ The Dutch started a thriving port colony called New Netherland which later became the city of Philadelphia.

16. _____ When the Pope created the Line of Demarcation, he divided the world in half, the East belonging to Spain and the West belonging to Portugal.

17. _____ The Portuguese navigator, Ferdinand Magellan, led the first expedition to sail around the world, thus proving that the earth was round.

18. _____ Native Americans sometimes fought each other for religious reasons or to enlarge or defend their territory.

19. _____ The colonization of the New World provided many economic benefits for both Europeans and the civilizations they encountered.

20. _____ The Columbian Exchange brought tobacco, chocolate, and tomatoes to Europe.

ECONOMIC OPPORTUNITY IN THE COLONIES

The desire for profit motivated the stockholders in the **Virginia Company** to colonize the New World. The king gave them the right to occupy and administer the land, and they made money from the products and raw materials that came from the colony. The king made money by taxing their profits. **Indentured servants** provided the labor in the colony and paid for their passage to the colonies by working for a landowner for four to seven years. At the end of the service, the worker was free to work his or her own land.

Tobacco was the main crop for the Virginia colony. As the European demand for tobacco grew, so did the need for laborers. In 1619, a Dutch ship brought the first Africans to Virginia as **slaves**. They were purchased as indentured servants, so they could eventually gain their freedom. However, by 1660 slavery was legal in Virginia, and by 1700 the English were heavily involved in the slave trade with Africa.

tobacco plants

On average, sixteen percent of the Africans died during the **Middle Passage** (the sea journey from Africa to the Americas). During the 1-2 month journey, men, women, and children lived in severely cramped quarters, and the men remained shackled. Many died of disease and malnutrition. It was said that sharks would follow each slave ship because so many bodies were thrown overboard.

Ironically, the year the first Africans arrived was the first year that the **House of Burgesses** met. The investors in the Virginia company had sent a governor to represent their interests and gave the settlers the right to elect **burgesses** (representatives). These representatives began meeting in the House of Burgesses in 1619. The House of Burgesses limited royal authority and increased citizen participation in the colonial government. This experiment in democracy became a living example for how to create a democratic government for the United States.

RELIGIOUS FREEDOM IN THE COLONIES

Puritans Arrive in Massachusetts

In 1620, settlers from England arrived in Massachusetts. They came seeking religious freedom more than economic opportunity. They were called **Puritans** because they believed the Church of England needed to be "purified" of anything that was not explicitly in the Bible. Tired of persecution, a group of Puritans wanted to go to the New World and create an ideal society based on their beliefs. Aboard the *Mayflower*, the Puritans and some other hopeful colonists left England in August 1620.

The **Pilgrims** (people who travel for religious reasons) arrived in the New World almost three months later, but before the passengers set foot on land, they struggled with disagreements. The Puritans drafted a document based on their religious belief that communities are formed by covenants. This document, known as the **Mayflower Compact** (November 21, 1620), provided that all the men who signed it would follow the "just and equal" laws established by the will of the majority. It was the first colonial agreement that formed a government based on consent of the governed.

Under this agreement, the group went ashore to what is now **Massachusetts**, established the **Plymouth Colony**, and suffered through a very harsh winter. The Native Americans of the region helped the Pilgrims survive, and the following year they celebrated the first **Thanksgiving** (1621) together.

To discuss matters of government, the Puritans held **town meetings** at which all male residents could speak. These meetings were important to the development of democracy in America. However, only male members of the Puritan church could vote or hold public office. Though the Pilgrims had come to America seeking religious freedom, they banished from their colony people who disagreed with them.

Roger Williams (1603?-1683) disagreed with the Puritans. He felt that all religions should be tolerated. He also believed that Native Americans should be paid for their land and that the church and the government should be separate. He was banished from the Plymouth Colony in 1635. Two years later, **Anne Hutchinson** (1591-1643) was banished for disagreeing with her ministers. These two established settlements in what became the colony of **Rhode Island** (1644). In Rhode Island, non-church members could vote, towns could reject laws of the colony's **legislature** (law-making body), and colonists enjoyed freedom of religion.

Proprietary Colonies

Some colonies were not founded by corporations, but by individuals called **proprietors**, who had sole authority in each colony. In 1632, Charles I appointed **George Calvert, Lord Baltimore** (1580?-1632), as the proprietor of a new colony called **Maryland**. In addition to making a profit from the colony, Lord Baltimore wanted to provide a safe place for Catholics, like himself, who suffered persecution in England. Many Catholics came to Maryland, but there was still a Protestant majority who took over the colony in 1689.

William Penn

The **Society of Friends**, whose members were known as Quakers, were the most radical dissenters from the Church of England. One Quaker **William Penn** (1644-1718) wanted to create a place of religious toleration where all people could enjoy freedom to worship and participation in lawmaking. In 1681, Charles II (1660-1685) named him proprietor of a new colony, Pennsylvania. When Penn arrived at the colony, he made agreements of peace with the Native Americans and paid them for their land. Penn wrote the Frame of Government (1682) which provided for an elected government to make and approve laws. This contract between Penn and the colonists also guaranteed freedom of worship, protection of property, trial by jury, and a role in government for all Christian men who owned property or could pay a tax.

James Edward Oglethorpe (1696-1785) was another proprietor who had high hopes for creating an ideal society in the New World. He wanted to provide a place for poor people to start over and a place for religious minorities to be free of persecution. So, in 1732, King George II gave Oglethorpe his wish. Oglethorpe named the colony **Georgia** in honor of the king. German Lutherans, Portuguese Jews, and a few Catholics and Scots Presbyterians came to the new colony, but financially, Georgia was a failure. By 1751, Oglethorpe and the other trustees of the colony gave up on their dream, and the king soon took possession of the colony.

EFFECTS OF RELIGION ON EDUCATION IN THE NORTH AMERICAN COLONIES

- The Puritans in New England emphasized knowledge of the Bible, so there were more elementary schools in Massachusetts than in any other colony. In 1647, Massachusetts passed a law that required all towns of 50 or more families to hire a teacher.
- Religious groups established the first schools in the Middle Colonies. The Dutch Reformed Church established a school in New Amsterdam in 1638. A Friends' School (Quaker) was started in Philadelphia in 1697, and Catholic priests (Jesuits) started the first schools in Maryland.
- In the South, there were only a handful of schools established for white boys. Some boys learned reading, writing, and math from their employers, and rich children had private tutors.
- Despite some missionary interest, the education of blacks and Native Americans was largely ignored.
- To educate religious ministers, colonists established colleges like Harvard, Yale, Columbia, Princeton, and William and Mary.

COLONIAL ECONOMY

The **Southern Colonies** were Virginia, North Carolina, South Carolina, and Georgia. Each colony was divided into large pieces of land, called **plantations**, owned by one wealthy person or family. The land owner grew **cash crops** (crops grown only for sale) like tobacco, rice, and **indigo** (a valuable color dye). This type of farming required a large labor force of indentured servants and slaves.

The **New England Colonies** included Connecticut, Massachusetts, New Hampshire, and Rhode Island. Settlers organized these colonies around small towns. Usually, one family owned a small farm and grew enough food for themselves and some local markets. This kind of limited food production is called **subsistence farming**. Other families owned a small shop for woodworking, glass blowing, weaving, or other craft. Fishing, lumbering, and shipbuilding were important industries in New England.

The **Middle Colonies** consisted of Delaware, Maryland, New Jersey, New York, and Pennsylvania. They enjoyed a diverse population and rich farmland. The economy was based on agriculture, but shipping, fishing, and trading were also important industries.

Colonial Trade

Initially, farming was the main industry of the colonies, but soon trade became very profitable. Colonists' involvement in trade resulted in the growth of large port cities like Boston, New York, Philadelphia, Baltimore, Newport, and Charleston. These cities developed commercial industries, like insurance, and small production industries related to shipbuilding.

· However, artisans and shopkeepers opposed British taxation and control, resented the rich merchants, and harbored strong revolutionary feelings. British merchants controlled the two most important items of colonial trade: tobacco and sugar. The American merchants had a smaller part of the trade: exporting rice to Europe and supplies to the Caribbean islands. New England traders would send finished goods and supplies to the island plantations in exchange for molasses, a byproduct of sugar processing. They would then take the molasses back and make it into rum, a very profitable product. The New England traders were also involved in a **triangular trade route** (see map at right) where they would bring rum to West Africa, exchange it for slaves, bring the slaves to the Caribbean, exchange them for molasses, and bring the molasses back to New England to be made into rum. All of this trading undermined England's economic system of **colonialism**. Under this arrangement, the colonies were supposed to supply England with raw materials. England would manufacture them and sell them back to the colonies as finished products. England was supposed to have exclusive control over colonial markets, but the Dutch violated England's trading monopoly. Dutch traders took advantage of trading routes while England was engaged in a civil war (1640s). England wanted to regain control.

Navigation Acts

In an effort to stop Dutch trading with the English colonies, Parliament passed the first **Navigation Act** (1651), requiring that only English ships carry goods to and from the colonies. England passed other Navigation Acts over the next 50 years which further restricted colonial trade. The **Navigation Act of 1696** allowed customs officials to seize any unlawfully shipped goods and required that merchants accused of smuggling be tried without a jury because colonists on the jury would not usually convict the merchants.

TENSION GROWS BETWEEN BRITAIN AND ITS COLONIES

Albany Congress

At this Congress, **Benjamin Franklin** (1706-1790) took the opportunity to propose a new form of government for the colonies. His **Albany Plan** (1754) recommended that each colony send delegates to a colonial assembly which would be led by a British governor-general. This unified government body would be responsible for policies regarding trade, defense, and treaties in the western regions of the colonies. The representatives at the Albany Congress accepted the plan, but the colonial assemblies either rejected or ignored it because they refused to give up any of their independence. The British also showed little support for the plan because they felt it put too much power in the hands of the colonies.

French and Indian War (1754-1763)

From 1689 to 1748, England and France engaged in successive wars both in Europe and in the colonies. After years of war, both France and Britain were reluctant to start fighting again. However, small, infrequent skirmishes in 1754 eventually developed into a war that spread across the globe and included France's ally, Spain. After Britain won victories in Canada, India, West Africa, the Caribbean Islands, and the Philippines, France and Spain surrendered and signed the **Treaty of Paris (1763)**. Under this agreement, France lost all of its land claims in North America. Britain obtained rights to the French portion of present-day Canada and to Florida which had been controlled by Spain. In compensation for Spain's loss, France gave Spain all of the Louisiana region west of the Mississippi. Britain returned Cuba and the Philippines to Spanish control.

Britain Tightens Reins On Its Territories

The British colonies in North America had long enjoyed a great deal of independence in their dealings with Britain because the relationship was profitable for both. However, when **George III** (1738-1820) became king in 1760, he tried to gain more control over colonial trade. The British government issued **writs of assistance**, search warrants that gave customs officials the right to search anywhere for **illegal goods** (goods that had been bought or sold without being taxed). **James Otis** (1725-1783),

James Otis makes his famous speech against the writs of assistance to English court officials in February 1761.

a lawyer representing Boston merchants who had their businesses searched under these writs, passionately defended the rights of the merchants and brought many important leaders into a larger discussion about personal liberties.

The British had been disappointed by the North American colonies' lack of support during the French and Indian War. The colonial assemblies had refused to send their **militias** (armies composed of citizens, not professional soldiers) into Canada, claiming that they needed to protect their home colonies. The colonists also demanded more control over their military and its funding. Further, colonial traders continued to do business with the French Caribbean colonies, which, in turn, helped supply the French troops. To Britain, this smuggling was **treason** (a betrayal of one's country).

At the end of the French and Indian War in 1763, Great Britain gained the French territory west of the Appalachians. However, Britain wanted to avoid conflict with the Native American nations, so, in the **Proclamation of 1763**, the British informed settlers that they could not move west. This proclamation infuriated settlers who wanted to move further west. To enforce this proclamation, Great Britain sent 10,000 troops to the colonies to uphold the law. These soldiers tended to stay in the cities. The British government also used these soldiers to enforce new taxes that Great Britain placed on the colonists to pay for its expenses during the French and Indian War.

Taxation Without Representation

The colonists were not allowed to have representatives in the British Parliament, so each tax became law without their consent. This policy of "taxation without representation" angered the colonists. This policy generated new laws and responses to these laws.

The Sugar Act (1764) - Previous to this time, the British taxed molasses at a high rate but did not enforce the law, so traders usually smuggled molasses into the colonies. This new act lowered the tax on molasses, but this time British troops strictly enforced the law.

The Stamp Act (1765) - This act created a tax on all items put on paper. Colonists had to pay a tax on their legal documents, newspapers, playing cards, etc. Because this was the first tax placed directly on the colonists, not just on trade, it led to riots in many colonies. A secret group of colonists called the **Sons of Liberty** came together to organize a **boycott**, refusing to buy British goods. The **Daughters of Liberty** did their part by weaving their own cloth, so they would not have to buy it from Britain. The British policy of taxation without representation began to unify the colonists in opposition to the British government. Due to colonial opposition, the Stamp Act was repealed in 1766. The Sons of Liberty were radicals who wanted to be free of British control. To keep the momentum of opposition to Britain, they organized **Committees of Correspondence** in each colony which spread ideas of independence.

British stamps placed on colonial paper under the Stamp Act.

The Townshend Acts (1767) - Though Parliament repealed the controversial Stamp Act, it established a tax on all imported glass, paper, lead, and tea sold in the colonies. With the authority of writs of assistance, British soldiers searched any home, building, or ship to see whether anyone had bought or sold goods without paying this tax. In response, mobs attacked British customs officials, and the colonists organized another boycott.

Trouble in Boston

The colonists in Boston regularly insulted the British troops who enforced the Townshend Acts. On March 5, 1770, things came to a head when colonists shouted insults at the troops at the Boston Customs House. For some reason, a soldier heard the word "Fire!" and began firing on the colonists standing there. In all, the soldiers killed five people, including **Crispus Attucks** (1723-1770), a free black sailor who was active in the Sons of Liberty. Infuriated at this action, the colonists held the soldiers responsible and called this event the **Boston Massacre**.

Boston Massacre

Because of colonial unrest and pressure from British merchants who were losing money from the colonists' boycott, the British removed all taxes, except the tax on tea. The colonists boycotted the tea because it reaffirmed the British Parliament's right to tax the colonies. On December 16, 1773, **Samuel Adams** (1722-1803) and other Sons of Liberty dressed up as Native Americans and boarded ships carrying tea. They cut open the crates of tea with their tomahawks and threw the tea into Boston Harbor. This action became known as the **Boston Tea Party**.

The Intolerable Acts (1774)

Many people in England and in the colonies thought that this outright destruction of property went too far. Thinking that a strong and swift reaction would put an end to the rebellion in Massachusetts, Parliament passed a series of laws to punish the people of Boston until they paid for the destroyed tea. These measures included forcing citizens to house British soldiers in their homes, shutting down the port of Boston to shipping, restricting town meetings and the colony's legislature, and ordering that British high officers charged with major crimes should be tried in the courts in England. Britain's harsh reaction to Boston encouraged support from all the colonies. Through the **Committees of Correspondence**, the other colonies provided Boston with food and supplies to withstand the British punishment.

The **Patriots** (colonists who wanted independence from Britain) called these laws the **Intolerable Acts**. Britain's attempt to crush the movement for colonial independence backfired and created more support.

Colonial Response

In response to the Intolerable Acts, colonial leaders organized the **First Continental Congress** (September/October 1774) in Philadelphia. At this congress, Joseph Galloway of Pennsylvania made a moderate proposal of creating a Parliament for the colonies like the one in Britain, both being subject to the English Crown. This proposal, similar to Benjamin Franklin's Albany Plan (1754), was defeated by one vote. The more radical Patriots then proposed their ideas, demanding a third boycott of all trade with Britain until the acts were repealed.

REVOLUTIONARY WAR (1775-1781)

The Fighting Begins

Patrick Henry (1736-1799) was a prominent **burgess** (representative) in Virginia. His "Give Me Liberty or Give Me Death!" speech in Virginia's House of Burgesses (March 1775) aroused colonial leaders to revolt against Great Britain and fight for freedom. Anticipating conflict with the British, colonists in Massachusetts strengthened their militia. The volunteer soldiers were called **minutemen** because they were ready to fight at a moment's notice. The conflict soon came. Shortly before midnight on April 18, 1775, about 700 British soldiers left Boston on their way to Concord, Massachusetts. They intended to confiscate the weapons stored there by the colonists. As soon as **Paul Revere** (1735-1818) saw the troops moving, he rode on horseback through the neighboring towns shouting, "The British are coming!" At this warning, the minutemen rushed to Lexington, a town between Boston and Concord.

"The British are coming!" Paul Revere rode on horseback to warn the villages of Lexington and Concord.

The British forces met the minutemen at Lexington on the morning of April 19. Later sources do not agree on who fired the first shot, but with this battle, the **War for Independence** began. After killing eight colonists and wounding ten others, the British soldiers marched on to Concord, where they met hundreds of minutemen waiting for them. The intense fighting of the minutemen forced the British to retreat, suffering 73 casualties and 200 wounded soldiers by the time they returned to Boston. A growing number of volunteers joined the Massachusetts militia, gathered around Boston, and surrounded the only British troops in North America.

The Second Continental Congress

The conflict in Massachusetts was important news for the delegates who gathered in Philadelphia on May 10, 1775 for the **Second Continental Congress**. The moderate members of the Congress wanted to negotiate a compromise with Britain. The radical members, led by **John Adams** (1735-1826) and his cousin Samuel Adams, called for independence even if it meant war. Public support for independence was growing.

As the delegates gathered on May 10, Ethan Allen and 83 volunteers called the Green Mountain Boys captured the British **Fort Ticonderoga** in upstate New York. The Congress unanimously chose **George Washington** (1732-1799) as commander of the Continental Army. The Congress chose Washington because he supported colonial independence, he was a strong leader, and, as a Virginian, he would help unite the southern colonies with the rebellion in New England. On July 3, 1775, he arrived in Cambridge, Massachusetts to take charge of the army.

Even as war preparations continued, the Congress sent one last peace proposal to King George III on July 8, 1775. It came to be called the "**Olive Branch Petition**." His response to the colonists' offer of peaceful reconciliation was the **Prohibitory Act** (August 1775) which declared that the colonies were in a state of rebellion and empowered royal officers and loyal subjects to "bring the traitors to justice." The king also hired 10,000 German **mercenaries** (soldiers hired to fight in foreign wars).

Thomas Paine

The king's policies angered the colonists, and the writings of another Englishman **Thomas Paine** (1737-1809) inspired them. In January 1776, he anonymously published a 50-page pamphlet called ***Common Sense***. Using forceful and dramatic language, Paine argued that the colonists should declare independence from Britain and form their own republican government. The pamphlet sold over 500,000 copies and energized the demand for independence.

FACTORS LEADING TO THE DECLARATION OF INDEPENDENCE

- growing public demand for independence, encouraged by *Common Sense*
- George III's refusal of peace and hiring of mercenaries
- strategic benefit of securing help from Britain's enemies
- efforts of John and Samuel Adams

The Declaration of Independence

By the spring of 1776, colonial legislatures and Committees of Correspondence were calling for independence. In addition to reflecting public opinion, a declaration of independence had strategic benefits. An independent nation could get support from Great Britain's enemies. Further, American soldiers captured by Britain could demand treatment as prisoners of war, rather than as traitors subject to the death penalty. Eventually, the moderates agreed with the radicals, and Congress created a committee to draft a formal declaration of colonial independence from Britain. The committee of **John Adams** (Massachusetts), **Benjamin Franklin** (Pennsylvania), **Robert Livingston** (New York), **Roger Sherman** (Connecticut), and **Thomas Jefferson** (Virginia) discussed their ideas and chose Jefferson to do the actual writing. Adams and Franklin made a few changes to the document and then submitted it to Congress. After little debate, Congress adopted the **Declaration of Independence** on July 4, 1776. It consisted of three parts: an explanation of the philosophy of human rights, government, and revolution; a list of grievances against the king; and a statement that the United States of America declared itself a nation independent from Britain.

Though Jefferson said he used no other book or pamphlet in writing the declaration, his document reflected the ideas of John Locke (see Chapter 1, page 19), Thomas Paine, and other Enlightenment writers (see Chapter 4, page 52). Along with these thinkers, Jefferson believed the following:

- that the natural world was organized in a logical and reasonable pattern;
- that this pattern was established by God but could be understood by human reason;
- that the power of government came from the consent of the governed;
- and that all men were created equal and given certain rights that are **unalienable** (can't be taken away by any human power); however, this last belief excluded all people of color and white women.

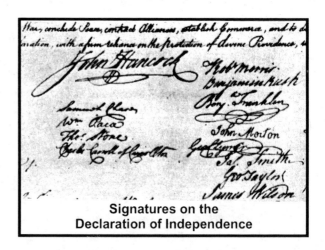
Signatures on the Declaration of Independence

Based on these beliefs and the king's abuses against the personal liberties of the colonists, Jefferson argued that it was clearly time for the colonies to revolt and establish an independent nation.

KEY FEATURES OF THE DECLARATION OF INDEPENDENCE

- written by Thomas Jefferson and signed on July 4, 1776
- inspired the colonists to fight for freedom from England
- became the foundation for a new American government that guaranteed life, liberty, and the pursuit of happiness
- Principles:
    1) All men are created equal.
    2) All people have certain unalienable rights.
    3) Government exists only by the consent of the governed.
    4) Government must be changed if it becomes unjust.

Reaction to the Declaration of Independence

The Declaration of Independence created a dramatic shift in the war. The colonists could not turn back from their chosen course. No longer were the colonists demanding protection of their rights as British subjects under British law. Now they were demanding independence based on God-given rights. The battle with Britain changed from a colonial dispute to a fight for liberty, justice, and democracy. The self-proclaimed independent nation could now seek foreign aid for its noble cause.

As news of the Declaration spread through the colonies, people cheered and bells rang out. Yet, only 50 percent of the colonial population actively participated in the war. About 30-50 percent of colonists remained neutral, including Quakers and Mennonites who opposed violence for any reason. Another 10-20 percent of colonists remained loyal to the king of Britain. These **Loyalists** or **Tories** were more numerous in some colonies than in others. By the end of the war, about 100,000 Loyalists left the colonies.

SUMMARY OF FACTORS LEADING TO COLONIAL SEPARATION FROM ENGLAND

1. **Colonialism**	- England bought raw materials from the colonies at low prices and sold products made from these materials back to the colonies at high prices.
2. **Navigation Acts** (1650s)	- England required American colonists to ship products only on English ships and trade solely with England.
3. **Writs of Assistance** (1751)	- British officials could search any home, building, or ship without the owner's permission.
4. **The Stamp Act** (1765)	- England placed tax on newspapers and other printed material.
5. **Boston Massacre** (1770)	- British troops killed five American civilians.
6. **Boston Tea Party** (1773)	- Colonists protested the tax on tea by dumping a shipment of tea into Boston Harbor.
7. **Intolerable Acts** (1774)	- British Parliament passed laws that limited trade and self-government in the colonies.

MAJOR EVENTS IN THE REVOLUTIONARY WAR

April 19, 1775 - The **Battles of Lexington and Concord** in Massachusetts began the war. **Paul Revere** and other **Patriots** (colonists who fought for independence) rode from Boston to Concord to warn the minutemen that the British were coming.

June 17, 1775 - At the **Battle of Bunker Hill**, Massachusetts, the British suffered heavy casualties even though the Patriots ran out of ammunition and retreated.

July 4, 1776 - The signing of the **Declaration of Independence** meant no turning back for the colonists. The war took on the character of a fight for liberty, and the colonists sought support from other countries.

March 17, 1776 - British troops retreated from Boston to Halifax, Nova Scotia. They were joined by over 1,000 Loyalists who feared that Britain had already lost the war.

September 1776 - British troops captured New York City and established their center of command, forcing Washington to retreat to New Jersey and then to Pennsylvania.

December 25, 1776 - Washington crossed the icy Delaware River to **Trenton**, New Jersey where he captured nearly 1,000 German **mercenaries** (soldiers hired to fight) who were sleeping after their Christmas celebration.

January 3, 1777 - Washington's troops moved on to **Princeton**, New Jersey and stunned the British with a terrible defeat.

October 17, 1777 - At the **Battle of Saratoga**, New York, the British General Burgoyne surrendered his 5,700 troops to the Patriots. This first major victory for the colonists was a turning point in the war.

December 1777 - At news of the Patriots' victory at Saratoga, the French offered a formal alliance with the United States to fight for the colonies' independence.

Winter 1777-78 - George Washington trained his tired and poorly equipped troops at **Valley Forge**, Pennsylvania. With the help of other foreign generals, General Washington was able to instill discipline and lift morale during that winter.

Summer 1778 - **George Rogers Clark** (1752-1818) led colonial troops to victory over the British and Native Americans in present-day Indiana and Illinois. His conquests here allowed the United States to claim this region after the war and develop it as the Northwest Territory. His younger brother, William Clark (1770-1838) later gained fame as an explorer.

Fall-Winter 1778-1779 - Having reached a stalemate in the North, Britain focused attention on the South with its valuable crops and many Loyalists. British troops captured Savannah, Georgia (December 1778) and Augusta, Georgia (January 1779).

September 23, 1779 - **John Paul Jones** (1747-1792), commander in the Continental Navy, tied his old merchant ship, the *Bonhomme Richard* (named after Benjamin Franklin), to the British man-of-war *Serapis*. In three hours of battle, 300 of 375 Americans were killed or wounded, but the British captain surrendered. Considered a pirate and a fugitive by the British, Jones was a hero of the United States Navy.

Summer 1780 - **General Cornwallis** (1738-1805) led British troops in the South. **Nathanael Greene** (1742-1786) took command of colonial forces and used **guerrilla war tactics**, that is, small groups of soldiers struck quickly and then disappeared into the woods or swamps. With this method, the colonists were unable to win but inflicted heavy losses on the British. Cornwallis retreated to Yorktown, Virginia.

September - October 1781 - French naval and army forces joined General Washington and the Patriots to defeat the British troops at **Yorktown**, Virginia. The British surrendered on October 18, 1781. This was the final blow to the British war effort.

The Treaty Of Paris (1783)

After nearly two years of difficult negotiations, all the representatives signed the **Treaty of Paris** on September 3, 1783. In this treaty, Britain recognized the independence of the United States and recognized the border of the new nation. The border extended to Canada in the north, to the Mississippi River in the west, to the northern border of Spanish Florida in the south, and to the Atlantic in the east. The victory of democracy over monarchy excited many in France, who would soon start their own revolution.

IMPORTANT CONTRIBUTIONS TO THE COLONIAL VICTORY

African Americans

From the beginning of the fight for independence, African Americans made sacrifices to free the colonies. **Crispus Attucks** (1723-1770), a free black sailor who was active in the Sons of Liberty, died in the Boston Massacre. Black minutemen fought at the Battles of Lexington, Concord, and Bunker Hill. On December 31, 1775, General Washington announced that black soldiers were welcome in the Continental Army. In 1778, Rhode Island formed an all-black regiment of freemen and slaves. About 5,000 blacks, free and slave, fought during the war.

The War for Independence encouraged northern states to end their practice of slavery, though blacks were still denied the right to vote. In the South, however, slavery was too important to the economy, so it remained. Thomas Jefferson called slavery "a necessary evil." The war, however, did change slavery from a national to a regional institution and created many opportunities for blacks in the North.

Women

As the struggle for liberty began, many women eagerly knit homemade clothes to avoid buying cloth from Britain. Once fighting broke out, women served in the army as doctors, nurses, seamstresses, cooks, guides, and spies. Other women stayed home to serve their families, always ready to flee from British invasion. When men left to fight, many women took their place in farming, business, and gun manufacturing.

A few women engaged in the fighting. **Deborah Sampson** of Massachusetts and **Sally St. Clair** of South Carolina disguised themselves as men and fought in the army. **Nancy Hart** of Georgia captured a group of Loyalist soldiers all by herself. **Mary Ludwig Hayes**, known as **Molly Pitcher**, fired her husband's cannon in battle when he became ill.

In the spirit of colonial independence, women called for their own liberty. **Abigail Adams** wrote to her husband, John Adams, that the Congress should include the liberties of women in the laws of the new country. In the name of women, she warned him: "[We] will not hold ourselves bound by any laws in which we have no representation." The framers of the new government, however, did not listen to the warning, denying women even the right to vote.

Alliance with France

France gave the most support to the colonists because it was still eager to avenge its losses to Britain in the French and Indian War. In 1776, a 19-year-old French soldier **Marquis de Lafayette** (1757-1834) came to North America to fight. General Washington befriended him and treated him like a son. Lafayette became a valuable asset to the Continental Army. The Battle of Saratoga (October 17, 1777) convinced French leaders that the colonists could defeat Britain with their help. Fearing invasion from France and its ally, Spain, Britain kept home a sizable portion of its navy which could have helped the British war effort. French military support was essential to the defeat of General Cornwallis at **Yorktown** (October 18, 1781). Encouraged by the victory of democratic principles, Lafayette returned to France and took a leading role in the **French Revolution** (1789-1799).

Benjamin Franklin

Benjamin Franklin's (1706-1790) interest in science and public service led him to help improve street paving and lighting in Philadelphia, organize the city's first fire company, and found what was probably the first public library in America. He also invented the Franklin stove and developed experiments to prove that lightning is electricity.

Benjamin Franklin

After his election to the Pennsylvania Assembly, he was sent to England where he was instrumental in repealing the controversial **Stamp Act** (1765).

During the **Revolutionary War**, he helped draft the Declaration of Independence and signed it as a representative of Pennsylvania. His most important task during the war, however, was his diplomatic mission in France. With wisdom and ingenuity, he gained generous help from France, which perhaps no other man could have obtained.

At the conclusion of the war, he took the leading role in negotiating the **Treaty of Paris (1783)**.

In 1787, he was selected as a delegate to the convention to draft the United States Constitution. Two months before his death in 1790, he petitioned the newly created Congress to abolish slavery and to end the slave trade.

As a printer, author, diplomat, philosopher, and scientist, Franklin played a crucial role in forming the government and character of the United States of America.

George Washington

George Washington (1732-1799) was selected to represent Virginia at both the **First and Second Continental Congresses**. Though divided on many issues, the Congressional delegates were unanimous in recognizing Washington's leadership skill. They selected him as commander-in-chief of the new Continental Army. Through the most difficult times, he held together the colonial military and government solely by the strength of his own character.

His military success in the Revolution made him the most revered man in the country. Desiring a strong central government to unite the newly independent states, Washington was influential in encouraging them to participate in the **Constitutional Convention** (1787). The new nation called again on Washington's strong leadership to be its first president. For eight years in office, he steered the young country through its difficult beginning. As the most powerful man in the early life of the United States, George Washington continually placed his power at the service of his country.

CHAPTER 3 REVIEW

A.   Define the following names, terms, and events:

indentured servants	Navigation Acts	George Washington
Middle Passage	French and Indian War	Olive Branch Petition
House of Burgesses	writs of assistance	Thomas Paine
Puritans	Sons of Liberty	Thomas Jefferson
Mayflower Compact	Crispus Attucks	Loyalists/Tories
town meetings	Boston Massacre	Declaration of Independence
Roger Williams	Boston Tea Party	guerilla war tactics
Proprietary Colonies	Intolerable Acts	Treaty of Paris (1783)
George Calvert	Patrick Henry	Abigail Adams
Society of Friends	minutemen	Lafayette
William Penn	Paul Revere	
James Edward Oglethorpe	Benjamin Franklin	
triangular trade route	First and Second Continental Congresses	

B.   On your own paper, write your response to each of the following:

1. Contrast the motivations the king had for colonizing the New World with those of the colonists.
2. What were the economic pressures that brought about the practice of using indentured servants and slaves?
3. List and briefly describe four early examples of democratic efforts in the colonies.
4. In what ways did religion influence the social and political structures of the New World?
5. Discuss how population and geography shaped the economic practices of the three different colonial areas.
6. What were the causes and effect of colonial disunity or rivalry?
7. List and describe 4 of the extreme laws or acts passed by the British Parliament and the colonial response to each.
8. Name two secret colonial groups and briefly describe their activities.
9. Discuss the significance and results of the First and Second Continental Congresses.
10. What were the events and pressures which made the writing of the Declaration of Independence advisable?

11. List the 4 key principles of the Declaration of Independence.
12. Briefly describe the significance of the following events and leaders of the Revolutionary War:
    a. The Battles of Lexington and Concord
    b. The Battle of Bunker Hill
    c. The Declaration of Independence
    d. Washington's crossing to Trenton, New Jersey
    e. The Battle of Saratoga
    f. George Rogers Clark
    g. John Paul Jones
    h. Nathaniel Greene
    i. George Washington at Yorktown
13. Trace the role played by African Americans in the Revolutionary War.
14. Identify and describe the leadership qualities present in Benjamin Franklin and George Washington.

C. Write True if the statement is correct and False if the statement is incorrect. Be prepared to state a reason for your false answers.

1. _True_ In 1619, a British ship brought the first Africans to Virginia as slaves.

2. _____ Religious beliefs affected how people organized colonies and governments.

3. _____ The Puritans obtained a land grant for their ideal society from the Plymouth group of the Virginia Company.

4. _____ All people aboard the Mayflower were in religious and social harmony.

5. _____ Roger Williams was banished from the Plymouth colony for disagreeing with the Puritan leaders.

6. _____ The proprietary colony named Maryland was created as a haven for Catholics, the majority group in the colony.

7. _____ James Olgethorpe wanted the Georgia colony to be a safe place for the rich, titled sons of the British monarchy.

8. _____ The Puritans in New England valued knowledge of the Bible, so there were more elementary schools in the Massachusetts colony than in any other.

9. _____ The Southern Colonies were divided into large pieces of land called tenant farms.

10. _____ Limited food production, common in the New England Colonies, is called subsistence farming.

11. _____ In large colonial cities, there was a large gap of wealth and power between the shopkeepers and the merchants.

12. _____ The social class of artisans and small shopkeepers had strong revolutionary feelings.

13. _____ The French gave large gifts to Patrick Henry in exchange for his support.

14. _____ In the Proclamation of 1763, the British, out of respect for Native American Nations and in the interest of collecting taxes in the cities, barred settlers from moving west.

15. _____ At the Boston Tea Party, the Sons of Liberty threw crates of tea into the Indian Ocean.

16. _____ The result of the "Olive Branch Petition" was that the British backed down from their hostilities and restrictions on the colonies.

17. _____ The language of Jefferson in the Declaration of Independence reflects the ideas of John Locke, Thomas Paine, and other Enlightenment writers.

18. _____ The words "All men are created equal," in the reality of the times, referred only to white males and white women.

19. _____ Loyalists were people who wanted to follow the other George (the king of England).

20. _____ Nancy Hart of Georgia single-handedly captured a group of Loyalists.

CHAPTER 4
AGE OF REVOLUTION

REVOLUTIONS IN EUROPE

COMMERCIAL REVOLUTION

During the 15th and 16th centuries, the rise of nation-states led to economic competition in Europe, as seen in the theory of **mercantilism**. Under this economic theory, a country's government regulated the economy to produce more exports than imports. In this way, the country hoped to develop a surplus of gold and silver. The resulting economic competition spurred European exploration and colonization around the world (1400-1700s). Colonization resulted in a huge increase in trade and money supply in Europe. All of these changes can be called a **Commercial Revolution**. The following are characteristics of the Commercial Revolution:

Mercantilism
* competition between nation states
* government control of the economy
* move from local to national and global economy

Increase in Trade
* discovery of New World greatly increased world trade
* investors took risks on explorers and new colonies, beginnings of capital investment

Changes in Money Supply
* increased trade created more wealth
* large amounts of silver and gold from Americas caused inflation in Europe
* Europeans brought silver and gold to Asia in exchange for goods

SCIENTIFIC REVOLUTION

The Renaissance ideas of curiosity and reliance on personal experience spread throughout Europe in the 16th and 17th centuries, creating a **Scientific Revolution**. Intellectuals of this time laid the groundwork for modern scientific theory by relying on **observation** and **experimentation**. They looked for observable, mechanical explanations of how the world works and discounted the authority of earlier philosophies. This revolution had the following characteristics:

* focus on the **scientific method**: knowledge of the universe is gained by 1) observing the world with one's senses, and 2) developing conclusions and generalizations based on these observations
* movement away from **superstition** (magical beliefs) and **speculation** (guessing) about the laws of nature
* less reliance on thinkers of the past such as Aristotle, Plato, and Thomas Aquinas
* the order and logic of the universe is fully understandable by the human mind
* natural rather than supernatural forces govern the universe

Contributions in Science and Mathematics

Chemistry
- **Robert Boyle** (1627-1691) experimented with gases, developed law of relationship between pressure and volume of a gas, and believed that matter is composed of "corpuscles" of various shapes and sizes (step toward atomic theory).
- **Jan Baptist van Helmont** (1580-1644) saw life as a series of chemical reactions, promoted treatment of disease with drugs, and was the first to distinguish between gases and air.

Medicine
- **Girolamo Fracastoro** (1478?-1553) developed the theory that disease is spread from person to person by small bodies that can reproduce, and he was medical consultant at the Council of Trent (1545).
- **William Harvey** (1578-1657) discovered that the heart pumps blood in continuous circulation through the body and laid the foundation for modern **physiology** (study of the body's functions).
- **Anton van Leeuwenhoek** (1632-1723) used the microscope to discover bacteria (1676) and the capillary system in blood circulation.

Physics, Astronomy, and Math
- **Galileo Galilei** (1564-1642) used experimentation, developed the telescope to study the moon, and promoted the **Copernican theory** that the earth revolves around the sun.
- **Johannes Kepler** (1571-1630) published the first textbook of astronomy based on Copernican principles.
- **Sir Isaac Newton** (1642-1727) developed the mathematical system known as calculus and developed the law of universal gravitation, which explains that all bodies in space and on earth are affected by the force called **gravity**. He is considered one of the greatest scientists in history.
- **Maria Agnesi** (1718-1799) wrote the first textbook for teaching calculus, including some of her original work in the field, and was elected to the Bologna Academy of Sciences – an exceptional event because universities excluded women.
- **Gottfried Leibniz** (1646-1716) developed calculus independently of Newton.
- **René Descartes** (1596-1650) proposed a mechanical view of the universe in all fields. His philosophy was based on experience, not the authority of other sources, and he contributed new ideas to the following areas of knowledge:
  1. Math - published first book on analytic geometry (1632), showed relationship between algebraic equations and geometric curves
  2. Medicine - believed that human body functions as a machine
  3. Chemistry - sought mechanical, not spiritual explanations for chemical processes

These many advances in science changed how people looked at the world. The religious world view based upon ancient authorities gave way to a mechanical view of the universe based upon personal observation. The earth was no longer the center of the universe. Disease was not a spiritual curse. Math could be used to explain very complex movements of planets. The laws of nature, which had been considered mysteries known only to God, could now be discovered by the human mind.

Sculpture of Sir Isaac Newton

51

AGE OF ENLIGHTENMENT

The **Age of Enlightenment** refers to the intellectual trends in Europe and the American colonies during the 18th century.

Enlightenment thinkers shared the following beliefs:

- People should examine all accepted ways of thinking and acting, and they should pursue new ideas and discoveries.
- There could be unending progress in science and the humanities.
- A person is not born with knowledge; it comes from experience.
- Truth is discovered through observing, not from authoritative sources like Aristotle or the Bible.
- The Roman Catholic Church had enslaved the human mind with superstitions.
- **Deism**: belief in God and an afterlife but not in specific religious practices or beliefs.

France was the home of the Enlightenment. One of the French leaders was Brancois Marie Arouet, who assumed the name **Voltaire** (1694-1778). He wrote various plays, novels, and poems, often with satirical wit. He believed religion led to intolerance, persecution, and wars. He rejected Christianity and the supernatural in favor of Deism and the power of human reason. He believed morality should be based on freedom of thought and respect for all individuals.

Jean Jacques Rousseau (1712-1778) was one of the most eloquent writers of the Enlightenment. In *The Social Contract* (1762), he argued for civil liberty and defended the democratic form of government. He opposed the **divine right of kings**, believing that the authority of government should come from the will of the majority. He believed that a democratic government embodied the will of the majority, so he felt the government could impose strict laws to enforce religious and political conformity.

Jean Jacques Rousseau

Sons of the Revolution crest coin

The Enlightenment movement had other proponents in various countries: **Immanuel Kant** (1724-1804) in Germany, **David Hume** (171-1776) in England, **Cesare Beccaria** (1738-1794) in Italy, and **Benjamin Franklin** (1706-1790) and **Thomas Jefferson** (1743-1826) in the English colonies in America. Europeans saw Enlightenment ideas put into practice in the **American Revolution** (1775-1783). This revolution further encouraged reforms in European governments that eventually led to the **French Revolution** (1789-1799), which ended the Age of Enlightenment.

FRENCH REVOLUTION (1789-1799)

Through the early part of the 18th century, France was the economic and cultural leader of continental Europe, but in 1789, political, economic, social, and philosophical trends converged to produce the **French Revolution**.

Causes of the French Revolution

Discontent of the People
- increasing and unequal taxes, wealthy nobility and clergy paid less than common people
- persecution of religious minorities, namely Jews and Protestants
- government interference in the private lives of citizens
- inefficient government administration and court system
- rising food prices because of inefficient government

Financial Crisis
- no national bank nor national treasury
- monarchy extravagantly spent more than it collected in taxes
- large war debts from the **War of the Austrian Succession** (1740-1748), the **Seven Years' War** (1756-1763), and the **American Revolution** (1775-1783); by 1789, France spent almost half its annual revenue paying interest on past loans

Enlightenment Writers
- declared people had certain natural rights, and the government's role was to protect them
- criticized the absolute rule of the crown, claimed a historically free France

Need for Reform

Many people sought political, social, and economic reforms in France. **King Louis XVI's** (reigned 1774-1792) opposition to reform added to the people's discontent with a poor economy and rising food prices. On July 14, 1789, a restless mob, hoping to release many political prisoners and to obtain munitions, stormed the royal fortress of the **Bastille**. Even though they found only seven inmates, the rebellion made a significant shift in the political movement from reform to outright revolution. The king withdrew his troops. The **National Assembly** (a newly formed representative government body) voted to end the **feudal system** in which people were legally defined by the class into which they were born. In the **Declaration of the Rights of Man and of the Citizen** (August 26, 1789), the National Assembly listed a number of "inalienable rights" granted to "all men" including black men in France. These rights were participation in government, due process of law and equal protection under the law, security of property rights, and freedom of religion, speech, and the press. These rights became part of the new constitution which also provided for a voluntary state religion: Roman Catholicism.

Cannonfire at Bastille

Changes in Government

On October 1, 1791, the new constitution took effect and the **Legislative Assembly** met for the first time. Despite apparent stability, an undercurrent of division continued between radical reformers who wanted a **republic** (nation governed by the people) and the **monarchists** who wanted to return all the political power to the king. Both these factions declared war on Austria and Prussia, beginning the **French Revolutionary Wars** (1792-1797).

Because the French military was in the middle of a reorganization, it suffered many defeats. The military losses, along with rising bread prices and the declining value of French currency, caused political power to shift to the local districts of Paris and to mobs of artisans and shopkeepers, called **sans-culottes**, who were fiercely devoted to the revolution. Two weeks before the meeting of a new representative **Convention**, sans-culottes mobs attacked the jails in Paris, murdering more than 1000 inmates who supported the king. The Convention tried the king for treason, and, on January 21, 1793, executed him by the **guillotine** (a device consisting of a heavy blade held up between upright guides and dropped to behead the victim below). Over the next six months, the new government suffered from military losses, a struggling economy, and various revolts against its authority. In this crisis, **Maximillien Robespierre** (1758-1794) led the radical members of the Convention, the **Jacobins**, to arrest the more moderate members and take control (June 2, 1793). Robespierre next led the **Committee of Public Safety** (a committee of the Convention) in the **Reign of Terror** (1793-1794), a policy which used violence, fear, and repression to stamp out all opposition to the new government. The result was 250,000 arrests, 30,000 executions by guillotine, and thousands of deaths in jails. The Jacobins had proposed the most democratic form of government; ironically, they used anti-democratic means to impose it.

The Rise of Napoleon

The Reign of Terror resulted in success for the French military. As the French armies moved through Europe, they instituted reforms based on the principles of the revolution, such as abolishing feudalism and guaranteeing basic individual rights. The most successful and popular general of the French army was **Napoleon Bonaparte** (1769-1821).

By the spring of 1799, however, France's enemies had forced the French Army back on all fronts. Because of these defeats, the French people lost faith in their government and voted for new representatives who began their own radical reforms. They drafted a new constitution and established a new government called the **Consulate**. Napoleon was named first consul and received almost dictatorial powers. This is considered the end of the Revolution.

Napoleon maintained many of the reforms of the Revolution and united them in one code. This **Code Napoleon** provided for the following:

Napoleon on Horseback, painting by Meissonier

- abolition of feudal privileges
- equality before the law
- freedom of conscience
- individual's free choice of occupation
- protection from arbitrary arrest and detention

Napoleon also established a central university to organize the public schools, a national bank, and a new unit of currency, the franc.

The Empire

Though initially supportive of the republic, Napoleon consolidated his own power and crowned himself emperor in 1804. He led France to dominate most of Europe through ten years of almost constant war. However, Britain, whose strength remained intact, perpetually formed new alliances to challenge Napoleon. In 1812, Napoleon launched an attack on Russia that ended in a terrible defeat for French troops. The other European nations united against Napoleon and finally defeated him at the **Battle of Waterloo** (June 1815).

The Constitutional Monarchy

After 25 years of revolution and war, the victorious allies wanted a stable France, so they established a **constitutional monarchy**. The new government incorporated ideas from the monarchy, the Revolution, and Napoleon. In this limited monarchy, the king's powers were checked by the constitution and parliament, and Napoleon's law codes were adopted. The democratic ideas of the French Revolution had changed France forever. The revolution also influenced political revolutions in Germany, Italy, and many Latin American countries.

EFFECTS OF THE FRENCH REVOLUTION

- **Promoted democracy**: despite the bloodshed and repression during the revolution, the abolition of feudal [class] privilege and experiments in representative government inspired democratic ideals throughout the world
- **Helped Equalize Society**: though the revolution did not distribute wealth equally, it encouraged legal equality of citizens by eliminating privileges associated with class
- **Hurt the Economy**: the disruption of war damaged the French economy, although the standardization of weights and measures, the development of a uniform civil law code, and the elimination of royal economic controls did later facilitate the Industrial Revolution in France
- **Promoted Nationalism**: described a nation not as a group of royal subjects but as a society of equal citizens; Napoleon's occupation encouraged nationalism in other countries
- **Provided a Model for Future Revolutions**: revolutionaries in later centuries drew instruction and inspiration from the French Revolution

---

KEY EVENTS OF THE FRENCH REVOLUTION

June 17, 1789	National Assembly is formed
July 14, 1789	Storming of the Bastille
August 26, 1789	Declaration of the Rights of Man and of the Citizen
October 1, 1791	New Constitution took effect; first meeting of Legislative Assembly
Summer 1792	Mobs attacked king's palace and jails in Paris
September 22, 1792	Convention declared France a republic
June 2, 1793	The radical Jacobins took control of the Convention
January 21, 1793	King Louis XVI executed
September 2, 1793	Reign of Terror began
November 9, 1799	Consulate established with Napoleon as first consul; end of revolution

---

REVOLUTIONS IN THE AMERICAS

Haitian Slave Revolt

The history of the slave revolt in Haiti provides an excellent example of the various economic, political, and social factors of colonialism in the Americas and its decline in the 19th century.

Using African slave labor in an extensive system of sugar and coffee plantations, the French colony of Haiti eventually exported more wealth than all thirteen of the British North American colonies combined. The wealth of the colony, however, came at high price to the African slaves who suffered greatly from overwork, lack of food, torture, and murder.

With the colony's leaders divided about the French Revolution (1789-1799), the black slaves revolted in 1791, killing whites and destroying plantations. By 1793, Haiti was involved in a full-scale civil war. Spain and Britain took advantage of the situation by trying to invade.

In the midst of this struggle, a great leader emerged, **François Dominique Toussaint L'Ouverture** (1743-1803). With the help of France, L'Ouverture defeated the British and the Spanish in 1801. He abolished slavery and declared himself governor-general of the island for life. As Toussaint L'Ouverture was gaining control of the island, Napoleon Bonaparte rose to power in France. Napoleon wanted to increase profits from Haiti by re-establishing slavery. Therefore, a large French army went to the island, tricked the loyal Toussaint, and brought him to France where he died in prison. The leaders of Toussaint's army, in retaliation, declared war on France and defeated Napoleon's army in a vicious war. On January 1, 1804, Haiti declared its independence, becoming the world's first black republic.

Toussaint L'Ouverture led Haiti in revolt against France.

The Haitian slave revolt produced the following outcomes:

- Black and white refugees fled to the United States bringing their culture to the lower South.
- Napoleon abandoned his plan for colonies in the Western Hemisphere and sold Louisiana in 1803.
- Some slaves in the United States tried to revolt.
- Fearing a massacre similar to Haiti, slave owners in the United States became even less willing to end slavery peacefully.
- Slave holders in the United States and the Caribbean islands isolated Haiti to keep ideas of emancipation from spreading.
- Haiti gave support to Simón Bolívar in his fight for South American independence from Spain; in return, Bolivar made abolition of slavery one of his goals.

Spanish Colonies in the New World Fight for Independence

In 1812, **José de San Martín** (1778-1850) returned to Argentina to help the South American colonies in their struggle for independence from Spain. He was soon joined by the exiled Chilean general of Irish heritage, **Bernardo O'Higgins** (1778-1842). Together, they led a revolutionary force over the Andes Mountains and liberated Chile and Peru from Spanish control.

Simón Bolívar of Venezuela (1783-1830) was called "The Liberator" because of his prominent role in the Spanish American colonies' struggle for independence.

Through more than 16 years (1809-1825) of repeated defeats and victories, Simón Bolívar's efforts led to the independence of Venezuela, Colombia, Ecuador, and Peru. A section of Peru became a separate country and was named Bolivia in his honor.

Bolívar's attempts to develop strong central governments of parliamentary democracy suffered from severe regional conflicts within each of the countries. This internal division further prevented the realization of his dream for a South American federation, united to insure prosperity and security. Despite his great role in the independence movement, he died an unpopular leader, due to political difficulties. Today, Latin Americans generally hold him in high esteem.

CHAPTER 4 REVIEW

A. Define the following names, terms, and events:

mercantilism	King Louis XVI	Maximillien Robespierre
Commercial Revolution	Bastille	Jacobins
Scientific Revolution	National Assembly	Reign of Terror
scientific method	Declaration of the Rights of	Napoleon Bonaparte
Galileo Galilei	Man and of the Citizen	Code Napoleon
Sir Isaac Newton	feudal system	Constitutional Monarchy
René Descartes	Legislative Assembly	Toussaint L'Ouverture
Age of Enlightenment	republic	José de San Martín
Deism	monarchists	Bernardo O'Higgins
Voltaire	sans-culottes	Simón Bolívar
Jean Jacques Rousseau	guillotine	

B. On your own paper, write your response to each of the following:

1. List and briefly discuss the three characteristics of the Commercial Revolution.
2. What were two causes and two effects of the Scientific Revolution?
3. List four scientists and their contributions to the scientific method.
4. What were four beliefs that defined the Enlightenment "attitude"?
5. Name and briefly discuss the three main causes of the French Revolution.
6. Discuss two ways that the French Declaration of the Rights of Man and of the Citizen and America's Declaration of Independence are similar and two ways that they are different.
7. Identify the significance of each of the following representative French governments or groups:

National Assembly	Legislative Assembly
Convention	Committee of Public Safety
Consulate	French Constitutional Monarchy

8. Based on its results, could the French Revolution be called successful in establishing a new republic? Why or why not?
9. What were two causes and the global effects of the Haitian slave revolt?
10. Identify Simón Bolívar's nickname and explain its significance.

C. **Write True if the statement is correct and False if the statement is incorrect. Be prepared to state a reason for your false answers.**

1. _____ King Louis XVI crowned Napoleon emperor in 1804.

2. _____ Historically, the Bastille was created and run as a "safe house" for French rebel forces.

3. _____ The Scientific Revolution included the belief in superstition and in Plato's works.

4. _____ One of the effects of the Haitian slave revolt was the Louisiana Purchase.

5. _____ Kepler published the first textbook of astronomy based on Copernican principles.

6. _____ The Enlightenment Movement occurred only in France.

7. _____ Bernardo O'Higgins helped free Chile and became its president.

8. _____ The Reign of Terror was designed to destroy any opposition to Napoleon.

9. _____ Napoleon reinstated feudal systems and denied equality under the law.

10. _____ Toussaint L'Ouverture, a former slave, became the great leader of Saint Dominique (Haiti).

11. _____ Voltaire believed that morality should be based on freedom of thought and respect for all individuals.

12. _____ A positive effect of the French Revolution was that it encouraged nationalism in other countries.

13. _____ Sir Isaac Newton is considered one of the greatest musicians.

14. _____ Maria Agnesi was one of many women during the Enlightenment who was elected to the Bologna Academy of Sciences.

15. _____ Napoloeon was finally defeated at the Battle of Waterloo.

CHAPTER 5
CONSTITUTIONAL ERA

GOVERNMENT FOLLOWING THE REVOLUTIONARY WAR

Following the Revolutionary War, thirteen independent states were left to figure out how to govern themselves. The colonists' chief loyalty was to the state in which they lived. Each state established its own government based on English traditions and colonial experiences. Most state constitutions included a bill of rights that guaranteed certain important rights. These rights included freedom of the press, freedom of religion, and the right to trial by jury.

First United States flag representing the 13 states.

Articles of Confederation

Following the Declaration of Independence (July 4, 1776), the Second Continental Congress appointed a committee to draft a national constitution. This first constitution was called the **Articles of Confederation**. It was **ratified**, or approved, by all thirteen colonies in March 1781, before the **Revolutionary War** ended later that year.

The Articles of Confederation proposed an alliance between the thirteen independent states. A congress much like the Continental Congress made up the central government. The following summarizes the powers of the national government under the Articles of Confederation:

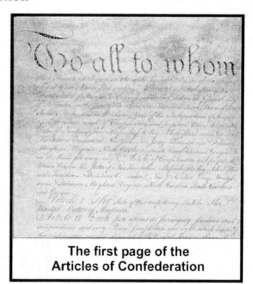

The first page of the Articles of Confederation

Gave Congress the power to
- declare war and make peace
- raise an army and navy
- make foreign treaties and alliances
- coin and borrow money
- regulate weights and measures
- establish a post office
- regulate Indian affairs
- pass laws by 9 of the 13 states
- make amendments only with a unanimous vote of all states

Prevented Congress from
- levying taxes
- regulating foreign or domestic trade
- settling disputes among states
- collecting state debts owed to the central government
- enforcing any of its powers

The Articles of Confederation had a few strengths and many weaknesses.

Strengths

- **States retained rights.** The Articles guaranteed that each state would retain its "sovereignty, freedom, and independence" and keep "every power, jurisdiction, and right" not given directly to Congress. This clause for reserved powers protected states' rights and made it more likely that state legislatures would ratify the Articles of Confederation. The Articles, while weak, did signify the desire of the states to work for unity.
- **The central government established a post office.** This development helped increase communication among the states.

Weaknesses

- **Loose bonds developed between independent states.** States became more independent and put less emphasis on sending delegates to represent them in Congress. The loose bonds that held the states together as a confederation began to break. Since the central government could not settle disputes between states, the states operated like small, weak nations. Taking advantage of the disputes, Spain and Great Britain began taking land claimed by the Confederation.
- **One vote in Congress was given to each state.** States had equal representation regardless of size. Larger states opposed this idea because they insisted that states with more people should have more influence. Smaller states supported equal representation because it gave them equal power. All states eventually agreed to equal representation. They felt an urgent need for a national government to face foreign aggressors.
- **There was no executive or judicial power.** The Articles of Confederation made no provision for a chief executive officer or a national court system. Only the states had executive and judicial powers. As a result, the central government could not enforce any law that it passed, and it had no way of interpreting the law. Without executive or judicial powers, the central government had no real power.
- **There had to be a unanimous vote for amendments.** All states had to approve any changes made to the Articles of Confederation. This requirement made any real changes impossible.
- **There was confusion over settlements west of the States.** The boundaries between the new states were not clearly defined. Two or more states often claimed the same territory. Other states claimed land to the Pacific Ocean. States had to voluntarily give up their individual claims to the United States government. Many states, however, were reluctant to do this, leading to disputes. Speculators also made money as the Congress, desperate for revenue, sold vast tracts of land to these speculators. These speculators had to compete with squatters, Native Americans, and other states for the rights to this land, leading to great confusion in the territories west of the original states.

Shays' Rebellion

During 1786 and 1787, poor farmers in Massachusetts under the leadership of Daniel Shays started a rebellion, closing down the courthouses in large cities of Massachusetts including the state supreme court in Springfield. Farmers were revolting because they faced excessive taxation of their farmland, high legal costs associated with debts owed on the land, and general economic depression in the area. The rebellion was easily put down during the early part of 1787, but it underscored common problems facing all of the colonies under the Articles of Confederation. Shays' Rebellion helped the leaders of the young nation realize that a more effective and centralized form of government was needed.

THE CONSTITUTIONAL CONVENTION

It became clear by the spring of 1787 that the Articles of Confederation needed to be changed if the United States of America was going to survive as a nation. Congress called on the thirteen states to send delegates to Philadelphia to revise the Articles of Confederation. Twelve states sent a total of 55 delegates. Only Rhode Island failed to send a representative. The convention in Philadelphia was called the **Constitutional Convention** (1787).

The Virginia delegates presented a plan for the new government called the **Virginia Plan**. Under this plan, representation in Congress would be based on the population of the states. This proposal satisfied states with large populations, such as Virginia, but angered small states who would have less representation.

Delegates from New Jersey countered this proposal with the **New Jersey Plan**. In this plan, each state would have an equal voice in Congress. This proposal satisfied the smaller states, who wanted representation equal to the larger states. However, the larger states were upset by this proposal, feeling that this proposed Congress would not reflect the nation's population.

States wanted to be sure their voices would be heard proportionately in the new federal government. Large states wanted to be sure their voices would be heard in proportion to their population. Small states also wanted to be sure that their voice would be counted in the new government. To accomplish this, the **Great Compromise** was reached. Congress was divided into two houses. In the upper house, the **Senate**, each state was represented by two senators. In the lower house, the **House of Representatives**, each state had representatives in proportion to its population.

The Great Compromise led to another question: How should slaves in the Southern states be counted in the population? Northern states said slaves should not be counted in the population since they were considered property. Southern states wanted them to be counted in the population in order to increase their representation in the House of Representatives. As a compromise between free and slave states in the House of Representatives, it was agreed that each slave counted as 3/5 of a person. For example, if a state had 5,000 slaves, they would count as 3,000 people in the state's population count. This statement set a precedent because it affirmed that the government believed a black slave was worth only 3/5 of any other person.

Another conflict between northern and southern states was the issue of slave trade. The northern states wanted to abolish slave trade, but the southern states insisted that it was a vital part of the southern economy. To compromise, Congress agreed not to interfere with the slave trade for 20 years.

To keep harmony between the northern and southern states, delegates also agreed to prohibit export taxes and to require a two-thirds majority vote in the Senate to pass any treaty. These agreements kept the northern and the southern states from passing taxes or treaties that would be harmful to another region.

UNITED STATES GOVERNMENT
UNDER THE CONSTITUTION

After many compromises, the delegates of the Constitutional Convention wrote the **United States Constitution** (1787) that governs our nation. The Constitution spreads the power between the national government and state governments. (Local governments are set up by the states.) The Constitution gives some powers to the national government, lets some powers stay with the state governments, and lets both share some powers. Shared powers, such as taxation, are called **concurrent powers**. This practice of dividing power is called **federalism**. Federalism keeps any one of the governments from gaining too much control. This system allows the people to have some power over the federal government at the state or local level.

Constitutionalism refers to a government in which power is divided among various groups, but all groups obey a system of laws called a **Constitution**.

The United States has three branches of government: the **executive**, the **legislative**, and the **judicial**. The Constitution divides the powers among these three branches, so one group will not have too much power. For example, the Congress can declare war, but the President commands the soldiers. The writers of the Constitution made a separate branch of government for each function or purpose of national government.

RATIFYING THE CONSTITUTION

Before the Constitution became law, it had to be **ratified**, or approved, by the states.

Supporters of the Constitution were called **Federalists**.

Madison

- Federalists believed that the United States needed to have a strong national government.
- They recognized the weaknesses of the Articles of Confederation through which individual states could reject national policy.
- Many prominent federalists such as **James Madison**,
Jay
Alexander Hamilton, and **John Jay** wrote a series of newspaper articles that became known as the **Federalist Papers**. These influential articles stated the advantages of a federal union under the Constitution. They were written to persuade the people of New York State to support the Constitution. The Federalist Papers are crucial to a discussion of the political theory behind the United States government.

Hamilton

Opponents of the Constitution were known as **Anti-Federalists**.

- Anti-federalists thought the new national government would be too powerful and that the states should retain more power.
- They believed the method of electing the President and the Senate was too far removed from the people.
- They opposed the longer terms of office outlined in the Constitution because longer terms of office might make representatives less responsive to the voters.
- Most importantly, anti-federalists argued that the Constitution lacked a specific bill of rights that protected individual liberties.

Despite opposition, all states eventually ratified the Constitution in 1788.

THE FIRST GOVERNMENT UNDER THE CONSTITUTION

The **electoral college** (a group of people representing each state) elected **George Washington** as the first President (1789-1797). President Washington appointed **Thomas Jefferson**, author of the Declaration of Independence, as **Secretary of State**, and **Alexander Hamilton** as **Secretary of the Treasury**. **James Madison** was a leader in the **House of Representatives**. As a leader in the lower house, Madison advocated ratification of the Bill of Rights. During his terms of service, he usually sided with Thomas Jefferson and the Democratic-Republicans, advocating states' rights over the rights of the federal government. Hamilton's goal was to build a strong economy, but he met with opposition in fulfilling his goals, especially from Madison.

The Whiskey Rebellion

In 1794, grain farmers in Pennsylvania rebelled against the federal government in protest of the new tax on whiskey. This tax discouraged sales of whiskey. This tax, in turn, hurt grain farmers who made their living by distilling their grain into whiskey. President George Washington ordered the state militias to serve the federal government by helping to end the rebellion. This action was important because it asserted that the commander-in-chief had the authority to act within a state and showed that the new government would act decisively in times of crisis.

Neutrality Proclamation

In 1789, the same year the Constitution was ratified, the French people revolted against the king and the aristocracy. Many people in the United States supported the revolt of the French people. Thomas Jefferson led the faction supporting the French Revolution. However, Alexander Hamilton led a faction opposing the attack on the French upper class. He feared United States involvement in the French Revolution might bring the United States into a war with Great Britain, which supported the French aristocracy. President George Washington believed that no involvement in Europe was the best course. In April 1793, he issued the **Proclamation of Neutrality**.

Jay's Treaty

President Washington sent representatives to Great Britain to gain recognition of the neutrality of the United States during the French Revolution. The statesman John Jay negotiated a treaty with the British which accomplished three objectives:

1. Settled northern boundary disputes with British Canada
2. Obtained British acknowledgment of the neutrality of the United States
3. Britain received most favored nation status with the United States

After much controversy, the United States Congress approved Jay's Treaty in 1796.

France was infuriated by Jay's Treaty between Britain and the United States. After this treaty, the United States ordered all French ships out of its ports. The French responded angrily by seizing shipping from the United States in the West Indies. To reach an agreement with the French, President Adams sent three representatives to France: John Marshall, Thomas Pinckney, and Eldridge Gerry. The commission arrived in Paris in October 1797. The French foreign minister, Maurice de Talleyrand, sent three secret agents to offer the representatives of the United States a deal. Tallyrand wanted $250,000 for himself and an additional $10 million as a loan to France. In this way, France would stop harassment of shipping with the United States. "Not a sixpence" replied one of the United States representatives angrily. When word of this event reached the United States, the newspapers reported the names of the secret agents as "X, Y, and Z." Citizens of the United States were outraged by this announcement, and a new campaign to build a large, impressive navy began.

WASHINGTON'S FAREWELL ADDRESS

When President Washington left office in 1797, after serving as President for eight years, he gave a farewell address which provided wise advice on several subjects.

- He emphasized that the United States should stay neutral and avoid permanent alliances with other nations.
- He spoke about the dangers of forming political parties. He warned that political parties would cause people to work for their special interests rather than for the public good, just as members of these parties had done in Great Britain.
- He believed that good government is based on religion and morality.

FORMATION OF PARTIES

Despite Washington's warnings, political parties arose in the United States quickly after he left office. Alexander Hamilton led one party supporting a strong federal government. They called themselves **Federalists**. Thomas Jefferson led the opposing party supporting strong state governments. They called themselves **Democratic-Republicans**. Political parties helped people to unite on common issues.

OPPOSING VIEWS OF HAMILTON AND JEFFERSON

Alexander Hamilton - Federalist

- favored a strong central government
- wanted power in the hands of the wealthy and well-educated rather than in the hands of the people
- thought the nation's economy should be based on manufacturing, shipping, and commerce and not on farming
- interpreted the Constitution loosely as giving powers not specifically stated

Thomas Jefferson - Democratic-Republican

- favored states retaining authority
- wanted power in the hands of the people because he felt the people were the safest store of power
- thought the nation's economy should be based on agriculture
- interpreted the Constitution strictly as giving powers only as stated

JOHN ADAMS AND JOHN MARSHALL

John Adams, a Federalist, became the second President of the United States in 1797. Adams appointed **John Marshall**, also a Federalist, as the Chief Justice of the Supreme Court. Marshall became one of the most influential people to hold that office. He established the supremacy of the national government over the states. His decisions showed that the Constitution could adapt to the changing size and needs of the nation.

**John Marshall
Chief Justice of
the Supreme Court**

- In the court case ***Marbury vs. Madison* (1803)**, John Marshall established the Supreme Court's right of **Judicial Review**. The court now had the right to declare whether laws passed by Congress were constitutional or not.
- In the case of ***Gibbons vs. Ogden* (1824)**, the Supreme Court ruled that Congress alone had the power to regulate interstate and foreign commerce. This decision allowed the building of roads and canals to increase without the restrictions of state monopolies.
- In other court cases, Marshall upheld the sanctity of contracts and established the right of the Supreme Court to declare state law unconstitutional.

Alien and Sedition Acts

In 1798, the Federalists passed a series of strict laws known as the Alien and Sedition Acts. These laws prevented immigrants from becoming citizens for 14 years instead of five and put citizens in jeopardy of fines and jail time for criticizing public officials. Federalists enacted this legislation to prevent new immigrants, most of them Democratic-Republican, from voting. The Alien and Sedition Acts outraged the Democratic-Republican party. Democratic-Republicans rallied against these laws, citing how they violated the first amendment right to freedom of speech.

Virginia and Kentucky Resolutions

Vice-President Jefferson believed that the Alien and Sedition Acts were unconstitutional. Because the federal government was controlled by the Federalists, Jefferson turned to the states for action. He believed that states had the right to reject or **nullify** a law passed by the federal government. In response, both the state legislatures of Virginia and Kentucky passed resolutions in 1798 proclaiming their right to decide for themselves whether a federal law is constitutional. While Kentucky and Virginia did not end up opposing the laws, later events would cause other states to bring up the question of states' rights of nullification.

CHAPTER 5 REVIEW

A. **Define the following names, terms, and events:**

Articles of Confederation	federalism	Democratic-Republicans
ratify	Constitutionalism	Marbury vs. Madison
Constitutional Convention	anti-federalists	Gibbons vs. Ogden
Virginia Plan	electoral college	XYZ Affair
New Jersey Plan	Whiskey Rebellion	Alien and Sedition Acts
the Great Compromise	Proclamation of Neutrality	Virginia and Kentucky
Senate	Jay's Treaty	Resolutions
Representatives	Federalists	nullify

B. **On your own paper, write your response to each of the following:**

1. List two strengths and two weaknesses of the Articles of Confederation.
2. Discuss the major differences between the Federalists and the Anti-Federalists, and name some prominent leaders of both sides.
3. How was support for the Constitution encouraged in New York?
4. Many important issues were debated at the Constitutional Convention of 1787. Describe one of the issues and how it was resolved.
5. Why would an Anti-Federalist be upset by the decisions made by the Supreme Court under John Marshall?
6. Contrast the first two political parties established in the United States.
7. What were President Washington's concerns about political parties?
8. What caused the Whiskey Rebellion?
9. Why were the people of the United States outraged by the XYZ Affair?
10. Describe the importance of the Virginia and Kentucky Resolutions.

C. **Write True if the statement is correct and False if the statement is incorrect. Be prepared to state a reason for your false answers.**

1. _____ Term limits were an issue during the debates over ratifying the Constitution.

2. _____ Daniel Shays began a rebellion of poor sailors, wanting government contracts.

3. _____ The Great Compromise divided the Congress into the Senate and the House of Representatives.

4. _____ During debates over representation, northern states wanted to include slaves in population counts since they were actual people.

5. _____ Western lands were settled in an unorganized fashion with states, speculators, squatters, and Native Americans all making claims to pieces of land.

6. _____ The Articles of Confederation considered one vote for each state to be equal representation.

7. _____ Political parties were formed because of differences between Hamilton and Washington.

8. _____ The Constitution ensures that most political power remains with the states.

9. _____ Opponents to the Constitution were known as Jay's Federalists.

10. _____ Madison believed that common people were fit to govern themselves.

CHAPTER 6
A YOUNG GROWING NATION

THE NATION GROWS AND DEFENDS ITS BOUNDARIES

Louisiana Purchase (1803)

President **Thomas Jefferson** (1743-1826) accepted Napoleon's offer to purchase not only New Orleans but the entire 900,000 square miles of the Louisiana region for the relatively small price of $15 million. The **Louisiana Purchase** was the United States' largest land purchase, nearly doubling the country's size. The purchase marked a turning point for the new nation as it began to seek its economic prosperity not from England but from the new western lands. It also marked a turning point for Native Americans living in this area. The United States did not consult them regarding the purchase, but the westward expansion of the United States which followed led to the Native Americans' destruction or expulsion to tiny parcels of marginal land called **reservations**.

Lewis and Clark Expedition (1804-1806)

Even before the Louisiana Purchase, Jefferson chose his personal secretary, **Meriwether Lewis** (1774-1809), to lead an expedition to find a water route to the Pacific Ocean. Lewis chose **William Clark** (1770-1838), the younger brother of George Rogers Clark, to help him lead 48 others on this great adventure. They left from St. Louis in May 1804. Along the way, they met a very talented Native American Shoshone woman named **Sacajawea** (1787?-1812). She became their translator and guide. With her help, they reached the Pacific coast in November 1805. Many people back home thought the explorers had died, but the group returned to St. Louis in September 1806 with valuable information on the geographic features and the native inhabitants of the Oregon and Louisiana territories. This exploration led to the rapid migration of settlers to the Pacific Northwest.

Sacajawea, child, and husband
Toussaint Charbonneau

The United States is Caught in the Middle Between Britain and France

During his second term (1804-1808) as president, Jefferson tried to keep the United States out of the war between Britain and France. As Britain and France fought on the open seas, neutral United States ships sailed into all the ports of Europe. The British navy retaliated by boarding American ships to search for British deserters. The British took all the sailors with British accents, without distinguishing between deserters and United States citizens. The people of the United States were outraged that American sailors were **impressed**, that is, forced to serve in the British navy. France and Britain continued to violate the United States' neutrality by boarding its ships, and the United States lost a great deal of money. Merchants from the East Coast believed that only war with the Europeans could protect their trading rights. Many Americans believed their nation's honor was at stake, but the new president, **James Madison** (1751-1836), knew his country was not ready for war.

Trouble Out West

Settlers in the West blamed the British for encouraging the Native Americans to resist westward expansion. Westerners soon began to call for war with Britain.

"**War Hawks**," like Henry Clay of Kentucky and John C. Calhoun of South Carolina were infuriated by the British not respecting the rights of United States sailors. They also felt that war with Britain could produce land gains for the United States in British Canada as well as in Spanish Florida because Spain was a British ally at the time.

The War of 1812 Begins

On June 18, 1812, Congress declared war on Great Britain for the following reasons:

- impressing United States sailors,
- violating the rights of neutral ships,
- requiring all trade to go through Britain,
- and stirring the Native Americans to violence.

Lacking a strong navy, the United States planned to invade the British colony of Canada and control it until Britain surrendered. This strategy failed, but **privateers** (private citizens who use their boats for naval battle) captured many British ships.

Important Events in the War of 1812 (1812-1818)

- **Battle of Horseshoe Bend (March 27, 1814)** - With the help of the **Cherokee** nation, **Andrew Jackson** (1767-1845) defeated the Creeks, Britain's allies in the South.
- **Battle of Fort McHenry (September 13, 1814)** - The British gave up their attack on this well-defended fort where Francis Scott Key wrote "**The Star Spangled Banner**," which later became the national anthem of the United States.
- **The Treaty of Ghent (December 24, 1814)** - The United States and Great Britain negotiated to end the war with the Treaty of Ghent. The treaty did not address any of the reasons for which the countries went to war.
- **Battle of New Orleans (January 8, 1815)** - Andrew Jackson's troops suffered 71 **casualties** (soldiers wounded or killed) while the British suffered over 2,000. This victory gave people in the United States great pride in their country and made Andrew Jackson a hero.

Francis Scott Key wrote "The Star Spangled Banner" from the Baltimore Harbor the morning after the British bombarded Fort McHenry.

Consequences Of The War of 1812

The following are results of the War of 1812:

- The United States and Great Britain agreed to return their land boundaries to pre-war agreements. The "War Hawks" hopes for land gains were dashed.
- Other European nations recognized the rights of the United States as a nation. Despite the fact that there was no clear winner in the war, the United States proved that it could defend itself.
- Feelings of **nationalism** (devotion to one's country) grew in the people of the United States because of the victory at New Orleans. The people felt the need to protect and promote the interests of the United States.
- The Federalist Party lost its power and disbanded. New England Federalists had been so angered by the war that they talked of **seceding** (withdrawing from the Union). The victory at New Orleans and the Treaty of Ghent embarrassed the angry Federalists and resulted in the end of their political party.
- The manufacturing industry grew in the United States. The lack of manufactured goods from Britain during the war pushed the United States to develop its own industries.

Henry Clay's American System

Henry Clay

Henry Clay (1777-1852), a prominent senator from Kentucky, proposed a balance of a rural economy and an industrial economy called the **American System**. The plan included a protective **tariff** (a tax on imports) to keep American manufacturing growing. The tariff would raise the prices of the imported European goods, making the American products more competitive. Congress passed the **Tariff of 1816** which raised tariffs on imports by 20 percent. Clay also proposed **internal** improvements (better canals and roadways) funded by federal government's tariff revenue to improve interstate commerce. In addition, Clay encouraged Congress to charter a **national bank**, the **Second Bank of the United States** (1816), in order to stabilize currency and to hold government funds.

Clay's vision was that the tariff would protect the growing manufacturing industries in the Northeast. The money from the tariff would pay for improvements in roads and canals. With these improvements in transportation, the South and the West could buy the Northeast's manufactured goods in exchange for food and raw materials. A strong national bank would stabilize this flow of commerce. His plan intended to bind the United States together economically and make it self-sufficient in war and peace.

The Growth of Manufacturing in the United States

During the 18th century, British manufacturers began replacing manual labor with machines, causing sweeping economic and social changes. This societal transformation would later be called the **Industrial Revolution** (1700s to present). These changes soon came to the United States.

In 1789, **Samuel Slater** (1768-1835) left Britain for the United States where he hoped to make money from his knowledge of textile machines. In 1790, he built a cotton mill in Pawtucket, Rhode Island. The nearby waterfall powered the factory to spin cotton into thread. The thread was then distributed to women who wove it into cloth in their homes.

In 1793, **Eli Whitney** (1765-1825) invented the **cotton gin**, a machine that separated the seeds from the cotton. The gin made cotton the most profitable crop in the South. Soon, manufacturers in the South copied his invention. In response, Whitney turned to the manufacture of **muskets** (long rifles). In this industry, he introduced the idea of **interchangeable parts**, that is, each part of the musket was produced with such precision that it could fit with all the other parts. Whitney's concept of interchangeable parts spread to other industries and became the basis for industrial development in the United States.

Eli Whitney's Cotton Gin

Transportation Improves

The need for transporting manufactured goods and raw materials drove the development of better transportation systems in the United States. The steam engine also made great changes in methods of transportation.

Roads and Canals

During Thomas Jefferson's presidency, Congress approved funding of the **National Road** (1811-1818) which stretched westward from Cumberland, Maryland to Wheeling, Virginia. The National Road was crude and often impassable, but by standards of that time, it was high quality. Under Henry Clay's initiative, the National Road was built to go further west. By 1852, the National Road stretched from Cumberland, Maryland to Vandalia, Illinois.

Completed in 1825, the **Erie Canal** provided a new shipping route from Buffalo, New York to Albany, New York. The canal's success contributed to establishing New York City as the major commercial center of the United States.

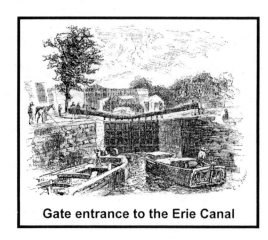
Gate entrance to the Erie Canal

The Steam Engine

Robert Fulton's *Clermont*

In 1807, **Robert Fulton** (1765-1815) used a steam-powered boat, the ***Clermont***, to travel up the Hudson River from New York City to Albany in record time. Fulton's journey showed that people could use the steam engine as a new means of power for transportation. Before this, crews would sail flat boats filled with cargo down the Mississippi River. When they reached their port, they would dismantle the boat, sell it for lumber, and travel by foot or horse back up the Mississippi. Fulton's invention led to the creation of the famous **Mississippi riverboat**.

In 1829, the British engineer **George Stephenson** (1781-1848) won a competition with his steam-powered locomotive, the *Rocket*. Also in 1829, the locomotive made its debut in the Western Hemisphere in Honesdale, Pennsylvania.

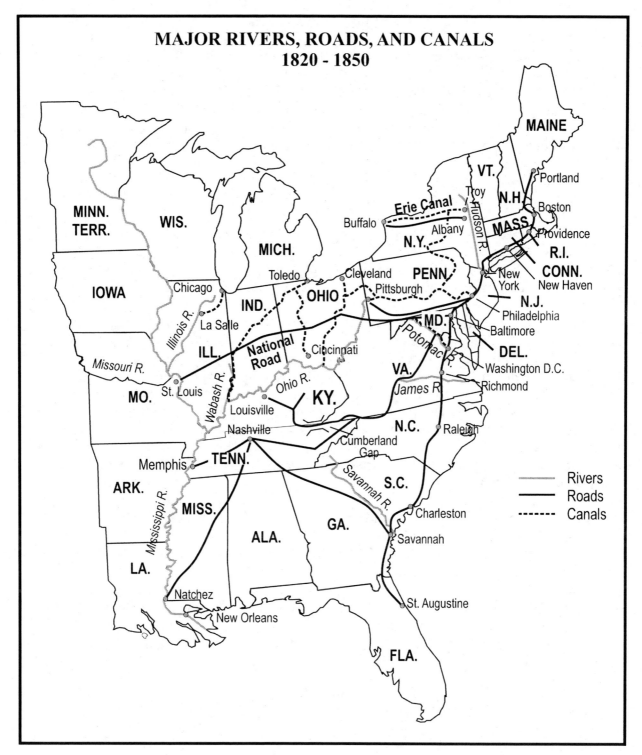

MAJOR RIVERS, ROADS, AND CANALS
1820 - 1850

Rivers

Roads

Canals

Consider the following:

If you were a manufacturer in the early 1800s, describe how you would transport your goods

1. from St. Louis to Toledo. _____

2. from Natchez to Louisville. _____

3. from Louisville to Washington, D.C. _____

Era of Good Feelings

Strong feelings of nationalism arose from the War of 1812 as well as an increased desire to defend the United States. President **James Monroe** (1758-1831) increased the strength of the army and navy, and Congress passed the **Tariff of 1816** to protect the young, but growing, manufacturing industries from foreign competition. In addition, states cooperated with one another in the construction of interstate canals and railroads. As people moved west, they began thinking of themselves as citizens of a nation, not a state. This national unity and optimistic mood during Monroe's presidency is known as the **Era of Good Feelings**.

The United States Gains More Land

Further land acquisitions added to national pride. The **Convention of 1818** settled the dispute between Great Britain and the United States over the northern boundary of the Louisiana territory. This agreement set the boundary at the 49th parallel from the Lake of the Woods to the Rocky Mountains. The two countries further agreed to occupy the Oregon territory jointly for 10 years.

For years, the border of Florida caused difficulties for the United States. Late in 1817, Andrew Jackson was sent to secure the border and, later, he invaded Florida. President Monroe condemned the action, but Secretary of State **John Quincy Adams** (1767-1848) offered an ultimatum to Spain: if you can't control Florida, give it to the United States. Busy with revolutions in its South American colonies, Spain agreed to sell Florida for 5 million dollars.

The **Adams-Onís Treaty (1819)** gave the United States rights to all of Florida as well as the southern parts of present-day Alabama and Mississippi. The treaty also defined, for the first time, the western boundary of the Louisiana Purchase (1803). Spain gave the United States its rights to the Oregon region, while the United States gave up its claims to Texas which had been included in the Louisiana Purchase.

Monroe Doctrine

Spain faced more territorial losses in its other colonies. Between 1810 and 1821, most of Spain's colonies in the Western Hemisphere revolted and declared their independence. Concerned that other European nations would try to establish control in the newly independent countries of Latin America, Secretary of State Adams proposed that the United States make a policy declaration. In his annual address to Congress (December 2, 1823), President Monroe included Adams' ideas and declared the following points in what came to be called the **Monroe Doctrine** (1823):

- The United States would not interfere in the internal affairs of European countries or the internal affairs of the independent countries in the Americas.
- The United States would use military force to oppose any European attempt to intervene in the Americas.

Monroe concluded his address by saying, "The American continents are henceforth not to be considered as subjects for future colonization by any European powers."

With this message, Monroe declared the Americas independent of all European nations. Filled with nationalistic feelings, the citizens of the United States supported the Monroe Doctrine with pride. Most European nations, however, did not support the policy, but Great Britain did.

POLITICS DIVIDES THE NATION AS IT AGGRESSIVELY GAINS MORE TERRITORY

Sectional and Political Divisions Grow

Despite the feelings of national unity and pride that grew strong during the presidency of James Monroe, **sectional** (regional) and political differences were beginning to divide the nation.

Democratic-Republicans (often called Republicans) were divided between states' rights supporters and federalists.

Southerners opposed **tariffs** (taxes on imports) because they raised the price on manufactured imports. Northerners supported these tariffs because they made imports more expensive than their own products.

The North and the South became more divided over the issue of slavery.

The Two-Party System Returns

Though all candidates were Republicans, the election of 1824 showed the growing division in the Republican party. The followers of John Quincy Adams and Henry Clay supported programs that were traditionally Federalist and called themselves **National Republicans**. Andrew Jackson's supporters believed they were the true followers of the Jeffersonian Democratic-Republicans. By 1828, they shortened their name to **Democrats**, thus reviving the two-party system in the United States.

President Andrew Jackson

In 1829, **Andrew Jackson** (1767-1845) became the first man to rise from childhood poverty to the office of President. His presidency, which consisted mainly of frontiersman and small farmers of limited education, became known as **Jacksonian Democracy** because property qualifications for voting white males were dropped during his administration. Jackson openly allowed his friends and supporters to have high positions in government office. This policy became known as the **spoils system**. The spoils system set a precedent for rewarding faithful supporters with government jobs and led to government corruption in some of the later presidential administrations.

Portrait of President Andrew Jackson on horseback, 1817

President Jackson experienced a serious test when South Carolina began protesting the high tariffs imposed on British goods. One of South Carolina's senators, **John C. Calhoun** (1782-1850), took center stage in promoting the **Doctrine of Nullification**. This doctrine states: "If Congress passes a bill that is very harmful to a particular state, that state is not obligated to enforce the federal law. In addition, if three-fourths of the states believe such a law to be unconstitutional, the law will be null and void." Jackson never debated this issue, but he was prepared to call federal troops if South Carolina chose to secede. Senator Henry Clay proposed a compromise tariff bill (the **Compromise of 1833**) that South Carolina could accept, ending the dispute. However, the issues of states' rights and secession would remain alive until the close of the Civil War.

The Indian Removal Act (1830)

President Jackson sympathized with white settlers in the South who were hungry for land and gold. He worked with Congress to pass the **Indian Removal Act** which ordered the forced removal of five Native American Nations from the Southeast: the Creeks, the Choctaws, the Chickasaws, the Seminoles, and the Cherokees. Most Native Americans resisted the new law and appealed to the United States Supreme Court. Chief Justice Marshall ruled that the Native Americans had a right

"The Trail of Tears" Painting by Robert Lindneux in the Woolaroc Museum in Bartlesville, Oklahoma

to their land and could not be forcibly removed. Jackson, however, completely disregarded the authority of the Supreme Court and sent troops to remove the Native American nations. Jackson's policies were especially harsh on the Cherokee Nation. These Cherokees were the same people that had previously helped Jackson win his battle against the Creeks of Alabama at Horseshoe Bend. Jackson now turned against this nation friendly to him and forced its people on a march of 800 miles to reservations in Oklahoma. On this **Trail of Tears** (1838-1839), over one quarter of the Cherokee people died from disease, starvation, and exposure to the bitter cold.

Jackson's Battle With the Bank

In 1832, President Jackson ordered all government funds to be removed from the national bank and placed in selected state banks that came to be called "pet banks." With the new funds, these "pet banks" gave loans easily, causing an increase in land speculation in the West. The loans, however, were far greater than the amount of gold and silver in the banks' vaults. This caused **inflation**: people lost confidence in paper money, so they spent it faster and prices rose higher. Jackson tried to control the inflation, but his policies made the situation worse. A financial crisis in Britain in early 1837 caused a decrease in foreign investment which created further problems in the United States. As a result, many state banks closed.

The Whig Party (1834)

President Andrew Jackson sometimes acted more like a king than a president. In 1834, Henry Clay of Kentucky, Daniel Webster of Massachusetts, and John C. Calhoun of South Carolina formed a new political party. Because they were opposing "King Andrew," they named it the **Whig Party** after the Whigs in England who had resisted King George III (1738-1820). Because of their varied backgrounds, the Whig Party could not unite to support one nominee in the election of 1836, so each section supported its own candidate.

The Democrats chose Jackson's trusted vice president, **Martin Van Buren** (1782-1862), as their candidate, and he won the election. However, the Whigs quickly blamed Jackson's policies for the economic crisis called the **Panic of 1837**, but due to party divisions, they offered no plan of their own. Regardless, the economic depression helped the Whigs win the White House in 1840.

The Move West

Fur trappers and traders were the first people to explore the western states. Their trails become routes for settlers who later went West. Settlers moved west for a variety of reasons.

WHY SETTLERS MOVED WEST

- Fur trappers and traders found profitable business.
- Explorers published descriptions of the natural beauty and rich resources of the West.
- Families sought new opportunities after suffering from the Panic of 1837.
- Missionaries hoped to bring the Christian faith to the Native Americans.
- Mormons moved west to escape persecution.
- Merchants wanted to participate in the Pacific Coast trade with Asia.
- Fortune seekers followed the Gold Rush of 1849.

Texas Independence (1836)

The Alamo

After an unsuccessful revolt by a small group of Texans in 1826, the Mexican government restricted further immigration (1830). In 1834, **General Antonio Santa Anna** (1794-1876) assumed dictatorial power over the Mexican government, dispensed with the Mexican constitution, and tightened his control over United States settlers in Texas which was then part of Mexico. In response, **Sam Houston** (1793-1863) led the settlers to fight and take over cities. Santa Anna answered with military force, killing all of the Texans in an old mission outside of San Antonio called the **Alamo** (March 6, 1836). Just four days earlier, a convention of 59 Anglo-American Texan delegates had declared the Republic of Texas to be independent from Mexico. After a series of battles, the Texans defeated Santa Anna at the **Battle of San Jacinto** (April 21, 1836) and took him hostage. In exchange for his freedom, Santa Anna promised to recognize the republic of Texas and withdraw his forces below the Río Grande. However, he still held claim to the land north of the Río Grande to the Nueces River. The Mexican congress rejected Santa Anna's agreement with the Texans and hoped to regain Texas. The Texans, however, applied to be **annexed** (added) to the United States.

The Annexation of Texas (1845)

President Jackson wanted to answer the new republic's request for annexation, but he could not overcome northern opposition. Northerners were hesitant because Texas would be admitted as a slave state. They feared that because of its large size, the state could even be divided into several smaller states and further disrupt the balance in the Senate between slave and free states. The day before he left office, President Jackson formally recognized Texas as an independent country and exchanged diplomatic relations with it. Soon, Britain did the same. From 1836-1845, Texas existed as its own country.

The next two presidents could not gain enough support to bring Texas into the Union, but the annexation was a determining issue in the **election of 1844**. The Democratic Party split regarding the issue, allowing **James K. Polk** (1795-1849) of Tennessee to become the first "dark horse" presidential nominee. (A **"dark horse"** is a candidate who unexpectedly wins support at a convention or in an election.) Polk took a strong stand calling for the annexation of both Texas and Oregon while Henry Clay and the Whigs tried to avoid the issue. In the election, a number of Whigs in New York took their support from Clay and cast their votes for James G. Birney of the anti-slavery Liberty Party. This move caused Clay to lose New York and, consequently, the election by less than two percent of the vote. Polk become a "dark horse" president.

In the spring of 1844, President **John Tyler** (1790-1862) had tried to push a treaty through Congress that would annex Texas, but he failed. Now he believed that the victory of his replacement, James K. Polk, meant that the voters wanted Texas admitted to the Union. In the last days of his term, Tyler called for a joint resolution of Congress admitting Texas to the Union. The joint resolution required only a simple majority in each house whereas a treaty required a two-thirds majority in the Senate. Congress passed the resolution and admitted Texas as a slave state in 1845.

Oregon Annexation (1846)

With the question of Texas settled, Polk set out to accomplish his other campaign promise of acquiring Oregon. In 1827, the United States and Great Britain had renewed their agreement of the **Convention of 1818** to occupy the Oregon territory jointly. Beginning in 1843, thousands of settlers from the United States moved to Oregon seeking a better life. President Polk approached Britain, arguing that the United States had rightful claim of the territory up to 54°50'N. Polk's aggressive tone irritated the British, but they were ready to give up Oregon because the fur trade there had dried up and was no longer profitable. Furthermore, the United States was an important customer for British manufactured goods, so Britain wanted to stay on good terms. Polk was not satisfied with the British offer of the 49th parallel as the boundary line, but, under the advice of the Senate, he accepted the treaty to obtain Oregon in the late spring of 1846.

The Mexican War (1846-1848)

Mexico considered the United States' annexation of Texas an act of aggression. Consequently, the Mexican diplomat in Washington, D.C. broke diplomatic ties and went home. This action did not weaken the territorial desires of President Polk, who, with many members of Congress, was a strong believer in Manifest Destiny. **Manifest Destiny** was the belief that it was God's will for the United States to expand and eventually possess the entire continent.

In June 1845, Polk ordered General Zachary Taylor to lead his troops to the Texas border. He also sent John Slidell to Mexico to settle the boundary dispute over the Río Grande river and to negotiate for the purchase of California and **New Mexico** (the area between Texas and California).

After the Mexican president refused to meet with Slidell, Polk ordered Taylor to move into the disputed territory between the Nueces and Río Grande rivers (March 8, 1845). In response, the Mexican troops crossed the Río Grande and attacked Taylor's forces. Immediately, Polk demanded that Congress declare war on Mexico because Mexicans had "shed American blood on American soil." Most members of Congress believed in the Manifest Destiny of the United States and supported the war. Though some representatives disagreed, Congress passed a declaration of war on May 13, 1846.

The Mexican War 1846-1847
Showing Territory Acquired by the United States

One month later, not knowing of the declaration of war, a group of United States settlers in **California** declared their independence from Mexico and formed the Bear Flag Republic (June 14, 1846). Their independence was short-lived because on July 7 the commander of the United States naval forces claimed California as a possession of the United States.

The **Mexican War** (1846-1848) was marked by victory after victory for the United States forces. The United States lost 12,000 soldiers in this war. The Mexicans lost even more lives. After fierce fighting, the Mexicans surrendered when United States General Winfield Scott marched into Mexico City on September 14, 1847.

The peace negotiations dragged on for several months, but finally, the United States and Mexico signed the **Treaty of Guadalupe Hidalgo** (February 2, 1848). In the treaty, Mexico gave up half its land, selling the territories of New Mexico and California to the United States for the equivalent of $18 million. This immense land purchase added 1,200,000 square miles to the United States, nearly completing the continental expansion of the United States and fulfilling its Manifest Destiny.

California Becomes a State

One week before the Treaty of Guadalupe Hidalgo was signed, James W. Marshall and John A. Sutter discovered gold in a river just north of Sacramento, California (January 24, 1848). By the following year, gold seekers came to California from all over the world in the **Gold Rush of 1849**. California's population rose to 90,000 by the end of 1849 and reached 220,000 by 1852. The tremendous growth in population produced a need for a stable government. The debate over slavery prevented the United States Congress from organizing California as a territory, so the Californians made their own arrangements. In September 1849, they drafted a

Courtesy Wells Fargo Historical Museum

**Placerville, California in the 1850s
(from a contemporary lithograph)**

state constitution, including a clause prohibiting slavery, which was approved by popular vote in November. Through a series of legislative compromises (**Compromise of 1850**), Congress admitted California as a free state on September 9, 1850.

Gadsden Purchase (1853)

In 1853, President **Franklin Pierce** (1804-1869) sent **James Gadsden** (1788-1858) to Mexico to settle the boundary disputes still remaining from the Treaty of Guadalupe Hidalgo and to purchase land for a southern transcontinental railroad. Over the objections of the Mexican people, the dictator Santa Anna accepted Gadsden's offer. In the **Gadsden Purchase** (1853), the United States paid $10 million to Mexico for parts of present-day New Mexico and Arizona. Northern

Gadsden Purchase

congressmen strongly opposed adding more slave territory, but President Pierce pushed the agreement through Congress. Eventually, the Southern Pacific Railroad built its tracks through this region.

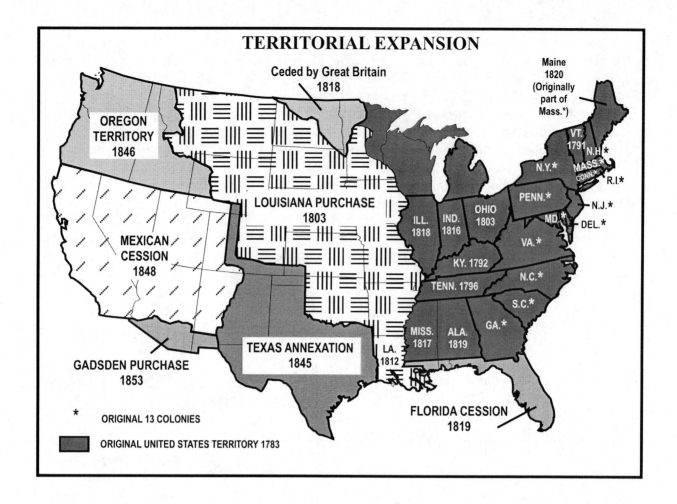

TERRITORIAL EXPANSION

Ceded by Great Britain 1818

Maine 1820 (Originally part of Mass.*)

OREGON TERRITORY 1846

LOUISIANA PURCHASE 1803

MEXICAN CESSION 1848

VT. 1791

N.H.*

N.Y.*

MASS.*

CONN.*

R.I.*

PENN.*

N.J.*

ILL. 1818

IND. 1816

OHIO 1803

MD.*

DEL.*

VA.*

KY. 1792

N.C.*

TENN. 1796

S.C.*

MISS. 1817

ALA. 1819

GA.*

LA. 1812

GADSDEN PURCHASE 1853

TEXAS ANNEXATION 1845

FLORIDA CESSION 1819

* ORIGINAL 13 COLONIES

ORIGINAL UNITED STATES TERRITORY 1783

SOCIAL PROBLEMS AND ANSWERS IN THE MID-1800s

Social Reform Movements

Inspired by religious and personal idealism, various reform movements gained momentum between 1830 and 1860. Supporters of these movements believed in the goodness of the human person and promoted changes in society to guarantee respect and dignity for all individuals regardless of race, gender, or class.

Second Great Awakening (1800-1860)

Periodically, from 1797 to 1859, fiery preachers would travel through the United States inspiring Christians with religious enthusiasm. Often they preached in meetings held outside, and they emphasized personal commitment to one's faith, not just membership in a church. They preached that God loved all people and that believers were to show their love for others through doing good works. They taught that God's love and grace changed people and that through good works people could change society to make it better. This revival of evangelical religion is called the **Second Great Awakening**. (The first Great Awakening peaked during the 1740s in colonial America.)

Transcendentalism

Also during the first half of the 19th century, a literary and philosophical movement developed called **transcendentalism**. Supporters of transcendentalism believed that all humans share in the spiritual unity of creation. They believed that human fulfillment would come through the awareness of truth and beauty found in nature and humankind. Suspicious of organized religion, they celebrated individualism and promoted self-reliance. The essayist and poet **Ralph Waldo Emerson** (1803-1882) was a leader in this movement, and promoted these ideas through his eloquent writings and

Ralph Waldo Emerson

lectures. In 1836, he helped found the Transcendental Club in Boston.

Henry David Thoreau

The writer, philosopher, and naturalist **Henry David Thoreau** (1817-1862) was also a member of the Transcendental Club. In 1846, Thoreau chose to go to jail rather than to support the Mexican War through paying taxes. He explained his reasons for nonviolent resistance to unjust laws in his famous essay "Civil Disobedience" (1849).

Transcendentalists believed that human beings could reach their full potential if they were freed from the artificial constraints imposed by society. This belief led them to support the movements for the abolition of slavery, women's rights, education, and temperance.

Educational and Social Reform

Horace Mann (1796-1859) was an influential American educator who advocated the education of both men and women through public schools. He believed that education was essential to the success of democracy claiming that "In a republic, ignorance is a crime." He opposed corporal punishment in schools, and he helped to create the state board of education in Massachusetts, the first in the United States. He also helped establish state hospitals for the insane and spoke against the sale of alcoholic beverages and lottery tickets.

Horace Mann

Dorothea Dix (1802-1887) impacted society by promoting legislation to improve mental institutions and prisons. Through her efforts, institutions for the insane and poor were created in 20 states and Canada. She also influenced improvements in prisons and housing for the poor in Europe.

Temperance Movement

During the early nineteenth century, the **temperance movement** began gaining momentum. Members of this movement wanted to moderate the use of alcohol. Later, they advocated total abstinence from alcohol. Several states passed laws prohibiting the sale of alcohol.

Abolitionist Movement

Abolitionists believed slavery was wrong, and they advocated laws to **abolish** it (put an end to it). The movement to abolish the **Atlantic slave trade** (bringing Africans to the Americas and selling them as slaves) grew strong in Europe in the late 1700s. The United States stopped trading Africans in 1808, but slavery persisted in the South until the mid-1800s.

Abolition In the United States

In the 1830s, the **abolitionist movement** gained momentum. Most people, however, viewed abolitionists as fanatics. Between 1833 and 1840, there were about 160,000 members of abolition societies. The white members were mostly middle class, educated, church people from Quaker or New England backgrounds. The black members were mostly former slaves. The following people were famous supporters of the Abolitionist Movement:

Frederick Douglass

1. **Harriet Tubman** (c. 1820-1913) was a hero of the abolitionist movement. She escaped slavery by running away to the North. Later, she returned secretly to the South nineteen times in order to lead other slaves to freedom by using the **Underground Railroad**. The Underground Railroad was not actually a railroad but a network of people who helped slaves escape to the northern United States or Canada.

2. **Frederick Douglass** (1817-1895) was so smart and so well-spoken that his opponents refused to believe that he had once been a slave. After escaping slavery in Maryland, he educated himself and became the most prominent African American speaker for the abolition of slavery. He worked with John Brown but would not support the Harper's Ferry raid (1859).

Published, 1852

3. **Harriet Beecher Stowe** (1811-1896) furthered the abolitionist cause through her novel, *Uncle Tom's Cabin* (1852). Though she was white and had never been a slave, her fictional account of the horrible experiences of a slave family motivated many people in the North and in Britain to support the movement to abolish slavery.

4. **Sojourner Truth** (c. 1797-1883) was born into slavery but was freed once New York emancipated slaves in 1828. Though illiterate, she became well-known and respected for her eloquent and charismatic speaking. As an abolitionist, she called for the equality of people of all colors. She also supported the equality of men and women by speaking for women's rights.

William Lloyd Garrison

5. **William Lloyd Garrison** (1805-1879) initially supported gradual emancipation but later came to believe complete and immediate emancipation was necessary. He founded an influential, anti-slavery newspaper called *The Liberator* (1831), and he helped establish the national **American Anti-Slavery Society** (1833).

Women's Rights Movement

As women participated in the abolitionist and temperance movements, they suffered discrimination from the men involved. Believing strongly in the equality of all persons, these intelligent and courageous women promoted the movement for equal rights for women and men.

With Lucretia Mott, **Elizabeth Cady Stanton** (1815-1902) helped organize the first women's rights convention, known as the **Seneca Falls Convention** (1848). Between 100 and 300 people attended, including Frederick Douglass. In her opening address, Stanton recalled the Declaration of Independence and proclaimed: "We hold these truths to be self-evident: that all men and women are created equal." When she advocated that women should have the right to vote, Mott told her she had gone too far. The delegates at the convention, however, agreed with Stanton. Women who supported the right to vote were known as **suffragettes**. They often suffered ridicule and physical violence from their opponents.

Susan B. Anthony (1820-1906) supported the temperance movement to ban alcohol, the abolition movement to free slaves, and the women's rights movement. She is best known for joining with Elizabeth Cady Stanton to fight for women's rights and, in particular, women's right to vote. While Stanton was busy with her young children, Anthony would often deliver speeches that Stanton had written.

Elizabeth Cady Stanton

Immigration versus Nativism

Between 1825 and 1855, more than 5 million immigrants entered the United States, mainly from northern Europe. Many **native-born citizens** (people born in the United States) felt threatened by the immigrants for the following reasons:

- Many immigrants settled together in neighborhoods where they preserved their language and culture. Native-born citizens feared the immigrants would change society, rather than assimilate into society.
- Coming to the United States with very little, immigrants often settled in city slums. Native-born citizens developed a prejudice that immigrants liked to live there.
- Native-born citizens feared that immigrants would take away their jobs.
- Most of the immigrants were Roman Catholic, which aroused the suspicion of Protestants in the United States.
- Southerners thought immigrants were anti-slavery because they settled in the North.
- Northerners thought immigrants were pro-slavery because they often tried to break up abolitionist meetings. (The immigrants feared that freed slaves would take their factory jobs.)

For these reasons, people developed feelings of **nativism**. Nativism is the opposition to foreigners and immigrants in order to protect the interests of native-born citizens in the United States. Because of this, many immigrants suffered discrimination and violence. During the 1840s and 1850s, many groups formed to oppose immigration. The most powerful of the groups was a secret society called the **Know-Nothings**. Members of the group vowed never to vote for a foreign-born or Roman Catholic candidate. The society's name came from the practice of members saying "I know nothing" when they were asked about the group. In the 1850s, Know-Nothing candidates won some state elections, but by 1861, the party had no representation in Congress and soon afterward it disappeared from the political scene. As more immigrants came from Southern Europe in the late 19th century, nativism grew again resulting in the immigration laws of the early 1900s.

The Arts in 19th Century United States

After the Revolutionary War (1775-1783), artists and writers followed European patterns, but in the mid-1800s, they began to develop a style unique to the United States. The seemingly unlimited possibilities of a new country with an expanding frontier captured the imagination of painters and authors.

Painting

In the late 1820s, **Thomas Cole** (1801-1848) began painting highly dramatic, romantic landscapes. He created unique paintings which displayed his vision of the awesome majesty of the United States wilderness. Other painters joined him near the Hudson River in New York and followed his style. This group of painters came to be called the **Hudson River School** (1820s-1880s). Their paintings were marked by meticulous and realistic attention to detail and a poetic feeling of nature. Their landscapes were the strongest and most original current in American painting.

Literature

Literature in the young republic flourished in the 1800s. Filled with the freedom of a vast frontier and the optimism of a fresh start, American writers created a literature that mirrored the newly forming nation. Their ideas reflected **nationalism** as they used settings and themes unique to the United States. Writers such as Cooper, Emerson, Thoreau, and Whitman envisioned an ideal America that questioned industrialization. Others such as Poe, Dickinson, and Hawthorne addressed the darker side of humanity.

Edgar Allen Poe

Emily Dickinson

During the early to mid-1800s, the following authors made significant contributions to the literature of the United States:

- **Noah Webster** (1758-1843) distinguished the language used in the United States from the language of Britain when he produced the first *American Dictionary of the English Language* (1828).
- **James Fenimore Cooper** (1759-1851) was a novelist who became known as the first great American writer. He idealized American life in his action-packed novels such as *The Last of the Mohicans* (1826).
- **Walt Whitman** (1819-1892) was a poet who emphasized the great worth of each individual in his poetry. He believed in a oneness of all humanity, and he captured the idealistic spirit of his time in his poetry. His break from traditional poetic styles of his day had a major influence on American literature.
- **Nathaniel Hawthorne** (1804-1864) was a novelist who wrote about sin, punishment, and atonement. Two of his most famous novels are *The Scarlet Letter* (1850) and *The House of the Seven Gables* (1851).
- **Edgar Allen Poe** (1809-1849) was a poet and also a master of the short-story. He is most famous for his mysterious and macabre tales such as "The Tell-Tale Heart" (1843) and his poem "The Raven" (1845).
- **Emily Dickinson** (1830-1886) wrote more than 1800 poems while living in seclusion, but only a few of them were published before her death. Her poems focused on love, death, and immortality. Today she is regarded as one of the greatest and most influential poets of the United States.

CHAPTER 6 REVIEW

A. **Define the following names, terms, and events:**

Thomas Jefferson	Adams-Onis Treaty	Panic of 1837
Louisiana Purchase	Monroe Doctrine	General Antonio Santa Anna
James Madison	John Quincy Adams	annexation
War Hawks	National Republicans	James K. Polk
Treaty of Ghent	Democrats	Manifest Destiny
Henry Clay	Andrew Jackson	Mexican War
tariff	spoils system	Treaty of Guadalupe Hildago
national bank	John C. Calhoun	Transcendentalism
Industrial Revolution	Doctrine of Nullification	Abolitionist Movement
National Road	Indian Removal Act	Seneca Falls Conference
Erie Canal	Trail of Tears	nativism
James Monroe	Whig Party	Know-Nothings
Convention of 1818	Martin Van Buren	

B. **On your own paper, write your response to each of the following:**

1. What were three results of the Louisiana Purchase?
2. Describe the British points of aggression upon which Madison and Congress based their call for war in 1812.
3. What were the direct and indirect results of the Treaty of Ghent?
4. Briefly discuss the three steps and the primary goal of Henry Clay's American System.
5. Identify two contributors to the Industrial Revolution, and describe the significance of their inventions or innovations.
6. What do you think was the impact of the National Road and the Erie Canal? Give details to support your answers.
7. What were four of the reasons that the United States experienced the "Era of Good Feelings"?
8. Name and discuss two major agreements made during Monroe's presidency.
9. What were the main points and the effects of the Monroe Doctrine?
10. Identify an unusual aspect of the election of 1824.
11. List and describe two positive and two negative contributions of President Andrew Jackson to democracy in the United States.
12. Discuss how and why the Whig Party was formed in America.
13. What were four of the reasons settlers moved west?
14. Contrast how and why the territories of Texas and Oregon were gained by the United States.
15. Explain how the self interest of the United States, in the form of Manifest Destiny, played a role in the Mexican War.
16. How did California become a state?
17. For each of the following movements, describe one person's contribution to it:
    a) Transcendental Movement, b) Educational and Social Reform, c) the Abolitionist Movement, and d) the Women's Rights Movement.
18. What were two effects of the vast immigration of the 1800s?
19. Why was the Hudson River School important?
20. Identify four key writers of the 1800s and their contribution.

C. **Write True if the statement is correct and False if the statement is incorrect. Be prepared to state a reason for your false answers.**

1. _____ Great Britain sold the Oregon Territory to the United States to maintain good trade relations.

2. _____ Native Americans were removed from their lands and settled on the fertile lowlands of Mississippi.

3. _____ The Second Great Awakening refers to the end of the slave trade in America, following Great Britain's lead.

4. _____ American writers such as Cooper, Thoreau, and Dickinson created a literature that mirrored the optimism of a newly forming nation.

5. _____ Samuel Slater established a cotton mill in Pawtucket, Rhode Island in 1790.

6. _____ Lewis and Clark were guided on their expedition to the Pacific by the Cherokee leader, Sequoia.

7. _____ Andrew Jackson won the 1828 election with the support of the North and East business special interests.

8. _____ The goal of the Temperance Movement was to ratify the 19th amendment, giving women the right to vote.

9. _____ In the Battle of Horseshoe Bend, Andrew Jackson defeated the Creeks with the help of the Cherokee people.

10. _____ Sam Houston led settlers in Texas to fight against Santa Anna.

11. _____ The trade of Africans as slaves stopped when the United States outlawed it in 1808.

12. _____ One cause of the War of 1812 was that French sailors deserted their navy to get higher wages on American ships.

13. _____ Thomas Cole wrote "The Star Spangled Banner" during the Battle of Fort McHenry.

14. _____ Texans defeated Santa Anna at the Battle of San Jacinto and took him hostage.

15. _____ One of the results of Henry Clay's American system was the creation of the Second Bank of the United States.

D. Matching: Write the letter in the blank which matches the description with the name or term.

1. _____ Walt Whitman

2. _____ John C. Calhoun

3. _____ Sacajawea

4. _____ Dorthea Dix

5. _____ Era of Good Feelings

6. _____ suffragettes

7. _____ Thomas Cole

8. _____ Noah Webster

9. _____ Henry Thoreau

10. _____ Transcendentalism

11. _____ Meriwether Lewis

12. _____ Samuel Slater

13. _____ Sam Houston

14. _____ Ralph Emerson

15. _____ Horace Mann

16. _____ Harriet Tubman

17. _____ W. L. Garrison

18. _____ E. Cady Stanton

19. _____ Eli Whitney

20. _____ Robert Fulton

A. senator of South Carolina - promoted states' rights and nullification

B. social reformer - promoted legislation to improve mental institutions and prisons

C. led an expedition to find a water route to the Pacific Ocean

D. women who supported the right for all women to vote - often suffered abuse by their opponents - but achieved their goal when the 19th amendment was passed

E. American poet who broke the rules of traditional poetry, writing with an idealistic view of the New World

F. invented the cotton gin, a machine which separated seeds from cotton so effectively that cotton became major crop in South - also invented muskets, long rifles with interchangeable parts, easy to manufacture and repair

G. led Texan settlers at the Alamo against Santa Anna in 1836

H. hero of the abolitionist movement - organized the "Underground Railroad" which planned and aided the escape of many slaves into freedom

I. literary and philosophical movement - belief that all humans share in the spiritual unity of creation - belief in individualism and self-reliance

J. used a steam- powered boat, the *Clermont,* as an effective means of transportation

K. artist whose creative work focused on dramatic wilderness landscapes: he inspired the Hudson River School, a group of artists who developed an American style of art

L. mood of national unity and optimism during Monroe's term

M. believed in immediate freedom for all slaves, founded an anti-slavery newspaper called the *Liberator,* and helped establish the National American Anti-slavery Society

N. talented Shoshone Native American woman - served as a translator and guide for Lewis and Clark on their expedition to find a water route to the Pacific Ocean

O. helped organize the first women's rights convention - believed women should have the right to vote

P. leader of the Transcendentalist movement - wrote in great detail on the beliefs of the philosophy

Q. produced a dictionary of American English, separating it from the "Queen's English"

R. textile worker who left England and also built the first cotton mill in this country

S. influential American educator - recommended education for both women and men through public funding

T. both lived and wrote about convictions concerning self-reliance and the unity of creation - this person's book *Walden* records observations made while living apart from society

CHAPTER 7
A NATION DIVIDED

In the early days of the United States, loyalty to one's state was often more important than loyalty to one's country. Neither North nor South had any strong sense of the permanence of the Union. New England, for example, once thought of **seceding**, or leaving the Union, because the War of 1812 cut off trade with England.

The economic, social, and political differences between the states in the South and the states in the North set the stage for conflict. The South and the North differed in several important ways:

SOUTH

- Agrarian, or farming, economy based on cotton, which represented 57% of all United States exports
- Cotton production was tied to the plantation system which relied on slavery
- Few immigrants from Europe
- Manufactured little, imported much; consequently, opposed high tariffs because they raised the price of imported goods
- Did not need strong central government and feared it might interfere with slavery

NORTH

- Industrial economy based on manufacturing
- Factories needed labor, but not slave labor
- Immigrants worked in factories, built railroads, settled the West
- Wanted high tariffs to protect its own products from cheap foreign competition
- Needed central government to build roads and railways, to protect trading interests, and to regulate the national currency

The United States required foreign companies bringing products into the United States to pay money to the government in order to sell them. The federal government relied on these **tariffs** for income because there were no taxes on personal or corporate income. The tariffs paid for infrastructure such as roads, canals, and turnpikes. Southerners preferred to do without these improvements in order to keep tariffs low.

The expanding **Northwest Territory**, made up of what is now Ohio, Indiana, Illinois, Michigan, Wisconsin and part of Minnesota, was far from the eastern markets that bought its grain and cattle. It relied on internal improvements to transport its goods, so it supported the Northeast's demands for high tariffs. In return, the Northeast supported most federally financed transportation projects in the Northwest Territory.

The various political, social and economic differences between the South and the North were underlying factors, if not always explicit issues, in the debate and controversy over slavery.

COUNTDOWN TO SECESSION

- **1820** - A debate raged in Congress over Missouri's application for statehood. Slave states and free states were equally represented in the Senate, though the more populous North held more seats in the House of Representatives. Missouri's admission would disrupt the balance of power. Senator Jesse B. Thomas of Illinois proposed a bill calling for the admission of Missouri as a slave state and Maine as a free state. In addition, the southern boundary of Missouri, 36°30'N, would become a dividing line for any new states admitted to the Union. All new states north of that line would be free states, while those to the south would be slave states. The bill passed through Congress and was signed into law by President Monroe in 1820. It became known as the **Missouri Compromise**.

- **1833** - A volatile dispute between South Carolina and the federal government occurred when a new law raised tariffs on items from Europe - sometimes as high as fifty percent. Because the South relied on Europe for manufactured goods, the residents of this region felt singled out by the federal government. For this reason, South Carolina threatened to **nullify**, or ignore the law altogether. As a compromise, the federal government agreed to reduce the tariffs over a nine year period, which appeased the people of South Carolina.

- **1850** - A new controversy arose as the United States gained vast territories of land from Mexico in the Southwest. Would Congress admit the new states and territories as slave or free? Having returned to the Senate after a seven year absence from Washington, Henry Clay of Kentucky proved his desire for national unity by proposing the **Compromise of 1850**. In this agreement, Congress would admit California as a free state, the unorganized territory of the West would be admitted as free territory, but the Utah and New Mexico Territories would be open to slavery by **popular sovereignty**. Popular sovereignty meant the people living in the area would vote on whether or not to allow slavery. Due to the support of Clay, Daniel Webster, and Stephen Douglas, as well as the death of President Zachary Taylor, the compromise resolutions were passed into law.

- **1850** - The **Fugitive Slave Law** was attached to the Compromise of 1850. Congress enacted the Fugitive Slave Law to mandate that northern states forcibly return escaped slaves to their owners in the South. This law was very unpopular in the North. Many northern states used the South Carolina Doctrine of Nullification to justify their position of not obeying this law.

- **1854** - Congress passed the **Kansas-Nebraska Act** which President Pierce signed into law. After fierce debate, this act allowed the previously free and unorganized territories of Kansas and Nebraska to choose whether or not to permit slavery. This act inflamed the smoldering slavery question by, in effect, repealing the Missouri Compromise. Settlers rushed into Kansas from both the North and the South. Kansas became known as **"Bleeding Kansas"** as armed clashes between pro-slavery forces and abolitionist settlers became commonplace. Because of illegal voting on the part of pro-slavery forces, two governments, one slave and the other free, were set up in Kansas. Kansas essentially existed as a state in civil war.

- **1854** - A coalition of Democrats, Whigs, and **Free-Soilers** (a party believing slavery must not be permitted in any new territory) formed the **Republican Party**. The party was most noted for opposing the extension of slavery in the territories.

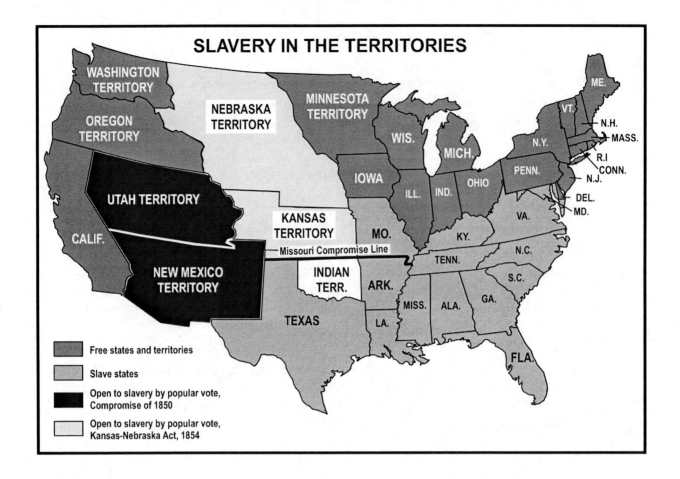

SLAVERY IN THE TERRITORIES

WASHINGTON TERRITORY

OREGON TERRITORY

NEBRASKA TERRITORY

MINNESOTA TERRITORY

WIS.

MICH.

ME.

VT.

N.H.

MASS.

N.Y.

R.I

CONN.

N.J.

PENN.

UTAH TERRITORY

IOWA

ILL.

IND.

OHIO

DEL.

MD.

CALIF.

KANSAS TERRITORY

MO.

VA.

KY.

Missouri Compromise Line

NEW MEXICO TERRITORY

INDIAN TERR.

ARK.

TENN.

N.C.

S.C.

TEXAS

MISS.

ALA.

GA.

LA.

FLA.

Free states and territories

Slave states

Open to slavery by popular vote, Compromise of 1850

Open to slavery by popular vote, Kansas-Nebraska Act, 1854

- **1856** - The violence in and around Kansas drew national attention. On May 21st, pro-slavery forces from Missouri and Kansas looted and burned the abolitionist town of Lawrence, Kansas. The next day, Republican **Senator Charles Sumner** (1811-1874) of Massachusetts addressed the Senate, denouncing the violence in Kansas and fiercely criticizing **Senator Andrew Butler** of South Carolina. Two days later, Senator Butler's nephew, a member of the House of Representatives, beat Sumner with a cane until he was unconscious. The beating was so severe that Sumner could not appear on the floor of the Senate for three years. This attack was seen as a setback for democracy in the nation.

- **1857** - The **Dred Scott Decision** threw the nation into turmoil. Dred Scott, a slave in Missouri, was taken by his owner onto Northern soil. In fact, he lived in the Wisconsin Territory for four years with his owner. When the owner returned to Missouri, Dred Scott sued for his freedom. Regarding Scott's case, the Supreme Court made the following rulings:

Dred Scott

  1. No slave or descendant of a slave was a citizen according to the Constitution.

  2. Dred Scott was not a citizen, so he had no right to bring a case to federal court.

  3. The time Scott spent on free soil did not make him free. As a resident of Missouri, he was governed by the state's laws which declared him a slave.

4. Under the Fifth Amendment, Congress could not deprive anyone of property, including slaves, without due process of law. The federal government was required to protect the property rights of slave owners regardless of where the owners took their slaves. Therefore, the Missouri Compromise, which had forbidden slavery above 36°30' N, was unconstitutional.

This ruling established that slave owners had the right to bring slaves into free territories and states. Further, the federal government would protect that right, including bringing runaway slaves back to their masters. Many were shocked by this decision which marked only the second time the Supreme Court had declared a piece of federal legislation unconstitutional. The Republicans opposed slavery in the territories and the northern Democrats supported popular sovereignty. The Supreme Court's decision undermined both positions.

- **1858** - Republican **Abraham Lincoln** (1809-1865) and Democrat **Stephen A. Douglas** (1813-1861) argued the opposing positions in their contest for a Senate seat in Illinois. In a series of public debates, their verbal skills and the importance of the issues argued brought national attention to this local election, and to the little-known Lincoln. "Honest Abe" held his own against "the Little Giant" especially when he asked how Douglas's support for popular sovereignty could withstand the Dred Scott Decision. With his eye on the 1860 Presidential race, Douglas tried to appeal to southern Democrats, as well as to the people of his home state. He argued that slavery could not be instituted without laws to govern it. If a territory had no slave laws, it could not have slaves. This idea, stated in a debate in Freeport, Illinois, became known as the **Freeport Doctrine**. The people of Illinois re-elected Douglas, but he lost his support in the South due to his ambivalence regarding slavery. Even though Lincoln lost the election, he proved to be a strong candidate, and he gained national notoriety.

Republican Abraham Lincoln and Democrat Stephen A. Douglas debated the opposing positions in their contest for a Senate seat in Illinois.

- **1859** - **John Brown** (1800-1859) took his fierce abolitionist ideas to the South where he hoped to arm the slaves and lead them in a rebellion. One October night, he led a band of followers to seize an **arsenal** (a place for making or storing weapons and munitions) at Harper's Ferry, Virginia. His group was soon captured by federal troops. The court found John Brown guilty of treason and hanged him. Though many northern leaders thought Brown was fanatical, his death helped galvanize the abolitionist movement. Southerners saw the northern sympathy for Brown as a sign that their security was at risk.

John Brown gathers supporters for his rebellion at Harper's Ferry, Virginia.

- **1860** - At its convention, the Democratic Party split along sectional lines over the issue of slavery. The northern Democrats supported slavery in the new territories as determined by popular sovereignty and nominated Stephen Douglas. The southern Democrats wanted federal protection of slavery in the territories, so they nominated John Breckinridge of Kentucky as their candidate. He was Vice President at this time. Meanwhile, the Republican Party chose Abraham Lincoln to run for the presidency because he opposed the extension of slavery into new territories, but he was not closely associated with abolitionists.

- **1860** - The South felt threatened by the candidacy of Lincoln. Unlike Douglas, who considered slavery a legitimate choice, Lincoln considered it a moral evil. The southern states feared that, as President, Lincoln would seek not only to prevent slavery in the new territories, but to dismantle it in the South. Consequently, South Carolina's governor declared his intention to secede if Lincoln won the election. Lincoln won easily due to the divisions in the Democratic Party, and the governor followed his intended course.

- **December 20, 1860** - At a special convention called by the state legislature, South Carolina declared its **secession** from the United States. By February 1, 1861, six other states had seceded: Mississippi, Alabama, Georgia, Florida, Louisiana, and Texas. As the states seceded, they proceeded to seize most federal forts within their borders.

FORT SUMTER

The day after his inauguration, President Lincoln learned that the soldiers at Fort Sumter had only one month of supplies remaining. Wanting to uphold the Union without provoking war, he notified the Governor of South Carolina that he was sending ships with food but no soldiers or munitions. On April 12, 1861, before the relief ships arrived, Confederate soldiers opened fire on the fort. After two days of fighting, the federal soldiers were forced to surrender. The shots fired here began the **Civil War (1861 - 1865)**.

Fort Sumter

BATTLE LINES ARE DRAWN

In response to the events at Fort Sumter, President Lincoln issued a call for 75,000 volunteer soldiers from all the states remaining in the Union. The so-called border states were forced to decide whether to support the Union or the Confederacy. With a great deal of controversy and division, Kentucky, Missouri and Maryland remained in the Union, while Virginia, North Carolina, Arkansas and Tennessee joined the Confederacy. The capital of the Confederacy was then moved from Montgomery, Alabama to Richmond, Virginia. Jefferson Davis, a senator from Mississippi, was elected president of the Confederacy.

Jefferson Davis, President of theConfederacy

THE UNION'S MILITARY STRATEGY

With the advantages of having over three times as many soldiers, supplies, and industries, the North had one goal: **Compel the Southern states to rejoin the Union.**

To reach this goal, the Union needed to accomplish the following:

- invade the South
- destroy the South's ability to wage war
- lower the morale of the South, so the South would no longer fight

The plan followed during the war was called the **Anaconda Plan**. The strategy was to squeeze the South by applying a naval blockade around the southern coast. In addition, the North would seize the Mississippi River to divide the western Confederate states from the eastern Confederate states. Like an anaconda, the Union wanted to circle the South in tighter and tighter circles with Northern troops until the Confederate supply lines were cut, and the fighting spirit of the South was crushed.

THE CONFEDERACY'S MILITARY STRATEGY

Because the South knew it was not strong enough to invade the North, the Confederacy had a different goal: **Force the Union to recognize the rights of southern states to secede.**

To reach this goal, the Confederacy needed to accomplish the following:

- prolong the War until the North tired of fighting and asked for peace
- convince European nations to support the South in its goals

Using the Revolutionary War as a model, the Confederacy hoped to win by wearing down the will of the stronger North, just as the colonies had done with Great Britain. They also hoped to secure the help of stronger nations such as Great Britain and France to break possible Union naval blockades.

The Confederacy had two distinct advantages over the Union:

1. The South would fight a defensive war. This meant that battles would occur over terrain and climate that were familiar to the Confederate soldiers.
2. The South had better educated and more competent generals than the North.

Both sides felt the war would be over quickly and decisively. Soldiers volunteered to serve by the hundreds of thousands. However, when the first fighting occurred in Virginia at **Bull Run** (July 21, 1861), both sides could see that a long and hard war lay ahead.

CHAPTER 7 REVIEW

A.   Define the following names, terms, and events:

secede	Fugitive Slave Law	Abraham Lincoln
tariff	Kansas-Nebraska Act	Stephen Douglas
Northwest Territory	Bleeding Kansas	John Brown
Missouri Compromise	Republican Party	Fort Sumter
Compromise of 1850	Charles Sumner	Anaconda Plan
popular sovereignty	Dred Scott Decision	

B.   On your own paper, write your response to each of the following:

1. List three differences between the North and the South prior to the Civil War.
2. Why did Northerners and Southerners disagree about tariffs?
3. How did the Missouri Compromise reduce conflict between the North and South?
4. Discuss Henry Clay's proposals in creating the Compromise of 1850.
5. Why did northern states ignore the Fugitive Slave Law?
6. Discuss two effects of the Kansas-Nebraska Act.
7. How did the Dred Scott Decision affect the North and the South?
8. In what ways did John Brown's raid at Harper's Ferry increase tension in the United States?
9. Why were the Lincoln-Douglas debates important?
10. List the major candidates in the election of 1860 and their position on slavery.
11. Discuss the formation of the Confederacy.
12. What two military advantages did the Confederacy have over the Union?

C.   Write True if the statement is correct and False if the statement is incorrect. Be prepared to state a reason for your false answers.

1. _____   Georgia was the first state to secede from the union in 1860.

2. _____   The primary goal of the Confederacy was to invade the North and win the right to end slavery.

3. _____   In the Dred Scott Decision, the federal government ruled that the property rights of slave owners must be protected regardless of where the owners take their slaves.

4. _____   The Kansas-Nebraska Act upheld the Missouri Compromise ruling, limiting slavery.

5. _____   One of the basic differences between the North and the South was that the North did not need a strong central government.

6. _____   The first shots of the Civil War were fired upon Fort Sumter by the Confederates.

7. _____   The Fugitive Slave Law was popular in the North as a good compromise to free states.

8. _____ Jefferson Davis, a senator from Mississippi, was elected President of the Confederacy.

9. _____ The Anaconda Plan, conceived by the North, was designed to circle the South cutting supply lines.

10. _____ Before the war, large waves of immigrants, seeking a more temperate climate, migrated to the South.

CHAPTER 8
CIVIL WAR AND RECONSTRUCTION

DECISIVE BATTLES OF THE CIVIL WAR (1861-1865)

- **First Battle of Bull Run (July 21, 1861)** - The Union and the Confederates fought this battle in Virginia, 30 miles south of Washington, D.C. It was a humiliating defeat for the North and almost led to a Confederate invasion of Washington, D.C.

- **Shiloh (April 6-7, 1862)** - This battle in Shiloh, Tennessee was the bloodiest of the Civil War. Total casualties for both sides numbered over 20,000. This battle ended without any clear winner in the West.

- **Antietam (September 17, 1862)** - **General George B. McClellan** (1826-1885) led the Union forces to victory here as commander of the Army of the Potomac. However, the Union casualties were so high from this battle that Lincoln had McClellan relieved of command. **Robert E. Lee**, a brilliant Southern general, planned an invasion of the North, but his battle strategies fell into the hands of a northern soldier. As a result, Lee met a larger force of Union soldiers than he had anticipated. The battle at Antietam Creek, Maryland is considered the bloodiest one day battle in the history of the United States. It was after this Union victory that Lincoln issued the **Emancipation Proclamation (1863)**.

- **Chancellorsville (May 1-4, 1863)** - General Hooker with his army of 130,000 soldiers, attacked the armies of Generals Lee and Jackson, which had 60,000 soldiers. Through deft maneuvering, the outnumbered Confederate forces defeated the much larger Union army. However, through a mistake, a Confederate soldier wounded General Jackson, leading to his death eight days later. Nevertheless, this Confederate victory persuaded General Lee to launch an offensive onto Union soil, resulting in the Battle of Gettysburg.

- **Vicksburg (May 15-July 4, 1863)** - After Union forces under General Farragut had taken the port city of New Orleans, they began moving north to gain control of the Mississippi River. The town of Vicksburg, Mississippi was very well guarded by the Confederacy and was the last major obstacle to total Union control of the Mississippi River. General Sherman and other leaders advised Union forces to retreat from the Vicksburg area in early 1863. However, Union General Ulysses S. Grant ignored this advice and began a bold siege of General Pemberton's Confederate forces at Vicksburg, lasting almost two months. On the fourth of July, Grant's forces conquered the city. Consequently, the Mississippi River came under the control of the Union.

Union forces led by General Ulysses S. Grant conquer Vicksburg, Mississippi and gain control of the Mississippi River.

- **Gettysburg (July 1-3, 1863)** - Union forces repeatedly defeated the Confederates as General Lee tried to take control of the city of Gettysburg, Pennsylvania. In November 1863, at this site, Lincoln gave **The Gettysburg Address**, which affirmed his belief in democracy and his desire to see the warring nation reunited in peace. This battle was considered the turning point of the war because the Confederacy no longer had the ability to launch an offensive into Union territory.

- **Chattanooga (November 23-25, 1863)** - After their defeat at Chickamauga in Georgia, Union troops retreated into Tennessee. A combined Union force from the armies of Sherman, Grant, and Hooker defeated the Southern forces occupying Lookout Mountain in Tennessee. Confederate forces fled Tennessee after this battle, placing the entire state in the hands of the Union and cutting off important railway supplies to Atlanta, Georgia.

- **Mobile Bay (August 5, 1864)** - Naval Admiral Farragut successfully attacked the Confederate forts defending Mobile Bay in Alabama, using his four armored warships and fourteen wooden vessels. After several months of fighting, Union troops occupied the city, thus cutting off an important supply port of the Confederacy.

- **Atlanta (September 2, 1864)** - Three months after Sherman's defeat at Kennesaw Mountain, he was able to advance against Atlanta, Georgia, which was a vital railroad terminal for the South. Sherman burned Atlanta to the ground, destroying the ability of the Confederacy to supply the war effort.

- **Sherman's March (May - December 1864)** - For this infamous march, Sherman hand-picked 60,000 soldiers to destroy everything in a 60 mile-wide path from Chattanooga, Tennessee, through Atlanta to Savannah, Georgia. Sherman wanted to destroy the railroad tracks and farms to disable the civilians from helping the Confederate army. The soldiers looted, raped, and murdered civilians and burned their towns from Chattanooga to the city gates of Savannah. Sherman then turned his forces north towards Virginia to meet with Grant and defeat Lee's army with their combined forces. Sherman's army continued its destruction as it moved north through the Carolinas, which included burning Columbia, South Carolina. Sherman's March and the burning of Atlanta broke the spirit of the Confederates creating bitterness and tension between the North and the South that exist to some degree even today.

SHERMAN'S MARCH (MAY - DECEMBER 1864)

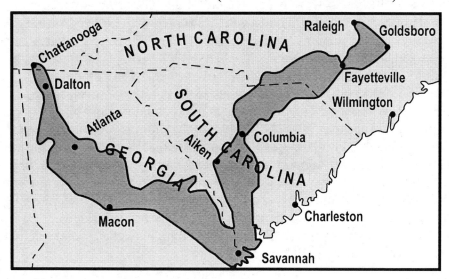

95

- **Surrender at Appomattox (April 9, 1865)** -
Realizing his army was outnumbered by more than two-to-one, General Lee surrendered to General Grant at the courthouse in Appomattox, Virginia. Grant offered generous terms of surrender, and the Civil War ended.

General Lee surrenders to General Grant at the Appomattox Courthouse in Virginia.

SOCIAL AND POLITICAL CHANGES DURING THE CIVIL WAR

As the battle lines were being drawn, Maryland was split between North and South. However, if Maryland joined the Confederacy, the Union capital, Washington, D.C., would be surrounded by Confederate territory. After Confederate sympathizers attacked Union troops in Baltimore, President Lincoln declared martial law in Maryland and suspended the right of **habeas corpus**. Habeas corpus guaranteed that a person could not be imprisoned without appearing in court. The President then jailed the strongest supporters of the Confederacy. As a result, the Maryland legislature voted to remain in the Union. The suspension was lifted at the end of the Civil War.

For the first time in United States history, men were **drafted** (forced to serve in the military) to fight the opposing side in the Civil War. The Confederacy started the draft first in April 1862. The draft did not produce many more men, and soldiers could hire someone else to take their place on both sides. When Lincoln initiated the draft in 1863, opposition was fierce. Lincoln included a provision allowing men selected to either serve in the military or pay 300 dollars. The poverty-stricken immigrant Irish resented this rich man's provision and held blacks responsible for the Civil War. Whites in New York City killed over 1,000 people over the course of three days of rioting. The rioters also made a point of looting the homes of the rich. Property damage from the riot was about 2 million dollars. Federal troops quelled the rioters, and order was restored.

Black Participation in the Civil War

During the war, blacks in the North volunteered for service in the army. In the beginning, they could only serve in non-combat roles. However, by the summer of 1862, Congress allowed blacks to serve in combat. They formed all-black units in many states. Led by white commanders, these units had to serve in harsh conditions. The army gave them half the pay of white soldiers. However, the 200,000 black soldiers served with bravery during the war effort. Black soldiers fought with such bravery during the war that Secretary of War Stanton said that blacks "have proved themselves among the bravest of the brave, performing deeds of daring and shedding their blood with a heroism unsurpassed by soldiers of any other race."

Some blacks—historians do not agree on the exact numbers— even served in the Confederate military While the Confederate States Army did not allow blacks to enlist until late in the war, both free and enslaved blacks did serve in the militias of some of the Confederate states from early in the war. Furthermore, some enslaved blacks went into battle with their masters. Other blacks indirectly supported the Confederate war effort through their work on plantations and in factories. However, they increasingly sabotaged their work or refused to work. The pace of defection to the Union lines increased once slaves received word of the Emancipation Proclamation. Because their labor was badly needed, slaves often went on strike or refused to work without being paid. Slaves in the South played a crucial role in both the support and later, the decline, of the Confederacy.

President Lincoln reads the Emancipation Proclamation for the first time to his cabinet members.

President Lincoln issued the **Emancipation Proclamation**, on January 1, 1863, freeing the slaves in the Confederate States, while maintaining slavery in the border states loyal to the Union. With this executive order, Lincoln hoped to give the war a moral focus beyond saving the Union and undermine the slave labor force supporting the Confederacy. He also wanted to insure the support of England and France which had already abolished slavery. Two years later, Congress passed the **13th Amendment** which abolished slavery throughout the United States.

IMPORTANCE OF RAIL AND SUPPLY LINES

During the war, the North had a clear advantage in both rail and supply lines. Seventy-five percent of the railroads were located in the North. These railroads enabled soldiers fighting far from home to have easy access to essential supplies such as food, clothing, and weapons. When Sherman marched through the South, Atlanta was targeted because it was the major railroad hub of the Confederacy. With Southern railroads destroyed and the naval blockade complete, Confederate soldiers were unable to continue the war effort.

COST OF WAR

More United States soldiers died in this war than in all the other wars in United States history combined. Over 600,000 men were killed during their time as soldiers in the Union or Confederate armies. Over half of these soldiers did not die in battle, however. Many soldiers died from common illnesses which were aggravated by the unsanitary conditions of life in the camps or in the war prisons. The major culprits in these soldiers' deaths were diarrhea, typhoid, measles, malaria, and dysentery.

The economic and social costs and gains of the war for each side were strikingly different.

The North

- At the start of the war, the Union federal budget was 63 million dollars. By the end of the war, the budget had grown 200 times larger to 1.3 billion dollars. To gain this money, the government began printing more dollars, causing inflation to increase quickly.

- Mostly due to wartime demands, industrial production increased to record high levels. International immigration increased in the urban North, and three new states joined the Union – Kansas, West Virginia, and Nevada.

- The Union was restored.

- Over 360,000 Union soldiers lost their lives.

- The return of 800,000 soldiers to work plus the slower demand for manufactured products in the North led to a short-lived **recession** (economic downturn characterized by higher unemployment).

The South

- The South lost its fight for independence, and its slave-based economy was abolished.

- Over 258,000 Confederate soldiers lost their lives.

- The South was devastated. With railroads and factories destroyed, banks closed.

- With farms destroyed and slaves emancipated, the agricultural economy declined.

- Some people feared retaliation from the North and from former slaves.

- Over ⅔ of southern wealth was destroyed. The majority of the wealth disappeared when the slaves, who were highly prized by their owners, received their freedom.

LIFE FOR EMANCIPATED BLACKS

Emancipated slaves were called "**freedmen**," and they experienced many difficulties even in their newly acquired freedom. Among these difficulties were:

- Illiteracy was widespread because teaching slaves to read and write had been illegal in most states.

- Freed slaves were skilled in farming but owned no land and had no money to purchase any land.

- Few people could afford to hire freedmen, and working for former masters was like going back to slavery.

After the Civil War, freed slaves were not given a portion of their masters' land. Instead, they had two choices. They either migrated to the North to work in factories, or they stayed in the South to work as **sharecroppers** and **tenant farmers**.

In **sharecropping**, blacks and poor whites cultivated a portion of a landowner's farmland. The crop, usually cotton, was then harvested and sold at the market. Once living expenses and tools were taken out of the earnings, the sharecropper received a portion of the profit.

photograph of a sharecropper

In **tenant farming**, the renter cultivates a parcel of land. After the harvest and the sale of the produce, the landlord is paid for rent of the land.

Under both systems, the harvests often did not pay for the expenses associated with the crop, so tenant farmers were given an amount of money to start the next year. In this manner, the sharecroppers and tenant farmers grew deeper and deeper in debt. This form of indebtedness put blacks in a condition of servitude similar to slavery.

In an effort to meet the immediate needs of those displaced by the war, Congress established the **Freedmen's Bureau** in March 1865. The Bureau was intended to aid both blacks and whites, but it served mostly blacks. The bureau provided clothing and surplus army food, five million dollars and agents to organize schools for black children and adults, medical care for over one million people, and agents to find work for freedmen and prevent exploitation. Some Southerners saw the Bureau as a Republican effort to help blacks at the expense of whites.

RECONSTRUCTION

Different Views of Reconstruction

Even before the Civil War ended, politicians in the North argued over how to readmit the rebellious states, or "reconstruct" the South. One reason the Executive Branch and Congress battled over Reconstruction was due to their differing understandings of the secession of the Southern states. President Lincoln and his successor, Andrew Johnson, believed that no state had a legal right to secede. Therefore, those individuals involved in rebellion were guilty of insurrection. The President was responsible for bringing those persons under the authority of the federal government and restoring the Union as quickly as possible.

Congress agreed that the President had authority to quell an insurrection, but they believed once the armed rebellion was thwarted, Congress should determine the political future of the "rebellious" states. According to the Republicans in Congress, the Confederate states forfeited their statehood when they seceded. In fact, Senator Charles Sumner of Massachusetts declared that the states had "committed suicide" by seceding, so they were to be treated like territories. Senator Sumner was a leader of the **Radicals** in Congress. Radicals were the Republicans who called for strict readmission standards and vigorous restructuring of the South.

President Lincoln wanted to restore the Union quickly while allowing for a gradual and peaceful restructuring of the South. Before the war, he believed that if slavery could be contained in the South, and not expanded to the territories, the moral evil of slavery would eventually be overcome. In a similarly patient way, he compared the rebirth of the South to the gentle process of hatching an egg saying, "We shall sooner have the fowl by hatching the egg than by smashing it." He considered reunification to be his duty as President.

The Republicans in Congress, however, feared the return of the Southern Democrats. The Republicans had gained control of Congress when the South seceded. During the war, they were able to push through legislation that the southern representatives had blocked previously, such as a national banking system, higher tariffs, and the Homestead Act. The Republicans did not want the Southerners to reverse these policies. Also, many of the Republicans were abolitionists, and they wanted to make sure blacks were guaranteed equal rights before the southern states were readmitted.

Different Plans for Reconstruction

Lincoln's plan for Reconstruction called for a generous way to readmit Southern states into the Union. For each state to be admitted, and for the occupying forces of the North to leave, 10% of the voting populace had to swear allegiance to the Union and the Constitution. Louisiana and Arkansas, both completely in Union control by 1864, were readmitted to the Union that same year in this fashion.

However, a twist of fate changed the tone of Reconstruction. On **April 14, 1865**, Lincoln and his wife attended a play at Ford's Theater. **John Wilkes Booth** (1838-1865), a Confederate sympathizer, killed Lincoln by shooting him in the back of the head during the performance. **Vice President Andrew Johnson** (1808-1875)

drawing of the scene in Ford's Theater as John Wilkes Booth flees after assassinating President Abraham Lincoln

became the new President for the remainder of Lincoln's second term. Johnson was sympathetic to white Southerners and advocated a mild form of Reconstruction that allowed the whites to maintain their power and keep blacks out of office. Before Congress could convene, the state governments in the South passed a series of **Black Codes**. While securing some basic rights for blacks, these codes, in effect, made blacks second-class citizens. For example, blacks could not own weapons, meet together after sundown, or marry whites.

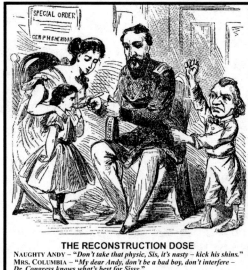

THE RECONSTRUCTION DOSE
NAUGHTY ANDY – *"Don't take that physic, Sis, it's nasty – kick his shins."*
MRS. COLUMBIA – *"My dear Andy, don't be a bad boy, don't interfere – Dr. Congress knows what's best for Sissy."*

1800s Political Cartoon showing the South as a little girl, Congress as a medical doctor trying to administer reconstruction, and President Johnson as a naughty little boy who is trying to interfere.

Many people in the North felt that the Civil War would be meaningless if blacks were not given citizenship rights in the South. In addition, the public outrage in the North over Lincoln's assassination was enormous. Politicians began demanding a harsher form of Reconstruction for the southern states. While Congress was not in session, President Johnson allowed all of the southern states to enter the Union under Lincoln's plan for Reconstruction. The states elected Democrats who supported keeping whites in power and keeping blacks in various conditions of servitude. Furious that the President did not seek Congressional approval, Congress refused to seat the representatives from the South and began its own stricter plan for Reconstruction.

Radical Reconstruction

On June 13, 1866, Congress passed the **14th Amendment** which stated, "All persons born or naturalized in the United States . . . are citizens." The amendment prohibited states from repaying the Confederacy's war debts and from compensating slave owners for the loss of the slaves. It penalized states for denying the voting rights of male citizens and required that government officials who had joined the Confederacy be pardoned by Congress before returning to public office.

During the summer of 1866, President Johnson offered strong opposition to the 14th Amendment and urged the southern states to reject it. Except for Tennessee, the southern states followed his advice. Riots in Memphis and New Orleans convinced Northerners that Johnson's leniency toward the South was not working. Northerners responded in the fall elections. Republicans won a majority in every northern state legislature, every northern governor's race, and more than a two-thirds majority in Congress, guaranteeing the ability to override Johnson's vetoes. In the spring of 1866, the Republican Congress passed its most radical plan for Reconstruction, despite Johnson's veto.

The main features of this **Reconstruction Act** (March 1867) were the following:

1) With the exception of Tennessee, which had ratified the 14th Amendment, all former Confederate states would be administered as five military districts;
2) Southern states would not be readmitted until they ratified the 14th Amendment;
3) Black citizens must be granted the right to vote;
4) Former Confederate officials could not hold public office.

Fearing that President Johnson would thwart the enforcement of the Reconstruction Act, Congress passed several laws which limited his power and strengthened the Reconstruction Act itself. While Congress was in recess for the summer, Johnson violated one of these laws by firing the Secretary of War. Upon returning to Washington, the House of Representatives threatened to **impeach** Johnson, which means removing him from office. On February 24, 1868, after several months of investigation, the House voted to impeach Johnson, even though the evidence against him was quite weak. He escaped a conviction in the Senate by one vote and finished his term as President. His political power had been significantly weakened by the whole process. At the end of his term, Johnson returned to Tennessee and was elected senator.

A New Kind of Politics

Ready to capture the presidency, the Radicals nominated **Ulysses S. Grant** to be the Republican candidate in 1868. Grant's popularity as a hero of the Civil War made him a strong candidate, and the 700,000 blacks voting for the first time ensured his victory. These new voters put a majority of Republicans in office, including many black officials who held office for the first time in the South. During the Reconstruction years (1868-1877), there were 14 black representatives elected to Congress and two black senators. Both senators were from Mississippi, including **Hiram R. Revels** who filled the seat last held by **Jefferson Davis** (former President of the Confederacy). On February 26, 1869, Congress passed the **15th Amendment** which guaranteed voting rights to all citizens regardless of "race, color, or previous condition of servitude." The amendment was ratified by the states within a year.

Bitter Feelings in the South

Throughout the South, whites had bitter feelings regarding the North and Northerners:

- The South was bitter about losing the war and losing its slaves.
- They were angry at Northerners for imposing Reconstruction on them.
- White supremacists called Republicans traitors to their race.
- They resented the high taxes which paid for the Reconstruction programs. These taxes were a double burden because of the economic hardships caused by the war.
- They blamed corruption in government on Reconstruction, Republicans, and black politicians.
- They resented carpetbaggers and scalawags.

Carpetbaggers were people who came from the North to do business in the South. Many were Union army officers who stayed in the South for the climate or the opportunities they saw. Others were teachers, ministers, or workers for the Freedmen's Bureau. It is estimated that B of them were trained as lawyers, doctors, and engineers. White Southerners derided them for supporting blacks and accused them of seeking opportunities for themselves at the expense of others.

Scalawags were Southerners who supported Reconstruction. Some scalawags had supported the Union during the Civil War and agreed with Reconstruction. Others accepted it as inevitable. Regardless of their reasoning, some newspapers would publish their names and recommend that they be shunned by the community.

Founded in 1866, the **Ku Klux Klan** (KKK), used terrorism and violence to intimidate blacks and other minorities. This secretive organization was designed to remove from power the people in Reconstruction governments who were giving rights to blacks. Dressed in hooded white robes, Klansmen would frequently burn crosses in the front yards of people they wished to intimidate or kill by lynching.

In response to the growing terrorist activities of the Ku Klux Klan (KKK), President Grant approved measures in Congress which made it a federal crime to interfere with the civil rights of blacks, especially the right to vote. In addition, the

Ku Klux Klan march in New York

President was authorized to declare **martial law** (military rule) if the rights of blacks in a particular state were violated. These measures were called the **Punitive Force Acts of 1870 and 1871**. Union forces in the South were small, so they were unable to stop the Klansmen from terrorizing blacks and preventing them from voting. Only in South Carolina, where Grant declared martial law, was the Klan's influence broken.

Corruption in Government During Grant's Presidency

Southerners blamed Reconstruction and black politicians for the corruption they saw in government, but there seemed to be a general moral lapse affecting the country after the war. Bribery, lying, and stealing infected all levels of government and business in both the North and the South. After the war, the government undertook many building projects. Schools, roads, and railroads that had been destroyed or left in disrepair during the war needed attention. This large scale building effort provided many opportunities for corrupt business dealings. In the building of the first transcontinental railroad, a small group of Union Pacific stockholders involved several politicians of both parties, including the Vice President, in swindling money from the government.

Though President Grant showed strong military leadership in the Civil War, he was a weak political leader who depended exceedingly on his advisers. These advisers proved to be inexperienced and corrupt. On a national level, excessive speculation and widespread corruption led eventually to an economic panic and depression in 1873.

Reconstruction Slows Down

As political corruption and economic difficulties began to claim attention, the memories of the Civil War faded and the drive for Radical Reconstruction weakened. The leading Radicals left Congress. Representative Thaddeus Stevens died in 1868, Benjamin Wade lost his seat in the Senate the following year, and Senator Charles Sumner died in 1874. In 1872, Congress passed a law which allowed almost all former Confederates to vote and hold public office again. That same year, the Freedmen's Bureau disappeared due to lack of funding from Congress. After years of fighting for civil rights for blacks, the members of the abolitionist movement ran out of steam. Business leaders wanted to invest in new enterprises in the South, but they feared the unsettled Reconstruction governments. They believed ending Reconstruction would stabilize the politics of the South, providing good opportunities for investment.

Southerners agreed, blaming Reconstruction and blacks for continued problems in the South. Building on the bitter feelings in the South and intimidating black voters, white southern Democrats gradually "redeemed" or regained power in state legislatures. In the presidential election of 1876, the Democrats returned to power.

Presidential Election of 1876

Because of the bad economy and the various scandals that had surrounded President Grant, the Democrats were hopeful that their candidate, **Samuel Tilden** (Governor of New York) would win the election. The Republicans put their support behind the Governor of Ohio, **Rutherford B. Hayes**. Tilden received almost 300,000 more popular votes than Hayes, but he needed one more electoral vote to win the election. Nineteen votes were disputed in South Carolina, Florida, and Louisiana. In these states, the Republicans and the Democrats had established rival boards of election officials, and each board was reporting different results. To settle the dispute, Congress appointed an Electoral Commission comprised of seven Republicans, seven Democrats, and one Independent. At the last minute, the Independent left the Commission, and he was replaced by a Republican. The Commission decided the votes belonged to Hayes, and he was elected President. The Democrats were outraged at the apparent dishonesty of this whole process. In order to keep the peace, the Democrats said they would let Hayes win if Republicans would end Reconstruction. This compromise is known as the **Compromise of 1877**.

Rutherford B. Hayes

The main points of this compromise were:

• The Democrats agreed to accept the election results.

• The Republicans agreed to
  1) appoint a Southerner to the President's cabinet;
  2) provide federal money for railroads in the South and for flood control along the Mississippi, and, most importantly;
  3) to withdraw federal troops from the South.

This compromise essentially ended Reconstruction.

When the South returned to the hands of white Southerners, blacks lost the support of the federal government and many of the social and political gains of the Reconstruction era. Freed slaves had their freedom, but it was severely limited. States passed laws requiring blacks and whites to use separate facilities in restaurants, hospitals, railroads, schools, and street cars. These laws, known as **Jim Crow Laws**, also imposed literacy tests and poll taxes which prevented blacks from voting, despite the 15th Amendment. The Supreme Court supported these laws, and they remained in effect until the 1950s.

103

CHAPTER 8 REVIEW

A.   Define the following names, terms, and events:

Robert E. Lee	sharecropper	carpetbaggers
General McClellan	tenant farmer	scalawags
Chancellorsville	Freedman's Bureau	martial law
Gettysburg Address	Radicals	Rutherford B. Hayes
Sherman's March	John Wilkes Booth	Compromise of 1877
habeas corpus	President Johnson	Jim Crow Laws
drafted	Black Codes	
Emancipation Proclamation	impeach	
recession	Ulysses S. Grant	

B.   On your own paper, write your response to each of the following:

1. Briefly explain the significance of the following battles:
    Vicksburg
    Gettysburg
    Sherman's March
    Mobile Bay
    First Battle of Bull Run
    Shiloh
2. Why is Appomattox Courthouse important?
3. How did Lincoln keep Maryland in the Union?
4. Discuss the contributions of black soldiers to the Civil War.
5. Contrast three losses of the North and the South in the Civil War. Were there any gains?
6. How did Lincoln's plan for Reconstruction differ from that of the Radicals?
7. Explain the significance of the 13th, 14th, and 15th amendments to the Constitution.
8. What kinds of political offices did blacks hold after the Civil War?
9. List four reasons for Southerners' bitter feelings toward the North after the Civil War.
10. How effective were the Punitive Force Acts of 1870 and 1871? Why?
11. List four factors which contributed to the end of Reconstruction.
12. Who won the presidential election of 1876? How were the election results settled?
13. Why were Jim Crow Laws a setback from blacks after the Civil War?

C.   Write True if the statement is correct and False if the statement is incorrect. Be prepared to state a reason for your false answers.

1. _____   For the first time in United States history, men and women were drafted, fighting the opposition in the Civil War.

2. _____   Emancipated slaves, male and female, were called "Freedmen."

3. _____   Sherman and his handpicked army of 60,000 soldiers entered Georgia from Tennessee and destroyed Atlanta and its railroads.

4. _____   President Grant was a weak political leader who depended heavily upon inexperienced and corrupt advisors.

5. _____ Jim Crow Laws were passed in the South to halt the illegal activities of carpetbaggers.

6. _____ Even though the South's railroads had been utterly destroyed, the region made a swift economic and political recovery.

7. _____ The Reconstruction Act readmitted all southern states right after the treaty was signed.

8. _____ The 15th amendment granted all male citizens, regardless of race, the right to vote.

9. _____ The Compromise of 1877 guaranteed that Maryland would be freed from martial law in exchange for its vote for the Freedmen's Bureau.

10. _____ "Radicals" were the Republicans who called for strict readmission standards and vigorous restructuring of the South.

CHAPTER 9
EXPANSION AND INDUSTRIALIZATION

THE RAILROADS

After Reconstruction, the people of the United States hurried to settle the West. To spur settlement of the West, Congress loaned hundreds of millions of dollars to railroad companies. Congress also gave these companies large parcels of land around their tracks. A company could sell this land if it needed to repay the loan. These incentives led to a boom in railroad construction. Railroads became the chief means of national transportation during the second half of the nineteenth century.

In 1862, Congress coordinated an effort among the railroad companies to build a transcontinental railroad. **Union Pacific** (an Eastern rail company) and **Central Pacific** (a rail company from Sacramento, California) joined their tracks at Promontory, Utah, in 1869. Other mergers followed creating a few huge rail companies. **Cornelius Vanderbilt** and his son, William, owners of the

Central Pacific Railroad through the Sierra Nevada Mountains

New York Central, became immensely rich through such mergers. Cities located at railroad hubs, such as New York, St. Louis, and Chicago, experienced explosive growth during this time.

Important Figures in Western Settlement

John Wesley Powell (1834-1902) - This **ethnologist** (one who studies human cultures) traveled the newly acquired Western frontier to classify the variety of languages spoken by the Native Americans. In 1891, he published the first complete classification and distribution map of the 58 language families of the Native Americans in the United States and Canada. In addition, his work as a geological surveyor of the Rocky Mountains provided valuable information about the mineral resources and topography of the West.

William Gilpin - After the gold rush to the Denver area of present-day Colorado in 1858-1859, the area experienced a great deal of problems. Miners from the East claimed rights to the land in the gold beds. However, Native Americans claimed the land had been rightfully given to them through various treaties with the United States. Miners ignored their claims and established the Jefferson Territory. However, the United States, in the middle of a break between North and South, ignored the miners' claims. In 1861, the federal government established the territory with William Gilpin as the first governor. William Gilpin formally requested Congress for the territory to keep the name given the river region by the Spanish, *Colorado*, meaning "red river."

Cattle Ranching

As gold rushes sent people from the west coast of California, eastward into the Rocky Mountains, another important movement, cattle driving, spurred people to move North from Texas to the Plains States. Many people made fortunes by raising cattle and sending them to large consumer markets in the East. However, the cattle needed to find a way to the nearest train depot. These depots, located in Kansas, were usually about 1,000 miles away from where the cattle were raised. Enterprising ranchers hired *vaqueros* (cowboys) to move the cattle north. These drives often took two months to complete. The life of the cowboy on the open plains became idealized in song and became embedded in the culture of the United States. With the severe winter of 1885-1886 and the use of barbed wire to fence off land, the days of cattle driving were over.

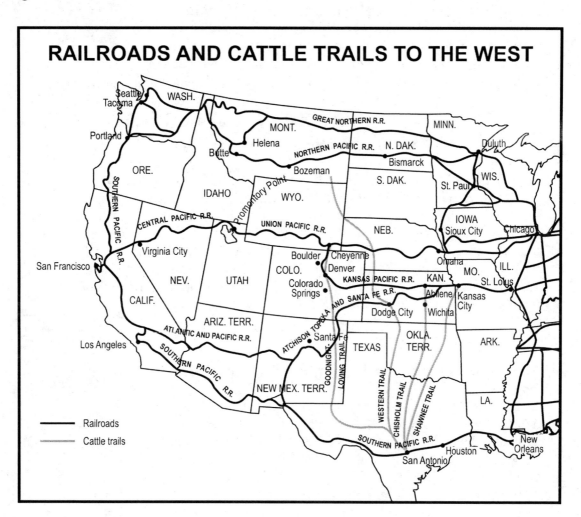

CONFLICTS WITH NATIVE AMERICAN NATIONS

As settlers began moving West with these railroads, they looked for land to farm. They also looked for gold in Colorado and the Black Hills of the Dakotas. Wave after wave of settlers and fur trappers came into the Plains, killed buffalo for their hides, and left the meat to rot on the land. Tragically, the Plains Indians depended on buffalo for their livelihood. As settlers from the East began taking away the livelihood and lands of Native Americans, Native Americans had the choice of either being forced onto **reservations** (parcels of wasteland set aside by the federal government for the Native Americans) or fighting back. When the Native Americans did fight back, the United States Army stepped in to protect the new settlers and forced the native populations to sign treaties giving up their land. The conflicts with those Native American nations that did fight back, lasting over thirty years, can be classified as the **Frontier Wars**. The United States Army conducted several costly campaigns in its fight with tribes resisting the move to reservations. One group of soldiers who served with distinction on the frontier were the **Buffalo Soldiers**. These soldiers, so named by the Native Americans, were members of four all-black regiments, the 9th and 10th Calvary and the 24th and 25th Infantry divisions and were well-known for their bravery in battle.

In the year 1800, approximately 60 million buffalo roamed the Great Plains from Canada to Mexico. Tribes, such as the **Sioux** and the **Ojibwa (Chippewa)**, depended on the buffalo for food, clothing, and shelter. As white settlers began killing the buffalo for sport and for hides, buffalo numbers dropped dramatically. By 1889, only 1,000 buffalo were left on the continent. As a result, the Plains Indians could no longer continue their ancestral way of life. They voluntarily moved or were forcibly moved onto reservations, where they became dependent on government assistance.

IMPORTANT INDIAN BATTLES AND CONGRESSIONAL ACTION

- **1860s -1870s - The Sioux Wars.** White settlers left the Sioux tribe alone until the 1870s when gold was discovered in the arid lands where the Sioux lived. Supporting the gold prospectors, the United States Army fought the Sioux tribes of the Dakota region. During one battle, **The Battle of the Little Bighorn** (1876), Sioux warriors surrounded a United States force led by General Custer, United States Army. Sioux warriors killed every soldier under Custer's command. However, the Sioux people were fighting a losing war with the United States Army. By 1877, the Sioux and Cheyenne had surrendered, and they were moved to reservations in the Dakotas or present-day Oklahoma.

- **1877 - The Nez Percé Trail.** The leader of the Nez Percé in the Oregon Territory, **Chief Joseph** (1840-1904), refused to give in to United States demands to resettle. Instead, he and his followers attempted to escape the federal government by fleeing to Canada. The United States Army stopped them 30 miles from the border. After they were moved to Oklahoma, the Nez Percé people almost completely died off due to sickness and malnutrition. White settlers eagerly claimed the rich farmland of the Oregon territory.

Chief Joseph

- **1887 - Dawes Act (General Allotment Act) -** This act of Congress was intended to assimilate Native Americans into the mainstream of society. Reservation lands were dissolved. Instead, each Native American family was given 160 acres to farm. Native American tribes having excess land were then forced to sell their land at outrageously low prices. The United States government did not provide the Native Americans with any training or tools for successful agriculture. As a result, the Native Americans were plunged deeper into poverty. Instead of being part of tribal nations, they now became wards of the state.

- **1890 - Wounded Knee.** **Wovoka** (c. 1856-1932) was a Paiute prophet of the Sioux who developed a religious ritual called the **Ghost Dance**. The Sioux believed this dance would bring back the buffalo and return the Native American tribes to their land. The dance alarmed white settlers around the Sioux reservations, and they called on the United States Army. The Army believed that the Sioux leader **Sitting Bull** (1834-1890) was using the Ghost Dance to start a Native American uprising. When the Army went to arrest Sitting Bull, a gunfight resulted, killing 14 people including Sitting Bull. The infantry soldiers pursued the Sioux men, women, and children to their camp at Wounded Knee Creek. A shot rang out, and the soldiers started firing. The United States Army killed between 150 and 370 men, women, and children who were mostly unarmed. This massacre marked the end of United States Army battles with Native Americans in the lower 48 states.

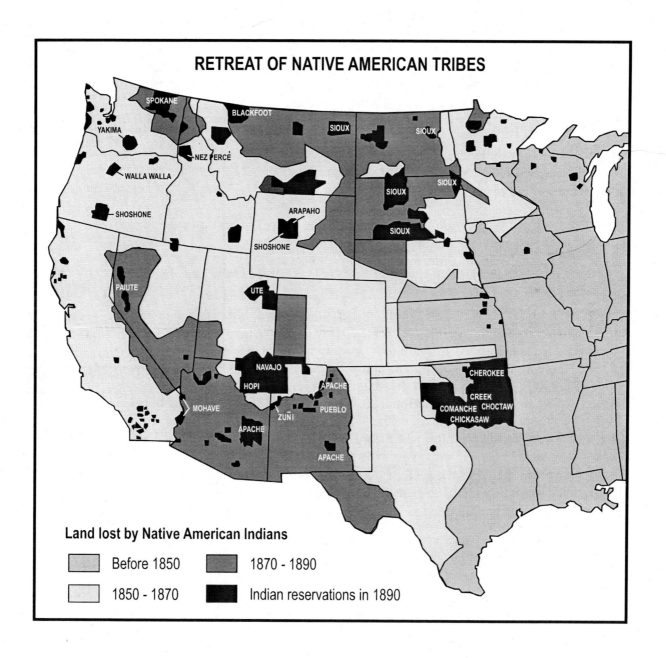

RETREAT OF NATIVE AMERICAN TRIBES

Land lost by Native American Indians

▦	Before 1850	▨	1870 - 1890
▢	1850 - 1870	■	Indian reservations in 1890

GEOGRAPHIC IMPACT OF WESTERN SETTLEMENT

In their move to the West, settlers cleared vast tracts of forested land that once belonged to the Native Americans. The settlers cut trees, planted fields, and bought and sold land to individuals and corporations. The great North American forests once covered one half of the continent. Today, forest covers less than one-third of the nation. Because of the lack of trees, precious farm land and topsoil are eroding away due to winds and flooding.

IMPORTANT DEVELOPMENTS USED
IN CONTINENTAL EXPANSION

The Bessemer Process - In the late 1850s, Sir Henry Bessemer (1813-1898) developed a faster and more efficient way of making steel. The process involved blowing air through molten iron to burn away impurities. Increased production of steel meant railroads could be expanded faster. Steel also made it possible to build sky-scrapers in the cities. Bessemer, Alabama, an important steel center, is named after Sir Henry.

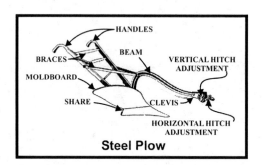
Steel Plow

The Steel Plow - Invented by John Deere (1804-1886) in the 1830s, the steel plow was strong enough to cut through the tough prairie sod of the Midwest and the Plains.

Barbed Wire - In 1873, Joseph Glidden developed a way of making fencing cheaply by twisting together sections of wire into barbed points. With this invention, farmers could cheaply and efficiently fence in 160 acres of land.

The Railroad - The early mechanization of agriculture gave farmers the ability to produce for themselves many times what they needed for survival. As a result, these surplus supplies of grain and animal products needed to be shipped to market. The best way to move these products to the major cities was by

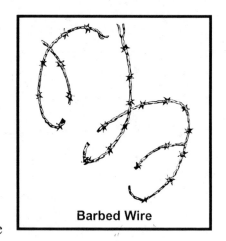
Barbed Wire

railroad. More than any other development, the railroad revolutionized the development of farming and industrial regions west of the Mississippi. Towns developed at the junctions of rail lines, and farmers could produce massive quantities of food for resale in the East.

Compressed Gas Refrigeration - Refrigeration proved to be very important to agriculture. Now, meat and produce could be processed and kept from spoiling by having railroad cars, ships, and meat processing areas equipped with these new cooling and freezing facilities. This development allowed farmers and ranchers to compete nationally and globally in different agricultural markets.

FARMING IN THE 1870s and 1880s

Farmers encountered problems in the 1870s and 1880s. Farming was a costly industry at this time. Farmers borrowed from banks so they could efficiently farm their land with the new machinery. However, large agricultural regions of the world were also investing in the mechanization of agriculture. Australia, Canada, and South America glutted the food markets with their surpluses resulting in far less profit for farmers in the United States. In addition, railroads held monopolies in the West. They often charged three times the price to haul grain and livestock as was charged in the East. With these kinds of conditions, farmers could not make a profit on the crops they produced or pay their debts.

Farmers began banding together to protect their interests from industries cutting into their farming revenue. Local farmers formed a co-operative called a **grange**. Through the grange, they pooled their resources to purchase new machinery, and together, the farmers could purchase supplies and machinery, as well as sell their produce, without paying other distributors. By 1874, farmers joined over 14,000 grange associations. Farmers founded other organizations on similar ideas including the **Northwestern Alliance**, the **Southern Farmers' Alliance**, and the **Colored Farmers' National Alliance**.

Organizing for business led to organizing for political action. A large portion of the Northwestern Alliance joined forces with the Southern Alliance, forming the National Farmers' Alliance in 1889. The following year, this organization met in Ocala, Florida to create a plan for political reform. This plan became known as the **Ocala Platform**. Its goals were the following:

1. Establish a government fund to help farmers when their debts grow too high.

2. Establish regional subtreasuries to allow farmers to borrow against 80% of their harvest. This would allow farmers to sell their crop when the prices were high instead of after harvest, when prices were low.

3. Have the government increase the number of silver dollar coins in circulation to cause inflation.

4. Increase fairness in the business world. At this time, industries were protected from foreign competition by tariffs. However, agricultural products were not protected by tariffs.

5. Change the federal tax from being based on amount of land owned to amount of income made during a given year, with the rich paying a higher percentage. This is known as a **graduated income tax**.

6. Have the government run the railroads to ensure fairness in pricing.

The **Greenback Party** formed in 1874. Members of this party believed that the issuance of large amounts of paper money, called **greenbacks**, would bring prosperity, especially to farmers, by raising prices and making debts easier to pay. Many farmers from the West and South joined the party, but by the late 1880s, the party had little power.

Under pressure from the National Farmer's Alliance, Congress passed the Sherman Silver Purchase Act in 1890. This act increased the amount of silver purchased yearly and allowed the U.S. Treasury to issue money backed by silver. Prior to this time, money was backed only by gold which had caused money to rise in value, making prices lower and debts harder to pay.

THE POPULIST PARTY

Reformers and farmers joined together to form a third party in 1892 called the **Populist Party**. For the presidential election that year, the party nominated two Civil War generals to run on the platform formulated at Ocala. Although the party did not win the presidential election, it received over one million popular votes. The Populists looked well poised to be a major contender for the 1896 elections, yet by 1897, the party disappeared completely as its momentum disappeared and the Republicans and Democrats adopted portions of the Populist platform.

THE SILVER QUESTION

President Grover Cleveland (1837-1908) faced a full scale depression in the United States economy during the first year of his term in 1893. The stock market had fallen, 500 banks failed, and 1,500 businesses went bankrupt. Cleveland believed the cause of the depression was the use of the silver standard set in place in 1890. He believed that the use of a **gold standard** (currency based on gold) was a necessity to a healthy economy. In 1893, Cleveland repealed the Sherman Silver Purchase Act and returned the nation to a purely gold standard. However, the depression continued after this change was implemented. As the depression deepened in 1894, more and more people blamed Cleveland's new policy for the worsening conditions. When the Democratic Party met in 1896, it was divided. The Eastern Democrats supported Cleveland. However, the Southern and Western Democrats supported a fiery speaker named **William Jennings Bryan (1860-1925)**. Bryan led his faction in decrying the use of the gold standard and backed a return to unlimited coinage of silver to spur inflation. In one of his speeches, Bryan is recorded as saying "You shall not press down upon the brow of labor this crown of thorns, you shall not crucify mankind upon a cross of gold." Supporters cheered him at the convention, yet many criticized him for using religious imagery to make a political statement. Because the Democratic Party was split on this question, the Republican candidate, William McKinley, won the presidential election of 1896.

THE NEW SOUTH

After the Civil War, the South refocused its efforts on rebuilding its economy primarily through the cultivation of the cash crops, cotton and tobacco. Southern manufacturing centered on factories which processed cotton, tobacco, and peanuts into other refined products such as textiles, oil, soap, cosmetics, cigarettes, peanut butter, fertilizer, and cattle feed. However, many of these agricultural-based industries were hit hard when the boll weevil ravaged the cotton crop in the South.

Industries also developed around other natural resources. Iron ore and coal deposits made steel manufacturing cheaper in Alabama than in Pennsylvania. Oil refining developed near oil deposits in West Virginia and Texas. Copper, granite, and marble extraction grew in Tennessee and north Georgia. Manufacture of hardwood furniture from nearby stands of trees grew in North Carolina.

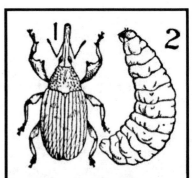

1) Boll weevil beetles feed on cotton plants and lay eggs in the cotton buds and bolls.
2) Boll weevil grubs hatch from the eggs and feed on the cotton.

However, these developments still lagged behind the rate of development in the North and the West. Northern bankers financed the businesses of the South, leading to a money drain which went North. In addition, manufacturers built plants in the South, but the final steps of processing were reserved for the factories in the North. The majority of the profit in manufacturing is found in the final steps of processing. This phenomenon kept the majority of the wealth in the hands of Northern industry. Also, Northern railroads charged higher prices for shipping goods towards the South. This fact discouraged businesses from locating production facilities in the South. It would be many more decades before the South became a high growth region.

IMPORTANT INDUSTRIAL INVENTIONS

Rich in natural resources, the United States used its spirit of invention to begin the process of industrialization during the 1800s. Large coal deposits found in the Appalachian Mountain region provided the energy for powering an industrial revolution. Large navigable rivers and canals made shipping products easier. Newly discovered at this time, many industries used oil as a source of power and as a lubricant for machine parts. Electricity lit and powered the cities so that work could easily continue in shifts, 24 hours a day if necessary.

Cyrus West Field (1819-1892) was a merchant and financier whose efforts led to laying the first telegraph cable beneath the Atlantic ocean in 1866. This **transatlantic cable** allowed the United States to hear of developments in Europe immediately through telegraph messages.

Ten years later, on March 10, 1876, **Alexander Graham Bell** (1847-1922) sent the first telephone transmission. It was a call to his assistant in the next room. With Bell's invention, the communication industry grew at a rapid pace. Soon, people could communicate across the nation and across the world.

Another form of widespread communication was the radio. **Guglielmo Marconi** (1874-1937), an Italian inventor, discovered that messages could be sent via radio waves in 1896. In the years following, Marconi's invention affected the lives of people in the United States in dramatic ways. Families purchased radios and received news and

Early American Radio

entertainment from area radio stations. Information could be spread to the general public in an instant. A new national culture was born based on sound.

MOVE TO THE CITIES

As industrialization continued in the United States, many people left their farms and moved to the cities for higher wages. In addition, new waves of immigrants from Europe, possessing no land, settled in the cities to find work. The result was unplanned growth of many urban areas in the East. The population explosion in the cities created many opportunities and many problems as well.

Cities became great sources of people, ideas, and cultures. People seeking a better life enjoyed the city because everything they wanted to do was in walking distance. Businesses and city officials located their shops, restaurants, parks, and amusement areas within blocks of each other.

As people moved closer together, businesses found new ways to accommodate these masses of people. One invention, the department store, allowed shoppers to do all of their shopping in one place. The store was divided into several departments, each of which was specialized to a specific need. This new level of convenience drew many people to the cities. Public transportation in the cities also allowed for fast, convenient travel. Subways, for example, allowed people to travel on tracks both above and below the city, avoiding all traffic. Because land was highly prized within a city, large corporations built skyscrapers in the city centers. These multi-story buildings increased the amount of people a city could support and increased the number of jobs available in an area. Other services, such as public libraries, parks, and sports facilities, became possible with massive numbers of people located in a small area. These additions to the city became a big draw for people living in outlying areas as well as for immigrants.

NEGATIVE ASPECTS OF URBANIZATION

Monopolies

The negative aspects of new industries and urbanization were numerous. Large companies would often squeeze out their competitors by lowering the price of their goods below cost. When the competitors went out of business, the large company would then raise its prices. This company would then have a **monopoly**, meaning that it was the only supplier for its particular industry. People like **John D. Rockefeller**, **Andrew Carnegie**, and **Cornelius Vanderbilt** acquired great wealth by forming monopolies. These nineteenth century capitalists were called **robber barons** because many of them acquired their wealth by exploitation and ruthlessness.

These business leaders became extremely rich because they could set their prices where they liked, and consumers would have to pay that price because these companies were the only supplier of their product.

For the first time in the history of the United States, a large number of millionaires, around 4,000, were able to live lavish lifestyles in this nation. About 1/8 of the families in the United States controlled 7/8 of the wealth. The phrase "the **Gilded Age**" came to be associated with the conspicuous wealth and power of the wealthy industrialists of this era.

These business leaders believed in the idea of **Social Darwinism**. Drawing from Darwin's observation of animals in the wild, this philosophy states that only the strongest survive. Life is a contest for survival of the fittest. The federal government at this time decided that the best way to promote business enterprise was to stay out of business activities. This hands-off policy is known as **laissez-faire economics**.

John D. Rockefeller

Andrew Carnegie

Cornelius Vanderbilt

POPULATION GROWTH
AND INDUSTRIALIZATION 1870-1920

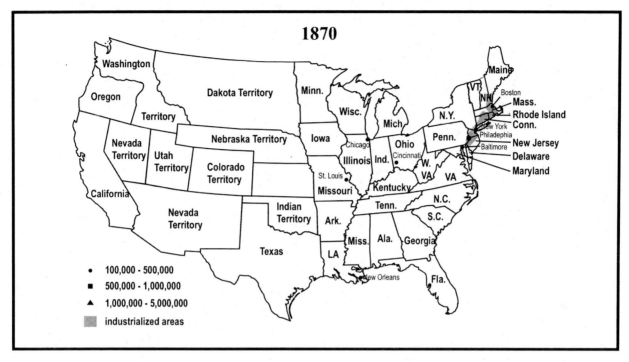

1870

- • 100,000 - 500,000
- ■ 500,000 - 1,000,000
- ▲ 1,000,000 - 5,000,000
- ▓ industrialized areas

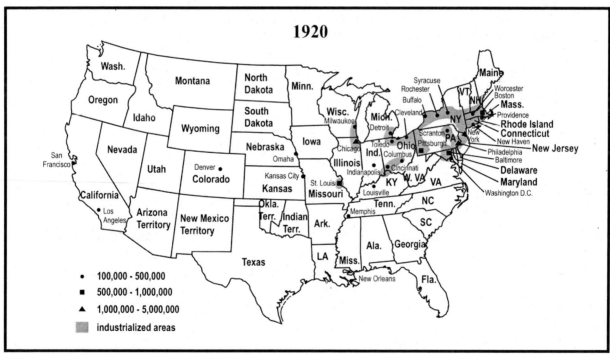

1920

- • 100,000 - 500,000
- ■ 500,000 - 1,000,000
- ▲ 1,000,000 - 5,000,000
- ▓ industrialized areas

Famous Robber Barons and Their Monopolies

- **John D. Rockefeller** (1839-1937) owned the **Standard Oil Company**. He created a monopoly in the oil industry by ensuring that his company was the only supplier of oil from the drilling to the refining.

- **Andrew Carnegie** (1835-1919) owned a steel company that controlled the iron and coal mines and owned railroads and steam ships. In this way, his company controlled the production of steel and forced out competition. Andrew Carnegie believed people with wealth had a responsibility to use it for the betterment of the poor. He called this idea the **Gospel of Wealth**.

- **Cornelius Vanderbilt** (1794-1877) and his son, William, owned the New York Central railroad.

Working Conditions

Located in the major cities, the large industrial corporations provided work for countless thousands. As there were no laws regulating the age or treatment of workers, many businesses allowed their employees to work in unhealthy conditions. Children worked in the factories as well. They worked at a fraction of an adult's wage and developed illnesses and deformaties in their bodies as a result of overwork. Women entered the workforce as well. They worked in traditionally female occupations such as clerical, teaching, and nursing. Usually, they were paid at a much lower rate than their male counterparts.

IMMIGRANTS

Life was extremely difficult for the newly arrived immigrants in the cities. New to the United States, immigrants worked twelve hours or more per day. Because they were desperate to find jobs, they were willing to work at lower wages and in worse conditions than native-born workers. The flood of immigration to the United States upset American workers, and they often initiated hate crimes against the immigrants. They felt the immigrants were taking away their jobs and forcing them to work for lower wages. Also, the new wave of immigrants came from countries that were generally non-English speaking and Catholic. They seemed strange and threatening to native citizens who spoke English and were generally Protestant. The working class did not see the great contributions immigrants were making to the nation. Then, as now, one immigrant generates more jobs on average than are created by one citizen born in the United States. In addition, a few wealthy immigrants brought hundreds of millions of dollars in foreign capital with them to invest in the United States.

When the immigrants arrived in the major cities, they often found that their language or nationality prevented them from getting jobs in the mainstream society of the United States. For example, in Boston, "Irish need not apply" signs were commonplace. In response to this environment, immigrants formed close communities in certain sections of a given city. This gave the immigrants an environment where they could obtain jobs and get acquainted with their new environment. While this situation did not exist because of government interference, it did create *de facto* **segregation** (segregation that exists without being mandated by the state).

The government responded to the outcry of domestic workers by placing restrictions on foreign immigration. As **racism** (prejudice) and **nativism** (favoring one's nation or region) rose in the United States, so did the restrictions on immigration. The following are examples of legislation that limited or sometimes stopped immigration to the United States:

- **1882 - The Chinese Exclusion Act** - Chinese were prohibited from legally immigrating to the United States.

- **1921 - The Emergency Quota Act -** To stop the tide of immigrants from Southern and Eastern Europe, Congress passed a law limiting the number of legal immigrants to 3% of the number of each nationality in 1910.

- **1924 - National Origins Act of 1924 -** Because the Emergency Quota Act did not substantially reduce the number of immigrants from Southern and Eastern Europe, Congress changed the quota to 2% of each nationality's population in the United States in 1890. In 1890, there were few immigrants from Southern and Eastern Europe, so immigration from those nations was reduced considerably by this law. In addition, the law prohibited all immigration from Asia.

CHAPTER 9 REVIEW

A. **Define the following names, terms, and events:**

Union Pacific	Battle of the Little Big Horn	William Jennings Bryan
Central Pacific	Dawes Act	Gilded Age
Cornelius Vanderbilt	Wounded Knee	laissez-faire economics
John Wesley Powell	Bessemer Process	*de facto* segregation
William Gilpin	refrigeration	Chinese Exclusion Act
vaqueros	Ocala Platform	Emergency Quota Act
reservations	Greenback Party	National Origins Act
Buffalo Soldiers	Populist Party	

B. **On your own paper, write your response to each of the following:**

Review the map on page 107. Then answer questions 1 and 2.

1. Which railroad had the longest route for transporting people and products?
2. Name four cities on this route.
3. What upset the Native Americans about settlers moving West?
4. Give three examples of how the United States government responded to the Native Americans' grievances.
5. Which state contains the most land dedicated to reservations?
6. Which tribes are represented in that state's reservations?
7. What did John Wesley Powell do to aid the settlement of the West?
8. What caused the ending of the cowboy era?
9. Describe three developments that aided continental expansion.
10. What impact did refrigeration have on the development of the United States?
11. Name the six points of the Ocala Platform.
12. What was William Jennings Bryan arguing for in his famous "Cross of Gold" speech?
13. Referring to the maps on page 95, how many more states had cities of 100,000 or more in 1920 than in 1870? Name those states.

14. How did railroads and the telephone contribute to the industrialization of American society?
15. Why were the years of industrial expansion in the late 1800s referred to as the Gilded Age?
16. How did the formation of monopolies affect business in the United States?
17. Describe the working conditions in American factories during this time period.
18. Describe four developments that drew rural people and immigrants to the cities.
19. What were the benefits of immigration on American society?
20. Why did Congress pass laws to limit immigration?

C. Write True if the statement is correct and False if the statement is incorrect. Be prepared to state a reason for your false answers.

1. _____ Barbed wire, used for enclosing property, was an important invention easing expansion to the West.

2. _____ The last Army battle opposing Native Americans took place at Wounded Knee Creek; the "battle" quickly became a massacre.

3. _____ Business leaders in the Industrial Revolution believed in the value of labor unions.

4. _____ Leaders of oil and steel interests joined forces and formed a third party called the Populist Party.

5. _____ Women became part of the workforce in factories, as well as in traditional female roles, earning the same level of pay as men.

6. _____ The rush to the Plains States was fueled by the demand for cattle meat in the East.

7. _____ The Sioux Wars began over the Central Pacific railroads crossing Sioux territory.

8. _____ Four all-black regiments serving with distinction in the Frontier Wars were called the Buffalo Soldiers.

9. _____ Children were allowed to work in factories since they made good wages in healthy job environments.

10. _____ The National Origins Act of 1924 encouraged immigrants to settle in rural areas such as the North Georgia Mountains.

CHAPTER 10
THE PROGRESSIVE MOVEMENT

LABOR UNIONS

1882 New York Freight Handlers' Union strike

In response to the worsening work conditions, workers organized into **labor unions**. Unions are organizations of workers who, together, put pressure on the employers in an industry to improve working conditions and wages. If employers do not want to cooperate, the union will organize a **strike**, meaning that workers will refuse to work until a set of conditions are met. Unions gained power during the Industrial Age in the United States as a reaction to the lack of safeguards in the workplace.

The first union to achieve national importance was the **National Labor Union (NLU)**. In 1866, this union united labor organizations on the national, local, and city levels. At its height, the NLU had a membership of 600,000. Because the Union became increasingly involved in politics, many unions left the NLU. Many union leaders felt that unions belonged strictly in the economic, not political, portions of society. As the NLU disintegrated, another larger organization gained prominence. In 1869, Uriah Stevens, a garment worker, founded the **Knights of Labor** as an organization dedicated to advancing the rights of the worker. It was the first labor organization to admit members regardless of trade, skill, national origin, color, or creed. It was also the first organization to press for an eight hour workday, the end of child and convict labor, and equal opportunities and wages for women in industry. Due to opposition from other labor organizations, the Knights of Labor lost its effectiveness and was disbanded in 1917.

Knights of Labor Contract

Many members from the Knights of Labor and other unions banded together to form the **American Federation of Labor (AFL)** in 1881. Union members from the skilled trades joined this organization to produce specific, measurable gains for their workers, such as shorter hours and higher wages. The organization worked by coordinating strikes in entire industries, such as car manufacturing. The AFL's demands were in sharp contrast to the sweeping reforms advocated by the Knights of Labor. However, this organization showed a high degree of effectiveness. In 1955, the AFL joined with the **Congress of Industrialized Organizations (CIO)** to form the largest union organization to date, the **AFL-CIO**. Examples of laws regulating the workplace include laws about the forty-hour workweek, a minimum age requirement for working, and workplace safety standards.

THE PROGRESSIVE MOVEMENT

Boss William Tweed

During the 1890s, a social and political movement called **Progressivism** developed in response to the growing corruption of politicians by the forces of big business. Progressives championed the causes of whoever was being oppressed in the society. They fought to bring down big city bosses who gained enormous wealth and power through bribery and corruption. This corruption often hurt the poor and immigrants the most. One of the most infamous big city bosses **Boss William Tweed** (1823-1872) stole over 100 million dollars from the treasury of New York City.

Many leading intellectuals wrote stories concerning the abuses of big business on workers and on the consumers. These journalists were known as **muckrakers**. The most famous example of this writing is *The Jungle* (1906), written by **Upton Sinclair** (1878-1968). *The Jungle* exposed the miserable working conditions and dangerous food quality in Chicago's meat processing plants. For example, rats and other rodents, who ran rampant in the plants, frequently were ground in with the beef for hamburger meat: fur and all. Sinclair's work prompted Congress to pass pure food laws. Another famous work exposing big business abuses is *The History of the Standard Oil Company* (1904) by **Ida Tarbell** (1857-1944). In this book, Tarbell exposes the ruthless practices of Standard Oil Company in its quest to gain a monopoly in the oil business. These and other writers raised the public's awareness of abuses occurring in trusted services and companies.

Legislation was passed targeting abuses caused by no competition in industries. For example, the railroads charged farmers high prices for shipping goods to market because there was little competition in the rail industry. In response to the abuse of rail freight fares, Congress passed the **Interstate Commerce Act** in 1887. This act established the Interstate Commerce Commission (ICC) to correct rail industry abuses. In addition, Congress also passed the **Sherman Antitrust Act** in 1890. This act made trusts, which destroy competition in business, illegal. This act was designed to allow the government to regulate unfair practices in industries such as steel, banking, and railroads.

Progressive reformers believed that each person had the right to a free education. They considered public education as instrumental to a democratic society where the citizenry was required to make informed decisions in voting for politicians and policies. While **Horace Mann** (1796-1859) had begun the push for public education earlier in the 19th century, Progessive reformers secured the opportunity of at least an elementary education for the vast majority of United States citizens. Unlike other countries where the educational curriculum was set by the central government, the United States entrusted local school districts with educational decisions.

During this time, corruption also plagued the federal government, as exemplified by the **spoils system** (the practice providing one's political supporters with government jobs). The first few months of James A. Garfield's (1831-1881) presidency were occupied with appointing his supporters to fill government positions. Angered that President Garfield did not appoint him to the position he wanted, Charles J. Guiteau shot the President on July 2, 1881. The assassination caused great public demand for reform. When Vice President Chester Arthur (1829-1886) assumed the presidency, he pressed Congress to pass the **Pendleton Civil Service Reform Act** and then signed the bill into law. This new legislation required rigorous testing of applicants for government positions. The **Civil Service Commission** oversaw the testing to ensure that government appointments were based on skill, not political dealings.

Both Democrats and Republicans considered themselves Progressives, concerned with correcting injustices in the United States society. The Progressive Movement mobilized bipartisan support for the passage of new amendments to the Constitution.

IMPORTANT AMENDMENTS TO THE CONSTITUTION

- **16th Amendment (1913)** - Congress now had the power to collect taxes on businesses and individuals. This amendment allowed the federal government to have access to vast amounts of money to be used in social programs and defense.
- **17th Amendment (1913)** - This law provided that the people of a state elect their senators instead of the state legislatures.
- **18th Amendment (1919)** - The government prohibited the making, selling, or transporting of alcoholic beverages. Labeled "Prohibition," this amendment was later repealed because of negative reactions.
- **19th Amendment (1920)** - Women received the right to vote.

PRESIDENT THEODORE ROOSEVELT

**Theodore Roosevelt
1858-1919**

Serving from 1901-1909, **President Theodore Roosevelt** was a progressive president who initiated several reforms while in office. An ardent lover of the natural environment, Roosevelt established a **National Park System** which protected huge tracts of land from development. He set aside 150 million acres in the continental United States and another 34 million acres in Alaska for conservation. He campaigned for the rights of workers and small businesses. For example, he prosecuted the **Northern Securities Trust** for violating the **Sherman Antitrust Act** (1890). A group of smaller railroad companies had formed this trust to set prices and eliminate smaller competitors.

Roosevelt promoted a policy called **The Square Deal**. This deal was a verbal contract with the people to maintain equality both for individuals and for businesses. His policy encouraged the popular press to expose corruption. After reading *The Jungle*, he also promoted the passage of the **Pure Food and Drug Act** (1906) to protect the health of United States consumers.

Roosevelt was also eager to promote legislation that would aggressively pursue the regulation of trusts in the railroad and other transportation facilities such as ferries and pipelines. When he signed the **Hepburn Act (1906)**, the Interstate Commerce Commission now had the power to set maximum freight rates and prevent the customer from paying unfair rates.

ELECTION OF 1912

William Howard Taft (1857-1930), Roosevelt's vice-president, was elected president after Roosevelt's second term. While in office, Taft, a Republican, lost Progressive support after backing a high tariff. In the next election, Roosevelt ran against Taft as the leader of the Progressive Party. Because the competition between the two split the Republican Party, the Democratic candidate, **Woodrow Wilson** (1856-1924), became the next president.

Wilson began his administration supporting many Progressive causes. He called his reform program **New Freedom**. His goal was to ensure that there was competition in the marketplace. At the same time, he did not want government to exercise too much power over business. He urged Congress to establish the **Federal Trade Commission (FTC)** (1914). This commission had the power to investigate companies for unfair business practices. In the same year, Congress passed the **Clayton Antitrust Act** (1914) which had been sponsored by the Alabama congressman Henry De Lamar Clayton. This act made sure that businesses could not use antitrust laws to break up labor unions.

RACE RELATIONS AFTER RECONSTRUCTION

After Reconstruction, the plight of blacks in the South steadily worsened. Once they were prevented from voting through practices of disenfranchisement, Southern states passed laws denying them many freedoms. The **Ku Klux Klan** (1867) increased its activities of terrorism and violence against blacks. Lynchings of blacks were commonplace, and their schools were frequently burned. In this atmosphere of violence, many blacks left the South. This journey to the cities of the North and West is known as the **Black Exodus**. One of the migrants testified in a Kansas courtroom in 1880 saying, "We can stand the climate North, East, or West as well now as when fleeing from the cruel yoke of bondage. We believe life, liberty, and happiness to be sweeter in a cold climate than murder, raping, and oppression in the South." (United States Government Printing Office 1880)

For blacks everywhere, two noted reformers provided them with hope. **Booker T. Washington** (1856-1915), a former slave, founded the **Tuskegee Institute** in Alabama for blacks. This school provided training in the industrial and agricultural fields. His dedication, in spite of threats and many discouragements, inspired blacks everywhere. His school became an important center for technical education in the South. His philosophy rested on maintaining a separation of the races. In a speech at the **Atlanta Exposition** in 1895, he said, "In all things that are purely social we (whites and blacks) can be as separate as the fingers, yet one as the hand in all things essential to mutual progress." Because his ideas appealed to many, black and white, this speech became known as the **Atlanta Compromise**. He taught that if blacks excelled educationally and occupationally in the **blue collar fields** (occupations requiring manual labor), they would eventually receive the rights of full citizenship. His ideas played well in both black and white communities because of his compromising, non-confrontational approach to race relations.

Dr. George Washington Carver

One of Washington's students at Tuskegee **George Washington Carver** (1864-1943) became famous for his agricultural experimentation with peanuts, soybeans, and cotton. He developed hundreds of uses for these crops and developed a new strain of cotton known as "Carver's Hybrid." His contributions enabled farmers in the South to grow different kinds of crops profitably besides cotton.

Another important black leader of this time was **W. E. B. Du Bois** (1868-1963). Dubois, the first black Ph.D. graduate from Harvard University, wrote several important papers attacking the philosophy of Booker T. Washington. He argued persuasively that blacks would be selling out their freedoms to whites by not pursuing occupations in the humanities and in **white collar fields** (clerical or professional). He believed Washington's work made accommodations to the wishes of the white majority which hindered efforts for black advancement and equality. He helped organize a group of black intellectuals known as **the Niagara Movement**. In 1905, these leaders met on the Canadian side of Niagara Falls after they were denied hotel accommodations in the United States. They outlined an agenda for black progress in the United States.

In 1896, the Supreme Court ruled in *Plessy vs. Ferguson* that **segregation** (separation of the races) is lawful as long as the separate facilities and services are equal. This ruling led to an increasing segregation of all facilities. Southern states segregated schools, bathrooms, restaurants, and even water fountains. Services, however, were not equal as the law required. Facilities provided for blacks were usually of lesser quality. In the North, neighborhoods also became increasingly segregated. This segregation led to an increase in racial tensions and misunderstandings throughout the United States.

CHAPTER 10 REVIEW

A. **Define the following names, terms, and events:**

National Labor Union	Sherman Antitrust Act	Atlanta Compromise
Knights of Labor	16th-19th Amendments	George Washington Carver
AFL	The Square Deal	W. E. B. Dubois
Boss Tweed	Pure Food and Drug Act	Niagara Movement
The Jungle	Hepburn Act	*Plessy vs. Ferguson*
Horace Mann	Clayton Antitrust Act	
Interstate Commerce Act	Black Exodus	
Civil Service Reform Act	Booker T. Washington	

B. **On your own paper, write your response to each of the following:**

1. What did President Chester Arthur do to lower the amount of corruption in the government?
2. What did workers do to improve their working conditions?
3. Describe three progressive reforms instituted by President Theodore Roosevelt.
4. Why did Congress approve the Interstate Commerce Act?
5. List two ways that President Woodrow Wilson affected business in the United States.
6. How did Booker T. Washington and W. E. B. DuBois differ in their views of race relations?
7. Describe the impact of the Supreme Court's decision in *Plessy vs. Ferguson*.

C. **Write True if the statement is correct and False if the statement is incorrect. Be prepared to state a reason for your false answers.**

1. _____ Booker T. Washington supported segregation during his speech at the Atlanta Exposition.

2. _____ The practice of segregation was declared illegal in the court decision *Plessy vs. Ferguson*.

3. _____ As a progressive president, Teddy Roosevelt was inspired to promote passage of the Pure Food and Drug Act after reading *The Jungle*.

4. _____ The Atlanta Compromise was an agreement ending the spoils system.

5. _____ Progressivism developed in response to growing unrest in the Western states.

6. _____ President Wilson began the Federal Trade Commission to regulate the cattle trade.

7. _____ An important change to the Constitution was the passing of the 19th amendment, giving women the right to vote.

8. _____ The Niagara Movement was established to set goals for the progress of blacks in America, including equal economic opportunities.

9. _____ After Reconstruction, many blacks moved North to find a better life in cities. This movement is known as the "Black Exodus."

10. _____ In the election of 1912, Wilson won as the leader of the Progressive Party.

CHAPTER 11
THE UNITED STATES BECOMES A WORLD POWER

IMPERIALISM

Imperialism is a policy by which one country takes control of another land or country. Several European countries controlled almost the entire continent of Africa between 1870 and 1914, as well as parts of Asia and the Middle East. For example, Great Britain controlled the Indian subcontinent, and several European nations controlled key ports in China. European nations colonized these 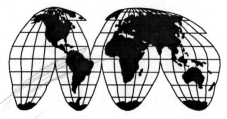 countries for their raw materials, so Europeans could expand their markets to other nations. They also felt it was their duty to spread their culture and religion in the colonies. The United States wanted to imitate its European counterparts.

At the turn of the 20th century, a growing number of people believed the United States should acquire overseas colonies to maintain a strong economy. These people were known as **imperialists**. There were several reasons for this desire to gain new territories and peoples:

1. The people of the United States felt they needed an additional source of raw materials so that they could produce finished goods.
2. Business leaders wanted an additional market for their surplus production of manufactured goods.
3. Politicians wanted to gain territory to maintain a global balance of power. They wanted to assure that no imperial power became too strong.

After the closing of the frontier by 1890, people in the United States were eager to find new lands and peoples to conquer. They looked overseas to find new avenues of expansion. In 1890, **Admiral Alfred Mahan** wrote a powerful book entitled, *The Influence of Sea Power upon History, 1660-1783*. This book told its readers that the way to influence the world is through control of the seas. This, in turn, helped people turn their eyes to overseas expansion as the way to increase the power and prestige of the United States. This book also influenced President Theodore Roosevelt to begin a massive naval buildup during his administration.

In 1885, **Josiah Strong** wrote a provocative book on Anglo imperialism called *Our Country: Its Possible Future and Its Present Crisis*. In this book, Strong explains that the Anglo race, personified by the United States, must continue its manifest destiny by taking over all of the nations of the world. He asserted that the Anglo race, with its Christian principles, was best fit to colonize the world.

The United States was particularly interested in Latin America and the Caribbean for two basic reasons. One, these nations were in close proximity to the United States. Two, the region was rich in natural resources as well as cheap labor. Large multinational corporations eyed the region hungrily and were at the front of support for any imperialistic expansion, either through military or economic means.

IMPERIALISM AND THE UNITED STATES 1850 - 1933

- **1850s** - Business leaders from the United States invested in sugar plantations on the Hawaiian Islands. As time passed, these owners gained economic control over the island and struggled for power with the Hawaiian monarchy.

- **1893 -** The wealthy white plantation owners rebelled against Queen Liliuokalani, who opposed the increasing control of the owners. With the help of United States troops from a nearby ship, the plantation owners seized the islands and deposed the queen. In 1898, Hawaii became a territory of the United States.

Queen Liliuokalani

- **1890s** - The Spanish government in Cuba violated the human rights of its citizens. To stir up their readers, two competing newspapers, the *New York World* and the *New York Morning Journal*, published the most sensational stories surrounding the abuses in Cuba. As a result, the people of the United States sympathized with the plight of the Cubans against Spain. This type of sensational writing with disregard for the truth is known as **yellow journalism**. On February 15, 1898, the United States battleship, *Maine*, exploded while anchored in a Cuban harbor. Immediately, the newspapers blamed Spain, and the United States clamored for war. On April 25, 1898, Congress adopted a resolution declaring war with Spain.

- **1898 - The Spanish-American War.**
The United States fought this war on two fronts: the Caribbean and the Philippines. Upon receiving word that the United States was at war with Spain, Commodore Dewey raced his warships out of Hong Kong and headed straight for the Philippine capital, Manila. Dewey's warships completely destroyed the Spanish fleet at anchor in Manila. With that battle won, and with the help of the Philippine people, the United States quickly seized all of the Philippines. Meanwhile, Lieutenant Colonel Theodore Roosevelt gathered volunteers for an invasion of Cuba.

The Rough Riders storm San Juan Hill.

Cutting though the government bureaucracy, Roosevelt organized his volunteers, called the **Rough Riders**, for combat in Cuba. Roosevelt shipped his Rough Riders from Tampa, Florida to Cuba. Through a series of daring maneuvers, United States troops and the Rough Riders liberated Cuba from Spanish control. Theodore Roosevelt became very famous for his role in the war including his bold charge of San Juan Hill.

- **December 10, 1898** - At the signing of the peace treaty, a defeated Spain relinquished control of Cuba and was forced to sell the Philippines, Puerto Rico, and Guam to the United States. On that day, the United States became a world power.

- **1899-1900** - United States Secretary of State John Hay promoted an agreement with the nations of Great Britain, Japan, France, Germany, Russia, and Italy that kept China open to trade with all nations. This policy is known as the **Open Door Policy**. This Open Door Policy assured that the United States would have opportunities equal to the other imperial powers in exploiting China for its material wealth. During the Boxer Rebellion, which followed in 1900, the United States sent troops along with the other imperial powers to fight the Chinese who wanted to stop the imperialistic expansion into China. The United States maintained an occupying force in Beijing (Peking), along with other imperial nations, for the next thirty years.

- **1902-1908** - President Theodore Roosevelt wanted to build a canal across the Isthmus of Panama. This waterway, to be called the **Panama Canal**, would ensure that the United States would have easy access to the Atlantic and Pacific Oceans for commerce and defense. When the Colombian senate refused to sell the land necessary to build the canal, Roosevelt was furious. He vowed to no longer work with the Colombian government. When the Panamanian people revolted against Colombian rule on November 3, 1903, United States warships made sure that Colombia could not send its troops to stop the rebellion. After the Panamanians gained their independence from Colombia, the United States leased the land they needed for the canal and began construction. Construction on

The Panama Canal

the canal started in 1905. However, the first task of the builders was to eradicate the malaria and yellow fever that had killed many workers and stopped other nations from building a canal there. **William C. Gorgas**, colonel of the United States Army Medical Corps, virtually eliminated these diseases by sanitizing and draining areas of standing water in the Canal Zone. Without standing water, the mosquitoes could not reproduce or live long enough to spread these diseases. With this problem eliminated, workers began construction in earnest. During construction, workers moved over 175 million cubic yards of earth. By the summer of 1914, the United States opened the canal.

- **1904** - President Roosevelt stated the new foreign policy of the nation. It was called **Roosevelt's Corollary** to the Monroe Doctrine. Where Monroe had said the United States would not allow European powers to colonize newly independent nations in the Western Hemisphere, Roosevelt said the United States had the right to intervene if a nation in the Western Hemisphere had trouble paying back its foreign creditors. The United States would intervene only to prevent European powers from colonizing the newly freed nations again. This doctrine led to increased United States involvement in the Caribbean and Latin America.

- **1909-1913** - In foreign relations, President Taft wanted to substitute dollars for bullets and promoted a policy of "**dollar diplomacy**." He believed the United States could control foreign nations by subjecting these nations to heavy investment from the United States. Taft promoted heavy investment in the Caribbean and made sure that United States financial institutions were in charge of financing in Latin America whenever possible. If the nations involved in these arrangements were not cooperative, such as Nicaragua in 1913, the United States landed Marines to enforce its control.

- **1915-1916** - President Wilson believed that the United States had the moral obligation to ensure that democratic governments would be fostered in Latin America and the Caribbean. This policy is known as "**missionary diplomacy**." In 1915, a series of revolutions and assassinations rocked the nation of Haiti. In response, Wilson landed United States Marines in Haiti to protect United States property and banking interests. The people of Haiti were not willing to become the next colony of the United States, so a series of bloody battles followed. To avoid further bloodshed, the Haitian government signed a treaty in September with the United States. Haiti submitted to becoming a protectorate of the United States.

  At the same time, civil war was tearing apart the nation of Mexico. In August 1914, with the help of the United States, Venustiano Carranza took over the government from the military dictator, Victoriano Huerta. Carranza, who was friendly to United States interests, had an enemy named Pancho Villa. In 1916, Pancho Villa crossed the Río Grande and set fires in Columbus, New Mexico, killing 19 people. In response, President Wilson sent a force of 6,000 troops under the leadership of General John Pershing to capture Villa dead or alive. These troops went 300 miles into Mexican territory. This reaction increased hostilities and almost led to war between the United States and Mexico. However, World War I drew Wilson's attention away from Mexico, and the United States troops left the following year.

- **1909-1933** - The United States took a controlling interest in Central America. For example, companies from the United States wanted to invest in Nicaragua. They saw advantages in its easy access to the Atlantic and Pacific Oceans. They also wanted to gain profits by developing the growing agricultural and mining industry there. However, Nicaragua's President Zelaya was not willing to work with the United States. In addition, he promoted nationalizing private businesses. Because of the pressure of business interests, the United States Navy supported efforts to overthrow Zelaya in 1909. However, the new government which was friendly to the United States was very weak. The majority of the population did not support it, so the United States Marines landed in Nicaragua in 1913. They quickly occupied the nation and insured that the conservative president remained in power. United States corporations invested heavily in Nicaragua, building railroads and improving ports in order to extract Nicaragua's mineral and agricultural wealth. The marines remained in Nicaragua in some numbers until 1925. Immediately after the marines left, liberal and conservative governments fought for power. Again, thousands of United States Marines landed in 1927 and kept the minority conservative party in power. The United States military then trained the conservative government in military readiness to ensure that the government, friendly to United States businesses and bankers, would remain in power. The last United States military forces left in January 1933. These conservative leaders in the Nicaraguan government were very corrupt, often using foreign aid given to the people of their nation for the leadership's own personal use. Throughout Central America at different times, the United States has intervened in promoting its interests ahead of the opinions of the people in the nations involved.

LONG-TERM CAUSES OF WORLD WAR I (1914-1918)

Nationalism

When Napoleon conquered much of Europe for a short time in the early 1800s, French ideals like democracy and self-determination spread to the regions conquered. Peoples of similar language and culture believed they had a right to be one nation. As the nineteenth century passed, the small city-states of central Europe became the nation of Germany (1861). The military state of Prussia convinced the other German city-states to unite. The result was a militaristic Germany that believed in its right to establish an empire.

The kingdoms of the Italian peninsula became a united nation largely through conquest by Sardinia. The miliary leaders who controlled the Italian government believed in improving the economy through conquest. The French speaking portion of the Netherlands formed its own nation called Belgium. This belief in national unity and, in some cases, racial supremacy is called **nationalism**. In time, each nation believed its culture was superior and so deserved the right to conquer other peoples. Darwin's (1809-1882) idea of "survival of the fittest" in the animal kingdom led many to believe the same held true for humans. The idea that only the strongest people are meant to rule is known as **Social Darwinism**.

Imperialism

European nations searched for colonies during the 19th century because they produced more industrial goods than they could use. Great Britain, France, and Germany competed with each other for control of Africa. These competitions increased the tensions between the nations in Europe, almost resulting in war several times between 1898 and 1914.

Military Expansion

Starting in 1874, Europeans maintained large standing armies in peace time in case of war. They also expanded their naval fleets. All of this military buildup among several nations in Europe made a war possible at a moment's notice.

Alliances

In 1882, the European powers of Germany, Austria-Hungary, and Italy formed an agreement of mutual protection called the **Triple Alliance**. If any one country was attacked, all three countries would fight. This alliance threatened all other powerful nations of Europe, so the countries of Great Britain, France, and Russia formed the **Triple Entente**. These competing alliances in Europe set the stage for conflict.

START OF WORLD WAR I

On June 28, 1914, **Archduke Francis Ferdinand** (heir to the throne of Austria-Hungary) was visiting one of his provinces, Bosnia. Serbian nationalists who wanted Bosnia to be part of Serbia shot the Archduke and his wife while they were riding in a car. This event caused a furor in Austria-Hungary. Austria-Hungary accused its neighbor, Serbia, of plotting to kill the Archduke and threatened war. Russia, which was allied with Serbia, threatened war with Austria-Hungary. Germany supported Austria-Hungary, and France mobilized its forces to help

128

Russia. By August 3, Germany and Austria-Hungary were at war with France and Russia. Crucial to Germany's strategy was the conquering of neutral Belgium and fighting France. When Germany attacked Belgium, Great Britain entered the war on the side of France forming the **Triple Entente**. Germany advanced on France until the French slowed them at **The Battle of the Marne (1914)**. For their next war tactic, the French dug trenches as defensive positions. The Germans did the same and soon lines of opposing trenches stretched from Switzerland to the North Sea.

BATTLE TACTICS AND NEW INNOVATIONS

Both sides primarily used **trench warfare** for the next three years. Each side's army lived in the trenches, which were usually infested with rats. A **no man's land** lay between the opposing trenches where soldiers placed barbed wire and land mines. When each side introduced **machine guns** and **poison gas**, the war turned especially deadly. Firing bullets in rapid succession, soldiers used machine guns to shoot massive amounts of ammunition at the enemy in a short amount of time, increasing the chances of hitting the enemy. Poison mustard gas, first used by the Germans, killed or disabled soldiers instantly. Artillery

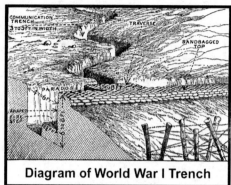

Diagram of World War I Trench

shells carried the gas to the enemy. When the artillery exploded, the gas would instantly engulf the soldiers. The gas would break down the internal organs of soldiers when they inhaled the fumes. Often, the gas destroyed the soldiers' lungs, causing them to fill with fluid. They literally drowned from the inside out. Soldiers died by the hundreds of thousands. In the **Battle of Verdun (1916)**, which lasted six months, 330,000 men died on the French and British side. Another 330,000 men died on the German side.

Another important development in the war was the use of the **airplane**. In 1909, Wilbur and Orville Wright built the first military airplane. By World War I, the warring powers on the Western Front used over 400 aircraft. At the beginning of the war, nations used these planes primarily for scouting and reconnaissance. By the end of the war, countries equipped airplanes with intermittent machine guns that could fire past an aircraft's propeller and attack enemy aircraft. The pilots of these armed airplanes were known as **Aces**.

CAUSES OF UNITED STATES INVOLVEMENT IN WORLD WAR I

From the onset of the war in Europe, the people of the United States took the position of neutrality. President Wilson urged people to resist war propaganda coming from both sides. However, many events and factors were pushing the United States towards war against Germany. For example, businesses interests were tied to Great Britain as they supplied the nation with weapons and other supplies. Corporations were eager for a war effort also because the nation was in a period of high unemployment, a **recession**. With a war, employment and productivity would increase. Moreover, wealthy bankers such as J. P. Morgan had loaned millions of dollars to Great Britain as it fought Germany. So, the banking elite had a vested interest in seeing Great Britain win the war and repay the loans with interest. Still, the United States watched the war from a distance for the next three years. Four events edged the United States closer to war:

1) The Sinking of the *Lusitania*

Sinking of the Lusitania

The United States sold and shipped military goods to the Triple Entente, especially Britain. The Germans, however, had a group of submarines, called **U-boats**, which they used to sink British and French merchant ships in the Atlantic. The Germans warned all nations that they would attack any ships entering or leaving British ports. President Wilson ignored the warning and continued commercial and military business with Great Britain. Without the knowledge of passengers, the United States had been shipping military supplies to Great Britain on cruise liners. For example, the passenger ship *Lusitania* carried 1,247 three-inch shells, 4,927 cartridges, and 2,000 more cases of small arms ammunition. On May 7, 1915, a German submarine torpedoed the *Lusitania* off the coast of Ireland. Twelve hundred people died in this attack, including 128 people from the United States. The people of the United States were furious. Unwilling to risk war with the United States, Germany agreed not to attack passenger ships in the Atlantic. A wave of anti-German feeling swept over the people of the United States.

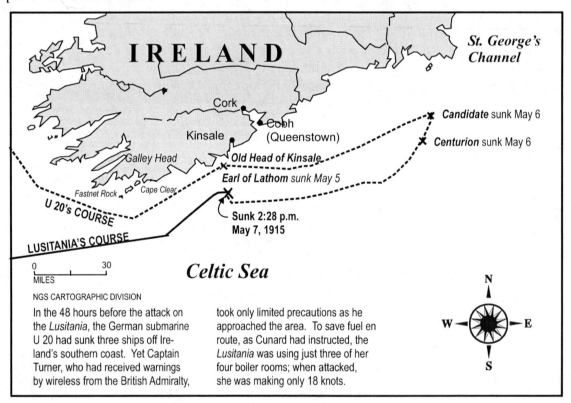

In the 48 hours before the attack on the *Lusitania*, the German submarine U 20 had sunk three ships off Ireland's southern coast. Yet Captain Turner, who had received warnings by wireless from the British Admiralty, took only limited precautions as he approached the area. To save fuel en route, as Cunard had instructed, the *Lusitania* was using just three of her four boiler rooms; when attacked, she was making only 18 knots.

2) The Zimmerman Telegram

In 1917, the United States intercepted a secret telegram between the German foreign secretary, Arthur Zimmerman, and his official in Mexico. The telegram stated that the German minister in Mexico should tell the Mexican government to attack the United States if the United

States declared war on Germany. In return, Germany promised to help Mexico win back the land the United States gained in the Mexican War (1846-1848). When the people in the United States heard about this telegram, they were very upset. As a result, President Wilson broke off diplomatic relations with Germany. This incident started another wave of anti-German feeling across the United States.

3)   German Aggression at Sea

In 1917, Germany began sinking United States merchant ships in the Atlantic. This German aggression against the United States was seen as a reason for immediate war.

4)   The Russian Revolution

In March 1917, revolutionaries in Russia overthrew the monarchy and strengthened the *Duma* as a temporary democratic assembly. With the monarchy of Russia gone, the Allied forces could present a united front for the ideals of democracy. With this event, Wilson asked the Congress to declare war on Germany, which Congress did on April 6, 1917.

President Wilson then embarked on a campaign to stir up support for the war. He proclaimed that the war was being pursued "to make the world safe for democracy." However, men in the United States did not rush to enlist. In the first six weeks after the war declaration only 73,000 men volunteered. At this point, Congress enacted the draft. To stir up support for the war, Wilson set up a Committee on Public Information to convince the public that they should fight in the war. As a result, 5,000 cities and towns across the United States heard from over 75,000 speakers on the subject. Despite all of this propaganda, there was a substantial movement of opposition to the war. To stop the opposition from gaining support, Congress passed, and Wilson signed, in June 1917, the **Espionage Act**. This act was used to imprison any citizen of the United States who publicly spoke or wrote against the war. Many anti-war leaders were imprisoned under this act, which effectively stifled any opposition to the war effort.

UNITED STATES INVOLVEMENT IN WORLD WAR I

By the time the United States sent troops to France to fight on the Western Front, the war on the Eastern Front had ended. Another revolution occurred in Russia. This time, a communist government came to power under the Bolsheviks. To stabilize the country, the Bolsheviks made a peace settlement with Germany. Now, all of the German army could focus on the Western Front. New to the war, the United States troops supplied much needed energy to the weary soldiers on the front lines. The United States soldiers did not build trenches. Instead, they fought through the enemy lines with heavy fighting. The United States, Great Britain, and France won a series of battles and forced Germany to negotiate an **armistice** (truce).

Memorial monument honoring first three Americans to die in World War I

COSTS OF THE WAR

The combined costs to all nations fighting in this conflict climbed to 186 billion dollars. In addition, over 20 million soldiers were casualties of the war. An additional 10 million civilians died as the war raged and caused shortages in food, housing, and medical supplies.

CONSEQUENCES OF WORLD WAR I

Political

Germany, Austria-Hungary, and the Ottoman Empire gave up parts of their land. Much of eastern Germany became the nation of Poland. The Austro-Hungarian Empire disappeared. The empire was divided into the countries of Austria, Hungary, Czechoslovakia, and sections of Serbia. In the event of future war, all men in the United States between the ages of 21 and 30 were required by law to register for the **draft**.

Economic

World War I ended when the defeated Germans signed an armistice (truce) on November 11, 1918. Later, at the **Treaty of Versailles (1919)**, the Germans reluctantly agreed that the war was entirely their fault. As a result, the treaty called for Germany to pay **war reparations** or costs to the victorious nations for its part in starting the war. These war reparations grew difficult for the Germans to repay, so they paid the reparations in yearly installments. In addition, Germany lost all of its overseas colonies and part of its land in Europe.

For the United States, the war produced an increase in industrial output and a decrease in unemployment. Trade with the Allies grew from $500 million in 1914 to $3.5 billion in 1917. The British, however, prevented the United States from trading with Germany and neutral nations by mining the North Sea. This policy upset Wilson, so Britain tried to soften the blow by purchasing the goods the United States normally sold to Germany.

Social

In peacetime, the European nations looked forward to the future and did not want to remember the war. The war reparations Germany was forced to pay were considered a humiliation to the German people. When the German dictator **Adolf Hitler** (1889-1945) rose to power, he used this bitterness to reclaim the achievements of Germany's past.

Achievements of the United States included an increased demand for workers to produce war materials which opened many jobs to women and blacks. Over 100,000 women worked in munitions factories, and many women found employment as steel workers. For the first time, the government began employing women doctors and lawyers. Blacks benefitted from the production boom. From 1914-1919, 500,000 blacks moved to the industrialized North and found jobs in the factories. However, factories removed both blacks and women once the war ended. With the consent of the unions, the factory owners replaced them with white men returning from the war.

POST WORLD WAR I ERA - THE LEAGUE OF NATIONS

On January 8, 1918, Woodrow Wilson spoke to Congress. He outlined the principles he considered to be the basis for bringing World War I (1914-1918) to an end and for maintaining world peace afterward. These principles became known as Wilson's **Fourteen Points**:

1. an end to secret treaties and alliances ("open covenants, openly arrived at")

2. freedom of the seas outside territorial waters in peace and war

3. removal of economic trade barriers among nations

4. reduction of national armaments to the lowest point consistent with domestic safety

5. colonial arrangements respecting the will of the peoples involved

6-13. **self-determination** for ethnic groups to establish their own governments, free from foreign rule

14. establishment of a League of Nations offering "mutual guarantees of political independence and territorial integrity to great and small states alike"

To insure that there would never be another world war, President Wilson promoted the **League of Nations (1920-1946)** as a way to foster understanding and discourage aggressions against other countries. Many countries around the world joined the League. However, Wilson could not get the United States Senate to agree that the United States should join the League. In fact, both the people of the United States and Congress believed strongly in a policy of **isolationism**, meaning that the people felt it best to stay out of international conflicts and events. Without the power of the United States, the League was virtually helpless to prevent any nation from committing aggressions against any other. For example, the League was powerless in stopping the Japanese takeover of Manchuria in 1931.

CHAPTER 11 REVIEW

A. Define the following names, terms, and events:

imperialists	dollar diplomacy	U-boats
Alfred Mahan	missionary diplomacy	*Lusitania*
Josiah Strong	nationalism	Zimmerman Telegram
yellow journalism	Social Darwinism	Espionage Act
Rough Riders	Triple Alliance	Treaty of Versailles
Open Door Policy	Triple Entente	League of Nations
Panama Canal	Archduke Ferdinand	isolationism
Roosevelt's Corollary	trench warfare	

B. On your own paper, write your response to each of the following:

1. List two reasons why the United States adopted a policy of imperialism.
2. Describe how Alfred Mahan influenced United States policy.
3. After the Spanish-American War, what territories did the United States gain?
4. How did the United States obtain land for the Panama Canal?
5. Discuss the significance of the Roosevelt Corollary.
6. Explain how Woodrow Wilson used "missionary diplomacy" in the United States occupation of Haiti.
7. Explain why bankers in the United States eagerly pushed for war with Germany.
8. Why did the assassination of Archduke Ferdinand cause World War I?
9. List four new battle tactics used during World War I.
10. Discuss the four events that led to United States involvement in World War I.
11. Describe three consequences of World War I for Germany.
12. Why was the League of Nations ineffective in preventing world conflicts?

C. Write True if the statement is correct and False if the statement is incorrect. Be prepared to state a reason for your false answers.

1. _____ The Open Door Policy was an agreement between the United States and China that the states would allow more Asian immigration to occur.

2. _____ One cause of the United States entering World War I was the sinking of the passenger ship *Lusitania* by a German U-boat.

3. _____ Before beginning work on the Panama Canal, the United States cleared both Colombians and mosquitoes from the area, by political and extermination methods respectively.

4. _____ The United States' anti-war leaders were protected by "missionary diplomacy."

5. _____ Germans believed themselves to have been abused in the Treaty of Versailles.

6. _____ The exclusive use of trench warfare limited casualties and helped the war to end quickly.

7. _____ Throughout Central American history, the United States, when sending military aid, has always bowed to the will of the people in how they wished to be governed.

8. _____ President Teddy Roosevelt created the "dollar diplomacy" policy in the early 1900s.

9. _____ Arguing against Imperialism, Josiah Strong wrote that all cultures have genuine value.

10. _____ Russia, France, and Great Britain formed the Triple Entente.

CHAPTER 12
BOOM AND BUST: 1920s and 1930s

POST WORLD WAR I CULTURE -
THE ROARING TWENTIES

Prominent Writers and Movements
in the United States

- **F. Scott Fitzgerald (1896-1940) -** A writer and novelist, Fitzgerald wrote works personifying the high society life of the 1920s. At the same time, the characters in his works mirrored his own life and that of his wife, Zelda Fitzgerald. Based on his experiences, his piercing portrayal of the materialistic excess and spiritual poverty of the wealthy brought his writings critical acclaim. He wrote his most famous work, *The Great Gatsby*, in 1925.

- **Ernest Hemingway (1899-1961) -** Regarded as one of the most influential writers of the twentieth century, Hemingway uses simple language to achieve a profound and complex effect. His novels grip the reader by adding realistic details to events, making the reader experience the actions in the stories. His most famous works include *The Sun Also Rises* (1926) and *The Old Man and the Sea* (1952).

- **The Harlem Renaissance (1920-1940) -** Beginning in Harlem, New York in the 1920s, an increase in black racial pride and awareness led many black intellectuals to write works portraying the daily lives of working class blacks in the United States. These writers used European literary styles to express their ideas and gained an audience in black and white circles of high society. Black painters, dancers, and musicians produced enduring works of art. Another important aspect of this renaissance was the introduction of **Jazz** and the **Blues** as new musical forms of expression. During and after World War I, musical artists from New Orleans and Mississippi brought their talents to the large cities of the North where they found a receptive audience of both whites and blacks.

- **Langston Hughes (1902-1967) -** a black poet and playwright of the **Harlem Renaissance**, Hughes wrote memorable poetry and short stories about the black experience in the United States.

Changes in Lifestyle and Education

In the 1920s, some women began wearing shorter skirts (knee length), cutting their hair short, and wearing makeup with loose-fitting, comfortable clothes. Women dressing in this manner were called **"flappers"** and received much attention. Women were also increasingly freed from housework with the production of ready-made clothes and the manufacture of canned goods. Many forms of music such as jazz became popular, and many prominent authors wrote critical works, calling the '20s youth part of the "Lost Generation."

Education gained importance after World War I. By 1918, every state had laws mandating that children must attend school up to a certain age. As a result, the number of secondary schools grew enormously. Children received more education than ever before, leading to a more learned and literate population.

Mass Media Entertainment

Radio - In the 1920s, radios became available for the households of the United States. Radio sales grew from less than 100,000 radios in 1922 to over 10 million radios in 1929. Radios changed the speed with which people gained information. In addition, national unity increased when radio stations transmitted the same programs into homes across the United States. Radio listeners enjoyed comedies, westerns, mysteries, music, and the latest news.

Movies - In the 1920s, movies became very popular. People came to see the famous movie stars and watch the fast action. In 1927, the first movie with sound, *The Jazz Singer*, made its debut. This new technology caused a sensation, and people flocked to the movies in greater numbers.

New Inventions

Important inventions changed the way people lived and worked. They also gave the people who used them more free time than they ever had before. Henry Ford's invention of the automobile allowed people to travel long distances for work or for pleasure. The airplane provided a way for many people to travel the United States or between continents in a matter of hours. Home appliances such as vacuum cleaners, mixers, and washing machines freed up more time for women working at home. The end result of these inventions was an increase in leisure time and leisure activities.

POVERTY IN THE 1920s

While many businesses flourished in the booming 1920s, many also did not. The new fashions of shorter skirts hit the clothing industry especially hard. These skirts required less material and created less demand for fabric. In addition, farmers produced an abundance of food during a time of falling prices for food. If any natural disaster occurred, such as a flood that destroyed their crops, many farmers would have to declare bankruptcy because they did not have any savings accumulated, and they had to sell their products very cheaply. The rail industry laid off railroad workers by the thousands as automobiles and trucks took the place of trains. Mining companies also laid off coal miners as the demand for coal fell because of the new production of oil.

In addition, immigrants and blacks did not fare well during this time. Wealthy white business owners made their fortunes by getting the work of their businesses done by blacks and immigrants at low wages. In addition, child labor laws were not yet enacted. Children continued working in hazardous conditions and brought home a meager wage. Labor at this time was largely unorganized. Employees who tried to organize at this time were generally seen as threats to the public order. As a result, employers could dictate the wages for their employees.

RACE RELATIONS

The Plight of Black Americans

Roughly 371,000 blacks served in segregated units in the armed forces, but only a few thousand black soldiers saw combat. The rest served in non-combat roles. Black Americans had hoped that their efforts to help make the world safe for democracy would gain them some recognition, but discrimination continued at home. Whites felt that blacks were now competing with them for jobs. However, this was not the case. Leaving the South for more employment in the North, blacks were only allowed to hold the most low-paying of jobs. In addition, whites discriminated against blacks in housing. Blacks could not rent in certain areas of the city, and where they were allowed to rent, landlords charged high prices for poor housing.

Racial Conflicts

Tension resulting from white mistreatment of blacks in the large industrial cities of the North increased after World War I. Denied almost all opportunities for advancements, blacks either decided to leave the United States or simply hoped conditions would improve. Eager for a new solution, hundreds of thousands of blacks joined **Marcus Garvey's Back to Africa Movement**. Although few blacks actually left for West Africa, the movement inspired unity among blacks and signaled their frustration with their lack of personal and economic freedom in the United States. Riots occurred in major Northern cities as mobs of whites invaded black neighborhoods and began killing blacks in anger for taking away low-paying jobs. In one race riot in East St. Louis (1917), for example, a white mob marched into a black neighborhood and killed over 200 people. That same year, in Houston, Texas, the government court-marshaled 63 black soldiers and hanged 13 without appeal for rioting in reaction to white harassment. Anti-black riots also occurred in Washington, D.C.; Chicago, Illinois; Knoxville, Tennessee; and Omaha, Nebraska.

The Growth of the KKK

Race relations reached what appeared to be an all-time low in the 1920s. Many white Protestant citizens were very afraid of what they perceived as the growing power of blacks and Catholic immigrants in the nation. Leaders in white communities both in the South and in the North joined the **Ku Klux Klan (KKK)** in massive numbers. The KKK claimed to have five million members during the 1920s. Many politicians became responsive to the KKK's increased numbers by limiting immigration from Eastern and Southern Europe. KKK members worked hard to attack Jews, Catholics, and blacks. Usually, they worked by intimidation and fear, burning crosses outside people's homes and sending hate letters. They put pressure on employers to fire black or immigrant workers. When this was not enough, Klan members resorted to **lynching** (putting to death by hanging) blacks and other minorities in order to frighten their communities into leaving the area.

The "Red Scare"

When the Communist Bolsheviks came to power in Russia in 1917, they promoted a worldwide movement of revolution. They asked that workers around the world revolt against their governments. In addition, **anarchists** (people who do not believe in any form of government) tried to assassinate John D. Rockefeller and Attorney General A. Mitchell Palmer. These two events led to a time of hysteria in the nation known as the "**Red Scare**." Between 1919 and 1920, the government arrested and jailed thousands of radicals including some foreign-born. Yet, these thousands had to be released because there was no evidence of conspiracy. Nevertheless, suspicion of foreigners was on the increase in the nation.

Sacco and Vanzetti Trial

While anti-foreign feeling was still high in the nation, two Italian immigrants were accused of robbery and murder in Massachusetts. These immigrants, named **Nicola Sacco** and **Bartolomeo Vanzetti**, were also **atheists** (those who profess no belief in God) and anarchists. Already prejudiced against them because of their ethnicity, their judge would not even admit their testimony into evidence when he discovered they were atheists. Evidence against them was very limited, but they were convicted and executed in 1927. Many people still debate today over whether they had a fair trial.

Scopes Trial

The **Scopes Trial (1925)** centered around John Scopes, a science teacher, who was accused of violating a Tennessee law. This law forbade the teaching of Darwin's theory of **evolution** (a belief that higher forms of life developed from lower forms of life). This famous trial pitted **creationists** who used the Bible's account of life's origins against those who believed in evolution. The trial ended with Scopes having to pay a fine. In addition, the law forbidding the teaching of evolution remained in effect.

IMMIGRATION LAWS OF THE 1920s

During the 1920s, the **nativists** (people who were afraid of foreigners entering the United States), coupled with the growth of the political power of the Klan, led Congress to almost completely restrict immigration to the United States from Eastern Europe, Southern Europe, and Asia. In 1921, Congress passed the **Emergency Quota Act** which set up a quota system favoring northern Europe for immigration. The United States government gave preferential status to immigrants from northern Europe and Britain because of their generally lighter complexions and Protestant beliefs.

PROHIBITION

In general, the public did not like the **18th Amendment** called **Prohibition (1919)**. Many simply ignored it by making and drinking their own alcohol. People went to hidden bars called **speakeasies** to drink and dance. Many people made huge fortunes by smuggling alcohol from Canada and the Caribbean into the United States. These people were called **bootleggers**. Crime families and mobsters proliferated. The most infamous of them was **Al Capone (1899-1947)**. Millions broke the laws against alcohol every day, which reduced respect for the law in general. The people asked that the prohibition against the sale of alcohol be lifted. Congress then passed the **21st Amendment (1933)**, which repealed the 18th amendment.

Al Capone

Women focused on two campaigns during the Progressive Era. One, the **temperance movement**, resulted in the passage of the 18th amendment, **Prohibition**. The second movement, **women's suffrage**, was a crusade to bring women the right to vote. For decades, women had struggled for this right. **Suffragettes** knew that they would lack any political power if they were not allowed to vote. In state after state, women campaigned in the legislatures to allow women the right to vote. Through continued pressure, the 19th Amendment was ratified by a majority of the states in August 1920. This amendment allowed women the right to vote.

CAUSES OF THE GREAT DEPRESSION

Disparity of Income

Throughout the Roaring 1920s, a select group of businessmen and professionals made large sums of money. However, the wages of their workers did not increase as fast as the price of the goods purchased. Businesses and farms produced a surplus of goods. At the same time, consumer spending on these goods steadily dropped. The government did not publish statistics on consumer spending, so few understood that the economy was slowing down.

The 1920s Economy

Many people made fortunes in the 1920s economy. Other people lived in deep poverty. Many people found work in the growing automobile and appliance industries. However, workers in these businesses did not receive wages that kept pace with the increases in cost of living. Farmers found themselves deeper in debt during this decade. In addition, blacks had a very difficult time finding work of any sort during this time. Latinos from Mexico worked as migrant workers, taking part-time work needed seasonally and receiving very low wages for their work. The majority of them lived in slums. Other people made fortunes investing in the stock market.

Stock Market Speculation

During the 1920s, the United States experienced a strong **bull market** (a market where stock prices are rising). Investors became accustomed to buying their stocks on margin, meaning purchasing stock for as little as 10% down. They borrowed the rest of the money from brokers and experienced huge profits when their stocks rose in value. When the **stock market crashed on October 29, 1929**, stock prices fell, and the majority of investors tried to sell all of their investments. Most investors received pennies on the dollar for their stocks. Others lost all of their money in stocks. Brokers, who financed the majority of the stock price for their investors, defaulted on their lines of credit with the banks. People holding savings accounts became worried that their money would not be there when the bank experienced so much loss of cash. They ran to the bank in huge numbers and withdrew all their money. As people pulled their money out, banks closed down. Businesses closed because they could no longer borrow money to cover their expenses. As a result, workers lost their jobs, and unemployment skyrocketed. This led to a long period of high unemployment and increased poverty called **The Great Depression** (1929-1941). European economies that were tied closely to the United States also experienced an economic depression.

Stock prices rise in a bull market.

Stock prices fall in a bear market.

The biggest problem for farmers during the 1920s and 1930s was that they produced more food than consumers needed. These surpluses drove down prices to the point that the harvest could no longer pay for a farm's operation. Many farms had to declare bankruptcy during this time. Between 1933 and 1936, the land between the Dakotas and Texas received little rain.

Because farmers did not know about stopping soil erosion, wind picked up this dry, loosened soil and spread it across the nation. Huge dust storms blew the precious topsoil away. Farmers refer to this experience and these lands as the **Dust Bowl**. Farmers across the center of the nation watched as the wind literally blew their farms away. They left their homes by the thousands and moved to the Pacific

Abandoned farm land in the Dust Bowl

Coast looking for work, further aggravating the problems of unemployment.

PRESIDENT HOOVER'S ADMINISTRATION (1929 - 1932)

Elected during a time of economic prosperity, Republican **Herbert Hoover** (1874 - 1964) received all of the blame when the economy was thrown into depression. Many people went from town to town in search of work. Children suffered greatly from hunger. Malnutrition rose from 18% to 60% in children. Between 1929 and 1933, 85,000 businesses shut down, 400,000 farmers lost their farms (no one had money to buy farm products), and soup kitchens started. Many people came to cities while looking for work. Outside the cities, they built communities of tents and shacks called **Hoovervilles**. People in the soup kitchens ate thin soup known as Hoover stew. In all areas of life, the nation's people blamed Hoover for the economic depression.

President Herbert Hoover

A group of World War I veterans, called the **Bonus Army**, marched on Washington in 1932 demanding early payment on a war bonus for their service to the country. The veterans were not supposed to be paid until 1945. The House passed a bill allowing the veterans to be paid early. However, the Senate did not pass the bill. The veterans camped in shacks and tents near the Potomac River and vowed to remain until they were paid their bonus. Alarmed by their action, President Hoover sent troops under General Douglas MacArthur to break up the camp. Using tanks, machine guns, and tear gas, MacArthur removed the protesters and burned the camp to the ground. Soldiers killed four people in the attack, and the people were outraged by Hoover's action. As a result, Hoover's popularity dropped very low. This made it easy for the Democratic Party to win the next presidential election.

ROOSEVELT'S NEW DEAL

In 1932, **Franklin D. Roosevelt** (1882-1945) was elected President on the promise to help "the forgotten man." People believed in him. He was enthusiastically **optimistic**. As governor of New York, Roosevelt had spent state government money to help those hurt by the Depression. Roosevelt won by a **landslide**, and became President during the worst year of the Depression.

Roosevelt went to work right away, using his famous **three R's: recovery, relief,** and **reform**. Based on these three R's, he created a series of federal programs fulfilling his campaign promise of "a new deal for the American people." As these **New Deal** programs were put in place, the size and scope of the government greatly increased. For the first time, the government was used to affect the economy. With the success of the New Deal, people in the United States increasingly demanded that the government take responsibility for safeguarding their economic well-being.

President Franklin D. Roosevelt

Relief measures were designed to stop suffering by:

1. providing direct money payments or jobs to the unemployed; and
2. providing mortgage loans to help farmers and homeowners in danger of losing their property.

Roosevelt wanted to bring about *recovery* by providing aid to farmers, business owners, and workers to get people back to work. The government provided many jobs for people in building roads, highways, public buildings, dams, and parks.

The third R, *reform*, was intended less to help with the Great Depression than to make sure there never would be another one. These measures **regulated** businesses and banks and protected bank depositors, investors, consumers, the aged, children, and the unemployed. Most of the New Deal (1933) measures were controversial, but they restored confidence at the time and improved the economy. A list of the New Deal programs follows:

*   Under the **Agricultural Adjustment Act (AAA)** (1933), the government gave loans to farmers, and the government paid farmers not to grow crops so food prices would go up.

*   Congress created the **Tennessee Valley Authority (TVA)** (1933). The TVA built hydroelectric dams to bring electricity to new parts of the South, including northern Alabama, and to provide employment and cheap electricity. The Southern Appalachians were historically one of the poorest areas of the nation. With the help of the TVA, this region prospered as it never had before.

*   The **Social Security Act (SSA),** passed in 1935, provides retirement income for all workers once they reach the age of 65.

*   Congress passed the **National Labor Relations Act (NLRA)** also known as the **Wagner Act** in 1935. It created a board to monitor unfair management practices such as firing a worker who joined a union.

*   The **Fair Labor Standards Act** (1938) raised the minimum wage to 40 cents per hour, set maximum work hours at 44 hours per week, and ended child labor under the age of 16.

*   Congress established the **Civilian Conservation Corps (CCC)** in 1933. The CCC provided employment for unmarried men between the ages of 17 and 23. These young men worked in the national parks installing electric lines, building fire towers, and planting new trees in deforested areas.

- Congress established the **Federal Deposit Insurance Corporation (FDIC)** in 1933 under the Federal Reserve Act to insure depositors up to $100,000.00 in case of bank failure. This insurance was intended to prevent people from running to the bank and withdrawing their money if banks were in danger of foreclosing.

- Congress established the **Works Progress Administration (WPA)** (1935) to provide jobs for unskilled workers. At one time, the WPA employed 2 of the unemployed of the nation (3.2 million people). The WPA constructed many government buildings during the 1930s.

The result of all of these projects was an improvement in the nation's industrial abilities and great improvements for the national parks. These works projects employed enough people to spur the economy back into action. By 1941, all economic signs indicated that the Great Depression was officially over.

African American Experiences During the Great Depression

During the Great Depression, it was the black workers who were first to lose their jobs. In addition, they were often denied the public assistance that the government made available, such as public works jobs. When blacks went to relief centers, they were threatened or beaten if they signed up for work. To make matters worse, some private charities refused to serve blacks in soup kitchens. President Roosevelt and his wife, Eleanor, looked for ways to alleviate the suffering in the black community. Roosevelt gathered a group of advisers together called the **black cabinet** that could help him find solutions to these situations. Black community leaders joined together in order to increase their community's strength and present grievances to the federal government. However, it would be many years before most of these grievances would be addressed.

The New Deal for Native Americans

President Roosevelt was concerned about the plight of Native Americans during the Depression years. In 1934, Congress passed the **Indian Reorganization Act**. This act protected and expanded the amount of land on Native American reservations. Congress also ended the policy of attempting to suppress Native American religious expression. Up until this point, it was illegal for Native Americans to freely practice their religions. Also, Native Americans received jobs on land conservation projects. These projects were coordinated by the Emergency Conservation Work group. In addition, Congress established the **Indian Arts and Crafts Board** to promote the sale of Native American arts and crafts.

CULTURAL DEVELOPMENTS

Movies

During the Depression, movie makers tried to revive people's faith in the nation. Movies told positive, uplifting stories about happy families in affluent households. The most popular movies included Walt Disney's *Snow White and the Seven Dwarfs* (1937). The first film going from black and white to the world of color was *The Wizard of Oz* (1939). This movie made people imagine what it would be like to walk on streets of gold somewhere over the rainbow. The most expensive and profitable production of the 1930s was *Gone With the Wind* (1939). This movie let people forget their lives and follow the story of love and loss across the war-ravaged South during the Civil War.

142

Radio

Radio broadcasts expanded during the Great Depression. Households listened with great enthusiasm for the latest news and entertainment. Radio personalities gripped the attention of listeners with exciting stories and various sound effects. One of the most famous stories broadcast was Orson Welles' *War of the Worlds* (1938). In the beginning of the program, the announcer told listeners that the story was fictional. However, listeners who tuned in late actually believed that space creatures were taking over the world. This caused a panic across the nation that demonstrated the influence of radio. In order to bypass the press, President Roosevelt often spoke directly to the nation using the radio. These radio programs were called **fireside chats**. The 1930s and early 1940s are known as the golden age of radio.

ECONOMICS

Producers and Consumers

The economy in the United States is based on a **mixed market economy**, meaning that the economy is a free market, with some public influence over that market. There are two groups which drive this market. One, the **producers**, provide the goods and services which the other group, the **consumers**, purchase. When producers sell an item, they aim for the **market price**. This price is the point at which the maximum number of items or services can be sold for the highest possible price.

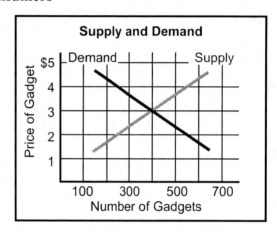

The Federal Reserve System

The **Federal Reserve System (Fed)** is an organization established by Congress in 1913 to regulate the economy. The Fed is organized into 12 central banks in the United States. Approximately one third of the banks in the United States are member banks. All national banks are required to join, and state banks have the option to do so. The Fed is led by a board of directors in Washington, D.C. This organization is not affiliated with any political party, and as a rule, politics are not discussed. The Fed relies on **open-market operations** (giving banks currency or taking currency away from banks to change the money supply and interest rates). The Fed uses three different tools to affect the economy in this manner.

The first way the Fed can affect the economy is through the buying and selling of **Treasury bills**, which are IOU's from the federal government to the holder. For example, if the Fed wants to increase the money supply, the Fed will offer to buy a certain number of Treasury bills from banks. The banks receive influxes of cash by selling the Treasury bills back to the federal government. The banks then use this money to loan to individuals and businesses. In this way, the money supplied by the Fed is multiplied throughout the economy.

The buying and selling of Treasury bills also affects interest rates. By purchasing a large quantity of Treasury bills, the Fed increases the demand for Treasury bills, thus increasing their price. As prices rise, interest rates fall because there is less return on the investment. This trend also works in the opposite direction. If the Fed decides to sell Treasury bills, the Fed effectively takes money out of circulation, reducing inflation. At the same time, interest rates increase because there is more return on the investment.

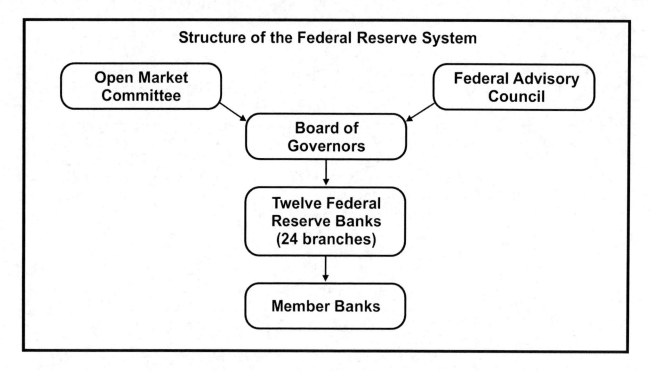

Structure of the Federal Reserve System

Open Market Committee

Federal Advisory Council

Board of Governors

Twelve Federal Reserve Banks (24 branches)

Member Banks

The Fed can also affect the economy by setting the **reserve requirement**. The reserve requirement is the minimum amount of money every bank must keep on reserve. By decreasing the amount of money every bank must keep on reserve, the Fed can increase the amount of money available for loans, increasing the amount of money in circulation. The Fed can also decrease the money available for loans by increasing the reserve requirement for banks.

The Fed has a third mechanism for affecting the economy, changing the percentage of the **discount rate**. The discount rate is the rate which the Fed charges banks who need to borrow money. As the discount rate of the Fed increases, the rate which banks charge businesses and individuals also increases. As the discount rate of the Fed decreases, the rate banks charge their customers also decreases.

The Fed uses all three tools to affect the economy by either encouraging spending or savings. The Fed can affect both the interest rates that banks charge and the amount of money in circulation in the United States. The Fed tries to follow an independent, cautionary policy in managing the national economy.

The federal government also uses other policies outside the control of the Fed to affect the economy in the United States. Historically, the government's policies of taxation, spending, and borrowing have had dramatic effects on the economy of the United States.

Economic Cycles

The national economy is always in an economic cycle consisting of periods of prosperity, known as **booms**, and periods of lower economic activity, known as **recessions**. Before the Fed existed, the United States economy went through periods of booms and recessions, and the government did not intervene. This policy is known as **laissez faire** economics. However, the amount of income and items the government has taxed has varied with time. Usually, when taxes are low, consumer spending increases because consumers have more income. When taxes are raised, however, people have smaller incomes and, consequently, spend less. The government has alternately lowered taxes as a way of stimulating the economy through consumer spending, and raised taxes improving the infrastructure of the country to facilitate economic development, such as through the building of roads.

Starting with the creation of the Federal Reserve in 1913, the federal government has been able to exert more direct influence over the economy. However, after World War I, the government did not control two vital aspects of the economy. One was the method of stock purchasing, and the other was the prevention of runs on banks. During the 1920s, stockholders increasingly bought stocks on margin, meaning they paid only a small percentage for stocks - usually 10%. When the stock market fell, these people did not have the money to pay for their stock losses. As a result, these stockholders went bankrupt, and banks were now required to pay these loans. People holding money in the bank became worried the banks would take their savings to pay for these bad loans, so millions of people withdrew their savings from banks and these banks then went bankrupt. These events started the Great Depression. At this point, the federal government took a more active role in these two parts of the economy. First, the Fed mandated a higher percentage be paid for any stocks bought on margin. In addition, the Federal Government insures every individual's bank account holdings up to $100,000.00. These two mechanisms serve to prevent another Great Depression.

Taxation

The government's policies of taxation profoundly affect the United States economy. During the early years after the country's founding, the United States government chiefly raised revenues through tariffs on imports. These tariffs discouraged foreign nations, particularly Great Britain, from being able to sell their manufactured goods in the United States. This situation allowed many domestic businesses to begin industrialization in order to provide those manufactured goods that the public in the United States demanded. Tariffs have also been used to protect home markets from competition. Currently, for example, the United States levies a high tariff on sugar. This tariff protects sugar growers in the United States from receiving low prices for their sugar harvests.

Shortly after the country's founding, both state and federal governments decided to tax items available for sale as a way of raising revenue. These taxes are known as **excise taxes**. Excise taxes, because they are levied as a percentage of goods sold, are called a **flat tax**. Regardless of income, all people are taxed at the same rate. Excise taxes are also used as a way to discourage the consumption of a particular item. Cigarettes, for example, have additional taxes levied on them to discourage their purchase.

Another and newer form of tax is the **income tax**. This tax, which is the 16th Amendment passed in 1913, is called a **progressive tax** because the wealthy have to pay a higher percentage of taxes than the poor. The income tax is used to provide the federal government with money. The majority of this money is allocated for defense, while smaller amounts are available for social programs, transportation, and education. Today, debate shifts between those that want to do away with the progressive income tax in favor of a flat sales tax and those who want to keep the progressive income tax system. While the income tax is designed to tax the rich at higher rates than the poor, many earnings, such as municipal bonds, treasury bills, and interest paid on house payments, are not taxed at all. Many believe these tax shelters allow the rich to, in some cases, pay less taxes than the poor.

National Debt

Another concern in the national economy has been the **national debt**. Every year, Congress creates a budget of expenditures to keep the federal government running. At the same time, the total money spent is then checked against the total amount of money collected in tax revenues. For many years, the government has progressively spent more than it takes in for revenue. This situation is known as **deficit spending**. People fear a continuation of deficit spending because it requires a portion of tax revenues to be spent on paying the interest on this debt. As a result, Congress is working to pass budgets that will allow a surplus to go towards paying off this debt.

Trade Imbalance

In international trade, the United States is concerned because it consistently has a **trade imbalance** with other nations, meaning that foreign nations are sending more goods to the United States than the United States is sending to foreign nations. This trade imbalance has caused concern in some arenas. Japan, for example, has consistently sold more goods in the United States than the United States has sold in Japan.

There are many reasons for this trade imbalance. People in the United States tend to spend most of the money they receive in their paychecks, whereas the people of Japan tend to save more of their income. As a result, demand for goods is higher in the United States. In addition, Japan has a large number of regulations that make it difficult to sell goods in Japan. However, the United States cannot follow a policy of **protectionism** (policy of raising trade barriers to protect domestic markets) because other foreign nations will also raise trade barriers against products from the United States. Instead, the United States has pursued a policy of eliminating all trade barriers. Starting in the 1980s, for example, each president of the United States has worked to reduce the established trade barriers in Japan.

Problems in Prosperity

The 1920s was a time of incredible prosperity in the United States. Businesses grew enormously, and the new confidence in this positive economy led many people to invest in stocks, land, and to purchase many new consumer products on credit. Both industrial and agricultural output soared during this time. They soared in the form of **consumable goods** (goods consumed by people directly, such as clothing, food, furniture, and cars) and **durable goods** (goods that may be used frequently over a long period of time). However, the demand for these new and abundant products did not keep up with supply. At this time, people could easily qualify for **credit**, meaning people could easily receive loans from a bank in order to purchase a certain product. As long as the economy continued to expand, consumers could continue to purchase items on credit.

However, during the second half of the 1920s, consumer demand dropped. People simply could not afford the products available, causing a slowdown in business. As a result, investors continued purchasing large amounts of stocks for as little as 10% of their actual value, artificially propping up the price of stocks more than they were actually worth considering the earnings of the companies they invested in. At the same time, tariffs for goods coming into the United States were kept high to prevent foreign competition. Consequently, countries around the world also imposed tariffs against goods coming from the United States, lessening the demand for United States goods worldwide. These situations contributed to the stock market crash of October 29, 1929.

146

CHAPTER 12 REVIEW

A. Define the following names, terms, and events:

Roaring Twenties	Scopes Trial	Hoovervilles	consumer
flapper	evolution	F. D. Roosevelt	open market
Harlem Renaissance	creationism	New Deal	reserve requirement
jazz	nativists	AAA	discount rate
Marcus Garvey	Al Capone	TVA	excise tax
Ku Klux Klan	Prohibition	SSA	income tax
lynching	suffragettes	NLRA	protectionism
Red Scare	bull market	FDIC	consumable goods
Sacco and Vanzetti	Great Depression	WPA	durable goods
atheists	Dust Bowl	fireside chats	
anarchists	Herbert Hoover	producer	

B. On your own paper, write your response to each of the following:

1. List three writers and describe how they influenced culture during the Roaring Twenties.
2. List the effects of three new kinds of technology during the 1920s.
3. Discuss two reasons for poverty in the 1920s.
4. Discuss two racial conflicts during the 1920s.
5. How did the KKK (Ku Klux Klan) affect blacks, Catholics, and Jews during the 1920s?
6. List two events that contributed to the anti-foreign feeling in the 1920s.
7. Discuss two results of the passage in 1920 of the 18th Amendment which prohibited the selling and manufacturing of alcohol.
8. Describe the debate that was highlighted by the Scopes trial.
9. Refer to the map on page 130. Is there enough information on this map to determine in which direction the Earl of Lathom was traveling when the U20 submarine sunk it? Explain your answer.
10. List three causes of the Great Depression.
11. Give two reasons why Herbert Hoover was an unpopular president.
12. Identify and describe three of Roosevelt's New Deal programs.
13. During the Great Depression, Hollywood made many films. Why were these films popular?
14. Describe the three ways the Fed can effect the economy.
15. Describe how the Fed is organized.
16. Explain how the income tax is a progressive tax.

C. Write True if the statement is correct and False if the statement is incorrect. Be prepared to state a reason for your false answers.

1. _____ The Federal Reserve is an institution which all national banks are required to join.

2. _____ The infamous trial of Italian atheists Sacco and Vanzetti, was tainted by anti-foreign feeling in the United States, following the Russian Revolution.

3. _____ During the 1930s, the United States enjoyed a bull market and healthy economic growth.

4. _____ The musical style called Jazz was created and played by New York musical artists

5. _____ The inventions of the radio and the motion picture increased national unity in the 1920s.

6. _____ The agricultural disaster known as the "Dust Bowl" took place in the lands between the Dakotas and Texas.

7. _____ President Hoover, who was the leader of the United States going into the Depression, was a Republican.

8. _____ The programs developed from President Roosevelt's New Deal were universally approved.

9. _____ European countries thrived economically as the United States suffered in the Depression.

10. _____ Crime families and mobsters flourished through illegal alcohol trade during Prohibition.

CHAPTER 13
WORLD WAR II

HISTORY AND ECONOMICS

Perhaps more than any other war in history, economics played a crucial role in World War II. Before discussing the specifics of the Second World War, it is important to have a brief review of economic policies and practices.

A Brief History of Economic Systems

In a **traditional economy**, the decisions are based on the customs and traditions of the society. One example of a traditional economy is the **feudal system** in Europe during the Middle Ages. People remained in the class into which they were born. A person who was born a serf, died a serf. The same held true for lords, warriors, and artisans. These traditions, and the lord, controlled the economy. Each estate was self-sufficient, producing its own food, shelter, fuel, and clothing. Consequently, for approximately 600 years, trade and communication were very limited.

As trade expanded during the 16th and 17th centuries, individual estates and cities formed larger nation-states. The government of these newly formed countries exercised control over commerce to maximize its benefits to the state. In 1776, the Scottish economist **Adam Smith** (1723-1790) published *The Wealth of Nations* which challenged this trend. He believed without government control that self-interest, private ownership, and market competition would guide the economy like an "invisible hand" to achieve the well-being of society. He thought that through expansion of manufacturing and markets, a nation's wealth could increase with almost unlimited possibilities. Smith's approach is called **laissez-faire** economics or a **free market economy** because the government enforces very little or no control over the economy.

During the Industrial Revolution, the use of mechanical power increased worker efficiency which made goods abundant and cheap. However, as the market demanded more and more goods at lower prices, factory owners forced workers to labor for very long hours in unhealthy, even dangerous, working conditions. The owners would often employ children whom they could pay much less than adults, and the government did little to change things.

Karl Marx (1818-1883) called the free market economy **capitalism** and criticized it for producing these terrible conditions for workers. He called the factory owners **capitalists** and blamed them for exploiting the workers. He believed that as machines replaced workers and as capitalists got richer, the workers would revolt and take control of the government. The workers would establish a **command economy** where the government owned the factories and set prices, wages, and production goals. Marx called this system **socialism** because society, not private individuals, controlled the economy. He believed once capitalism was destroyed that there would be no need for a strong government. It would wither away and people would work according to their abilities in order to provide for the needs of the other people. He called this utopian stage **communism** because people owned property in common and worked to serve one another.

Karl Marx

All societies participate in the following economic activities: **production** (making goods or providing services); **consumption** (using up goods or services); **exchange** (paying for goods, services, or resources); and **distribution** (sharing income and wealth within a society). Each society organizes these activities according to the following different models:

	Property Ownership	Income Distribution	Government's Role	Economic Incentives
Traditional Economy (Tribal or Feudal Society)	rich elite, nobility	the few landowners and nobles are rich, and the many peasants are poor	the king, lord, or chief is the government and controls the economy	in exchange for work, the peasants get protection from lord and soldiers
Market Economy (Free Enterprise, Capitalism)	private individuals own land and means of production	determined by the **market mechanism** (interaction of supply and demand)	government is only needed to protect rights of private property, guarantee contracts, and provide military protection for nation; buyers and sellers free to make choices of purchase and production	self-interest motivates people to pursue profit
Command Economy (Central Planning, Communism)	government owns factories, farms, and large retail establishments	regulated by government	government plans production, prices, and the distribution of income and wealth	people work for the betterment of society as a whole or for rewards given by the state

No economy is a pure form of a traditional, command, or market economy. An economy which involves some combination of these practices is called a **mixed economy**. For example, even in a free market economy, the government will usually regulate "natural monopolies" such as railroads or utilities (electricity, natural gas, water). The investment in these industries is so large that it doesn't make sense to have competition, so the government regulates it.

POLITICAL AND ECONOMIC UPHEAVAL AFTER WORLD WAR I

The devastation of World War I, the Communist revolution in Russia, and the problematic peace agreements of the Paris Peace Conference created great political and economic struggles in Europe. The Great Depression of the 1930s only made things worse. The economic crisis appeared to show the failure of the liberal ideals of democracy, free market economies, and international agreements of peace. People suffering from poverty and starvation received little help from their elected governments that were divided by factions. The people turned to strong leaders who promised to restore economic prosperity and national pride, even while limiting civil liberties.

The Rise of Communism

In late February 1917, the Russian workers in the capital city of Petrograd (later Leningrad, now St. Petersburg) took to the streets. Czar Nicholas II (1868-1918) called out the army to stop the uprising, but within 24 hours, the soldiers joined the workers in the revolution and took control of the city. After several months of political instability, the **Bolsheviks** (Russian for majority) took control in November 1917 and chose **Vladimir Lenin** (1870-1924) as the leader of the new government.

Vladimir Lenin

Lenin had gained power under the slogan "Peace, Bread, and Land." He opposed World War I, believing that it forced workers to fight against workers to the benefit of the rich. He called for the soldiers to fight for a workers' revolution instead. A follower of Marx, he said that only the destruction of capitalism would bring lasting peace. In his desire to end the war, Lenin negotiated peace with Germany, signing the **Treaty of Brest-Litovsk** on March 3, 1918. Angered and insulted by this treaty, many Russians fought the Bolshevik Party (which changed its name to the **Russian Communist Party**) in a civil war from 1918 to 1920. Lenin and the Communist Party defeated their opponents and took strict control of the government. They quickly crushed workers' strikes, peasant uprisings, and a sailors' revolt.

Lenin's **New Economic Policy** (1921) encouraged limited private enterprise, establishing a **mixed economy** that was partially nationalized and partially market-based. It also provided for more pluralism in society but established one-party rule, banning all factions within the Communist Party. On December 30, 1922, the ethnic territories of the former Russian empire joined with Russia to form the **Union of Soviet Socialist Republics** (USSR).

Problems Created by the Paris Peace Conference

When World War I ended, representatives from the Allied nations met at the **Paris Peace Conference** (January 18, 1919- June 28, 1919). President Woodrow Wilson called for a "peace without victory," believing that only a peace between equals could last. He encouraged the other Great Powers (France, Great Britain, Japan, and Italy) not to impose a harsh peace on Germany, but to work together toward an equal arrangement for a lasting peace. Having suffered years of war on their own soil, the nations of Europe could not share in Wilson's generosity or idealism. Each nation pushed for its own interests, creating peace agreements that satisfied no one. Because **Germany** had signed an **armistice** (truce) and created a democratic government, it hoped for a favorable peace agreement. Instead, the Allies excluded the Germans from the negotiations and from the League of Nations. The Allies' threat of invasion forced Germany to accept the **Treaty of Versailles**. The treaty debilitated the German military, crippled the German economy with war reparations, and humiliated the German people by requiring them to admit sole responsibility for causing World War I.

Also at the conference, the Allies broke up the Austro-Hungarian empire, drawing national boundaries without respect for the ethnic composition of the area's population. These false divisions later caused serious boundary disputes.

At the conclusion of the Paris Peace Conference, the commander of the Allied forces, Ferdinand Foch, prophetically said, "This is not peace, but a truce for 20 years."

Economic Crisis

World War I seriously damaged the economies of the European nations. Both the winners and the losers came out of the war with large debts. The defeated countries struggled to pay reparations while the victorious nations counted on those reparations to repay the United States.

Many soldiers could not find jobs after the war as economies struggled to change from war production to peacetime industries.

On October 29, 1929 the New York Stock Market crashed, beginning a world-wide economic crisis called the **Great Depression (1930s)**. Production dropped and unemployment skyrocketed. In the midst of these problems, the United States put into effect the highest tariff law in its history, the Smoot-Hawley Tariff (June 17, 1930). Other countries responded with their own tariffs and developed policies of protection and self-sufficiency to isolate themselves from the collapsing world economy.

Nationalism

The Great Depression caused mass unemployment and spread poverty and despair. As democratic governments struggled to restore economic and social stability, people lost confidence in their elected officials. They turned instead to extreme political movements that promised to end the economic problems and to restore national pride. The more people suffered, the more they wanted to see their country restored to strength, even through domination of other nations. **Nationalism** (pride in one's country) grew strongest in countries that suffered the greatest economic problems and had the deepest resentment of the Paris Peace Treaties.

Nationalism, plus the lack of United States participation, limited the effectiveness of the **League of Nations**. Each country pushed for its own interests at the expense of other countries. Weak nations relied on the League because they had no other options. Strong nations maintained their rights through threats or the use of force.

THE RISE OF TOTALITARIANISM

The Allies in World War I fought in the name of democracy, but the economic and political instability following the war led to the rise of totalitarian regimes. In a **totalitarian government**, one political party or group maintains complete control under a dictatorship and bans all others. The government exerts strong influence over all aspects of society, restricting personal freedom.

Italy

After World War I, **Benito Mussolini** (1883-1945) further developed his political ideas, which he called **fascism**. Mussolini dreamed of revitalizing an Italian empire from the heritage of the ancient Romans. He hoped to accomplish this by strict government controls and a strong military both directed toward nationalistic goals. His Fascist Party (1919) opposed workers' strikes in the cities and peasants' strikes in the country. Mussolini gained the support of those who feared the spread of communism, namely, conservative business leaders and landlords, the Roman Catholic Church, and the army.

In 1921 and 1922, Italy's democratic constitutional monarchy was in crisis. Mussolini established himself as dictator by banning all political parties, except for the Fascist Party, abolishing labor unions, forbidding strikes, and silencing political opponents. His government preserved a capitalist economy and pursued increased military power for the nation. As dictator of Italy from 1922-1945, Mussolini transformed the state into a militaristic and nationalist instrument of conquest.

Benito Mussolini

Japan

In 1925, Japan responded to the growing popularity of democratic ideals by granting the right to vote to all males. This was a great change from the previous government of the nobility and military. The following year, **Emperor Hirohito** (1901-1989) was enthroned, and he claimed *Showa* ("enlightened peace") as the motto for his reign. However in 1931, the Japanese army, without any authority from the Japanese government, occupied the Chinese province of **Manchuria**. Split by party divisions, Japan's democratic government was not strong enough to resist the military. As a result, Japanese military leaders established their own national cabinet and dispensed with democracy.

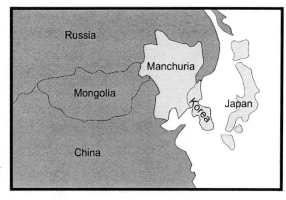

Germany

Economic hardship followed Germany's humiliating defeat in World War I. The democratic government established in 1919 failed to provide solutions, and the problems worsened. As Germany suffered through the Great Depression, armed gangs of fascists and communists roamed the streets forcing the government to use emergency measures. The fascists, called **Nazis**, steadily gained support. The Nazis' **Führer** ("leader"), **Adolf Hitler** (1889-1945), preached a message of racist fascism. He claimed that the so-called **Aryan race** (Caucasian people of non-Jewish descent) was superior and deserved to conquer other nations. He blamed Germany's economic struggles on Jews and on the nations who imposed harsh **war reparations** (money penalties) at the **Treaty of Versailles** (1919). His message of national superiority and **scapegoating** (displaced blame) attracted Germans who were suffering economic and patriotic hardship. In January

Adolf Hitler

1933, the German president responded to Hitler's strong popular support by appointing him chancellor of Germany. In a series of political moves, Hitler dismantled all opposition to the Nazis and established himself as dictator. Fulfilling his promise to rebuild Germany, Hitler violated the Treaty of Versailles by rejuvenating the military, creating a new air force, and re-establishing the draft. The **Gestapo** (secret police) helped Hitler suppress dissenters, putting all aspects of society under Nazi control.

The Union Of Soviet Socialist Republics (USSR)

Vladimir Lenin, the first Communist leader of Russia, had encouraged **Joseph Stalin** (1879-1953) and supported his leadership in the new Bolshevik government. Later, Lenin tried to remove Stalin from leadership, but Stalin secured his position by fierce political maneuvering. By 1930, Stalin had eliminated his political opposition and established himself as the sole leader of the USSR.

In 1928, the Soviet Union was not producing enough food to feed its people, the majority of whom were peasants working on small farms. Stalin forced many peasants from their own land to work on collective farms. In an effort to industrialize the nation, he sent others to work

Joseph Stalin

in factories. Stalin's efforts failed, and the Soviet Union produced even less food, leading to a period of famine. Millions of peasants died as food supplies dwindled. Despite these failures, Stalin held onto his power with brutal violence. From 1934-1938, Stalin purged the military and the Communist Party leadership of anyone he considered disloyal to him. Between 1.5 million and 7 million Soviet citizens were arrested and executed in this purge.

FASCISM VERSUS COMMUNISM

Though the theories of fascism and communism are opposed to each other, when put in practice, the systems look quite similar.

COMMUNISM	FASCISM
Goal Marx's goal was for the factory workers to unite in a violent revolt to overthrow the wealthy capitalists. The workers would then set up a strong central government to control production, own all property, and eliminate capitalism. This central government would later pass away leaving a communal utopian society. Marx was a materialist who considered religion "the opiate of the masses" and called for its elimination. Marx was not nationalistic; he believed that the unity of economic classes crossed national boundaries.	**Goal** Both Mussolini and Hitler saw themselves as heirs to the great empires of their nations' past. They sought to re-establish national dominance through a strong central government exerting strict control over society and a mighty military capable of dominating neighboring countries. They required the desires and rights of individuals subordinated to the benefit of the state.
Practice In practice, Stalin succeeded in eliminating private enterprise and establishing strict government control over the economy and all other aspects of society. Where Marx had envisioned the socialist government to be a dictatorship of the workers moving toward utopia, the reality in Russia was one party rule by an elite inner circle. Stalin's goal was to maintain governmental power and spread Russia's Communist domination to other countries.	**Practice** Mussolini gained control of the government and exerted strict influence over society, but he did not use the brutal means of Hitler or Stalin. Although he had pledged his support to the lower classes, once in power, he aligned himself with big business, giving free rein to large cartels to control the economy. Hitler also aligned himself with big business to the detriment of small business owners. He used torture and murder to place the entire country under the control of his Nazi Party.
Result The result was increased industrial production, failure of agricultural reform, uniform control of society, elimination of church influence, development of a strong military, and the creation of a huge monolithic empire with no civil liberties for its citizens.	**Result** Under Mussolini, Italy plunged into an economic decline. While he allowed the rich to hold their wealth and property, the workers and farmers suffered poverty due to the country's economic failure. Mussolini made Roman Catholicism the state religion. Hitler's policies, on the other hand pulled Germany quickly out of depression, almost eliminating unemployment, increasing production to record levels, and developing a strong military. Through tyranny, he succeeded in restoring national pride in the German people. With growing nationalism and a strong military he led Germany to far reaching conquests of other nations. Hitler united the Protestant churches and put them under government control.

REJECTION OF PEACE

Sixty-three nations (except for the USSR) signed the **Kellogg-Briand Pact** or **Paris Peace Pact** in 1928. The ratifying countries promised to use negotiations rather than war to resolve political differences, except for cases of self-defense. Though they signed this pact, the militaristic governments of Italy, Germany, and Japan rejected the spirit and letter of this agreement as they strove to exert influence beyond national boundaries through war. The pact said nothing about enforcement, so other countries were unable to unite in opposition.

Japanese Aggression

Soon after Japan invaded Manchuria (September 1931), the League of Nations demanded that the Japanese withdraw their troops. Japan responded to the demand by announcing its diplomatic withdrawal from the League of Nations. The League proved powerless to stop international aggression.

Receiving little help from the League of Nations and unable to fight the Japanese because of its own civil war, China signed a treaty with Japan in May 1933, formally giving up claims to Manchuria. In July 1937, Japan began military operations to seize the rest of China. By the end of 1938, Japan had captured all the major cities along the Chinese coast but could not control the inland countryside.

Italian Aggression

Early in 1935, Mussolini agreed to support an independent Austria against German interference if France would allow Italy's invasion of Abyssinia (present-day Ethiopia). On October 3, 1935, Italian forces moved into Abyssinia. Four days later, the League of Nations condemned Italy for its aggression. The League imposed economic **sanctions** (economic penalties) which only irritated Mussolini and did little to help Abyssinia. Hitler had already withdrawn from the League, so he offered help to Italy. The leading democracies failed to prevent the invasion and pushed Mussolini and Hitler together as allies.

Later, Italy, Germany, and Japan signed an anti-communist pact, thus, forming the **Rome-Berlin-Tokyo Axis**. These nations and their allies were later called the **Axis Powers**. Opponents of the Axis were called the **Allied Powers** or **Allies**. At this time, Britain and France were the leading Allied Powers. Backed by the Axis nations, Italy invaded Albania in 1939.

German Aggression

In 1936, Hitler further violated the Versailles agreement by moving German troops into the Rhineland. Fearing another war with Germany, Britain and France did nothing. In March 1938, Hitler tested his boundaries by **annexing** (adding) Austria to Germany. He convinced other countries that this move was an internal German affair, and again, he met no resistance. In September, he demanded the right to annex the Sudetenland, the western border of Czechoslovakia where 3.5 million ethnic Germans lived.

The British prime minister **Neville Chamberlain** (1869-1940) and the French premier **Edouard Daladier** (1884-1970) hoped to avoid war through a policy of **appeasement**, that is, giving in to Hitler's demands. At the **Munich Conference** (September 29-30, 1938), they ignored Stalin's offer of military aid to Czechoslovakia and agreed to Hitler's capture of the Sudetenland. In exchange, Hitler promised to claim no further land in Czechoslovakia or anywhere else. The British were very happy to avoid war. Chamberlain spoke to cheering crowds in Britain, calling the Munich Agreement a "peace with honor" and a "peace for our time." Hitler soon proved him wrong.

155

The Invasion Of Poland - World War II Begins

Less than six months later, Hitler broke his promise and invaded the rest of Czechoslovakia. On September 1, 1939, Germany invaded an unsuspecting and unprepared Poland. Hitler moved his forces quickly, using a technique called **blitzkreig**, which means "lightning war." Joint forces of armored tanks and bombers raced through the countryside of Poland. On September 3, Great Britain and France declared war on Germany, but the element of surprise put them at a disadvantage. They could not assemble forces quickly enough to match Hitler's attack. The USSR assured Poland's defeat by invading on September 17. Poland surrendered three weeks later, concluding the first battle of World War II.

THE UNITED STATES REMAINS NEUTRAL

Despite the rise of the Axis Powers in the 1930s, the United States maintained strong **isolationist** policies, not wanting to become involved in European conflicts for the following reasons:

- United States citizens had sad memories of the lives lost in the World War I.

- Citizens were bitter because three fourths of the war debts of European countries remained unpaid.

- During the Great Depression, United States citizens were struggling just to survive from day to day and had little concern for international affairs.

- People in the United States increasingly believed the theory that arms manufacturers and Wall Street investors had pushed the United States into the World War I.

Responding to isolationist feeling, Congress passed the **Neutrality Act** (1935), forbidding arms sales to warring nations. Anti-war feeling in 1937 provided strong support for the **Ludlow Amendment** to the Constitution. The amendment required a national vote before the United States could declare war. It failed in Congress by only a narrow margin.

Germany's invasion of Poland spurred the United States to institute a **"cash and carry"** policy on munitions. By allowing the Allies to buy munitions with payment up front and requiring the nations to provide their own transport, the United States hoped to retain neutrality while helping to defeat Germany. However, the inactivity in Europe after the conquest of Poland led some United States newspapers to label the conflict a "Sitzkrieg" or "Phony War."

Germany Attacks France and Britain

The lull in fighting proved to be a calm before the storm. On April 9, 1940, Germany invaded Denmark and Norway. On May 10, Hitler's troops launched a surprise attack on Belgium and Holland. That same day Neville Chamberlain resigned his position as British prime minister, having failed terribly with his policy of appeasement. The king, George VI, asked **Winston Churchill** (1874-1965) to be the new prime minister. Churchill accepted, and three days later, he told the House of Commons, "I have nothing to offer but blood, toil, tears, and sweat." This was but the first of Churchill's many inspiring wartime speeches.

Winston Churchill, Prime Minister

German troops soon forced France to surrender. After the **Fall of France** (June 22, 1940), Britain remained as Germany's only active enemy in Europe. Hitler knew that he had to destroy Britain's mighty Royal Air Force before he could cross the English channel and invade the island country. In the **Battle of Britain** (July-September 1940), thousands of German planes bombed British airfields and cities. During the almost nightly air raids, residents of London slept in subways and woke up to smoke and rubble. However, with high quality aircraft and radar, the British destroyed much of the powerful German air force, compelling Hitler to give up his plans for invasion.

United States Tries to Help

Shocked by the Fall of France, the United States began the first peacetime draft in its history and greatly increased its military budget. Public opinion, however, still opposed United States involvement in the war. In the fall of 1940, **Franklin D. Roosevelt** (1882-1945) was elected to an unprecedented third term of office with the promise, "I have said this before, but I shall say it again and again: Your boys are not going to be sent into any foreign wars." Despite this promise, the United States began strengthening its military forces and providing even more support to Great Britain.

President Franklin D. Roosevelt (right) meets with Prime Minister Winston Churchill (left).

Roosevelt realized that the United States policy of neutrality had hurt the countries suffering aggression more than the aggressor countries. He tried to show people this strategic problem as well as the moral difficulties of neutrality. As Britain struggled in its fight against Germany, Roosevelt told the people of the United States, "If Great Britain goes down, all of us in the Americas would be living at the point of a gun. . . . We must be the great arsenal of democracy."

In response, Congress passed the **Lend-Lease Act** (March 1941). To justify the Act, Roosevelt offered the reluctant American public the analogy of a neighbor's house being on fire. He said that you would lend them a hose, not try to sell it. This loan of supplies is a help to your neighbor, it protects your house, and nothing is lost to you as the supplies are to be returned. This specific act gave the President the authority to lend or lease war supplies to countries who were out of money but whose survival was vital to United States defense. When Hitler betrayed Stalin by invading the USSR in June of 1941, the United States sent large amounts of supplies to Stalin to prevent a German victory.

Problems In Southeast Asia

The United States struggled with its policy toward Japan. The United States was sympathetic to China in its conflict with Japan, but the United States policy of neutrality allowed Japan to get 90 percent of its scrap metal and 60 percent of its oil from the United States. After the United States declared an embargo on scrap metal, oil, and aviation fuel to Japan, the Japanese announced a military alliance with Italy and Germany. Later that year (November 1941), Japanese diplomats came to Washington, D.C. for negotiations which proved unsuccessful. Meanwhile, army general **Tojo Hideki** (1884-1948), the new prime minister of Japan, was planning a surprise attack on **Pearl Harbor**, Hawaii, the primary naval base for the United States in the Pacific.

Tojo Hideki

PEARL HARBOR – THE U.S. ENTERS THE WAR

A few minutes before 8 a.m. on December 7, 1941, Japanese airplanes began the first wave of bombings at Pearl Harbor. United States intelligence had known of the impending attack but was unable to get the message to the military base before the attack began. In less than two hours, the Japanese forces sank or seriously damaged eight battleships and 13 other naval vessels, destroyed almost 200 warplanes, and killed or wounded over 3,000 military personnel. The next day, President Roosevelt emotionally described December 7 as "a day which will live in infamy." Both houses of Congress approved a declaration of war against Japan and later against Germany and Italy.

The Japanese bombing of United States naval base at Pearl Harbor, Hawaii.

Suddenly, the United States had plunged itself into the middle of World War II (1939-1945).

ON THE HOMEFRONT

Isolationist feeling in the United States after World War I had led to a sharp reduction in military personnel and equipment. President Roosevelt had already initiated some strengthening of the armed forces, but the United States still had a long way to catch up to the Axis powers. The people of the United States joined together with great dedication and sacrifice to succeed in the war.

The Armed Forces

Six million men and women volunteered for service while Congress drafted 10 million more men. At one point, the army alone had to provide housing for 5 million personnel.

Wartime Production

President Roosevelt set very high production goals for 1942 including 60,000 airplanes, 45,000 tanks, and 20,000 anti-aircraft guns. Industrial workers met or surpassed these goals and reached even higher goals in 1943 and 1944.

Roosevelt created the **War Production Board** (WPB) to manage and control the economy. The WPB supervised the conversion of industry from peacetime to wartime production.

Increased Prosperity

The increase in production ended the Great Depression and brought unemployment to an extremely low 1.9%. Between 1939 and 1945 the **Gross National Product** or **GNP** (a nation's total production of goods and services) rose from $91.1 billion to $213.6 billion. The United States produced more than Germany, Italy, and Japan combined. The wages of most workers rose steadily from 1941 to 1945, and the demand for manufactured goods increased. Farmers also benefitted as demand for agricultural products caused crop prices to double between 1940 and 1945.

Making Sacrifices

In an effort to focus all resources on the war, the government created a **rationing system** which limited the use of certain critical foods and materials. People could not purchase coffee, sugar, meat, rubber, or gasoline without using a government-issued coupon. To conserve resources, industries encouraged people to put off purchases until after the war. One tire company asked people to conserve rubber by driving less, using the slogan, "Hitler smiles when you waste miles."

Paying for the War

To pay for the war, the government raised taxes, especially on the incomes of high-salaried workers. It also issued **war bonds** to finance the war. The government used posters and other forms of advertising to convince citizens to purchase war bonds. Movie stars and entertainers boosted patriotic feelings by helping to sell war bonds. In this way, the government was able to borrow large amounts of money for the war effort.

Photograph taken circa 1943 shows men and women standing in line to purchase United States defense savings bonds.

Women's Participation

When the United States entered World War II, women responded with great eagerness to the war effort. More than 200,000 women served in special units of the Army, Navy, Marines, and Coast Guard. As men left for the front, women took their places in offices and factories. The great need for labor provided opportunities for women in new areas of work. By the end of the war, women made up one-third of the work force. The government maintained that women should get paid the same as men for the same work, but many employers found ways to avoid paying women fair wages.

"Rosie the Riveter"

Blacks in the War

One reason the United States fought in World War II was to oppose Hitler's racism, but blacks suffered racism at home. Nearly one million African Americans served in the United States armed services during World War II. However, most blacks were restricted to low ranks, served in segregated units under white officers, and lived in segregated camps surrounded by segregated civilian towns. Even the Red Cross separated blood donations according to race. Desegregation of the armed forces began on a trial basis during the war and became a permanent policy in 1948.

The expansion of defense-related industries during the war encouraged about one million blacks in the rural South to seek jobs in the industrial cities of the North. However, discrimination prevented many of them from getting work. The mass movement of blacks into the northern cities increased racial tensions as whites and blacks competed for housing and jobs. The summer of 1943 saw race riots in Detroit and Harlem. Even still, blacks were free from worse oppression in the South, and they enjoyed much larger incomes.

Mexican Americans Suffer Discrimination

The labor demand during the war opened industrial jobs in the Southwest to Mexican Americans, and the increased need for food to feed the army created new agricultural jobs. Tensions rose as Mexican Americans and whites competed for jobs and housing. In July 1943, some servicemen on leave in Los Angeles attacked Mexican American youths, setting off a week of rioting.

Japanese Internment

The Japanese attack on Pearl Harbor fueled suspicion and dislike of Japanese immigrants in the United States. On February 19, 1942, President Roosevelt signed **Executive Order 9066**, ordering all Japanese Americans away from military facilities. Under authority of this order, the United States military forced 110,000 Japanese Americans from their homes and, during the war, placed them in camps on federal land, including deserts and swamps, in the nation's interior. Two-thirds of the interned Japanese were United States citizens, but in 1944 the Supreme Court declared the order a justifiable war measure.

TURNING THE TIDE

After some initial setbacks, the United States soon showed its military might and provided the energy and resources the Allies needed to push back German and Japanese forces.

North Africa

When the United States entered the war, Generals **George C. Marshall** (1880-1959) and **Dwight D. Eisenhower** (1890-1969) urged an invasion of France across the English channel. Joseph Stalin supported this plan enthusiastically, hoping that the invasion would force Hitler to divert some of his troops from the USSR back to France. British Prime Minister Winston Churchill argued that the Allies were not ready to go into France but should focus their attention on North Africa. German advances in Egypt convinced the Americans to invade North Africa.

Operation Torch began in November 1942, when troops from Britain and the United States landed on the beaches of North Africa and began fighting the German army. After many victories, the Allies encountered stiff resistance in Tunisia from the German Afrika Corps of General Rommel. After a few preliminary delays, the Allied troops drove the Germans north towards the Mediterranean Sea. In May 1943, the greatly outnumbered Axis forces surrendered. This victory opened the Mediterranean Sea to Allied shipping. In addition, the Allies could now invade Southern Europe. This first major victory of the war lifted the spirits of the Allies.

Italy

Two months after his victory in North Africa, Eisenhower sent paratroopers to attack the Italian island of Sicily. From here, the Allies attacked Italy's mainland assaulting Salerno in September 1943. Due to the successful invasion, Mussolini was overthrown. The new Italian government joined the Allies in fighting Germany, but Hitler ordered his troops in Italy to keep fighting. German troops defended Rome for almost one year, and they continued fighting fiercely until the end of the war.

Allied soldiers land in Salerno, Italy.

160

Normandy

Allied invasion fleet near Normandy, France.

While fighting continued in Italy, General Eisenhower was called away to lead an invasion of France. Promoted to Supreme Allied Commander of the European theater of operations, he coordinated **Operation Overlord** (1944), the largest amphibious assault ever undertaken. Encouraged by the victories in the Mediterranean, Eisenhower was ready to return to his first plan of invasion.

By June 1944, the Allies had assembled close to three million troops. Allied bombers began the attack destroying many railroads in northwest France, thus cutting off German supply lines. Planes also bombed insignificant targets, so the Germans would not know the landing point of the coming invasion. On June 6, 1944, **D-Day**, weather conditions and the tides were right. A fleet of 6,000 Allied ships launched the great invasion of the beaches of **Normandy**. The first soldiers ashore received withering gunfire. Allied losses were very high, and it took six weeks to secure landing areas. From this foothold, the soldiers were able to advance further into France. On August 25, 1944, the Allies fought their way into Paris, liberating the city from four years of German occupation.

Wounded American soldiers receive first aid on the beach of Normandy after the D-Day invasion of France.

GERMANY'S DEFEAT

Yalta Conference (February 4-11, 1945)

Anticipating Germany's defeat, the **Big Three** (popular name for the leaders of Great Britain, the USSR, and the United States), met in February 1945 at the Black Sea resort city of **Yalta** to discuss military strategy and postwar policies. In the negotiations, Stalin restated his promise to declare war on Japan 90 days after the defeat of Germany. He also agreed to hold free elections to establish democratic governments in Eastern European countries liberated from German occupation. In return, Roosevelt and Churchill conceded

The "Big Three": Churchill, Roosevelt, and Stalin (from left to right) at the Yalta conference.

that the USSR would retain land in Poland and have special rights to certain Japanese islands and parts of the Chinese mainland. Further, because of the tremendous losses inflicted on the USSR by Germany, the Soviet Union would receive half of the war reparations from Germany.

At the conclusion of the conference, the leaders issued the **Yalta Declaration** which stated the Allied intention to "destroy German militarism and Nazism and to ensure that Germany will never again be able to disturb the peace of the world"; to "bring all war criminals to just and swift punishment"; and to "exact reparation in kind for the destruction wrought by the Germans." The document described how Germany was to be divided into four zones administered by the United States, Britain, France, and the USSR. In addition, the leaders scheduled a conference in San Francisco for April 1945 to establish the United Nations as a permanent peace-keeping organization.

Victory in Europe

The victory in France was costly to the Allies. General Eisenhower lacked sufficient supplies to launch an offensive into Germany. While holding northern France, he ordered an invasion across the Mediterranean into southern France. Meanwhile, the Soviet army was pushing across Poland, Czechoslovakia, and Hungary. By March 1945, Eisenhower's troops were resupplied and ready to move into Germany.

Winston Churchill wanted Eisenhower to make a narrow path to Berlin. The British Prime Minister didn't trust Joseph Stalin and did not want Soviet troops to gain control of Germany. Eisenhower believed military strategy should outweigh politics, so he spread his troops throughout southern Germany. They eventually met the **Red Army** (as the Soviet troops were known) at the Elbe River, 100 miles west of Berlin. Together they marched to Berlin.

In the face of certain defeat, Hitler committed suicide on April 30, 1945. One week later, Germany surrendered unconditionally, ending the European conflict. President Roosevelt died on April 12 and never saw the day of victory. Fate thrust Vice-President **Harry S Truman** (1884-1972) into a challenging position of leadership. After many long years of war, people in Allied countries celebrated **V-E Day** (Victory in Europe Day, May 8, 1945) with great joy. But joy turned to shock and horror as eyewitnesses viewed the secret atrocities of Hitler's reign.

THE HOLOCAUST

As Allied soldiers began liberating areas of Europe formerly held by Germany, they encountered many disturbing sights. They found **concentration camps** that housed ghost-like people with hollow eyes and bony frames. Gas chambers and ovens only hinted at the horror perpetrated in these camps, but the hundreds of thousands of bodies buried in mass graves confirmed the soldiers' suspicions.

At the beginning of the war, Hitler had instructed German soldiers to kill Jews and other social undesirables on the spot. Many soldiers, however, became demoralized by shooting these unarmed people. Hitler then devised a strategy to kill those deemed socially inferior by building concentration camps. The Nazis herded people into rail cars by force and told them they were going to work camps. As the people entered the camps, they were divided into two groups: those with skills and those who were unskilled. The unskilled were herded to gas chambers to be killed. Those with skills underwent slower deaths through starvation diets combined with overwork. German scientists also used these people for grotesque experiments of torture and genetic alteration. Almost six million Jews died in

After Germany surrendered, male prisoners walk out of a German concentration camp.

Hitler's network of camps. Other groups labeled socially inferior or dangerous such as gypsies, Slavs, prostitutes, the handicapped, homosexuals, and political dissidents also suffered torture and execution.

JAPAN'S DEFEAT

The defeat of Germany was a great victory for the Allies, but it did not end the war. Japan remained a formidable enemy in the Pacific.

General Douglas MacArthur

General **Douglas MacArthur** (1880-1964) led the Allied forces in the Pacific. The Allies secured their first victory in June 1942 at **Midway**. For the next eight months, United States Marines engaged in fierce battle at **Guadalcanal** (1943). The Allied forces used a "leap-frog" technique of invading one island, defeating the Japanese, and "hopping" to the next island. By August 10, 1944, the Allies had gained control of the key islands of Saipan, Tinian, and Guam. From these bases, Allied planes made regular bombing runs over Japan.

As the Allied forces moved closer to Japan, the Japanese recognized defeat and forced General Tojo Hideki to resign as prime minister. However, the Japanese soldiers continued to fight ferociously. In desperation, Japanese pilots resorted to **kamikaze** (Japanese for "divine wind") missions, loading their planes with explosives and willingly crashing into Allied naval ships. The heavy damage inflicted by the Japanese caused Allied military leaders to look to the United States' secret weapon.

The Atomic Bomb

Soon after entering the war, the United States had enlisted the help of German scientists and the cooperation of Great Britain and Canada to design and build three atomic bombs. The secret operation was named the **Manhattan Project** (1942-1945).

During the **Potsdam Conference** (July 17-August 2, 1945), President Truman, Winston Churchill, and Joseph Stalin issued the Potsdam Declaration (July 26, 1945), which restated many of the agreements made at Yalta. It also included an ultimatum to Japan saying that "the alternative to surrender is prompt and utter destruction." When the Japanese did not surrender, President Truman authorized the dropping of an atomic bomb on Japan as soon as possible.

Churchill, Truman, and Stalin at the Potsdam Conference

On August 6, 1945, a specially equipped B-29 bomber, the *Enola Gay*, dropped an atomic bomb on **Hiroshima** leveling the city. Two days later, the Soviet Union declared war on Japan and invaded Manchuria. On August 9, the United States dropped an atomic bomb on **Nagasaki**. Japan estimated that 240,000 Japanese died from the two bombs while the United States estimated half that number. Thousands more civilians suffered sickness and death from the radiation left after the bombing. In the face of these atomic disasters and the Soviet declaration of war, Japan surrendered to General Douglas MacArthur on August 14, 1945. World War II was over.

The Atomic Bomb dropped on Nagasaki

Why the Bomb?

Some people still question why the United States dropped the bomb in August, and why it chose these cities.

Before becoming President, Truman knew very little about the secret Manhattan Project. By the time he replaced Roosevelt, the billions of dollars and work hours spent on the project had created a great deal of momentum toward using the newly developed atomic bombs.

President Truman claimed that Hiroshima was a military target, but an official government report stated that Hiroshima and Nagasaki were "chosen as targets because of their concentration of activities and population." The United States knew that these cities, previously not bombed, would clearly show the destructive force of the new atomic weapons.

Based on the fierce fighting from Japanese soldiers in previous battles, some military advisers estimated 500,000 to 1,000,000 Allied casualties would be suffered in a ground assault of the Japanese mainland. However, the first invasion wasn't scheduled until November on the island of Kyushu, with casualties estimated at 31,000. By July, the United States held the key islands of Iwo Jima and Okinawa and had established a secure naval blockade around Japan. The Japanese military was weakening and in need of raw materials. Japan had begun discussing peace through its diplomat in Moscow. Before the scheduled invasion, there was time for the beleaguered Japan to surrender.

However, Stalin's promise at the Yalta Conference meant that on August 8, the USSR would enter the war against Japan. If the United States could defeat Japan without the USSR, then it could control post-war arrangements in eastern Asia without Soviet interference.

EFFECTS OF WORLD WAR II

The First and Second World Wars moved from traditional battle techniques to **total war**. Total war was fought without limitations. It was a battle involving not just armies, but entire societies. In this kind of war, total victory was the only acceptable outcome.

Immediate Effects of World War II

- **Defeat:** the militarily aggressive Axis Powers (Japan, Germany, and Italy) and their allies suffered defeat
- **Death**: over 60 million soldiers and civilians died in the conflict: over 20 million from the USSR, 290,000 from the United States, and 6 million Jews in Germany
- **Displacement**: about 60 million people of 55 ethnic groups from 27 countries were uprooted: 45 million people were homeless, 15 million soldiers were prisoners of war, and 670,000 survivors of Nazi death camps
- **Destruction**: about 23 percent of Europe's farmland was out of production, half its shipping vessels were destroyed, coal production was down 40 percent, and transportation and communications systems were severely damaged; Japan suffered similar devastation
- **Collapse of colonial empires**: Asia and African nations sought independence from imperial nations (France, the Netherlands, Germany, Italy, Japan, and Great Britain) weakened by the war
- **Rise of Two Superpowers:** the Soviet Union became the dominant power in Europe, while the United States possessed the strongest military and economy
- **Atomic Power**: the atomic bomb brought an end to the war, but it increased political tension and fear of world destruction

Lasting Effects of Word War II on Life in the United States

- After fighting in the war and working in non-traditional jobs, women began to think about pursuing careers along with having a family.
- Wartime production rejuvenated the United States economy, making it the world's strongest.
- Participation by blacks in the military and wartime industries helped the movement for civil rights, though discrimination still continued.
- The Servicemen's Readjustment Act of 1944 or "GI Bill" provided former soldiers with financial aid for college and special loans to buy homes or start business.
- Post-war prosperity and increased manufacturing led to the growth of suburbs, a consumer society, and middle-class America.
- As soldiers returned home, they married, had children, and focused on family, increasing the population and creating the so-called "Baby Boom" generation (1947-1960).
- As the truth about the destructive capability of atomic weapons was revealed, people began to fear this new technology.

CHAPTER 13 REVIEW

A.   Define the following names, terms, and events:

traditional economy	Adolf Hitler	Dwight D. Eisenhower
free market economy	Gestapo	D-Day
Karl Marx	Joseph Stalin	Normandy
capitalism	Kellogg-Briand Pact	Big Three
command economy	Rome-Berlin-Tokyo Axis	Yalta Conference
socialism	appeasement	Red Army
communism	Munich Conference	Harry S Truman
mixed economy	blitzkreig	V-E Day
Vladimir Lenin	Winston Churchill	concentration camps
Paris Peace Conference	Fall of France	Douglas MacArthur
nationalism	Battle of Britain	kamikaze
totalitarian government	Franklin D. Roosevelt	Manhattan Project
Benito Mussolini	Tojo Hideki	Potsdam Conference
fascism	Pearl Harbor	*Enola Gay*
Hirohito	Gross National Product	Hiroshima
Manchuria	rationing system	Nagasaki
Nazis	Executive Order 9066	total war

B.   On your own paper, write your response to each of the following:
1.   How did Karl Marx think capitalism would come to an end?
2.   What is the major difference between a command economy and a free market economy?
3.   Define the four economic activities of all societies.
4.   Describe three problems created by the Paris Peace Conference.
5.   How did economic issues contribute to worldwide unrest before World War II?
6.   How did rising nationalism decrease the effectiveness of the League of Nations?
7.   How did Mussolini stop the threat of communism in Italy?
8.   Describe how the Japanese military took control of the government in Japan.
9.   Why were Hitler's ideas attractive to the German people?

10. What did Mussolini, Hitler and Stalin have in common? How were they different?
11. Compare the goals and practices of fascism and communism.
12. Describe one example of the League of Nations' failure to stop territorial aggression.
13. Evaluate the effectiveness of the policy of appeasement regarding territorial aggression.
14. What event started World War II? Why?
15. List three reasons why the United States wanted to remain neutral in World War II.
16. Discuss the moral and strategic challenges to isolationism in United States foreign policy.
17. Compare and contrast United States foreign policy in the 1920s and 1930s with United States foreign policy before the First World War.
18. What role did the government play in the United States economy during World War II?
19. In what ways did women in the United States contribute to the war effort?
20. Describe the how the war affected the lives of African Americans and Mexican Americans.
21. Discuss the effects of Executive Order 9066.
22. Discuss two military turning points during World War II.
23. Describe the agreements made at the Yalta Conference.
24. Describe the disagreement between Churchill and Eisenhower regarding the invasion of Germany.
25. List two reasons Hitler created concentration camps.
26. How did the atomic bomb influence the United States' dealings with Joseph Stalin?
27. What military contributions did the United States make to the Allied victory?
28. Evaluate the impact of total war.
29. List four lasting effects of World War II on life in the United States.

C.   Write True if the statement is correct and False if the statement is incorrect. Be prepared to state a reason for your false answers.

1. _____ Mussolini gained control of the Italian government through brutal means, surpassing both Hitler and Stalin.

2. _____ Eisenhower passed the Lend-Lease Act, giving the president the authority to lend or lease war supplies to countries whose survival was in the United States' best interests.

3. _____ The Treaty of Versailles, ending World War I, was so harsh that it bred resentment and anger in the German people.

4. _____ In addition to raising taxes, the United States government issued War Bonds in order to finance World War II.

5. _____ D-Day is the name given to the Allied invasion on enemy soil in Guadalcanal.

6. _____ The militarily aggressive Axis powers Japan, Germany, and Russia suffered a collective defeat in 1945.

7. _____ Karl Marx wrote *The Wealth of Nations*, outlining the economic philosophy of laissez-faire.

8. _____ Germany's invasion of Poland spurred the United States to initiate a "cash and carry" policy on munitions.

9. _____ Immediately after Pearl Harbor was bombed, the United States declared war on all the Axis powers at once.

10. _____ The Allies defeated General Rommel in North Africa for their first major war victory.

11. _____ Nazis were members of the fascist party in Germany who followed Hitler.

12. _____ Democratic governments of the 1930s developed successful economic programs to help ease the suffering of poverty-stricken citizens.

13. _____ One cause of the isolationist policy in the United States was the fact that three-fourths of the European war debts remained unpaid as World War II began.

14. _____ World War II's first battle began and ended with Germany's invasion of Czechoslovakia.

15. _____ The Second World War ended soon after a nuclear bombs were dropped on two Japanese cities: respectively, Nagasaki and Hiroshima.

16. _____ In 1917, the Bolsheviks (majority) held a successful uprising against the monarchy and nominated Lenin as their leader.

17. _____ The League of Nations condemned Italy for its invasion of Abyssinia and imposed an embargo on all food and medical shipments to both countries.

18. _____ After the Fall of France, Italy remained as Germany's only active enemy in Europe.

19. _____ The "Big Three" was a code name given to the important invasions of the Allied powers: Operation Torch, Operation Overlord, and D-Day.

20. _____ By the end of World War II, women made up one-third of the work force in the United States while being paid less than their male co-workers.

CHAPTER 14
THE COLD WAR

LOOKING FOR PEACE AND JUSTICE

Creation of the United Nations

Despite the failure of the League of Nations to prevent the Second World War, the flame of hope still flickered for an international organization that could promote peace in the world. Following the intentions of the Yalta Conference (February 4-11, 1945), delegates from 50 countries gathered in San Francisco on April 25, 1945, to develop the purpose, principles, and organizational structure for the **United Nations (UN)**, an organization of nations dedicated to work for world peace and security and the betterment of humanity.

In an effort to ensure its success, the UN opened membership to all nations. The UN was, and still is, set up in the following manner. In the **General Assembly**, representatives from the member nations discuss any issue that is within the scope of the UN charter, and each nation has one vote. The General Assembly can make recommendations, but it has no power to enforce them, except through the leadership of moral authority.

Perhaps more important to the UN's success was securing the support of the world's strongest nations by giving them special powers. China, France, Great Britain, the Union of Soviet Socialist Republics (USSR), and the United States of America (US) were named permanent members of the **Security Council**. (Other members are elected to the council for two-year terms.) The Security Council investigates disputes between nations, recommends solutions, and can take military action with a force made up of troops from member nations. In order to take action, all five permanent members of the council must agree. One member's veto prevents any action.

Strengths and Weaknesses of the United Nations

The United Nations was strengthened by two factors:

- It offered membership to all the nations of the world.
- It enjoyed the participation of the strongest nations at that time: China, Great Britain, France, the United States, and the USSR (also known as the Soviet Union).

However, the United Nations was also weakened by the following factors:

- The General Assembly had no power to enforce its decisions.
- The Security Council had authority to enforce decisions, but any one of the five permanent members could **veto** (stop) an action.
- The United Nations could invite countries to contribute military personnel and equipment, but it had no military force of its own.

These last two weaknesses meant that the division between the US and the USSR could prevent the United Nations from taking action.

War Crimes Trials

Fulfilling the intention of the Yalta Conference to "bring all war criminals to just and swift punishment," representatives from the United States, Britain, France, and the USSR established the **International Military Tribunal** on August 8, 1945. From November 1945 to September 1946, the tribunal held trials in **Nuremberg**, Germany for 24 individuals and seven organizations. Twelve defendants were sentenced to death by hanging, three were acquitted, and the others received prison sentences ranging from ten years to life. Following Nuremberg, twelve more trials were held in each of the four zones in Germany. The tribunal tried one hundred eighty-five other individuals for various crimes committed during World War II.

From May 1946 to November 1948, the International Military Tribunal for the Far East carried out trials in Tokyo for the 28 individuals accused of crimes during the war in the Pacific. The tribunal sentenced **General Tojo Hideki** to be executed on December 23, 1948 as punishment for his crimes.

The war crimes trials following World War II set an important example for international law. Respect for the trials suffered, however, because they were biased. Rather than an impartial body examining the crimes of all parties in the war, the victors of the war prosecuted the defeated. For example, the international tribunal did not address the destruction of civilians caused by the two American atomic bombs dropped on Japan or the Allied fire bombing of Tokyo which preceded them.

The Potential for Peace in the Aftermath of WWII

People rejoiced with much enthusiasm at the end of World War II. The Allies had defeated the militaristic dictatorships of Germany, Italy, and Japan, and the nations of the world had joined together hoping to promote peace and prevent further wars. After the devastation of more than six years of world war, people longed for peace. However, there were many obstacles to overcome.

The following were obstacles to peace after World War II:

- After the defeat of their common enemy, tensions arose between the USSR and the US.
- China resumed its civil war.
- Tens of millions of people had been uprooted from their homes and lost loved ones.
- Most of Europe and Asia suffered from destroyed homes, land, and industries.
- The collapse of the European and Japanese empires led to strong independence movements around the globe.
- The US economy was strong, but it faced the challenge and danger of converting from wartime production to peacetime production.
- The Soviet Union took control of eastern Europe to rebuild its economy.
- The world lived in fear of the destructive power of nuclear weapons.

THE COLD WAR IN EUROPE

The United States (US) versus the Soviet Union (USSR)

Given the vast differences between the United States and the Soviet Union, it is hard to imagine how the two countries could have negotiated post-war arrangements in a friendly way. The following historical differences led to contrasting post-war goals:

	United States	**Soviet Union**
Government	founded on the principles of representative government, developed competitive party system	long history of autocratic government from the Byzantine emperors to the Mongol Khans to Communist dictatorship
Economy	free market economy, progressive and prosperous	strong government control, technologically and economically underdeveloped
National Interests	expanding world trade: New England colonists were traders, and Southern colonists were exporters Strong European economies provided profitable markets for goods from the United States.	had always lacked warm water ports for commerce Because of a long history fighting Germans, the Soviets wanted to keep Germany weak.
Approach to the World	crusading message for the world: Revolution established a new kind of government, manifest destiny of 1800s, and US fought 20th century wars to "make the world safe for democracy"	Centuries of various invasions led to a fear of outsiders, a desire to protect borders, and an inward focus.

Different Post-War Goals

During World War II, the United States made great gains economically while the Soviet Union expanded territorially. These differences led to different post-war goals.

	United States	**Soviet Union**
Gains	**Economic:** As European nations had destroyed each other's factories, US industries increased production to fill the gap. US businesses pushed into market and resource areas previously dominated by Europe: Africa, Latin America, and the Middle East.	**Territorial:** The Red Army occupied eastern European countries as it pushed back Nazis in defeat. Shortly before Japan's surrender, Soviet troops invaded Manchuria.

	United States	**Soviet Union**
Goals	After defeating the Axis dictatorships, the US pushed for free elections in previously occupied territories.	Stalin feared that the influence of ideas from the non-communist West would weaken his domestic hold and wanted to surround the USSR with "friendly" governments.
	After record high war time production, the US needed strong and expanding world markets for its products, so as to move smoothly to peacetime production.	The USSR wanted to rebuild its economy through strict control and domination in a closed sphere of influence.
	National ideals promoted the worldwide spread of democracy and a free market economy.	National ideals promoted a worldwide Communist revolution.

The conflicting histories and political goals of the USSR and the United States contributed to a post-war struggle over Eastern Europe.

Origin of the Term "Cold War"

The term **"Cold War"** was used first by the American financier and presidential advisor Bernard Baruch (1870-1965) during a congressional debate in 1947. That same year, the well-known journalist Walter Lippmann (1889-1974) published a book entitled *Cold War*. Both used this term to describe the hostile relationship between the United States and the Soviet Union. The battle between the two superpowers and their respective allies was fought primarily through political and economic means, not erupting into actual warfare between the two countries.

President Truman invited former British prime minister Winston Churchill to speak at Westminster College in Fulton, Missouri. In his speech on March 5, 1947, Churchill said, "A shadow has fallen upon the scenes so lately lighted by Allied victory. . . an **iron curtain** has descended across the [European] Continent." The image of an iron curtain caught the imagination of many people and became a popular way of describing the growing division between Eastern and Western Europe. The United States, the nations of Western Europe, and other nations opposed to Soviet expansion were called the "West," while the Soviet Union and its allies were known as the "East."

At another time Churchill said, "I do not believe that Soviet Russia desires war. What they want is the fruits of war and the indefinite expansion of their power and doctrines." The United States ambassador to Russia, **George F. Kennan** (1904 -) agreed with Churchill's assessment and recommended a policy of **containment**, by which the United States would strategically resist any attempts by the Soviet Union to expand its influence. The supporters of the containment policy believed that World War II might have been prevented if western leaders had opposed Hitler's expansionist aggression during the 1930s. They were determined not to make the same mistake with Stalin.

The Truman Doctrine

The first opportunity for the United States to exercise its new policy of containment came in early 1947 when Britain told the United States it could no longer support the monarchy in Greece against attacks from Communist rebels. Neither could it help Turkey resist Soviet demands to establish a naval base in its territory. On March 12, 1947, President Truman asked Congress to approve $400 million in aid to Greece and Turkey. In his speech, he described what later came to be called the **Truman Doctrine**: "I believe it must be the policy of the United States to support free peoples through economic and financial aid, which is essential to economic stability and orderly political processes. . ." This new policy contradicted the Monroe Doctrine's pledge that the United States would not interfere in European affairs. The fighting in Greece continued for two years until the Greek Communists gave up.

The Marshall Plan

After the announcement of the Truman Doctrine, the next step in containment was the economic recovery of Europe. Some members of Congress argued that the United States could not afford the aid to Europe, but President Truman said that strong European economies would resist the temptations of communism, build strong militaries to defend themselves, and provide good markets for products from the United States.

After the Communists overthrew the democratic government of Czechoslovakia in February 1948, Congressional opposition to the plan dwindled. In April 1948, Congress approved the **European Recovery Plan**, developed by Secretary of State **George C. Marshall** (1880-1959), which sent $12 billion over four years mostly to Britain, France, and Germany. Also known as the **Marshall Plan**, this financial aid sparked economic revival and prosperity in these countries, alleviating the suffering of many people. The Marshall Plan became the crowning achievement of the containment policy, preventing Soviet advances into Western Europe. For his efforts, Secretary Marshall received the Nobel Prize for Peace in 1953.

Unifying Latin America Against Communism

In September 1947, the United States and 18 other American republics signed the **Río Treaty**. The signing nations pledged to come to each other's aid, stating that an attack "against an American state shall be an attack against all American states." The following year these nations established the **Organization of American States (OAS)** to oversee the treaty's guarantee of mutual defense, to prevent military conflicts in the western hemisphere by promoting peaceful negotiations, to promote respect for human rights and democratic government, and to support regional efforts for economic, social, and cultural development.

Berlin Airlift and NATO

After fruitless discussions with the Soviets regarding Germany's reunification, France, Great Britain, and the United States decided in the spring of 1948 to unite their zones and establish an independent nation. On June 24, the USSR responded by denying all road, rail, and river access to Berlin. The United States and Britain responded with the **Berlin Airlift**, a massive campaign of transporting food and supplies by plane into West Berlin. For 321 days, planes brought thousands of tons of supplies to the city's 2 million residents.

On April 4, 1949, while the Berlin Airlift was under way, the United States signed the North Atlantic Treaty with Belgium, Britain, Canada, Denmark, France, Iceland, Italy, Luxembourg, the Netherlands, Norway, and Portugal. The treaty stated that each nation would come to the defense of any member nation, and it formed a combined military force to be administered by the **North Atlantic Treaty Organization (NATO)**.

Following President Washington's warning about "entangling alliances" with European nations, the United States had avoided any peace time treaties since 1800. World politics following World War II forced the United States into new directions in foreign policy.

Realizing the strong resolve of the Western nations, the Soviets ended their blockade of Berlin on May 12, 1949. Eleven days later, the Federal Republic of Germany, known as West Germany, was officially formed. The Soviets responded on October 7, 1949 by organizing the German Democratic Republic, or East Germany.

Soviets Explode Their First Atomic Bomb (Summer 1949)

The United States had felt confident as the only nation in possession of nuclear weapons, but that confidence disappeared when the Soviet Union exploded its first atomic bomb in the summer of 1949. With both nations possessing atomic weapons, conflicts between the United States and the USSR became much more threatening. Both countries raced to make more weapons and more powerful weapons in case war did break out.

THE COLD WAR IN ASIA

Occupation of Japan

At the conclusion of World War II, the United States Army under General Douglas MacArthur occupied Japan. The Allies gave MacArthur authority over Japan, and representatives from Britain, China, and the USSR formed a council to assist MacArthur in bringing democracy to Japan and rebuilding its economy.

Hoping that the emperor would help the transition to a new democratic government, MacArthur made sure that **Emperor Hirohito** was not prosecuted in the war crimes trials. Under the new constitution, the emperor became merely a symbol for the nation.

MacArthur supervised the following changes to Japanese society:

- dissolved large industrial and banking trusts (monopolies) and revived the economy
- established a democratic government
- reformed the traditional educational system
- broke up land trusts to give tenant farmers the opportunity to buy the land they worked
- disbanded the military
- forbade state supported religion
- gave women the right to vote and other protections against discrimination

By the beginning of 1949, the United States was sending more than $1 million in aid each day to Japan. The United States also maintained military bases and troops in and around Japan to protect the disarmed country from foreign attacks or large national disturbances.

China

During the 1930s, China was divided by fighting between the Kuomintang Party (KMT) or Nationalist Party led by **Chiang Kai-shek** (1887-1975) and the Chinese Communist Party (CCP) led by **Mao Zedong** (1893-1976), also known as **Mao Tse-tung**. When China entered World War II (December 8, 1941), the KMT and CCP joined together to fight the Japanese, but shortly after the war's end, fighting broke out again between Nationalist and Communist forces.

General George C. Marshall

In 1946, United States General **George C. Marshall** traveled to China, but he was unsuccessful in his attempt to negotiate peace between the warring factions. In an effort to stop the spread of communism, the United States sent more than $3 billion in aid to Chiag Kai-shek from 1945 to 1949. Despite this financial and military aid, the Chinese Communist Army steadily gained ground in China.

China under Mao Zedong

On October 1, 1949, Mao Zedong stood before a crowd of hundreds of thousands in Bejing's Tian'an Men Square and announced the establishment of the **Communist Peoples' Republic of China**. By the end of the year, Mao's troops forced the Nationalist government of Chiang Kai-shek to flee to the island of Taiwan.

The new Communist government strictly controlled schools and universities, religious practices, economic production, and foreign policy. To enforce these reforms, eliminate all opposition, and establish its authority, the Communist government also resorted to terror, killing nearly two million anti-Communists.

The United States refused to recognize Mao's Communist government and provided military aid to Taiwan. The United States maintained the Nationalist government's seat on the Security Council of the United Nations. In response, the Soviet Union **boycotted** (refused to participate in) the Security Council.

The Korean War (1950-1953)

Apparently without the knowledge of Communist China or the Soviet Union, Communist North Koreans invaded neighboring South Korea. Under the leadership of the United States, troops from the United Nations (UN) entered the battle on the side of the South Koreans and eventually drove the invaders out. Seeking more gains, however, the UN troops moved into North Korea, drawing China into the battle. After three years of fighting up and down the Korean peninsula and President Eisenhower's hint at using nuclear weapons, the Koreans signed a cease fire on July 27, 1953, re-establishing the 38th parallel as the boundary line between North and South Korea.

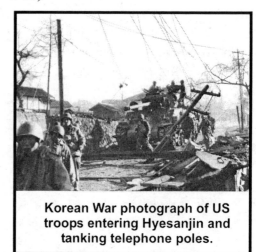

Korean War photograph of US troops entering Hyesanjin and tanking telephone poles.

The Impact of the Korean War

The UN forces repelled the invasion of South Korea, and the United States government demonstrated its determination to stop armed aggression. However, the Soviet Union's voluntary absence from the UN Security Council made it easier for the United Nations to join together in acting on common goals. Also, by crossing the 38th parallel, the United States and the UN showed their own aggression by invading an independent nation.

When President Truman ordered US troops into South Korea, he also ordered a fleet of the US navy to protect Taiwan and more military aid to the French who were fighting the Vietnamese Communists. The declared aim of the UN intervention was to bring peace and stability to Southeast Asia, but the following negative results came from the Korean War:

- The war inflicted untold damage to the Korean nation and its people.
- The United States damaged relations with China by invading North Korea and by providing naval protection for Chiang Kai-shek on Taiwan.
- The United States support for French domination of Vietnam prolonged the conflict there.
- The war increased hostilities and diplomatic tensions between the United States and the USSR.
- The North Koreans and Communist Chinese suffered over 2 million casualties, including the death of Mao Zedong's son. The South Korean and UN forces suffered nearly 1.5 million casualties, including the deaths of 33,629 United States soldiers.
- The United States increased its involvement in Southeast Asia.

Increased United States Involvement in Southeast Asia

The events in China and Korea encouraged the United States to increase its involvement in Southeast Asia. Despite billions of dollars of aid from the United States, the French continued to lose ground against **Ho Chi Minh's** (1890-1969) Communist forces in Vietnam. Fearing a repeat of the Korean War, President Eisenhower refused to commit ground troops to Vietnam or to use nuclear weapons against the Vietnamese. When the French finally admitted defeat in 1954, Ho Chi Minh led the Communist government in North Vietnam, and the United States supported the government in South Vietnam with military and economic aid. President Eisenhower justified the United States presence in Southeast Asia with the **domino theory**, the belief that if South Vietnam "fell" to Communists, then the other nearby nations would soon follow just like a line of falling dominoes.

SEATO (September 8, 1954)

In an effort to prevent the spread of communism after France's withdrawal from Vietnam, the United States formed the **South East Asia Treaty Organization (SEATO)** with Australia, New Zealand, Philippines, Thailand, Pakistan, France, Great Britain. Unlike NATO, SEATO did not require members to assist one another against military aggression. However, SEATO did support US intervention in South Vietnam, and several other member nations also sent troops. US involvement would continue into the 1970s with the **Vietnam War** (1957-1975).

Warsaw Pact (May 14, 1955)

Events in Korea increased fear of Soviet-led Communist aggression. The United States tried to strengthen its position in Europe by admitting Greece and Turkey to NATO in 1952 and West Germany in 1955. The USSR responded with its own military alliance called the **Warsaw Pact**. On May 14, 1955, Albania, Bulgaria, Czechoslovakia, East Germany, Hungary, Poland, Romania, and the USSR signed the Warsaw Treaty of Friendship, Cooperation, and Mutual Assistance.

COMPARISON OF UNITED STATES
FOREIGN POLICY IN EUROPE AND IN ASIA

Europe	Asia
1. **Soviets in Europe:** Because the Red Army was in Germany, the United States faced strained negotiations with Stalin about German rebuilding and unification. 2. **Truman Doctrine:** Congress agreed to President Truman's request for economic and military aid to governments like Greece and Turkey that were fighting Communists. 3. **Marshall Plan:** The United States gave billions of dollars in aid to help the European people and to oppose Soviet influence in Western Europe. 4. **NATO (1949):** In an effort to oppose Communist governments in Europe, the United States formed its first peacetime alliance since 1800. The treaty required the US to come to the aid of any other member nation and led to US troops being stationed in Europe. 5. **Response to Communist Aggression:** Communists gained power in countries already under Soviet control, so the United States did not interfere. Even when Soviet tanks rolled into Hungary to stop a revolt (1956), the United States sent no troops. (However, thousands of Marines fought in Lebanon in 1958.)	1. **The United States in Japan:** United States troops gained control of Japan without the presence of Soviet troops. The United States controlled the rebuilding of Japan. 2. **Aid to China:** The United States sent economic and military aid to help Chiang Kai-Shek in his fight against Maos Tse-dung's Communists. 3. **Occupation of Japan:** The United States gave billions of dollars to rebuild the Japanese society and economy, as well as establishing a military presence in that country. 4. **SEATO (1954):** This treaty was also intended to combat Communist governments, but it did not require member nations to aid each other militarily. However, SEATO did support and contribute to the United States military involvement in Vietnam. 5. **Response to Communist Aggression:** In 1950, Communist North Koreans invaded South Korea, a country that had been under United States control. President Truman sent United States troops to fight the Communists.

THE FEAR OF COMMUNISM AND THE McCARTHY ERA

Fears of a Communist takeover in the United States increased in the 1950s. In 1950, Alger Hiss, a state department official, was convicted of perjury in an investigation by the House Un-American Affairs Committee into his alleged delivery of classified documents to the Soviets during the 1930s. That same year, the United States Justice Department arrested an American couple, **Julius** and **Ethel Rosenberg**, for giving secret information about the atomic bomb to the Soviet Union. Many questioned the fairness of their subsequent trial and the severity of the resulting death sentence. Despite these objections, the Rosenbergs were executed by electrocution in 1953.

Senator **Joseph R. McCarthy** (1908-1957) of Wisconsin seized on the growing fear of communism and almost overnight became the most controversial senator in the nation. On February 9, 1950, he claimed to have in his hand a list of 205 State Department employees who were members of the Communist Party. The next day, he changed the numbers to 205 people who were "bad security risks" and 57 people who were Communists. State Department investigations showed no basis for his charges. Nevertheless, over the next four years, McCarthy enjoyed great popularity as he continued to accuse people of Communist activities. Though he was unable to provide solid evidence for his claims, his accusations ruined the reputations of many public figures.

After nationally televised hearings in 1954, the Senate **censured** (officially disapproved of) McCarthy for "conduct . . . unbecoming a Member of the Senate," and his popularity declined. People came to use the term **McCarthyism** to describe sweeping accusations of betrayal based on little or no evidence.

THE ATOMIC ARMS RACE AND THE SPACE RACE

The United States produced the first atomic bomb in 1945, but the Soviet Union soon followed in 1949 with its own atomic bomb. The **arms race** (competition between the US and the USSR to build more weapons) was off and running, despite pleading from other countries. To maintain its nuclear superiority, the United States greatly increased spending on the development of a **hydrogen bomb** or **H-bomb**, a thousand times more powerful than the first atomic bombs. By November 1952, the United States exploded its first hydrogen bomb, and the following year, the USSR did the same. By 1964, Britain, France, and China all had nuclear weapons.

Once the two superpowers had developed their own H-bombs, they fiercely competed to design rockets and missiles to deliver these smaller nuclear warheads. In 1955, both the United States and the Soviet Union announced programs to launch artificial satellites. The Soviets won the **space race**, launching **Sputnik I** on October 4, 1957. The Soviet satellite was the first spacecraft to orbit the earth. One month later, the Soviets launched a dog, Laika, into space inside Sputnik II.

Effects of Sputnik

The Sputnik launches had the following significant effects upon the course of the Cold War:

- **Soviet Policy of "Peaceful Coexistence":** Joseph Stalin died in 1953, and **Nikita S. Khrushchev** (1894-1971) became the new leader of the Soviet Union. He claimed that the Soviet development of the H-bomb and the launching of Sputnik neutralized the United States' nuclear threat. He advocated a policy of "**peaceful coexistence**" by which the Soviet Union would show the superiority of the communist system through economic and political competition with the West.

- **Soviet Split with China:** For the leader of Communist China, Mao Zedong, Sputnik was not an opportunity for "peaceful coexistence," but an opportunity to press for worldwide Communist revolution. To that end, Mao demanded that the Soviets give China atomic bombs and the rockets to deliver them. When the Soviets refused, the Chinese pledged to create their own nuclear weapons. This split sparked a competition between China and the Soviet Union for the leadership of Communist parties around the world, thus contradicting the ideal that communism went beyond national self-interest.

- **Increased Spending on Education and Space Program in the US:** The United States believed it was ahead of the Soviet Union in the fields of science and technology until the launching of Sputnik. A surprised public blamed the education system in the United States and called for a stronger curriculum emphasizing science and math. In 1958, Congress passed the **National Defense Education Act**, giving federal aid to schools and colleges, especially for projects designed to improve instruction in math and science. Congress also increased the budget of the National Science Foundation which provided grants for scientific research and curriculum development.

- **Increased Speed of the Space Race:** Less than four months after Sputnik I, the United States sent up its first satellite, Explorer I (January 31, 1958). Later that year, the United States government established the **National Aeronautics and Space Administration (NASA)** to direct the United States space program. On April 12, 1961, the Soviets launched Vostok I, and Yury A. Gagarin became the first human to orbit the earth. Less than a month later, Alan B. Shepard circled the earth in the United States Mercury Capsule. On July 20, 1969, astronauts Neil A. Armstrong and Edwin E. Aldrin became the first humans to walk on the moon.

Impact of the Arms Build Up

The nuclear arms race and the space race had a significant effect on the US economy. Increased military spending created high-paying jobs for Americans and added to post-war prosperity in the United States. Among the important effects of the arms race were the following:

- increased tensions between the Soviet Union and the United States
- large increases in military spending, initially aiding economic prosperity, later causing economic drain
- the possibility of world destruction caused the anxiety of the "atomic age"
- the destructive arms potential, ironically, has prevented all out war, each side avoiding open conflict out of fear of nuclear destruction

HOT SPOTS IN THE COLD WAR

Iran, 1953 - When the Prime Minister of Iran ousted the Shah and nationalized the British oil industry, the United States **Central Intelligence Agency (CIA)** organized a coup d' état and restored the Shah to power, protecting western oil interests in the Middle East.

Guatemala, 1954 - The progressive government of Guatemala distributed unused land to the poor, including 400,000 acres of government land and 225,000 acres from the United Fruit Company, based in the United States. United Fruit called the government Communist, which resulted in a United States backed overthrow of the government and the establishment of a military dictatorship. The new president, Colonel Carlos Armas, then returned the land to United Fruit Company.

Hungary, 1956 - Soviet tanks and troops moved swiftly into Hungary and crushed a rebellion against the Communist government. The Western nations welcomed refugees from Hungary but offered no direct aid.

Suez Canal, 1956 - The Suez Canal is an important shipping route between the Mediterranean Sea and the Red Sea. When Communist influences caused the Egyptians to seize the canal, Israel invaded Egypt. After a cease fire, President Eisenhower pressed Congress to pass the **Eisenhower Doctrine** (March 1957), authorizing the United States to give military and economic aid to Middle East countries that requested help against Communist aggression.

Lebanon, 1958 - When rebels smuggled Egyptian arms into Lebanon and civil war broke out, President Eisenhower sent thousands of United States Marines to Lebanon. The Marines brought an end to the fighting, eliminating any threat of Communism and securing United States oil interests in the Middle East.

Cuba, 1959-1963 - **Fidel Castro** (1926-) led a revolution to establish a new government in Cuba in 1959. President Eisenhower recognized the new government a week later. Castro executed more than 700 opponents of the revolution and jailed many more. The new government improved health care in rural areas and took land from the rich to give to the poor. The United States had much to lose from Castro's land reform. By 1958, United States businesses owned 40 percent of Cuba's sugar industry, 80 percent of its utilities industry, and 90 percent of its mineral resources. Although Castro emphasized that his revolution was not Communist, the United States government was suspicious and applied economic pressure on Cuba by reducing its imports of Cuban sugar.

Before breaking off diplomatic relations with Cuba, Eisenhower authorized the CIA to begin training anti-Castro Cuban exiles for an invasion of Cuba. When **President John F. Kennedy** (1917-1963) came into office, he commanded the invasion force to attack, landing at the **Bay of Pigs** on April 17, 1961. However, the failure of this undercover military operation greatly embarrassed the new Kennedy administration.

Fearful of further plans of attack from the United States, Castro sought economic and military aid from the Soviet Union. When US spy planes spotted Soviet nuclear missiles in Cuba, Kennedy responded with a naval blockade of the island, resulting in the **Cuban Missile Crisis** (October 1962). The two superpowers avoided nuclear war when the Soviet leader Nikita Khrushchev agreed to recall the Soviet ships and missiles. In return, the US agreed to remove its missiles from Turkey and not to invade Cuba.

CHAPTER 14 REVIEW

A. Define the following names, terms, and events:

United Nations	Marshall Plan	SEATO	Nikita S. Khrushchev
General Assembly	Río Treaty	Warsaw Pact	peaceful coexistence
Security Council	Berlin Airlift	censure	NASA
Nuremberg war trials	NATO	McCarthyism	Fidel Castro
Cold War	Chiang Kai-shek	arms race	John F. Kennedy
iron curtain	Mao Zedong	H-bomb	Bay of Pigs Invasion
containment	Ho Chi Minh	space race	Cuban Missile Crisis
Truman Doctrine	domino theory	Sputnik I	

B. On your own paper, write your response to each of the following:

1. Compare the strengths and weaknesses of the United Nations.
2. What was the significance of the war crimes trials that followed World War II?
3. List four obstacles to world peace following World War II.
4. Contrast the different post-war goals of the United States and the Union of Soviet Socialist Republics.
5. Explain the origins of the term "Cold War."
6. List two significant changes in United States foreign policy after World War II.
7. Describe the impact of United States' occupation on Japanese society.
8. Describe Mao Zedong's takeover of China.
9. Evaluate the effectiveness of the United Nations in stopping aggression in Korea.
10. Evaluate the impact of the Korean War on international relations.
11. Contrast the United States' foreign policy in Europe with its policy in Asia.
12. What conclusions can be drawn from the fear of communism in the United States and the McCarthy era?
13. How did the possibility of nuclear war influence competition between the United States and the USSR?
14. List four effects of the Soviet launch of the Sputnik satellites.
15. List three effects of the nuclear arms build up.
16. Compare United States interventions in Guatemala in 1954 and Hungary in 1956.

C. Write True if the statement is correct and False if the statement is incorrect. Be prepared to state a reason for your false answers.

1. _____ The Organization of American States (OAS) was formed to provide all of the American nations with nuclear weapons.

2. _____ The Nuremberg war trials, held in the USSR, dealt swift and just punishment for all crimes committed in WWII.

3. _____ Julius and Ethel Rosenberg, a married couple, were tried, convicted, and electrocuted in 1953 for the crime of giving secret information to the Soviets.

4. _____ A policy of appeasement, rather than containment, was used by the West to limit communism.

5. _____ Leader of communist Cuba , Khrushchev directed a nuclear missile buildup on the island.

6. _____ Protecting western oil interests, The CIA organized the fall of the prime minister of Iran.

7. _____ One of the historical influences on the Soviet Union's goals, was the centuries of invasions, producing a distrust of outsiders and an inward focus.

8. _____ In order to smooth the transition to democracy in Japan, Emperor Hirohito of Japan was protected from prosecution in the war crimes trials after World War II.

9. _____ The National Defense Education Act was a United States. response to the Cuban Missile Crisis.

10. _____ After WWII, both the United States and the Soviet Union strove to promote their very different forms of economics and government throughout the world.

11. _____ France's reunification was difficult, so Germans sent aid by plane, which was called the Berlin Airlift.

12. _____ John F. Kennedy ordered the completion of an Eisenhower secret invasion at the Bay of Pigs in Cuba, which was a huge success in fending off communism.

CHAPTER 15
THE POWER OF PROTEST

PART I: WORLD-WIDE UNREST

The following consequences of World War II provided the opportunity and inspiration for nationalist independence movements to gain strength in African and Asian countries controlled by European nations:

1. The destruction, displacement, and economic decline due to World War II laid the groundwork for unstable situations around the globe.
2. Wartime occupation intensified the desire for independence among natives in former European colonies.
3. The right of **self-determination** (people governing themselves) was proclaimed through the charter of the United Nations (1945).
4. The war had drained European nations of their resources for managing colonies.
5. The United States and the Soviet Union dominated the world scene and both opposed colonial empires for ideological reasons.

LEADERS OF INDEPENDENCE MOVEMENTS IN FORMER EUROPEAN COLONIES

The leaders of the independence movements were usually educated in European schools and universities. They became familiar with European customs and policies. As natives, they could command the respect of their peers, as well as deal with the Europeans. Often these leaders developed a strong nationalistic political party which organized strikes, boycotts, and other political actions to pressure the European governments to grant independence to the former colonies. Some leaders resorted to violent revolution to force out the Europeans.

THE EMERGENCE OF THE THIRD WORLD

Once the European nations left their former colonies, several problems followed, including one-party rule, **neo-imperialism** (continued dependence on European goods and investments), and violence between tribal groups and revolutionaries.

During the Cold War, scholars came to call the bloc of nations led by the United States the **First World**, and the bloc of nations led by the Soviet Union, they called the **Second World**. **Third World** became the name for technologically and economically underdeveloped nations who belonged to neither camp. Both the United States and the Soviet Union tried to entice these nations to follow their ideals, but often the emerging nations chose to create their own institutions based on **indigenous** (native) traditions, needs, and hopes.

AREAS WHERE NATIONALISM RESULTED IN THE REVIVAL OF OLD OR THE CREATION OF NEW NATIONS

Indian Subcontinent

Mohandas K. Gandhi (1869-1948) led **India** to independence from British rule through a powerful campaign of nonviolent civil disobedience. Gandhi had worked more than 30 years uniting India, but India and **Pakistan** became separate states when the British granted India its independence in 1947. Gandhi's sadness only increased when Muslims and Hindus began killing each other in riots. Gandhi was able to prevent some of the fighting by traveling to Muslim territory and **fasting** (refusing to eat). Shortly after one of these fasts, a Hindu who opposed Gandhi's tolerance of Muslims shot and killed Gandhi.

Mohandas K. Gandhi

In 1948, Britain granted partial independence to **Malaysia** and full independence to **Ceylon** (now Sri Lanka) and **Burma** (now Myanmar).

Southeast Asia

During World War II, Japan invaded French Indochina, Indonesia, and the Philippines. The United States regained the **Philippines** before the end of the war and granted the country independence on July 4, 1946. In 1945, the Dutch tried to re-establish colonial control in **Indonesia**, but the native people fought back, eventually gaining independence in 1949. Similarly, the native peoples of Indochina resisted French efforts to re-establish colonial control in that area. Despite large amounts of aid from the United States, the French admitted defeat in 1954 and granted independence to **Cambodia, Laos,** and **Vietnam. Ho Chi Minh** (1890-1969), the Communist leader of the Vietnamese independence movement, won control of North Vietnam. The United States tried to preserve the government of South Vietnam during the **Vietnam War** (1957-1975). However, after the United States withdrew its troops, Ho Chi Minh united North and South Vietnam.

Middle East

After World War I, hundreds of thousands of Jews came to **Palestine** to escape persecution, especially from Hitler's Germany. Under British control, this area was primarily inhabited by Muslim Arabs. When the British failed to resolve continued conflicts in Palestine, the United Nations (UN) proposed two separate states, one Arab and one Jewish. On May 14, 1948, the Jewish population proclaimed the formation of a new nation, **Israel**, according to the UN guidelines. The United States, the USSR, and other nations quickly recognized the new government. The surrounding Arab nations, however, declared war and attacked the next day. During more than seven months of war, the people of Israel resisted Arab attacks, gaining more territory than the original UN plan had outlined.

The island nation of **Cyprus**, west of Syria in the Mediterranean Sea, gained independence from British rule in 1960 through extreme terrorist activity and aggressive political negotiations, aided by UN guidelines.

Africa

Since the late 1800s, European nations controlled almost the entire African continent. However, African independence movements gained strength after World War II.

Kwame Nkrumah (1909-1972) led the independence movement in the British colony of Gold Coast by vigorously organizing strikes and boycotts. In 1957, he was elected president of the newly independent nation, renamed **Ghana**.

Soon, other African nations gained their independence. In 1960, **Nigeria** gained independence from Britain, and the Belgians left their colony of the Congo, now called **Zaire**. After eight years of a terrible war with France, **Algeria** gained its independence in 1962. By the end of the 1970s, almost all the African nations were free from European colonial rule. In South Africa, however, a white minority continued to rule a black majority.

Nelson Mandela (1918-) led black resistance to the policy of **apartheid** (forced segregation of the races) imposed by the white government of **South Africa**. Because of his activities, the South African government arrested him in 1962 and sentenced him to life in prison. Mandela became a symbol of resistance to apartheid, and people from around the world called for his release. Under the leadership of President **F. W. de Klerk** (1936-), the South African government released Mandela in February 1990.

After his release, Mandela helped whites and blacks work together to end apartheid. Both Mandela and de Klerk were honored for their efforts with the Nobel Peace Prize in 1993. The following year, the people of South Africa voted in the first multiracial elections and elected Mandela as the first black president of the Republic of South Africa.

PART II: POST-WAR SOCIAL PROTEST MOVEMENTS IN THE UNITED STATES

For most people in the United States, the 1950s was a period of general stability. However, beneath the calm surface, blacks, women, young people, and social critics were calling for change.

THE CIVIL RIGHTS MOVEMENT

The **civil rights movement** is the political, legal, and social struggle of blacks in the United States to gain racial equality and full citizenship rights. The movement was strongest during the 1950s and 1960s, but blacks resisted racial injustice before that time and continue to struggle for justice to this day.

Integration Starts in the Military (1948)

In July 1948, President Truman issued **Executive Order 9981**, declaring that "there shall be equality of treatment and opportunity for all persons in the armed services." He ordered that desegregation of military facilities "be put into effect as rapidly as possible." However, desegregation was slow in the 1940s. By 1951, most of the units in Korea were integrated, but, in 1960, the armed forces still were not entirely integrated.

Separate But Equal

The **National Association for the Advancement of Colored People (NAACP)** challenged the laws of **segregation** (separation of the races) through court cases, winning small but important victories through the first half of the 20th century. In May 1954, the NAACP won a major victory in a case where the Board of Education of Topeka, Kansas would not let a black girl, **Linda Brown**, attend an all-white school that was near her home. In *Brown vs. Board of*

Education of Topeka **(1954)**, the Supreme Court ruled that racial segregation in public schools, based on *Plessy vs. Ferguson* **(1896)**, is unconstitutional, claiming that "in the field of public education the doctrine of 'separate but equal' has no place."

The Montgomery Bus Boycott (1955-1956)

Segregation laws in the city of Montgomery required black passengers on buses to sit in the back and to give up their seats to white passengers if the bus was crowded. Many of the white bus drivers enforced this law by cursing and humiliating blacks. On December 1, 1955, a white bus driver ordered **Rosa Parks** (1913-), a leading member of the local branch of the NAACP, to give up her seat to a white passenger. When she refused, the bus driver called the police who arrested her and took her to jail.

Rosa Parks

Rosa Parks was very popular and highly respected. Local leaders of the NAACP saw that her arrest could unite Montgomery blacks in a citywide protest. The leaders formed the Montgomery Improvement Association to direct a boycott of city buses and selected the young Baptist minister **Dr. Martin Luther King, Jr.** (1929-1968) as its president. Having only recently arrived in Montgomery, King had not made any enemies and could unify the community. He was also a great public speaker. Almost overnight, the city's 50,000 blacks united in walking to work or coordinating informal taxi service with people who owned cars, rather than ride the bus.

The boycott lasted over a year until, in November 1956, the Supreme Court ruled that buses in Montgomery must be integrated. Because of the bus boycott, the black community won its battle, and Martin Luther King, Jr. became a national figure.

In 1957, Dr. King helped found the **Southern Christian Leadership Conference (SCLC)**, an organization of black churches and ministers devoted to challenging racial segregation. By encouraging the use of nonviolent direct action, such as demonstrations, marches, and boycotts, the leaders of SCLC hoped to complement the NAACP's efforts to fight segregation through the courts. As president of the SCLC, King strongly influenced the goals and actions of the organization, drawing on the teachings of Jesus Christ and Mohandas Gandhi.

Little Rock Central High School (1957)

In 1957, national attention turned to Arkansas where Governor Orval E. Faubus refused to obey a federal court order to integrate Little Rock Central High School. He called out the Arkansas National Guard to prevent nine black students from entering the school. President Eisenhower did not think the federal government should enforce desegregation, but in the face of this open defiance of federal authority, he sent federal troops to escort the black children into their school.

Sit-ins and SNCC (1960)

On February 1, 1960, four black college students from North Carolina A&T University protested racial segregation in restaurants by sitting at a "whites only" lunch counter in Greensboro, North Carolina. They waited to be served and when the management ordered them to leave, they refused. Within days, "**sit-ins**" (nonviolent protest by sitting in segregated places) had spread across North Carolina, and in a few weeks they were taking place in cities across the South. As the movement spread, the long-time civil rights leader **Ella Baker** (1903-1986) called the students together to coordinate their efforts. The students gathered in Raleigh, North Carolina in April 1960 and formed the **Student Nonviolent Coordinating Committee (SNCC)**.

Freedom Rides (1961)

In 1960, the Supreme Court ruled that segregation was illegal in bus stations open to interstate travel. The **Congress of Racial Equality** or **CORE** (an organization founded in 1942 and devoted to social change through nonviolent direct action) organized **Freedom Rides** to test that decision. In the summer of 1961, black and white Freedom Riders boarded a bus in Washington, D.C. and traveled south. The trip was mostly peaceful until the bus reached Anniston, Alabama where a white mob attacked the bus, burning it and beating the riders as they fled the flames.

Alabama's violent reaction to the Freedom Rides attracted national attention. When the state officials refused to protect the riders, Attorney General **Robert Kennedy** (1925-1968) sent 600 United States marshals. When the riders reached Jackson, Mississippi, state officials arrested them and imprisoned them at the state penitentiary, ending the protest. The federal government did not try to stop these arrests, fearing that doing so would disrupt public order.

The Freedom Rides resulted in the desegregation of some bus stations, but more importantly, the courage and dedication of the riders drew national attention and support to the cause of civil rights.

The March on Washington (August 1963)

Illustration of Dr. Martin Luther King, Jr. giving "I have a dream. . ." speech

Civil rights protests continued through 1962 and 1963, forcing the federal government to protect blacks from mobs and police in the South. National civil rights leaders wanted to keep pressure on **President John F. Kennedy** (1917-1963) and the Congress to pass civil rights legislation, so they planned a march for August 1963. On August 28, 1963, Martin Luther King, Jr. addressed a crowd of more than 200,000 black and white civil rights supporters. Standing in front of the Lincoln Memorial, King proclaimed: "**I have a dream. . .**" He challenged his listeners to dream with him of a day when white and black people would live peacefully together as brothers and sisters with equal rights and equal justice under the law. His stirring words continue to influence oppressed peoples around the world. Along with Dr. King's speech, the peaceful and orderly demonstration gained more support for the civil rights cause.

Reform and Riots

Partly as a result of the March on Washington, President Kennedy proposed new civil rights laws. After Kennedy was assassinated on November 22, 1963, the new president, **Lyndon B. Johnson** (1908-1973), strongly urged Congress to pass the laws in honor of Kennedy. Despite fierce opposition from Southern members of Congress, Johnson pushed through the **Civil Rights Act of 1964** (July 2, 1964). The act prohibited segregation in public housing and discrimination in education and employment. It also gave the president the power to enforce the new law.

Less than a month after the passage of the Civil Rights Act, a white, off-duty police officer killed a 15-year-old black in Harlem, New York. The incident led to five days of rioting. Over the next month, race riots spread to other cities in New York and New Jersey, as well as Chicago and Philadelphia.

Voting Rights

The passage of the Civil Rights Act of 1964 turned the focus of the civil rights movement to voting rights. Civil rights leaders believed that securing the right to vote for blacks was key to the civil rights movement. With the power to vote, blacks could change the laws that affected them. However, Southern society prevented blacks from even registering to vote.

Some counties required a **literacy test** before a person could register to vote. The literacy tests were given by white officials who gave easy questions to whites and very difficult questions to blacks to prevent them from registering. Even if blacks registered, some counties required a **poll tax** (a fee charged for a person to vote). Most blacks in the South were too poor to pay the poll tax, so they couldn't vote. On top of these obstacles, **intimidation** stopped many blacks from voting. White racists threatened to fire blacks from their jobs, beat them, or hang them if they tried to vote or even register to vote.

The Freedom March from Selma to Montgomery (March 1965)

Early in 1965, the people of Selma, Alabama asked Martin Luther King, Jr. and the SCLC to join a voter registration drive begun by SNCC. After over a month of protests, arrests, and the death of one civil rights activist, the protesters decided to bring national attention to their cause by marching 50 miles to the state's capital, Montgomery. John Lewis of SNCC and Hosea Williams of SCLC led the march on Sunday, March 7, 1965. When the 500 marchers reached Selma's city limits, 200 state troopers and sheriff's deputies beat them with clubs and whips, stomped them with horses, and showered them with tear gas. People across the United States were shocked by the televised scenes of this violent event, later called Bloody Sunday. President Johnson said that "what happened in Selma was an American tragedy."

Thousands of whites and blacks came to Selma to continue the march. Two weeks after Bloody Sunday, Martin Luther King, Jr. led more than 3000 marchers out of Selma, including a core of 300 people who walked the entire journey. Four days later they arrived in Montgomery, where King addressed a rally of nearly 40,000 people in front of the capitol building. The final victory of the march came on August 6, when President Johnson signed the **Voting Rights Act of 1965**. It authorized the president to suspend literacy tests for voter registration and to send federal officials to register voters where county officials refused to do so. This new law led to the registration of many black voters who began electing black officials into office.

Continued Problems for Blacks

Despite legislative victories and the success of the growing black middle class, the majority of blacks remained poor and dispossessed in the cities of the United States. Blacks' frustration with their desperate situation in urban poverty exploded in the **Watts Riots** (August 11-16, 1965). Just days after President Johnson signed the Voting Rights Act, the arrest of a black man in the Watts section of Los Angeles touched off six days of rioting. Tragically, thirty-four people died, 1,032 people were injured, and 3,952 people were arrested before the National Guard stopped the rioting. Urban violence continued in 1966 and 1967. Race riots in over 100 cities killed 94 people and injured hundreds more.

Broadening the Nonviolent Campaign

With other civil rights leaders, Dr. King became increasingly opposed to the war in Vietnam. He was greatly disturbed by the pictures of Vietnamese children burned by United States bombing, and he saw the poverty in United States cities tied to the large amounts of money spent on the military. He warned that "the security we profess to seek in foreign adventures, we will lose in our decaying cities."

Addressing the Violence

President Johnson established a commission to find the causes of urban violence. After a seven-month investigation, the **Kerner Commission** reported (February 29, 1968) that the United States needed to "make good the promises of American democracy to all citizens–urban and rural, white and black, [Hispanic], American Indian and every minority group."

To address these problems, Martin Luther King, Jr. announced (March 4, 1968) a **Poor People's Campaign**. Poor whites, blacks, and Hispanics would march on Washington, D.C. and demand that the United States spend money on the problems of the poor, not on the military.

Before the Poor People's Campaign began, Dr. King was shot and killed in Memphis, Tennessee on April 4, 1968. In the resulting riots, forty-six persons died in riots in Washington, Chicago, and other cities, while many other people held marches and rallies. President Johnson declared Sunday, April 6, to be a national day of mourning. More than 300,000 people followed Dr. King's casket in a funeral procession through the streets of Atlanta.

Black Militancy

By 1965, a growing number of blacks began to advocate a more militant approach to civil rights, disregarding nonviolence.

Malcolm X (1925-1965) was born Malcolm Little. While in prison for burglary, he became interested in the teachings of **Elijah Muhammad** (1897-1975), the leader of the **Nation of Islam** or the Black Muslims. Black Muslims called white people "devils" who enslaved all nonwhites. Under the religion of Islam, they advocated black self-sufficiency, even calling for the establishment of a separate African American homeland in the United States. In contrast to the nonviolence taught by other religious leaders of the civil rights movement, Malcolm X said that blacks should use "any means necessary" to secure their rights, including fighting back against violence. At the same time, Malcolm X was becoming increasingly dissatisfied by Muhammad's failure to participate in

Malcolm X

the civil rights movement. In 1964, Malcolm X left the Nation of Islam and founded the secular black nationalist Organization for Afro-American Unity (OAAU). He then went on a **pilgrimage** (a journey for a religious purpose) to the Islamic holy city of Mecca, Saudi Arabia. After seeing black and white Muslims praying and living together in Africa and Europe, he stopped teaching that all white people are evil and began calling for whites and blacks to work together. On February 21, 1965, three men killed Malcolm X while he was speaking at an OAAU rally. His assassination and the publication of *The Autobiography of Malcolm X*, later that year, increased the popularity of his teachings.

Inspired by the teachings of Malcolm X, some workers in SNCC came to believe that future progress in civil rights would come from independent black political power. The continued resistance of southern whites caused members of SNCC to reject the method of nonviolent protest as being too slow and ineffective. This militant faction took over leadership of the group when **Stokley Carmichael** (1941-) was elected chairman of SNCC in May 1966. He called for **Black Power**, a term that included pride in African heritage, separate black economic and political institutions, self-defense against white violence, and sometimes violent revolution. The theme of Black Power dominated SNCC and CORE in the late 1960s.

Achievements and Challenges of the Civil Rights Movement

Blacks made great gains in the 1960s. Federal legislation outlawed segregation and freed blacks from the humiliation of Jim Crow laws. Blacks secured the right to vote and significantly influenced the political process. In 1972, there were more than twice as many black-elected officials than there were in 1964. Blacks also made economic and educational progress. By 1970, 28 percent of black families earned over $10,000 per year, compared to 11 percent in 1960. In 1971, 18 percent of young blacks were in college, compared to about 10 percent in 1965.

However, the great mass movement of the 1960s faded for the following reasons:

1. **Assassination of leaders:** Malcolm X and Martin Luther King, Jr. were sorely missed.
2. **Loss of energy:** By 1970, blacks had struggled for 15 years and still did not have equality.
3. **Decline of black family life:** Unemployment rates of young black males rose to 40 percent. Drugs, crime, and single parent homes increased in black neighborhoods. A NAACP report stated that the employment situation of "urban blacks in 1971 was worse than at any time since the Great Depression of the thirties."
4. **Loss of white support:** There seemed to be a white consensus that the United States had done enough for blacks, as shown by the election of President Richard Nixon. He attacked civil rights policies and social programs.

These factors impacted blacks. Relative to whites, black unemployment rates rose and black incomes declined during the early 1970s. However, the number of black elected officials increased, especially mayors (8 in 1971 and 135 in 1975). Also, the number of black students in college increased by 56 percent between 1970 and 1974. Racial inequality remained in the United States, but the civil rights movement had made significant progress.

Civil Rights Movements Among Other Groups

Blacks' struggle for civil rights inspired similar movements among other groups like Hispanics and Native Americans.

In 1962, **Cesar Chavez** (1927-1993) began to organize grape pickers into unions. The majority of grape pickers were Mexican Americans who were mistreated and underpaid. Chavez led sit-ins and a nationwide boycott of grapes. These nonviolent protests forced more growers to accept unions and provide better pay and working conditions for their workers.

By 1969, a majority of Native Americans lived in urban areas, mostly in the eastern United States. City life weakened the traditional practices of Native Americans. Many young people reacted by taking great pride in their heritage and strongly demanding rights for their people. The **American Indian Movement (AIM)** formed in 1968. In March 1973, some members of AIM seized the trading post at Wounded Knee (South Dakota), the site of an 1890 massacre by the United States Army. The AIM members did not have the support of other Native Americans, and federal officers forced them to leave after a gun battle causing two Native American deaths.

The Ongoing Struggle for Civil Rights

Jesse Jackson (1941-) was a close friend and co-worker of Dr. Martin Luther King, Jr. In 1971, Jackson established Operation PUSH (People United to Save Humanity) to help gain economic advancement for racial minorities. In 1984 and 1988, he ran for the Democratic presidential nomination. He did not win the nomination, but he led efforts to register more black voters and to increase the number of minority groups represented at the Democratic national conventions.

As the leading spokesperson for the Nation of Islam, **Louis Farrakhan** (1933-) gained popularity during the 1980s as he established new **mosques** (Islamic houses of worship) around the country. He advocated moral and economic responsibility, encouraging blacks to avoid drugs and crime while staying in school or providing for their families. He also caused controversy with anti-semitic remarks, calling Judaism a "gutter religion" and Hitler a "great man." Other black leaders condemned his comments, though Farrakhan said that news reports misrepresented his statements. In October 1995, he organized the **Million Man March** in Washington, D.C. The event was designed to encourage black men to take personal responsibility for themselves, their families, and their communities. Crowd estimates ranged from 400,000 to over one million.

Strategies of Civil Rights Organizations

NAACP (New York City, 1909) used mainly a legal strategy, challenging segregation and discrimination in courts to obtain equal treatment for blacks through national laws.

SCLC (Atlanta, 1957) wanted to add to the NAACP's legal strategy by protesting segregation through nonviolent, direct actions such as marches, demonstrations, and boycotts.

SNCC (North Carolina, 1960) used nonviolent, direct action and voter registration drives; it focused on changing local communities rather than national laws; the group turned away from nonviolence in the late 1960s.

CORE (New York City, 1942) used nonviolent direct action to create a society in which "race or creed will be neither asset nor handicap"; it promoted "black power" in the late 1960s.

Nation of Islam (Detroit, 1930) advocated black dignity, responsibility, self-reliance, and separation from whites, even establishing a separate nation in the United States.

Black Panther Party (Oakland, California, 1966) promoted the idea of Black Power and black self-defense; the party used armed patrols to confront police brutality; it later developed community programs to provide food, clothing, and medical care for the poor.

"Firsts" for African Americans

- **Benjamin O. Davis, Sr**. - first black general in the army, October 16, 1940

- **Camilla Williams** - first black woman to perform with a major opera company, 1946

- **Jackie Robinson** - first black player in modern Major League Baseball, April 10, 1947 – Rookie of the Year, 1947 – first black inducted into the Baseball Hall of Fame, 1962

- **Ralph J. Bunche** - first black to receive the Nobel Peace Prize, September 22, 1950, for negotiating a cease fire in 1948 between Israel and its Arab neighbors

- **Althea Gibson** - first black person to win a major tennis title, French Open, 1956

- **Martin Luther King, Jr.** - youngest person to receive Nobel Peace Prize, December 10, 1964

- **Patricia R. Harris** - first black woman ambassador (Luxembourg), May 19, 1965

- **Bill Russell** - first black to coach a professional athletic team, April 18, 1966

- **Edward W. Brooke** - first black senator since the Reconstruction era and first black senator to be elected by popular vote, elected from Massachusetts, November 8, 1966

- **Constance Baker Motley** - first black woman to be named federal judge, August 30, 1966

- **Carl B. Stokes** - first black mayor of a major city (Cleveland, Ohio), November 13, 1967

- **Thurgood Marshall** - first black Supreme Court Justice, confirmed by Senate August 30, 1967

- **Shirley Chisholm** - first black woman US representative, elected from Brooklyn, New York, November 5, 1968

- **Andrew Young** - first black US representative from the Deep South in the twentieth century, elected from Georgia in 1972

FEMINIST MOVEMENT

The **feminist movement** or **women's liberation movement** is a social and political movement that seeks equality of rights and status between women and men, giving women the freedom to choose their own careers and life patterns. In the 1960s, the feminist movement gained energy from the civil rights movement in much the same way as the women's suffrage movement of the mid-1800s was invigorated by the abolitionist movement. (see pp. 80-81)

Springing from the civil rights movement, the push for women's rights came up from the grass-roots level, but it also came down from government policies. At the suggestion of Esther Peterson, director of the Women's Bureau of the Department of Labor, President John F. Kennedy set up the first national Commission on the Status of Women in 1962. The following year, the commission reported employment discrimination, unequal pay, legal inequality, and insufficient support services for working women. The commission's report led to the **Equal Pay Act (1963)** which made it illegal to pay different wages to men and women who performed the same work. The new law had little effect, however, because most women remained in traditionally female occupations which offered low wages and little opportunity for advancement. In 1963, women were paid, on average, 41 percent less than men.

Title VII of the Civil Rights Act of 1964 prohibited employment discrimination based on sex as well as race, color, or ethnic origin. The act also established the Equal Employment Opportunity Commission (EEOC) to enforce the new law.

Betty Friedan (1921-) promoted opportunities for women beyond the roles of wife and mother in her book, *The Feminine Mystique* (1963). In 1966, she helped found the **National Organization of Women (NOW)** and served as its first president. NOW promotes the equality of men and women through elections, legislation, rallies, and marches.

Gloria Steinem (1934-) became a leader in the feminist movement after 1968. With Betty Friedan and Shirley Chisholm (the first black woman elected to Congress), Steinem helped found the National Women's Political Caucus (1971) to encourage women to seek political office and to work for women's rights laws.

Friedan, Steinem, and NOW supported a new amendment to the Constitution, the **Equal Rights Amendment (ERA)**, which would guarantee women's equal rights. Congress passed the ERA in 1972 and extended the deadline for states' ratification by three years, but the ERA failed to become part of the Constitution.

Phyllis Schlafly (1924-) founded Stop ERA in 1972 to prevent the ratification of the new amendment. In 1975, Schlafly founded the **Eagle Forum** to support the preservation of traditional morality and the traditional American family.

Title IX of the Education Amendments of 1972 banned discrimination on the basis of sex by schools and colleges that receive federal money.

The Supreme Court's decision in *Roe vs. Wade* (1973) ensured a woman's right to get an abortion. NOW and other women's groups support this decision while other women oppose abortion.

Impact of the Feminist Movement

Change in attitudes regarding the roles of men and women have occurred in society. Men are more active in parenting and childbirth while women more often pursue careers. Schools have developed women's studies programs, and they encourage using language that includes women: for example, "fireman" is changed to "firefighter."

Workplace: From 1940 to 1989, the percentage of employed women rose from 28 percent to 57 percent. Many more women are becoming lawyers and doctors. However, most women are still limited to jobs like nursing, teaching, retail sales, and secretarial work, earning less than men do. Women also suffer the **"double burden"** of being the primary homemaker as well as working outside the home.

Politics: By participating in government, elections, and political organizations, women greatly influence government policies and legislation.

Family Life: Before women entered the workforce in large numbers, employers paid men enough to support their families. Now the economy often requires that both men and women must work. With both parents working, children are placed in daycare.

PART III: THE RISE OF A COUNTERCULTURE IN THE UNITED STATES

After suffering the economic hardship of the Great Depression, people in the United States continued to make spending sacrifices during World War II, delaying purchases to support the war effort. When the war was over, Americans were ready to spend the money they had saved. The transition from wartime to peacetime caused some economic difficulties in the late 1940s, but in the 1950s, the United States economy peaked, reaching its highest levels of production and prosperity to date.

Characteristics of the 1950s in the United States

- Young couples created a **baby boom** by focusing on marriage, family, and children.
- Blacks moved to cities for work while many whites moved to the rapidly growing suburbs.
- Shopping plazas and malls made suburbs self-contained.
- The number of cars and highways increased.
- Society clearly defined social roles: women at home, men outside the home, children obedient at all times.
- A mass consumer culture developed around television programs and commercials; during the 1950s, almost 7 million television sets were sold each year.
- Religion grew more important; in 1954, Congress added the words "under God" to the Pledge of Allegiance to the Flag.

One result of all this prosperity was the time and money that many would spend on entertainment and others would spend searching for a deeper meaning in life.

SOCIAL CRITICISM

In *The Lonely Crowd* (1950), David Riesman argued that many Americans cared too much about pleasing others, and he criticized the power of advertising to shape the tastes of the public. William H. Whyte's *The Organization Man* (1956) argued that large business and government organizations tended to discourage creativity and individualism.

Artists offered social criticism with new art forms. **Abstract expressionism** moved away from realistic pictures and expressed emotions with swirling lines of color. **Pop art** commented on commercialism by portraying items like soup cans and soda bottles with camera-like precision.

ROCK AND ROLL

When hundreds of thousands of blacks left the rural South to seek jobs in Northern cities during World War II, they brought their music with them. Record producers saw the potential of teen buying power and promoted singers like Elvis Presley, Chuck Berry, Buddy Holly, and Little Richard to popularize the new music called **rock and roll**. The music's strong beat and loud volume marked a sharp contrast from the soft singing of Frank Sinatra and Bing Crosby, who were popular among adults at the time. The hair styles, clothing styles, and sexually suggestive movements of some performers caused many people in the United States to complain about the music.

Although some had thought rock and roll would be a passing fad, rock musicians continue to create new musical forms. Rock music became a symbol for youth, encouraged social criticism, and remains internationally popular today.

COUNTERCULTURE

During the 1950s and 1960s, young people, especially college students, tried to live their lives differently. They created a **counterculture**, a lifestyle with values and customs opposed to those of established society.

The **beat movement** was a social and literary movement that began in the 1950s and was centered in San Francisco's North Beach and New York's Greenwich Village. Members of this movement, called "**beatniks**," wore informal, "hip" clothes and used colorful language to express their feelings of alienation from conventional society, which they called "square." They were generally unconcerned with politics or social problems but focused on intense experiences of the senses enhanced by drugs, sex, or meditation. They described these experiences in unstructured poems and books, writing about thoughts and feelings without plan or revision.

The counterculture grew in the 1960s as college students strongly questioned the standards of society. Called "**hippies**," these young people criticized the materialism of the consumer culture and rejected traditional occupations (jobs) which they felt limited creativity and individualism. Rejecting traditional roles and styles, young men grew long hair and beards while young women wore peasant-like clothes with bright colors. Seeking a deeper meaning in life, they experimented with drugs, sex, and rock music. Often groups of hippies fled from traditional society to rural areas where they lived together in communes, sharing resources and work, often growing their own food.

Believing in respect for all people, hippies supported the civil rights movement and gained energy from it. Pursuing the ideal of a society based on peace and love rather than money and violence, hippies joined others in protesting the Vietnam War with marches and demonstrations. They had "sit-ins" and "teach-ins" to influence university policies that affected them. Many people of mainstream culture criticized the hippies for being lazy, dirty, and disrespectful.

Rock was the music of the counterculture during the 1960s. The musician **Bob Dylan** (1941-) wrote serious poetic songs that criticized war, prejudice, and injustice. Some called him the Shakespeare of rock music. The high point of the youth counterculture in the United States was the **Woodstock Music and Art Fair** (August 1969) where more than 400,000 young people gathered for a three-day outdoor concert near Woodstock, New York.

Anti-War Movement

After 1965, the United States' increased involvement in the **Vietnam War** (1957-1975) divided the nation between so-called "hawks" and "doves." The "hawks" agreed with the United States decision to fight the Communists in Vietnam and called for stronger action. The "doves," on the other hand, opposed US involvement in Vietnam, questioning the necessity and morality of the war. Some opponents of the war, like the boxer Muhammad Ali, refused to be drafted into the military and joined mass demonstrations. In October 1967, over 50,000 anti-war demonstrators marched in Washington, D.C.

photograph of a Vietnam War protest

Opposition to the war and distrust of the government increased dramatically in the early 1970s. On May 4, 1970, National Guardsmen fired into a crowd of students demonstrating against the war at Kent State University in Ohio. In June 1971, a government official (Daniel Ellsberg) leaked a secret study of the Vietnam war to the press, revealing questionable practices by the United States government. In the face of growing opposition at home and continued defeat in Vietnam, the United States withdrew all of its troops from Vietnam by March 1973.

Effects of the 1960s Counterculture

Most counterculture organizations did not last beyond the 1960s. However, the counterculture movement made several changes, both positive and negative, in American life:

- Hippies and political activists encouraged a movement toward peace and social justice.
- People questioned government policies as well as unrestrained capitalism and militarism.
- Drug use became more wide-spread.
- The drive for freedom of expression reduced government censorship, making explicit language and photography more wide-spread.
- Sexual experimentation changed attitudes about traditional sexual roles and led to an increase in sexually transmitted diseases.
- The number of couples living together before marriage and divorcing rose significantly.
- Freedom of expression and lifestyle became more tolerated.
- There was an increased tolerance of persons with diverse religious, racial, and ethnic backgrounds.

CHAPTER 15 REVIEW

A.   Define the following names, terms, and events:

self-determination	SNCC	feminist movement
Third World	CORE	Betty Friedan
Mohandas K. Gandhi	Freedom Rides	NOW
Kwame Nkrumah	John F. Kennedy	Gloria Steinem
Nelson Mandela	March on Washington	ERA
apartheid	"I Have a Dream" Speech	Phyllis Schlafly
F. W. de Klerk	Lyndon B. Johnson	rock and roll
civil rights movement	Selma March	counterculture
Executive Order 9981	Poor People's Campaign	beat movement
Brown vs. Board of Education	Malcolm X	hippies
of Topeka (1954)	Cesar Chavez	Bob Dylan
Rosa Parks	Jesse Jackson	Woodstock Music and
Martin Luther King, Jr.	Louis Farrakhan	Art Fair
Montgomery bus boycott	Million Man March	anti-war movement
SCLC	Thurgood Marshall	
sit-in	Shirley Chisholm	

B.   On your own paper, write your response to each of the following:

1.   List five factors that contributed to worldwide unrest following World War II.
2.   Describe common qualities of many leaders of independence movements in Asia and Africa.
3.   Discuss the factors which led to the emergence of the Third World.
4.   Identify the areas where nationalism resulted in the revival of old nations or the creation of new nations.
5.   What was the significance of *Brown vs. Board of Education of Topeka*?
6.   List two important outcomes of the Montgomery bus boycott.
7.   Describe the goals and method of protest used by Dr. Martin Luther King, Jr. and SCLC.
8.   Describe the racial dispute at Central High School in Little Rock, Arkansas and its resolution.
9.   What events led to the formation of the Student Nonviolent Coordinating Committee?
10.   What were the goals and accomplishments of the Freedom Rides of 1961?
11.   What two major events led to the passage of the Civil Rights Act of 1964?
12.   What obstacles to voting did blacks face in the South?
13.   What civil rights legislation followed the Selma march and what were its effects?
14.   Why did race riots break out in cities even after Congress passed civil rights laws?
15.   Why did Dr. Martin Luther King, Jr. oppose US involvement in the Vietnam War?
16.   Describe the change in the goals and strategies of SNCC during the course of the 1960s.
17.   List three gains of the civil rights movement.
18.   List four reasons why the civil rights movement weakened.
19.   How did the civil rights movement for African Americans affect other minority groups?
20.   How did the goals and strategies of the Nation of Islam and the SCLC differ?
21.   Discuss the impact of the feminist movement on life in the United States.
22.   Identify five significant characteristics of life in the United States during the 1950s.
23.   Why did some people oppose rock and roll music?

24. Compare and contrast the "beatniks" and the "hippies."
25. List three criticisms of life in the United States during the 1950s.
26. List four effects of the counterculture movement of the 1960s.

C. Write True if the statement is correct and False if the statement is incorrect. Be prepared to state a reason for your false answers.

1. _____ All the citizens of the United States were supportive of sending troops to Vietnam.

2. _____ The "Freedom Rides" were organized by CORE, traveling from Washington D.C. to the South.

3. _____ Pop art, as a method of expression, comments upon commercial images in the United States culture.

4. _____ Despite Arab resistance, the nation of Israel was established after World War II, in the year 1948.

5. _____ The Equal Pay Act was an effective law passed to ensure equal opportunity for Native Americans in the work force.

6. _____ Dr. King gave his "I have a dream . . ." speech at the Lincoln Memorial to an orderly crowd of demonstrators; the speech and the dignity of all involved gained support for Dr. King's message.

7. _____ Hippies were the young people of the 1950s who dressed in odd clothes and focused on a perceived heightened level of creativity brought by various chemicals and altered mental states.

8. _____ Ho Chi Minh led the people of India in a campaign of nonviolent civil disobedience.

9. _____ In 1957, President Kennedy sent federal troops to escort Linda Brown, a black child, into her classes at Little Rock Central High School.

10. _____ New nations, which had been European colonies, tended to still rely on European goods and monetary investments for economic support, a situation known as neo-imperialism.

11. _____ True democracy, in the sense that all citizens have the right to vote, was achieved in the United States with the passage of the Voting Rights Act of 1965.

12. _____ The presidential campaign of Jesse Jackson led to his working to increase the number of registered black voters and minority groups represented in the Democratic national conventions.

13. _____ The Supreme Court case *Roe vs. Wade* ensured that every woman would get equal pay for equal work.

14. _____ Black Muslims, the group with which Malcolm X was first associated, advocated black self-sufficiency and a separate African-American homeland in the United States.

15. _____ The Woodstock Music and Air fair, a peaceful but muddy event, was held at Kent State University in Ohio.

16. _____ The policy of apartheid ended in South Africa when the country gained its independence from Britain in 1990.

CHAPTER 16
CHALLENGES AND CONCERNS
OF THE MODERN WORLD

THE GLOBAL ENVIRONMENT

As industrialization has increased worldwide, so have the problems associated with this growth - air pollution, acid rain, habitat loss, water contamination (1.5 billion people lack safe drinking water), and species loss (between 4,000 and 50,000 species are dying out each year). Because the pollution produced in one nation often affects another, international organizations such as **United Nations Environmental Program (UNEP)** and political parties such as the **Green Party** have formed to regulate and combat these unhealthy aspects of industrialization. As the developing countries of East Asia, Latin America, and Africa continue the process of industrialization, international organizations are imposing tighter safeguards through agreements to ensure that levels of toxic air emissions and habitat destruction of endangered species are minimized. However, problems such as increased **global warming** (global temperature has increased 1 degree Celsius within the last century) , the depletion of the **ozone layer** (holes in the ozone layer have been expanding at the north and south poles) and the **extinction** of increased numbers of species, both plants and animals, continue to cause concern and problems for people around the world.

The United States has been a source of both negative environmental practices and positive activism for the good of the global environment. Environmentalism arose as a social and political movement in the 1960s and continues to influence national environmental policies. The size and reach of the United States demands that it address the worldwide effects of its wasteful practices. Organizations within the United States dedicated to worldwide ecological conservation include **Greenpeace** (organization committed to ensuring that corporations follow ecologically sound practices, sometimes using civil disobedience) and the **Sierra Club** (group sponsoring talks, exhibitions, and environmental activism in local communities). Also included were the **Environmental Defense Fund** in 1967, **Friends of the Earth** in 1968, the **Natural Resources Defense Council** in 1970 and the **Sierra Club Legal Defense Fund** in 1971. All of these groups work to educate people and raise awareness about environmental issues and promote political change to protect the global environment.

Growing interest in environmental issues led to the following changes in United States governmental laws and policies:

- **Wilderness Act (1964)** - its goal was to set aside "an area where earth and its community of life are untrammeled [undisturbed] by man."

- **Environmental Protection Agency (1970)** - independent agency of the United States government responsible for protecting and maintaining the environment by seeking to control and lessen pollution from radiation, pesticides, and noise.

- **Clean Water Act (1972)** - made provisions for clean water as the Clean Air Act (1970) had done for air, including establishing national standards and time limits for these laws to be obeyed.

- **Endangered Species Act (1973)** - provided laws to prevent the destruction of certain plants and animals in danger of disappearing from the earth.

- The growing interest in environmental issues led to the celebration of the first **Earth Day**.

On April 22, 1970, approximately 20 million people gathered at various places around the United States to protest abuse of the environment by businesses and the government. The annual celebration of Earth Day continues to be an important way for environmentalists to educate people about environmental problems such as pollution, destruction of plant and animal species, and using up non-renewable resources, like oil.

The efforts of environmentalists have led to much greater awareness of environmental issues, as well as legislation and agencies designed to protect the environment. Despite these efforts, the industrial use of resources continues to harm the natural health and beauty of the whole earth.

THE GROWTH OF NUCLEAR AND BIOLOGICAL WEAPONS

After World War II, both the United States and the Soviet Union began massive buildups of nuclear weapons stockpiles. The end result was the promise of world destruction should these weapons ever be used. Secretly, however, other nations began acquiring the technology to manufacture these weapons as well. For example, China, India, Pakistan, and Israel are also nuclear powers today. This increase in the number of nations with these weapons of mass destruction increases the likelihood of nuclear conflict in the future. Biological weapons, also capable of killing entire cities with one explosion, are being produced secretly in many nations. Iraq, for example, was suspected of producing missiles which could carry the deadly biological agent, anthrax, during the Persian Gulf conflict (January 17-February 28, 1991). Because biological weapons are relatively inexpensive to produce in comparison with nuclear weapons, they are now easily available in Third World nations. Technology is providing faster and less expensive ways to kill massive numbers of people in a matter of moments, while also destroying the environment.

Several nations have attempted to limit the spread of nuclear and biological weapons. In addition, worldwide agreements have focused on reducing the size of existing stockpiles of these weapons:

- **Limited Test Ban Treaty** (1963) - this agreement limited atmospheric testing of nuclear weapons.

- **Nuclear Nonproliferation Treaty** (1968) - this agreement attempted to restrict the keeping and testing of nuclear weapons to five countries: Great Britain, France, China, the United States, and the Soviet Union.

- **Strategic Arms Limitation Talks** (SALT, 1972) - the agreement limited the number of nuclear weapons the United States and the Soviet Union could possess.

- **INF Treaty** (1987) - this agreement between the United States and the former Soviet Union banned nuclear missiles with a range of 300-3400 miles.

ADVANCES IN SPACE EXPLORATION AND TECHNOLOGY

During the **Cold War**, the United States and the Soviet Union competed against each other in outer space. Starting in 1957, Soviet rockets launched satellites, the series called Sputnik, into orbit around the earth. In 1961, the Soviets launched Vostok and placed the first human into space. In the United States, Kennedy vowed to put an astronaut on the moon by the end of the decade. On July 20, 1969, the **Apollo 11** mission landed on the moon, and Neil Armstrong became the first person to walk on its surface. After this feat was achieved, NASA began a shuttle program, while the Soviet Union focused on satellite production and a space station. Under the Reagan administration, the United States began developing a system that could destroy nuclear warheads in space before they could reach the ground called the Strategic Defense Initiative, or **Star Wars**. However, this system proved to be too costly and limited in effectiveness, so it was canceled. The focus turned from competition and defense to profitability. The United States began its shuttle program as a means of conducting experiments at zero gravity and as a means Of releasing satellites. As a result of these missions, communication has increased its pace all over the world. Satellites, launched into space,

**Apollo 11 launch
to the moon**
(Photograph compliments of NASA)

could relay messages from one side of the world to the other. For the first time, programs on television could be broadcast live from the other side of the world. Telecommunications was improved in both the commercial and military arenas. With the help of microprocessors and computer chips, engineers built the first telescope for use in space, the **Hubble Space Telescope** (1990). After some minor corrections, the telescope now beams crystal clear images of the planets, stars, and other galaxies free of the interference from the earth's atmosphere. Through space exploration and technology, scientists are finding innovations which improve the quality of life on earth.

The Hubble Space Telescope
(Photograph compliments of NASA)

INTERNATIONAL TRADE

Communications through telephone and wireless services have increased the degree of interaction that is possible worldwide. With the creation of the **Internet** (an organization of computer links worldwide), international trade and business becomes more feasible as the world becomes more interconnected. Businesses in the world desire to reach as many customers as possible, and with the Internet, businesses can receive worldwide attention at a fraction of the usual marketing cost. Also, the increase in air travel, as well as the development of more roads, has improved the speed and accessibility of products to consumers.

A number of world trade organizations and agreements have developed to help foster trade internationally and remove protective tariffs. However, these organizations, especially the **World Trade Organization (WTO)**, have increasingly come under attack for two reasons. First, the WTO has not adequately addressed the environmental impact of these business arrangements. Second, the WTO does not prohibit companies from paying unfairly low wages in poor working conditions as benefits of these trade agreements.

The following organizations are important for business and trade today:

- **General Agreement on Tariffs and Trade** (GATT, 1948-1994) - This is an organization of several nations established to reduce trade barriers on merchandise between member states. In 1994, member nations, including the United States and seven additional organizations, reorganized into a new organization, the WTO.
- **World Trade Organization** (WTO, 1994) - This organization was established by GATT member nations to supervise existing trade agreements. In addition, the organization also oversees agreements on services and intellectual rights, as well as trade in merchandise.
- **European Union** (EU,1992) - This organization was created by a merging of several other European organizations in 1992. This Union works towards the complete economic and partial political unification of all European nations. Currently, member nations are in Western Europe. However, Eastern European nations are being considered for membership. Many of these member nations have agreed to form a united currency, the euro, which is already in use electronically and will be printed in 2002. Member nations also work to resolve political differences and reduce immigration restrictions between member states.
- **North American Free Trade Agreement** (NAFTA, 1994) - This is a pact between the United States, Canada, and Mexico which calls for the complete elimination of all tariffs between the three nations within 15 years. This agreement is designed to form the second largest economic block in the world.
- **Organization of Petroleum Exporting Countries** (OPEC, 1960) - This organization of oil-producing countries sets quotas to determine how much oil should be produced per member country. This organization wields enormous influence because it literally sets the price for oil, gasoline, and other products essential in transportation and manufacturing. OPEC members agreed to raise oil prices dramatically in the 1970s by cutting production. This event led to shortages in the United States and Western Europe.
- **Association of Southeast Asian Nations** (ASEAN, 1967) - This organization of Southeast Asian nations was first organized as a military alliance to prevent the spread of communism. However, in 1992, ASEAN member nations agreed to create a free trade area and to cut tariffs on non-agricultural goods over a fifteen year period.
- **Organization of American States** (OAS, 1948) - An organization composed of the nations of North America, South America, and the Caribbean which is dedicated to fostering democratic political institutions, as well as promoting trade between member nations and cooperation in eliminating illegal drug trafficking between member nations.

DEPLETION OF NATURAL RESOURCES AND ENERGY SUPPLIES

In modern times, industrialized nations are becoming increasingly dependent on fossil fuels to power society. Nations in the Middle East, Nigeria, Venezuela, and the North Sea area control access to vast reserves of petroleum. The United States, Western Europe, and East Asia are increasingly dependent on these oil-producing nations to meet their energy needs. While the

United States has produced more fuel efficient vehicles and machinery, there are more vehicles on the road, offsetting this increased efficiency. The world oil supply continues to grow as more fields are discovered, and this is a large problem for two reasons:

1) The first world nations are increasingly dependent on oil-producing nations to supply them with oil-based products such as gasoline. If OPEC agrees to lower or suspend oil shipments, the economies of industrialized nations could be crippled.
2) Because fossil fuels release harmful chemicals into the air, the continued use of these fuels contributes to unhealthy conditions around the world associated with global warming and acid rain.

Another global problem is the depletion of natural resources, such as timber and **old growth forests** (forests that have not been cut down and replanted). In Indonesia, Malaysia, and Brazil, multinational corporations are destroying forests that support a wide variety of plant and animal life in order to make paper or to clear land for commercial farming. The loss of these forests contributes to the loss of wildlife habitat, **erosion** (soil loss), and destruction of more than 50 percent of the world's renewable oxygen supply. Efforts in the conservation movement have focused on purchasing land in endangered areas or promoting select cutting of timber in which a portion of the old growth trees remain while new ones are planted in the surrounding area.

TERRORISM WORLDWIDE

During the second half of the twentieth century, acts of terrorism have greatly increased, driven by both nationalism and ideological reasons. Terrorist acts have been made easier to commit with the use of advances in telecommunications and microprocessors. These developments allow terrorists to coordinate their activities in an instant and to deliver explosives in small, concealed containers. After the creation of Israel following World War II, terrorism in the Middle East rose up against this 1948 creation of a Jewish nation in an Arab region. During the 1970s and 1980s, **PLO (Palestine Liberation Organization)** members took their terrorism to Western European nations who supported the existence of Israel. The members used terrorism to protest the Israeli takeover of their homeland, Palestine (the West Bank). In the United States, Germany, Italy, and Japan, individuals have attacked their own nations' governments because they oppose the increasing power of the national government and corporations. Within the United States, the **Patriot Movement**, a loose alliance of groups calling for resistance to government laws and institutions, has been linked to acts of terrorism, including the Oklahoma City bombing.

Notable Acts of Recent Terrorism

- The 1988 bombing of Pan Am Flight 103 over Lockerbie, Scotland killed 259 people on the plane and 11 persons on the ground. Libyan terrorists, angry over the United States' support of Israel, were responsible for this incident.
- The 1993 bombing of the World Trade Center in New York City killed 6 people and caused over 600 million dollars in property and financial damage. Middle Eastern terrorists were responsible for this act.
- The worst act of terrorism in the history of the United States was committed on April 19, 1995. Timothy McVeigh, a former soldier, executed the bombing of the Federal Building in Oklahoma City. In all, 168 people died in this attack, and the blast injured 850 others. McVeigh received the death penalty for his crime. He planned this attack to protest the increasing power of the federal government in the lives of people.

HUMAN RIGHTS ABUSES

An area which is receiving increased international scrutiny is human rights. The **United Nations (UN)** charter, signed by all member nations in 1945, prohibits the abuse of human rights, particularly in relation to race, sex, language, or religion. Since that time, however, each nation has adopted its own policy on this subject. The governments of China, Libya, Iraq, and the former Soviet Union, to name a few, have systematically denied the human rights of political, ethnic, and/or religious minorities in their nations through false imprisonment, forced reeducation, torture, expulsion, and murder. Iraq, for example, promoted the wholesale killing of an ethnic minority, the Kurds, in northern Iraq using chemical weapons. The United States is not immune from these abuses, either. The National Guard of Ohio fired on citizens of the United States during anti-war protests at Kent State University on May 4, 1970, killing four students. Since 1946, the United States government has also supported harsh military control in Latin America through the training of forces at the **School of the Americas (SOA)**, located at Fort Benning, GA since 1984. Graduates of this school have been linked to wholesale murders of different populations in Guatemala, El Salvador, and Chile. In one case, the United Nations Truth Commission, in a 1993 session, indicted 35 former graduates of the SOA for the high profile murders of religious and political leaders in El Salvador during the years 1980-1991.

Regrettably, the UN has no power to enforce its laws within member nations such as the United States. Nevertheless, the UN does increase awareness of human rights abuses and will often attempt to exert international pressures to create change within a nation. For example, the UN condemned the **apartheid** (systematic segregation of the races in South Africa; the white minority was the only group allowed in power) government of South Africa. The international community responded by imposing **sanctions** (agreements to conduct no trade with a particular offending nation). This international pressure led to the accelerated pace of true democracy in South Africa and the ending of apartheid. Another organization instrumental in increasing awareness of human rights groups is **Amnesty International**. This group works to end the imprisonment of political dissidents as well as the abolishment of the inhumane treatment of prisoners through torture and/or cruel, degrading living conditions. Amnesty International has intervened on behalf of about 30,000 prisoners in over 100 countries.

WORLD HUNGER

During the last decades of the twentieth century, world food production soared far faster than the population increased. At the beginning of the 21st century, the food supply surpassed the needs of the population. The credit can be given to advanced agricultural practices, such as the use of **herbicides** (weed killers), **pesticides** (insect killers), and **fungicides** (plant disease killers). In addition, the increasing use of **irrigation** (diverting water sources to farmland) and genetically engineered crops have helped to increase crop yields. This movement, beginning in the 1960s in the Third World, has been called the **Green Revolution**. However, the main obstacle to eliminating world hunger is the distribution of this food. Because some nations have poorer soils, they cannot produce the crop yields necessary to sustain their population. At the same time, many of these nations, for example, Sudan, suffer from few roads. As a result, the food grown in one region cannot reach certain populations in other regions. Another obstacle is the distribution of wealth. Many people living in these poor nations with poor agricultural resources cannot afford to purchase the food they need. The distribution of the world's food supply is uneven, which sometimes leads to world hunger.

POPULATION GROWTH

The world's population is currently above 6 billion and is continuing to grow. By 2025, the world population is expected to increase to between 7.9 and 9.1 billion inhabitants. A growing world population places additional stresses on the world's resources. However, population growth is not even. Many industrialized nations of the world are at zero or negative growth levels, while developing nations have populations that grow rapidly. Africa, for example, is expected to double its population in 35 years. This growth is attributed to higher rates of live births, lower infant and childhood mortality, and higher life expectancies. Most of these advances are caused by medical developments. These growing populations in Third World nations make the problems facing people with limited resources even more stressed. However, it is the abuse of the world's resources that cause even larger problems. The average person in the United States uses 100 times the resources of the average person in Bangladesh, for example. These disparities and their impact on the environment are the actual problems the world will face in the coming years. Due to the promoting of methods of contraception in the developing world, world population growth is expected to slow considerably around the world during the 21st century.

WORLD DISEASE

Many developments have changed the course of world events in the field of disease. After World War II, doctors began prescribing bacteria-killing **antibiotics** such as penicillin to combat many diseases such as strep throat, staph infections, and meningitis. In addition, vaccinations have virtually wiped out dangerous viruses such as polio and smallpox. A new concern at the turn of the twenty-first century is the emergence of bacteria which are resistant to all antibiotics. These new bacteria could potentially cause a public health crisis, easily passed from one person to another, killing thousands without any medical treatment which could combat the disease. A further concern has been the continuing spread of sexually transmitted diseases, particularly **HIV (Human Immunodeficiency Virus)**, which causes **Acquired Immune Deficiency Syndrome (AIDS)**. HIV destroys an individual's immune system, allowing him or her to be susceptible to any disease. After a certain number of years, the disease is lethal. Because no vaccine has been developed, it is likely that this virus will continue spreading. This virus is spread principally through intravenous drug use, blood transfusions, homosexual activity, and promiscuous heterosexual activity. This virus, while lethal, can go unnoticed for years within a person because there are no immediate symptoms. The spread of the virus has been greatest in the countries of sub-Saharan Africa, the point of origin for the virus. Efforts in eradication have focused on educating people on how the virus is spread. These efforts have lessened the rate of the spread of this disease in the countries which have implemented educational programs. The **Centers for Disease Control and Prevention (CDC)**, in Atlanta, Georgia, monitors the spread of diseases such as AIDS and develops methods for their control and prevention.

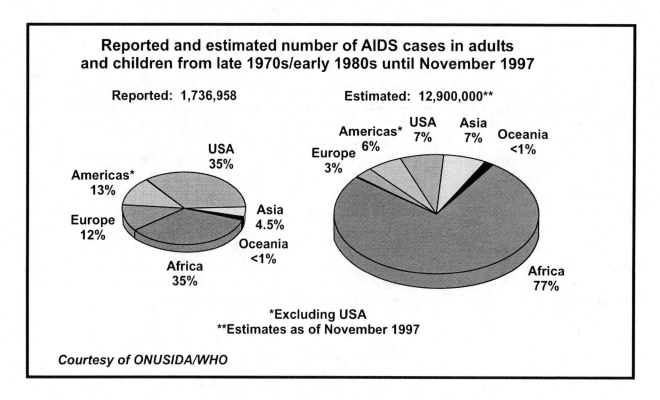

Reported and estimated number of AIDS cases in adults and children from late 1970s/early 1980s until November 1997

Reported: 1,736,958

USA
35%

Americas*
13%

Europe
12%

Asia
4.5%

Oceania
<1%

Africa
35%

Estimated: 12,900,000**

Americas*
6%

USA
7%

Asia
7%

Oceania
<1%

Europe
3%

Africa
77%

*Excluding USA
**Estimates as of November 1997

Courtesy of ONUSIDA/WHO

CHAPTER 16 REVIEW

A. **Define the following names, terms, and events:**

environmentalism	WTO	School of the Americas
Greenpeace	EU	apartheid
Sierra Club	NAFTA	sanctions
Earth Day	OPEC	Amnesty International
INF Treaty	ASEAN	Green Revolution
Apollo 11	OAS	antibiotics
Star Wars	old growth forests	HIV
Hubble Space Telescope	PLO	CDC
Internet	Patriot Movement	

B. **On your own paper, write your response to each of the following:**

1. Evaluate the impact of the environmentalist movement on the United States.
2. How are nations dealing with growing environmental problems?
3. Why is the spread of nuclear and biological weapons to other nations alarming?
4. Why have space missions become important in recent years?
5. What two main attacks are international trade organizations experiencing from some members of the public?
6. What two problems are associated with the continued use of oil as the preferred energy source?
7. How have advances in technology made the work of terrorists easier?
8. Explain why the UN is limited in its ability to punish nations violating human rights.
9. Describe the method of international pressure which helped end the undemocratic government in South Africa.

10. What is the main obstacle today to the elimination of world hunger?
11. What methods have helped make farmland more productive in the Third World during the last forty years?
12. What advances have helped increase the population growth rate in the developing world?
13. What other problem besides population growth is adversely affecting natural resources?
14. Why are disease-producing bacteria again becoming a problem at the beginning of the 21st century?
15. What method has been effective in limiting the spread of the Human Immunodeficiency Virus?

C. Write True if the statement is correct and False if the statement is incorrect. Be prepared to state a reason for your false answers.

1. _____ Middle Eastern terrorists are the main problem facing nations today.

2. _____ The UN charter prohibits the abuse of human rights by member nations.

3. _____ One of the world's environmental problems has been the increase in old-growth forests.

4. _____ ASEAN is a communist organization of member states in Southeast Asia.

5. _____ The Iraqi government used chemical weapons on the Kurdish minority in Northern Iraq.

6. _____ The Star Wars defense plan proved to be a great seller at the ticket booth.

7. _____ Graduates of the School of the Americas have been linked to murders in Latin America.

8. _____ NAFTA will eliminate trade barriers between Canada, the United States, and Mexico.

9. _____ The nations of China, India, and Pakistan now possess nuclear weapons.

10. _____ HIV can be spread through the air, mosquito bites, and touching the hand of an infected person.

CHAPTER 17
CIVICS AND CITIZENSHIP

HISTORIC FOUNDATIONS OF AMERICAN GOVERNMENT

Here are some of the main influences on the development of government in the United States:

1. The English people had already fought and won some rights from their kings: **Magna Carta** (1215) and **English Bill of Rights** (1689). The English settlers coming to America brought these ideas about representative government and **civil liberties** (individual freedom) with them.
2. The challenging life on the frontier taught the colonists the values of independence and self-reliance.
3. Many colonists were running from religious and political persecution. Puritans settled in Massachusetts, and Catholics settled in Maryland.
4. European philosophers **John Locke** (England) and **Jacques Rousseau** (France) influenced American thought. They believed that all people had certain rights and liberties and that a ruler must satisfy the will of the people.
5. Great Britain's **colonial policy** of heavy taxation on sugar, tea, and paper, to support its empire, helped shape our revolution and ultimate freedom.
6. The **social contract theory** of Rousseau expressed the idea that there should be an agreement between the people and the government that limits the rights and duties of each.
7. The formation of American government was greatly influenced by the writings of Thomas Jefferson who wrote the **Declaration of Independence** (1776). Jefferson, James Madison, Alexander Hamilton, John Adams, and Benjamin Franklin contributed their ideas to the **Constitution** (1787).
8. In *The Spirit of Laws* (1748), the French philosopher, Montesquieu, proposed three branches of government: the legislative, the judicial, and the executive.

THE SYSTEM OF GOVERNMENT

As the new nation's leaders met in 1787 to write the Constitution, they agreed to establish a **democratic republic**, meaning that the people as a whole exercise important controls over their elected leaders through elections, lobbying, and other processes. The leaders are expected to represent the interests of the people who elected them. If the voters believe that their interests have not been represented well enough, they may decide not to reelect the leaders. In this way, the voters in a democratic republic have some control over their government. This system is different from **popular sovereignty**, which allows the people to vote on the laws directly through a referendum. The United States government is federal in nature, with power shared between the national government, the states, and local jurisdictions. However, Article VI of the Constitution states that if there is a conflict between the state and national governments, the national government is "the supreme law of the land."

The Constitution spreads the power between the national governments and state governments. (Local governments are set up by the states.) The Constitution gives some powers to the national government, lets some powers stay with the state governments, and lets both share some powers. This practice of dividing power is called **federalism**.

Federalism keeps any one of the governments from gaining too much control. This system allows the people to have some power over the government at the state or local level.

Constitutionalism refers to a government in which power is divided among various groups, but all groups obey a system of laws called a **Constitution**.

Separation of Powers - The Three Branches of Government

The United States has three branches of government: the **executive**, the **legislative**, and the **judicial**. The Constitution divides the powers among these three branches, so one group will not have too much power. For example, the Congress can declare war, but the President directs the soldiers. The **War Powers Act** is a law that controls the war powers of the branches.

STRUCTURE AND FUNCTION OF GOVERNMENT

The writers of the Constitution made a separate branch of government for each function or purpose of national government.

THE THREE BRANCHES OF THE FEDERAL GOVERNMENT

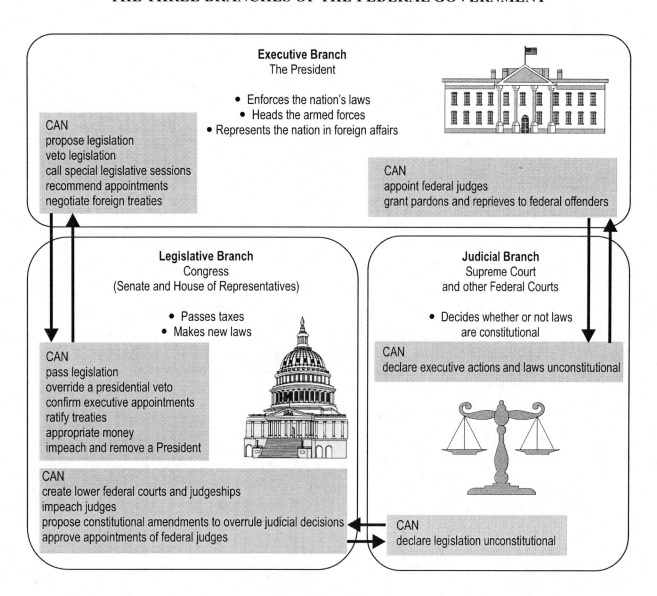

The writers of the Constitution knew that the limits of the powers and responsibilities of each branch were not always clear. To keep the branches equal in power, the writers developed a system of **checks and balances**. These checks and balances include the following elements:

- The President can choose his own Cabinet members and ambassadors, but the Senate must give advice and can approve or reject the choice (by majority vote).
- The Congress can pass laws, but the President can **veto** them.
- The President can make treaties with other countries, but the Senate must give advice and can approve or reject these treaties (by majority vote).
- The Congress can pass laws, and the President can sign them, but the Supreme Court can say they are unconstitutional.

This system of checks and balances and separation slows the process of making decisions and taking action. This can be good because it gives citizens time to learn about the issues and to give their opinions. It also gives the government time to think about the effects of any new law.

THE CONSTITUTION

The Constitution includes a **Preamble**, or introduction, followed by **Articles** that describe how the federal government will function.

- The **Preamble** states the purpose of establishing a new government under the Constitution. The Preamble does not establish any law.

- **Article 1** establishes the **Legislative Branch,** the branch of the federal government which makes the laws. This branch consists of a two-house Congress. The two houses are the **Senate** and the **House of Representatives**. Section 8, Clause 18 of Article 1 is known as the **Elastic Clause**. The Elastic Clause gives Congress the power to pass legislation that is "necessary and proper" for doing its job. It allows Congress to stretch the meaning of its delegated powers outlined in Section 8, Clauses 1-17.

- **Article 2** outlines the **Executive Branch**. It gives executive power to the **President of the United States** who is responsible for enforcing the laws passed by Congress.

- **Article 3** explains the **Judicial Branch**. The judicial branch of the federal government is the federal court system. The Constitution establishes the **Supreme Court** which is responsible for interpreting the laws made by Congress.

- **Article 4** gives the **Relations Among the States and Between States and Federal Government**. It ensures that each state recognizes the acts of other states. For example, a state must recognize a marriage license issued by another state.

- **Article 5** provides for **amendments** to the Constitution.

- **Article 6** covers other miscellaneous provisions like prior public debts, supreme law of the land, and oaths to support the Constitution.

- **Article 7** explains **ratification** of the Constitution. Ratification of 9 out of the original 13 states would establish the Constitution as law in those states.

POLITICAL PARTIES

A **political party** is a group of people who seek to dominate or control a government. The party selects candidates to run for public office and finances their campaigns.

Growth of Political Parties

Early political leaders like Washington opposed political parties. However, people with similar political, social, or economic interests soon formed political organizations. The **Federalists** under Alexander Hamilton wanted a strong central government. The **Democratic-Republicans** led by Thomas Jefferson believed in less central government and more power for the people.

In 1828, the current **Democratic Party** was formed. Like the Federalists, **Democrats** believe in a strong central government. They also support the rights of the poor and minorities and heavier taxes for the wealthy.

In 1854, the current **Republican Party** was formed. Like the Democratic-Republicans, **Republicans** believe in a smaller central government, more state and local control, and less taxation for the wealthy and businesses.

Reasons for a Two-Party System in the United States

- Offers two or more viewpoints on an issue
- Allows citizens to challenge how their government functions
- Allows political power to pass from one group to another without violence

---

THE LEGISLATIVE BRANCH

The primary responsibility of the **legislative branch** is to make and pass laws. However, the legislature carries out other important laws including the ability to **impeach** (charge with official misconduct) federal officials, including the president, as well as to decide how and where the federal money will be spent. Congress also confirms federal appointments to the Supreme Court and can propose constitutional amendments.

Article One of the Constitution explains the **expressed powers** of Congress, such as imposing taxes, borrowing money, regulating international and interstate commerce, establishing post offices, maintaining a military, and declaring war. Article One also states that Congress has the right to make laws deemed "necessary and proper." These laws are called **implied powers**. This section of Article One is also called the **elastic clause**. The broader the implied powers of Congress, the greater the amount of control Congress and the federal government have. For example, Congress approved the creation of a **national bank** - an institution not specifically named in the Constitution.

Congress is divided into two houses: the lower house, the **House of Representatives**, and the upper house, the **Senate**. Members of the House of Representatives are elected by members of their district. Each state is allotted a certain number of district representatives based on population. Thus, the House of Representatives reflects the population of the United States. In the Senate, each state is allowed to send only two representatives, so each state, regardless of size, has equal weight. A bill must pass both the House and the Senate to become law.

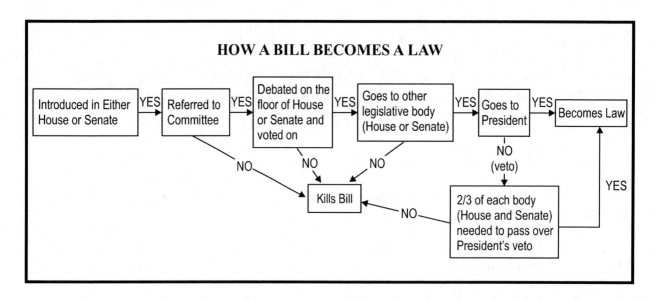

HOW A BILL BECOMES A LAW

Congressional Committees, which are groups of congresspersons, focus on a specific subject and decide whether or not a bill should be voted on in Congress.

Today, there are many groups that focus on a certain political issue. These groups are called **special interest groups**. These groups voice their view and attempt to influence members of Congress on a particular issue. These groups often receive more attention and support from their representatives because these special interest groups help to fund the election and reelection campaigns of members of Congress.

Congress has the power to pass laws with a majority vote. However, to protect the rights of individuals, the Constitution also provides a list of ten amendments, known as the **Bill of Rights** (1791), to protect such fundamental individual rights as rights of assembly, freedom of speech, and freedom of religion. This Bill of Rights also protects individuals who may be in the minority in the United States.

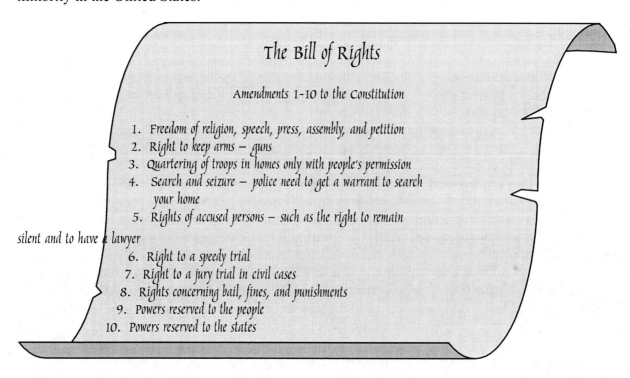

The Bill of Rights

Amendments 1-10 to the Constitution

1. Freedom of religion, speech, press, assembly, and petition
2. Right to keep arms – guns
3. Quartering of troops in homes only with people's permission
4. Search and seizure – police need to get a warrant to search your home
5. Rights of accused persons – such as the right to remain silent and to have a lawyer
6. Right to a speedy trial
7. Right to a jury trial in civil cases
8. Rights concerning bail, fines, and punishments
9. Powers reserved to the people
10. Powers reserved to the states

LIMITS ON GOVERNMENT

The government cannot tell Americans what to think, what to say, what to write, or what to read. It also cannot tell us which job we must take. **Immigrants** come to the United States because they want the personal freedom, economic freedom, and religious freedom guaranteed by our Constitution. They appreciate the limits on government power in the United States.

We do not live alone in this country. We live with other people. Because we live in society, the individual does not have unlimited rights. If we use a right to do some action, and that action hurts another person, then we cannot practice that right. For example, if we belong to a religion that practices human sacrifice, we cannot say that **Freedom of Religion** gives us the right to kill another person. But, if we cannot say the Pledge of Allegiance because of our religion, we are protected by the Constitution. **Freedom of Speech** does not give us the right to say or write anything we want about our neighbor. If we hurt another person with lies, we can have a problem with the law.

In conclusion, the Constitution protects the individual person and society. It balances personal liberty with the needs of the nation. The individual cannot always do whatever he or she wants, if the action conflicts with the rights of another person. Just as the Constitution limits powers of branches of government, it also limits the government's power over individuals.

EXECUTIVE BRANCH

The president plays a powerful role as chief of the **executive branch**. To prevent the military from running the nation instead of the people, the Constitution clearly states that the elected civilian president holds the highest office in the military – **commander-in-chief**. In addition, the president has power over the legislature allowing the veto of any bill placed before him or her. The executive also has power over the judicial branch because the president appoints nominees to the Supreme Court, the final authority in the judicial branch.

As a law enforcer, the president can decide whether or not to enforce the law. In one important example, President Andrew Jackson went against the ruling of the Supreme Court preserving the land rights of the Cherokee Nation. Instead, he defied the order and undermined the power of the judiciary.

In addition to the presidency, the executive branch of government includes the administrative directors of the executive departments of the federal government. These directors form the **presidential cabinet**. They are appointed by the president and must be confirmed by Congress. Below is a list of the current presidential cabinet departments:

Secretary of State	Secretary of Veterans Affairs
Attorney General	Secretary of Defense
Secretary of Labor	Secretary of Housing and Urban Development
Secretary of Energy	Secretary of the Interior
Secretary of Agriculture	Secretary of Commerce
Secretary of Education	Secretary of Health and Human Resources

These officers serve as long as the president is in power unless they are impeached or resign. Cabinet members do not have any executive authority by themselves. They serve as trusted advisors to the president in their fields of expertise.

FOUNDATION OF AMERICAN JUDICIAL / LEGAL SYSTEM

Purposes of American Judicial/Legal System

- Resolve conflicts
- Protect individual rights
- Control crime

The Rule of Law

Laws are rules that guide our actions in society. The Constitution is the supreme law of the country. All other laws must agree with the Constitution. The **rule of law** means that everyone, even the President, must follow the Constitution. The early colonists borrowed this idea from English common law.

Due Process

The principle of **due process** protects citizens from the government. How does it do this? **Due process** means that the government must follow accepted rules and procedures when acting against a person. For example, all people have the right to a fair hearing in court before the government may take away their rights, freedom, or property. The **5th** and **14th Amendments** guarantee that the government cannot take someone's life, liberty, or property without the **due process** of law.

Before a Trial:
- The **5th Amendment** says: An accused person does not have to say anything when the police or the judge ask him or her questions.
- The **6th Amendment** says: When a person is arrested, he or she has the right to have a lawyer immediately.
- The **8th Amendment** says: A judge cannot make a person pay an unfair bail.

During a Trial:
- The accused person is innocent until proven, in court, that he or she is guilty.
- Everyone has the right to a speedy and public trial by jury.
- Everyone can have a witness on his/her side.
- The accused person's lawyer can question all witnesses.

After a Trial:
- The **Bill of Rights** protects people who are found guilty of a crime.
- A judge or jury cannot make you pay an unfair fine nor give you an unfair punishment.
- In some states, it is legal to punish people for certain crimes by death.

THE JUDICIARY BRANCH

The **judiciary branch** of the United States government is a federal court system divided into two branches: the **federal** and the **state** branches. The federal courts have **jurisdiction** (the authority to settle cases) over federal crimes and interstate disputes. The state courts have jurisdiction over crimes against the state laws. The vast majority of criminal accusations and legal disputes are settled in state courts. Each state organizes its courts differently. However, most try to model their system after the federal process.

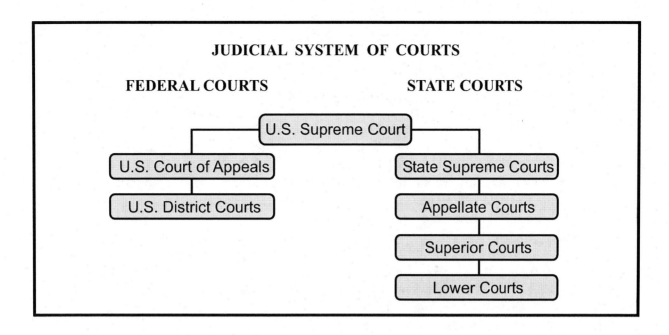

JUDICIAL SYSTEM OF COURTS

FEDERAL COURTS   **STATE COURTS**

U.S. Supreme Court

U.S. Court of Appeals   State Supreme Courts

U.S. District Courts   Appellate Courts

Superior Courts

Lower Courts

As the highest court in the United States, the **Supreme Court** follows a special procedure in deciding which of the cases to hear. The Supreme Court is the final appeal for cases in the federal courts. The **Solicitor General** acts as the advocate for the government's position in cases involving the federal government in the Supreme Court. This position is the third highest in the Department of Justice. In addition, the Supreme Court can rule over matters that have not been placed under any other state or federal court. For example, the Supreme Court can hear cases of disputes between states as well as disputes concerning foreign officials in the United States, such as ambassadors.

The Supreme Court, however, exercises its most powerful right in the form of **judicial review**. This right, established by the Supreme Court in the case *Marbury vs. Madison* (1803), gives the Supreme Court the power to declare laws passed by Congress and by other states as unconstitutional. For example, in the 1954 case *Brown vs. Board of Education* racial segregation was declared unconstitutional. These types of rulings have a profound impact on the society and laws of the United States.

Cases that are presented before the Supreme Court are tried at the court's discretion. Thousands of cases are petitioned to be heard before the Supreme Court in a given year, yet the court will usually only hear about 125 of those cases. These cases must satisfy the following criteria:

1) The case must fall within the court's jurisdiction.
2) The case must be **justiciable**, meaning it raises questions appropriate for the court to answer.
3) The case must pass a **ripeness test**, meaning it presents an actual or substantial threat to individual rights.
4) The case must meet the **mootness standard**, meaning it presents a current problem that needs to be solved.
5) The party bringing the case must have **standing**, or vested interest, in the issues raised in the case.
6) The issue cannot be military or political in nature.

CITIZENSHIP

A **citizen** is defined as a person who is a member of a particular nation. Citizens enjoy both the rights and responsibilities associated with that citizenship. For example, citizens enjoy the right to vote and run for office in United States elections. Under the Fourteenth Amendment, citizens also possess the rights of due process under the law. However, **legal residents** of the United States cannot participate in the political process and do not enjoy full legal protections.

A person can become a United States citizen in two ways: 1) By birth; 2) By naturalization. A citizen by birth is any person born to parents who are already citizens. A person born to non-citizens who are legally in the United States is also a citizen. These two circumstances are called the **rule of birth** and **rule of soil**, respectively.

A **resident immigrant** can also become a citizen through naturalization. First, a resident must submit a statement of intent indicating that he or she wishes to initiate the citizenship process. After living in the United States for five years, passing a citizenship test, and taking the oath of allegiance, a resident can become a citizen of the United States. Children under the age of eighteen from resident immigrant households also become citizens when their parents complete the naturalization process.

EQUALITY OF OPPORTUNITY VERSUS EQUALITY OF WEALTH

The preamble of the Constitution states that the rights of "life, liberty, and the pursuit of happiness" should be available to anyone. The pursuit of happiness clause implies equal opportunity to pursue material gain. However, the wealth in this nation is not evenly distributed. For over one hundred and fifty years since the country's founding, minority groups such as Native Americans, blacks, and women, have been systematically denied equal economic opportunity through slavery, confinement to reservations, Jim Crow Laws, segregation, and denial of the right to vote. Even for those that have historically enjoyed equal access to wealth, not all have chosen to take advantage of the opportunity, leading a simple life – which is a freedom too.

CHAPTER 17 REVIEW

A. **Define the following names, terms, and events:**

Magna Carta	legislative	amendment	solicitor general
federalism	judicial	electoral college	rule of birth
constitutionalism	implied powers	veto	rule of soil
democratic republic	expressed powers	cabinet	
popular sovereignty	House of Representatives	jurisdiction	
executive	Senate	judicial review	

B. **On your own paper, write your response to each of the following:**

1. Describe the social contract theory.
2. Name the basic beliefs of a democratic republic as it is practiced in the United States.
3. What is federalism? What is constitutionalism?

4. How many branches are there in the United States government?
5. Explain the function of each branch of our government. Explain checks and balances.
6. Give two reasons why there is a two-party system in the United States.
7. What is one power the Legislative Branch has over the Supreme Court?
8. What is one example of Congress's use of the implied powers (elastic clause) in the chapter?
9. What is the purpose of Congressional committees?
10. How does the Constitution protect the individual? How does it protect society?
11. Name five rights or freedoms granted by the Bill of Rights.
12. How does the Constitution insure that civilians control the military?
13. Name four positions in the presidential cabinet.
14. What protections does a person have during the judicial process?
15. What is the role of the Solicitor General?
16. What six requirements must a case pass before it will be heard before the Supreme Court?
17. List two ways to become a citizen of the United States.
18. Name two privileges citizens of the United States have that are not available to residents of the United States.

C. Write True if the statement is correct and False if the statement is incorrect. Be prepared to state a reason for your false answers.

1. _____ In a clear majority vote, the will of the citizenry is all that is required to impeach a president.

2. _____ The 5th amendment guarantees the right of an accused citizen to remain silent when questioned by the police or any court official.

3. _____ According to Article VI of the Constitution, the state of Georgia has supreme sovereignty over its use of the Chattahoochee River within its borders.

4. _____ There are 100 senators in the Senate at this time, two from each state.

5. _____ The United States' presidents have always upheld the legal rulings of the Supreme Court.

6. _____ The main purpose of the Constitution is to balance the personal liberty of citizens with the freedom of legal aliens.

7. _____ One reason for having a two-party political system is the benefit of two points of view.

8. _____ Special interest groups have grown because of the need for an unbiased government.

9. _____ Voting by all eligible citizens will promote a democratic government.

10. _____ A citizen is a person born and raised in the United States, and all others are immigrants.

CHAPTER 18
WORLD GEOGRAPHY

TYPES OF GEOGRAPHY

Geography is the study of land, bodies of water, climate, and the people living in these environments. **Physical Geography** is the study of how physical characteristics (landforms, climate, and ecosystems) define a region. **Cultural Geography** is the study of cultural characteristics (ethnic origins, language, religion, historical settlements, and political and economic patterns) that may define regions. Geography uses both of these characteristics to accurately define regions of the world.

A **region** is a cultural and geographic area that has common features which are different from the surrounding areas. Based on physical and cultural similarities, geographers divide the world into **ten regions: North America, Central and South America, Europe, Central Eurasia, Middle East, North Africa, Sub-Saharan Africa, South Asia, East Asia**, and **Australasia**. These regions are basic units of study for geographers. However, regions can also be used to designate smaller portions of a continent or nation. For example, the region of the north Georgia mountains is different from that of the south Georgia plains.

REGIONS AND THEIR FEATURES

- **Region** - an area of land that shares a common feature different from the surrounding area: For example, **mountains** are in **north Georgia**, but they are different from the **rolling hills of the Piedmont region** or the **plains of south Georgia.**

- **Physical features** - parts of the land made by nature: These natural features include **landforms, rocks, soil, water, plants, animals, climate, and weather.**

- **Cultural features** - objects made or changed by human beings: Examples of these features include **farms, cities, canals, dams, and roads.**

North America

North America composes one region. This region is united by being part of one continuous mass of land, mostly surrounded by water. It is made up of Canada, the United States, and Mexico. These nations share important physical features such as coastlines and the Rocky Mountain chain. In addition, the region was colonized by Europeans, and the majority of the population shares certain Christian beliefs and holidays such as Christmas and Easter.

Central America and South America

Central America and South America compose another region. This region is united by being part of one continuous mass of land, the majority of it being south of the equator. Most of the people are Catholic and speak a Latin-based language, usually either Spanish or Portuguese.

216

Europe

Europe is united by being located in the western section of the Eurasian continent. The region shares important physical features including a mountain chain, the Alps, a temperate climate, and excellent access to freshwater. The majority of Europeans also share certain Christian beliefs and holidays as in North America. In addition, the region is united by a shared history of unity in both the Roman Empire and, later, the Catholic Church and the Latin language.

Central Eurasia

Central Eurasia, located in Central Asia and Eastern Europe, is united by being part of one continuous land mass. However, this region has little access to the sea. The region is isolated because it has few accessible sea ports and few features which provide defense, such as mountain chains. The people of this region are united in their understanding of their isolation and also that they can be easily conquered by other nations because of their lack of geographic defenses. This region was overrun at different times by the Muslims, the Mongols, the Tartars, the French, the Germans, and the Russians.

Middle East

The Middle East is united by several important features. This region has access to sea water, but the majority of the land is desert. The people of this region have had to adapt to conditions of scarce water. Irrigation is extensively used to produce crops in this region. The Middle East is also rich in one important resource, oil. In addition, the majority of the people here follow a religion called Islam and worship one God, Allah. This religion also defines the law in many parts of the Middle East. The region is united though the Arabic language, and the people share common beliefs and customs.

North Africa

North Africa is similar to the Middle East in many ways. North Africa is rich in oil and enjoys abundant coastline. Most of the land is desert and requires irrigation to produce crops. Most of the people speak Arabic and follow the Islamic religion. However, North Africa is separated from the Middle East by being part of the African continent.

Sub-Saharan Africa

Africa south of the Sahara is a separate region from the rest of the continent because the region has a climate with abundant rainfall. The area enjoys fertile land and abundant coastline. The region is culturally diverse, reflecting the influence of indigenous, Arab, and European cultures. The people of this region tend to speak either native or European languages. The majority of the people either follow tribal beliefs, Christianity, or a mixture of both.

South Asia

South Asia, comprised of the Indian subcontinent and Southeast Asia, is noted for remarkable rainfall. The annual heavy rainfall is caused by seasonal winds called **monsoons**. Rice is an important crop in this region. This region is also one of the most densely populated in the world. The people of this region speak a variety of languages and practice religions of Eastern origin, such as Hinduism and Buddhism.

East Asia

East Asia, comprising China, Korea, Taiwan, and Japan, is the most populous region in the world. The region is similar geographically in that East Asia has a large amount of coastline. The culture has been influenced the most by Confucian philosophy. While the spoken languages of East Asia are not similar, most East Asians can communicate because, with the exception of Koreans, they share the same character language in which each character stands for a different word.

Australasia

Australasia is a world region which lies south of the equator and north of 47 degrees south latitude in the Pacific Ocean. The area is composed of the Australian continent, plus surrounding islands. Most of the nations in this region share English as a common language and have populations with a Christian majority.

PHYSICAL GEOGRAPHY

Physical geography determines how a region develops in terms of its housing, isolation, food sources, and clothing. Below are a list of **physical features** that are important to a region.

Land Areas

Cape - a piece of land projecting into a body of water.

Continents - largest land masses on earth. The seven continents are **Europe, Asia, Africa, North America, South America, Australia,** and **Antarctica.**

Islands - land areas smaller than continents and surrounded by water. Examples: **Cuba, Taiwan, Ireland, Hilton Head Island**

Archipelago - chain of islands. Example: **Hawaiian Islands, Aleutian Islands**

Peninsula - piece of land surrounded on three sides by water. Examples: **Florida, Italy**

Isthmus - narrow strip of land joining two larger land areas. Example: **Isthmus of Panama**

Landforms

Landforms are measured by their **elevation** (height above sea level).

Mountains - high, rocky land forms. Examples: **Appalachians and Himalayas**

Hills - raised areas of land smaller than mountains. Example: **Piedmont region of Southeastern United States**

Plateaus - high, flat area of land. Example: **Colorado Plateau**

Plains - level or rolling lands lower than mountains, hills, or plateaus. Examples: **Great Plains of North America, savannas of central Africa**

Bodies of Water

Oceans - largest bodies of salt water in the world. The four oceans are the **Atlantic, Pacific, Indian, and Arctic** and cover more than 70 percent of the earth's surface.

Sea - an area of salt water partly surrounded by land. Examples of seas: **Arabian, Bering, Caribbean, Labrador, Mediterranean, Philippine, Red, Sea of Japan, and South China Sea**

Gulf	- an area of an ocean that reaches deep within a land area, such as the **Gulf of Mexico**.
Bay	- a bay is similar to a gulf but smaller. Examples: **Hudson Bay** and **Bay of Bengal**
Strait	- a narrow stretch of water that leads from one body of water to another. Examples: the **Strait of Gibraltar** and the **Strait of Suez**
Lake	- a body of fresh water surrounded by land. Examples are **Lake Superior** in the United States and **Lake Victoria** in Africa.
River	- large natural stream of water that flows into an ocean, lake, or other body of water. Branches of a river are called **tributaries**. Two of the longest rivers in the world are the **Nile** in Africa and the **Amazon** in South America.

WEATHER PATTERNS AND CLIMATE

Dry Climates

Desert	- less than 10 inches of rain per year, wide range of temperature, cactus, few trees
Steppe	- semi-dry, 10-12 inches of rain per year, short grasses
Mediterranean	- hot, dry summers, mild and rainy winters, long growing season

Wet Climates

Tropical rain forest	- rainy and warm all year, heavy vegetation
Tropical savanna	- always hot but with wet and dry seasons, grasses and trees

Humid Climates

Humid subtropical	- mild winters, humid summers, mixed forests
Humid continental	- hot summers, cold winters, located in middle of large land masses
Humid marine	- mild, rainy winters, cool and rainy summers, mixed forests

Cold Climates

Subarctic	- long, cold winters, short summers, **conifer forests** (pine trees)
Tundra	- temperatures below 50° F all year, land is always **permafrost** (frozen), small trees and mosses
Ice Caps	- constant cold, temperatures below freezing, snow all year long

ECOSYSTEMS

An **ecosystem** is the relationship between living and non-living things in a particular environment. Factors that influence an ecosystem include climate, soil, water, plants, and animals.

Forests and grasslands provide the best resources for supporting human, plant, and animal life.

Arctic, mountain, desert, and oceanic ecosystems are less favorable for human and animal life. Climates are harsher, and fewer people live in the environment.

Changes in ecosystems can affect the balance of nature. For example, a hurricane or forest fire can disrupt an ecosystem. Humans who dump harmful chemicals in a river will affect the quality of the water, as well as the plants and fish in the river. **Acid rain**, a product of exhaust, can damage trees and lakes over a large area.

NOTABLE INTERNATIONAL LAND AREAS, LAND FORMS, AND BODIES OF WATER

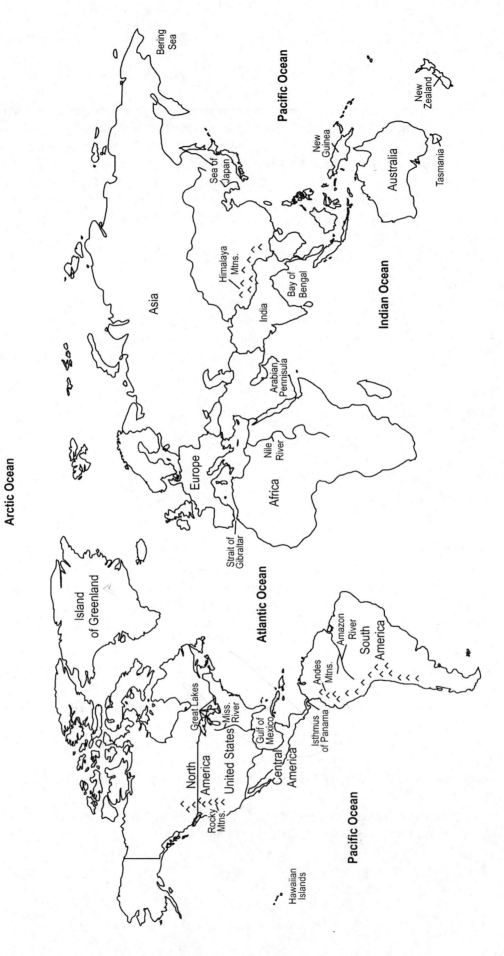

Bering Sea

Pacific Ocean

New Zealand

New Guinea

Australia

Tasmania

Sea of Japan

Himalaya Mtns.

India

Bay of Bengal

Indian Ocean

Asia

Arabian Peninsula

Nile River

Europe

Africa

Arctic Ocean

Island of Greenland

Strait of Gibraltar

Atlantic Ocean

Amazon River

South America

Andes Mtns.

Great Lakes

Miss. River

North America

United States

Gulf of Mexico

Central America

Isthmus of Panama

Rocky Mtns.

Pacific Ocean

Hawaiian Islands

220

CLIMATE MAP OF NORTH AND CENTRAL AMERICA

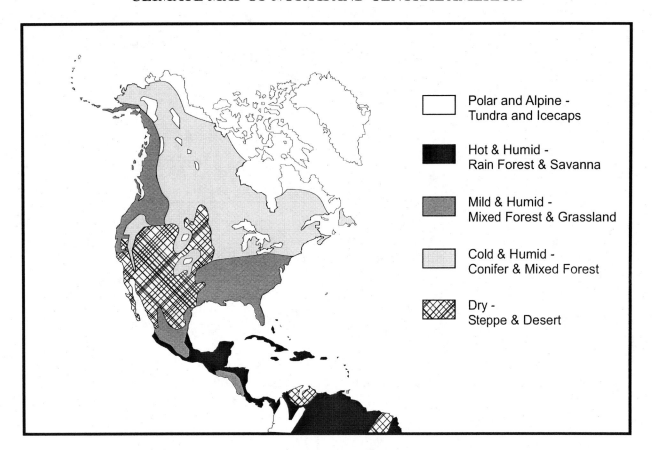

Polar and Alpine - Tundra and Icecaps

Hot & Humid - Rain Forest & Savanna

Mild & Humid - Mixed Forest & Grassland

Cold & Humid - Conifer & Mixed Forest

Dry - Steppe & Desert

EFFECTS OF PHYSICAL GEOGRAPHY ON CULTURE

Physical features affect how the people living in a region adapt to their environment. There are many examples of how physical characteristics of a region affect the human activities in that region. For instance, people living on islands or next to rivers have many of their activities centered on the water. Japan, for example, relies on seafood for its primary protein source because it is an island nation which has little land for agriculture. Britain, another island nation, has historically relied on overseas business as its principal activity because the island is small. In other areas of the world, the people have had to adapt differently. For instance, people living in mountainous regions focus on activities associated with mountainous living. The people of China need more land to feed the people, so farmers have terraced the mountainsides to open more land up for farming. The Incas of South America have lived in the Andes Mountains for centuries. Therefore, their houses and places of worship are made out of the most plentiful material, stone.

Land regions also serve as a way to open or isolate cultures as well. **Land features** such as mountains or islands often serve to isolate cultures from other influences. The people of Tibet, for example, have a very distinct culture because they live on the Himalayan Plateau, near the highest mountain range in the world. The people of India, on the other hand, show considerable cultural diversity because the flat plains and river systems allowed for immigration and invasion by peoples from all over Asia. In addition, their long coastline has helped to promote trade overseas.

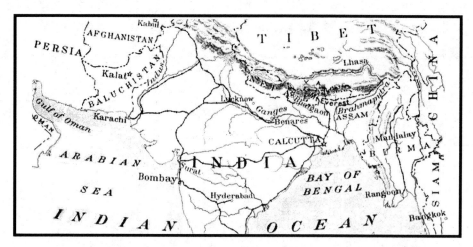

The direction a human settlement takes in its economic development depends on the resources around the settlement. If resources such as water, good soils, and mineral resources are located close to the settlement, the settlement will have all the factors needed for self-sufficiency. However, if a settlement is not in close proximity to these resources, the settlement will have to rely on other areas to supply those needs. The settlements in the North American region, for example, have an abundance of water, farming areas, forest resources, and some mineral sources. However, North America does not meet its needs for one mineral product, crude oil.

Other regions of the world lack many of the resources necessary for human settlement, yet because they possess one vital resource, they have settlements. One of these regions, the nation of Kuwait in the Middle East has a scarcity of water, farming soil, and forests. However, Kuwait possesses an overabundance of crude oil. Kuwait relies on its markets, for example, the United States, to sell its crude oil in order to purchase the food, water, and textiles the desert nation needs as necessities for life.

Another important factor related to self-sufficiency and industrialization is the amount of **infrastructure services** (facilities promoting growth) in the region. Other regions of the world, such as Central Africa, have an abundance of natural and mineral resources. However, the region is not self-sufficient because vital transportation, communication, and power services are not in place. The region has the ability to industrialize, but this lack of infrastructure prevents it from achieving more rapid industrialization.

People, however, are sometimes able to bring natural resources into areas where these resources have never been before. Through the use of both ancient and modern innovations, increasing areas of land have been brought into cultivation or somehow changed to increase business and productivity. For thousands of years, the Egyptians have dug waterways extending out from the Nile River to irrigate their crops. This practice allowed arid land to become land suitable for farming. In the past five hundred years, the small coastal nation of the Netherlands has increased its land size by one third by pumping sea water off of the land and using this new land for agriculture.

Holding a vast array of different resources, the world does not have an even distribution of those resources. In addition, different nations have different degrees of ability in providing for the needs of their citizens. Some nations are more industrialized than others. Nations are grouped as being either **First World (industrialized)** or **Third World (developing) nations**. Nations considered First World have already undergone industrialization and have a large service sector. Third world nations are in the process of industrialization and are generally poorer economically, with the majority of the population focused on subsistence agriculture. However, Third World nations often have large supplies of raw materials, which the First World nations need to produce finished goods.

222

NATURAL RESOURCES AFFECT HOW HUMANS LIVE

Natural resources - include **plants, animals, bodies of water, and mineral resources** like rocks and soils, hills, mountains and plains as well as **weather and climate**. For example, oil, natural gas, and coal are very important sources for fuel. Water and metals are important for manufacturing.

Cultural resources - include things made by people such as **roads, cities, buildings, dams**

Human Activity	Resources Needed
farming	fertile soil, adequate water, moderate climate, fuel, roads
fishing	oceans, lakes, and rivers, forest (for ships), fish, roads
manufacturing	water, fuel, roads, raw materials, machinery, people
services	hospitals, railroads, fuel, people, paper, water

As a result of these conditions, global trade and business have become a necessity. Global links of communication, such as those provided by the Internet, satellites, telephone, and fax machines, have allowed for an almost instantaneous communication of ideas, services, and business transactions. With the development of highways and air transport, rapid advances in transportation have increased the pace of business and extended the amount of international trade worldwide. Coupled with this high degree of international trade is the trade of cultures and ideas. People from different countries come together out of economic necessity in international commerce. This contact with other cultures promotes understanding and a greater sense of how a local decision can be perceived around the world.

FACTORS AFFECTING INTERDEPENDENCE AMONG NATIONS

In today's world, nations are becoming increasingly **interdependent**. Few nations possess all the natural resources that are required to prosper. In addition, their isolated location will require them to exchange goods so they can provide for their people.

For example, Japan is isolated and has few trees and must, therefore, buy lumber and paper products from tree-producing countries. The United States is dependent on Middle Eastern countries for oil. Inland nations are dependent on coastal nations for fish. England must trade with a country in a warmer climate such as India for tea and so on.

The following list includes factors that affect how people live:

Natural Environment - climate, land, and natural resources
Level of Technology - tools and machinery for production of goods
Government - social and political organization of society, customs, and values
Interaction with Other Societies - trade, communication, and transportation
Population Size - fertility rates, health, and family values

CHAPTER 18 REVIEW

A. Define the following names, terms, and events:

physical geography	isthmus	river	land features
cultural geography	plateau	desert	infrastructure services
region	plain	steppe	first world nation
physical feature	ocean	rain forest	third world nation
cultural feature	sea	savanna	natural resources
cape	gulf	continental climate	cultural resources
continent	bay	tundra	interdependence
archipelago	strait	ice caps	
peninsula	lake	ecosystem	

B. Study the map below. Then write the number from the map that matches the following continents, land features, or bodies of water.

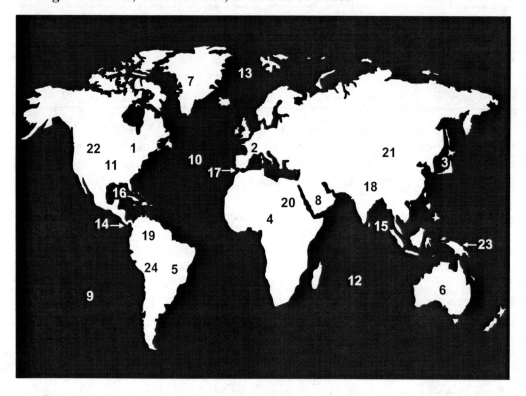

1. _____ Indian Ocean
2. _____ South America
3. _____ Arabian Peninsula
4. _____ Atlantic Ocean
5. _____ Pacific Ocean
6. _____ Bay of Bengal
7. _____ Amazon River
8. _____ Rocky Mountains

9. _____ Gulf of Mexico
10. _____ Isthmus of Panama
11. _____ Island of Greenland
12. _____ Asia
13. _____ Australia
14. _____ Strait of Gibraltar
15. _____ Nile River
16. _____ Sea of Japan

17. _____ Europe
18. _____ Africa
19. _____ North America
20. _____ Arctic Ocean
21. _____ Andes Mountains
22. _____ Himalayan Mountains
23. _____ Mississippi River
24. _____ Island of New Guinea

NAMIBIA

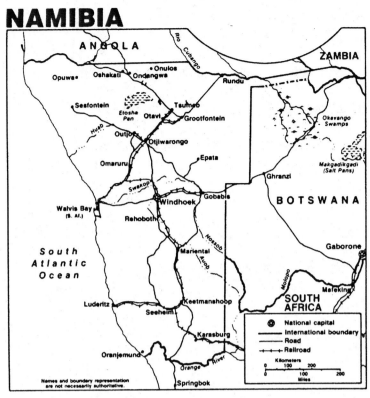

C. Study the large political map of Namibia at the left. Then answer the questions.

1. What is the capital of Namibia?
2. Trace the international boundary of Namibia on the map.
3. Name the four countries that border Namibia.
4. Which river forms the southern border of Namibia?
5. Which two seaport cities have railroads?

NAMIBIA:
Vegetation and Rainfall

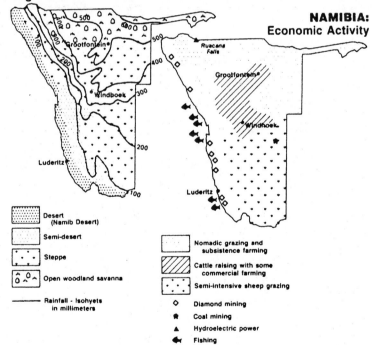

D. Study the smaller vegetation and economic maps of Namibia at the left. Then answer the questions.

1. Trace the part of Namibia that has the most rain.
2. Outline the part of Namibia that has the least amount of vegetation.
3. Circle Namibia's diamond mining areas.
4. Most of Namibia's land is used for three activities. What are they?

E.   **Write True if the statement is correct and False if the statement is incorrect. Be prepared to state a reason for your false answers.**

1. _____   Tropical savannas are rainy and warm all year and have heavy vegetation.

2. _____   One of the world's ten regions is the region of North and South America.

3. _____   The underwater tunnel dug beneath the English Channel, connecting Britain and France, is an example of infrastructure.

4. _____   The physical characteristics of a region affect human activity in that region.

5. _____   The European region is characterized by the Islamic faith.

6. _____   Cultural geography is the study of how physical characteristics define a region.

7. _____   Two of the longest rivers in the world are the Nile and the Amazon.

8. _____   One example of the independence of the United States is that the country supplies its own oil.

9. _____   Landforms are measured by their elevation (height above sea level).

10. _____   Many ancient Hindu documents have been discovered in South Asia, preserved by its dry and hot climate.

11. _____   Because Japan has few trees, it depends on other countries for lumber and paper.

12. _____   Acid rain's greatest impact is on the air we breathe.

13. _____   The main religions of South Asia are Hinduism and Buddism.

14. _____   Because it lacked geographic defenses, Central Eurasia was overrun by Muslims, Tartars, Germans, and other groups during its history.

15. _____   An archipelago is a chain of islands, but a peninsula is a large, mountainous island.

CHAPTER 19
MAP AND GLOBE SKILLS

CARDINAL AND INTERMEDIATE DIRECTIONS

A **map** is a flat drawing of all or part of the earth. A **globe** is a model of the earth shaped like a ball or sphere. North, south, east, and west are called **cardinal directions**. North is usually at the top of a map or globe, south is at the bottom, east is to your right, and west is to your left.

Maps and globes also contain a symbol to help you find directions. This symbol is called a **compass rose** like the one shown on the world map below. A compass rose shows the four cardinal directions. It may also show the **intermediate directions** (in-between directions). These intermediate directions are **northeast (NE), northwest (NW), southeast (SE), and southwest (SW)**.

Now practice finding directions on the world map shown below.

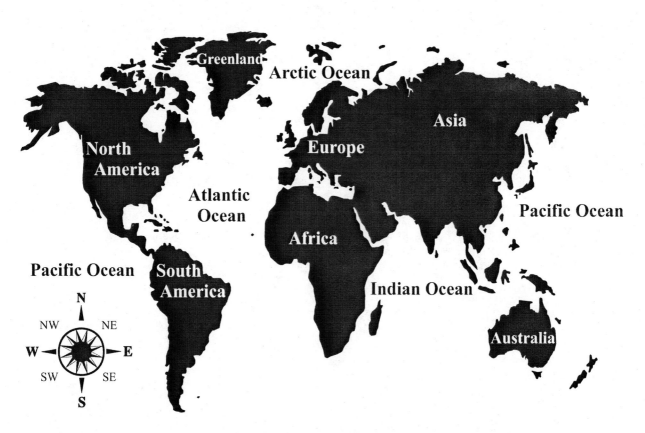

1. Which continent is south of Europe?
2. Which ocean is north of Europe?
3. Which continent is east of Europe?
4. Which continent is west of Europe?
5. What ocean is northwest of Australia?
6. What continent is southeast of Asia?
7. What direction is Africa from South America?
8. What direction is South America from Europe?
9. What island is northeast of North America?
10. Which ocean lies east of Asia?

READING A GRID MAP

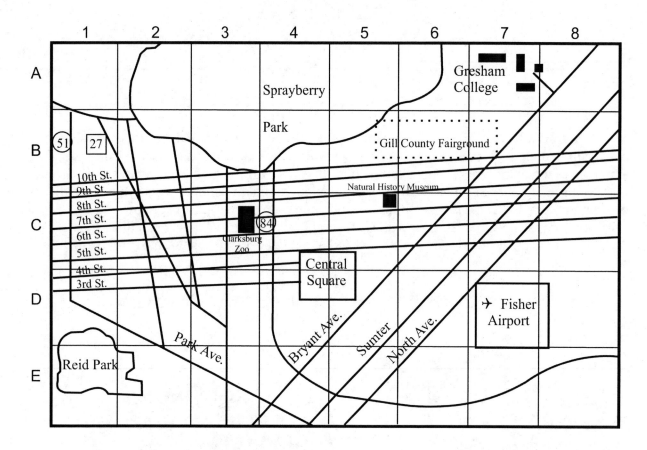

A **grid** is a pattern of lines drawn to make rows and columns on a map. These lines divide the map into squares. Each square can be identified by numbers and letters. The numbers appear on the top of the map, and the letters are located on the left side of the map.

Look at the letters on the side of the map above. The letters identify the rows of squares. The numbers label the columns of squares. If you were asked to locate Reid Park on the map, you would look to see which row and column it is in. Most of Reid Park is at the intersection of row E and column 1. Therefore, the answer is E-1.

Identify the row and column for each of the following places.

1. Gresham College _____

2. Fisher Airport _____

3. Natural History Museum _____

4. The center of Gill County Fairground _____

5. The intersection of Bryant Avenue and 6th Street _____

6. The intersection of 10th Street and Highway 27. _____

7. Clarksburg Zoo _____

DEGREES OF LATITUDE AND LONGITUDE

World maps and globes contain two sets of lines that form a grid around the earth. This grid helps us locate places. Horizontal lines that run parallel around the earth are called **lines of latitude**. The 0^0 line of latitude is the **equator.** It divides the earth into the **Northern Hemisphere** and the **Southern Hemisphere**. Lines of latitude are numbered 0^0 to 90^0 north and 0^0 to 90^0 south. The United States is in the Northern Hemisphere because we are north of the equator.

The second set of lines on the global grid is **lines of longitude**. The 0^0 line of longitude is the **prime meridian** which goes through Greenwich, England. It divides the earth into the **Eastern Hemisphere** and the **Western Hemisphere**. Lines of longitude are numbered from 0^0 to 180^0 east and 0^0 to 180^0 west. The United States is in the Western Hemisphere because we are west of England. The latitude measurement for a location is always listed first, followed by longitude.

Now look at Mexico's lines of latitude and longitude. Then answer the questions about this part of the globe. Example: Monterrey is located at 27^0 N 102^0 W.

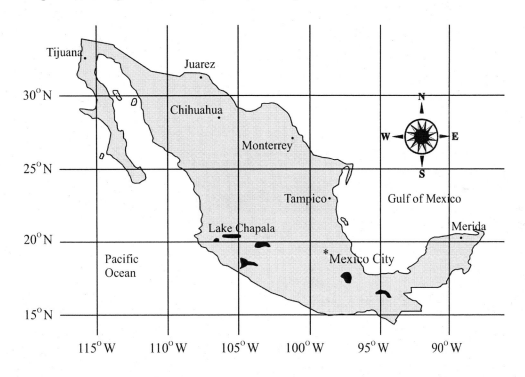

1. What body of water is at 110^0 W longitude? _____

2. Is Mexico north or south of the equator? _____

3. Is Mexico east or west of the Prime Meridian? _____

4. Estimate the longitude of these cities: Monterrey _____, Chihuahua _____, Mexico City _____.

5. Estimate the latitude of these same cities: Monterrey _____, Chihuahua _____, Mexico City _____.

6. Estimate the latitude and longitude of Juarez _____, Tampico _____, and Merida _____.

7. What city lies at latitude 34^0 N and longitude 116^0 W ? _____

DEGREES AND MINUTES LATITUDE AND LONGITUDE

The area on a map between each degree latitude or longitude is divided into 60 minutes. The area of each minute is divided into 60 seconds, just like time on a clock. On the maps below, we will look at just the division of minutes. On the map of Belgium on the right, notice the city of Genk. It lies about 9/10 of the way between 50^0 and 51^0 latitude. That position would be 50^0 54'N because 9/10 of 60 minutes is 54. It lies about 1/4 of the way between 5^0 and 6^0 longitude. Its position is 5^0 15'E because 1/4 of 60 minutes is 15. (Use an apostrophe to denote minutes.) Therefore, the position of Genk on the map is written 50^0 54' N 5^0 15' E.

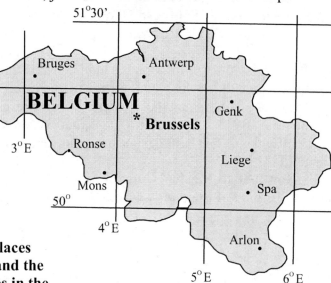

Find the locations of the following places in Belgium in the Northern Hemisphere and the fictitious country of Geil, below, which lies in the Southern Hemisphere.

1. Mons   _____

2. Brussels   _____

3. Arlon   _____

4. Antwerp   _____

5. Spa   _____

6. Ronse   _____

7. Bruges   _____

8. Liege   _____

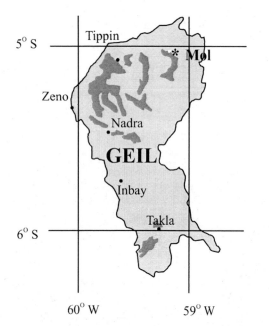

9. Tippin   _____

10. Takla   _____

11. Inbay   _____

12. Zeno   _____

13. Mol   _____

14. Nadra   _____

USING A MAP SCALE TO FIND DISTANCE

By using a **map scale**, you can determine the distance between two places in the world. A **map scale** can show distances in both miles and kilometers. You will need the edge of a piece of paper to do these exercises. To find the distance between Calgary and Ottawa, mark on the piece of paper the distance between the two cities. Then use the scale to figure the distance. The cities are about 2,000 miles apart.

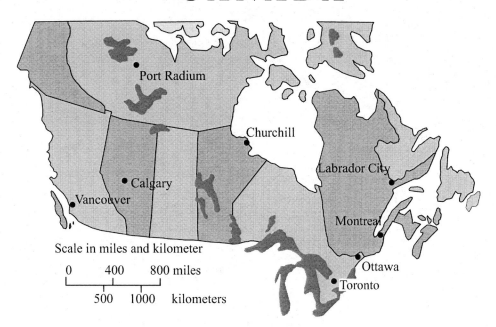

CANADA

Find these distances in miles.

1. Calgary to Churchill _____

2. Churchill to Ottawa _____

3. Port Radium to Churchill _____

4. Port Radium to Ottawa _____

5. Labrador City to Ottawa _____

6. Calgary to Labrador City _____

7. Vancouver to Montreal _____

8. Montreal to Toronto _____

Find these distances in kilometers.

9. Churchill to Labrador City _____

10. Ottawa to Port Radium _____

11. Port Radium to Calgary _____

12. Churchill to Ottawa _____

13. Calgary to Churchill _____

14. Calgary to Ottawa _____

15. Toronto to Vancouver _____

16. Montreal to Churchill _____

READING A PHYSICAL MAP

A **physical or topographic map** shows land features and elevations: Sometimes it includes cities, mountain ranges, boundaries, and rivers. The physical map below shows the United States. **Study this map. Then answer the questions that follow.**

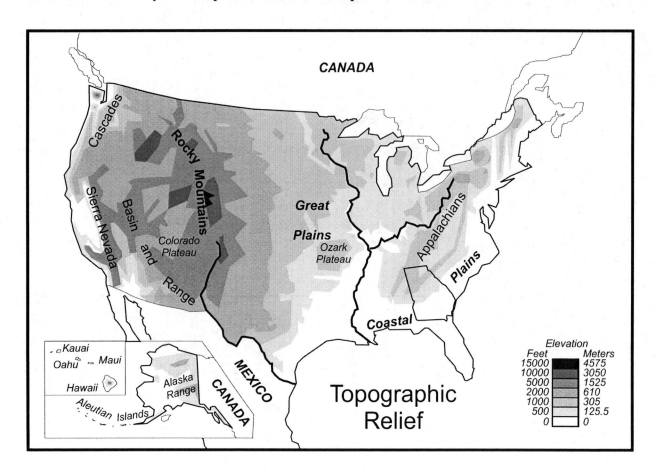

1. Which region has the highest elevation?

2. Locate the area where you live. What is the approximate elevation?

3. Trace and label the five Great Lakes. Which one is located entirely within the United States?

4. Label the following: Atlantic and Pacific Oceans, Gulf of Mexico, Mississippi River, Ohio, and Río Grande Rivers.

5. Circle the five mountain ranges in the United States.

6. What is the approximate elevation of the Great Plains?

7. What do the elevation levels tell you about the differences between the East Coast and the West Coast?

READING A POLITICAL MAP

A **political map** shows how a country is organized. At the side or corner of this and other types of maps, you will find a guide for understanding the map. This guide is called a **map key** or **legend**. The legend will often explain **symbols** such as those representing cities, boundaries, or landforms.

Study this political map of the Ukraine. Then answer the questions.

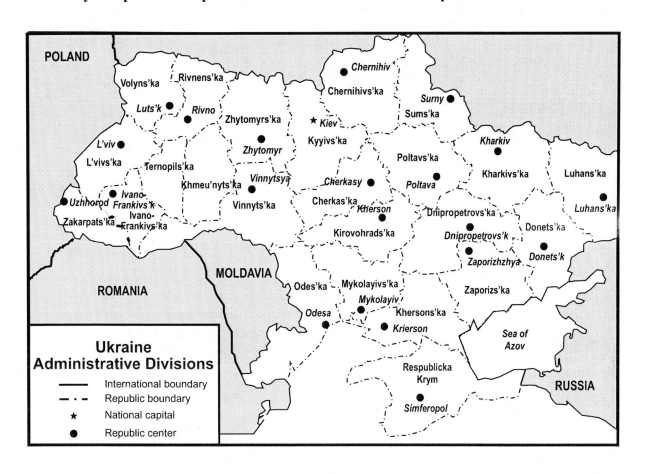

1. What is the capital of the Ukraine? _____

2. What small country is directly south of the Ukraine? _____

3. What is the republic center for Odes'ka? _____

4. Which large body of water lies in southeastern Ukraine? _____

5. Name any two countries that lie west of the Ukraine. _____

READING AN ECONOMIC MAP

An **economic map** shows resources and products of a country. These resources and products provide an income and standard of living for the people. **Study this map of Tunisia. Then answer the questions.**

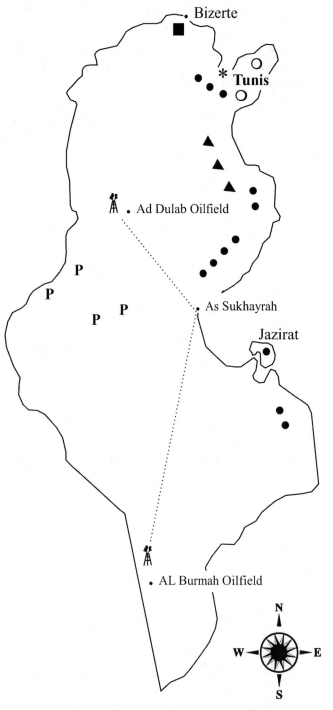

1. In what part of Tunisia are the olive oil processing plants?

2. Where are Tunisia's phosphate deposits?

3. Based on the map, what is Tunisia's most important agricultural product?

4. List the main oilfields in Tunisia.

5. Near which city are citrus trees grown?

6. In which city is the country's steel mill?

7. How is oil transported to the port of As Sukhayrah?

8. On which island are olives grown?

Economic Activity

Industry

.... Petroleum Pipeline
■ Steel Mill
▲ Olive Processing Plant

Mining
⚒ Oilfield
P Phosphate Deposits

Commercial Agriculture
● Olive-Growing Area
○ Citrus

READING A HISTORICAL MAP

A **historical map** shows places and events from the past. The purpose of this kind of map is to help us understand and interpret historical events.

Study the historical map below. It shows how the German submarine U 20 sank American and British ships during World War I. **Then answer the questions that follow.**

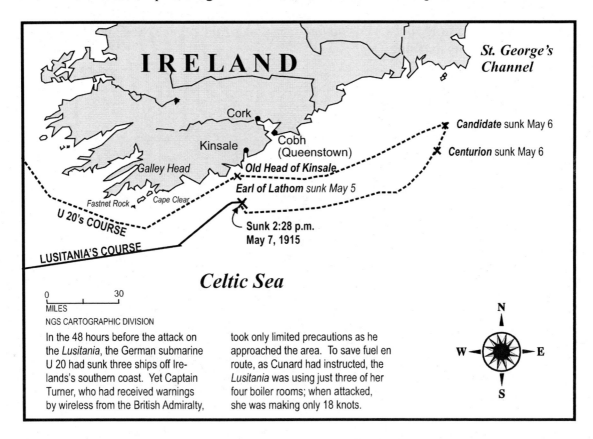

In the 48 hours before the attack on the *Lusitania*, the German submarine U 20 had sunk three ships off Ireland's southern coast. Yet Captain Turner, who had received warnings by wireless from the British Admiralty, took only limited precautions as he approached the area. To save fuel en route, as Cunard had instructed, the *Lusitania* was using just three of her four boiler rooms; when attacked, she was making only 18 knots.

1. Which line shows the U 20's course?

2. In which direction was the U 20 moving the day it sank the *Candidate*?

3. Name the ships that the U 20 sank.

4. When was the *Lusitania* sunk?

5. In which body of water was the *Lusitania* sunk?

6. Why was the *Lusitania* traveling so slowly?

7. Which ship sank the closest to land?

8. In which direction was the *Lusitania* moving when it was sunk?

9. In which direction was the U 20 moving when it sank the *Lusitania*?

TIME ZONES

A **time zone** is a division of the earth's surface in which standard time is kept. This time zone is generally 15 degrees of longitude in width. The earth is divided into **24 time zones** or one time zone for each hour of the day.

The United States mainland (excluding Alaska and Hawaii) has four time zones. As you move from east to west, you subtract an hour as you enter each new time zone. As you go from west to east and change time zones, you add an hour. **For practice, use the United States map to answer the questions that follow.**

1. In which time zone is Georgia?
2. In which time zone is Butte, Montana?
3. How many hours later is it in Jacksonville than in Seattle?
4. If it is 3:00 p.m. in New Orleans, what time is it in Denver?
5. If it is 10:00 a.m. in Boise, what time is it in Atlanta?
6. Todd leaves Atlanta at 8 a.m. and arrives in Reno at 1:00 p.m. How long did the flight take?
7. Reggie wants to fly from Denver to Columbia. If he leaves Denver at 10:00 a.m. and arrives in Columbia at 2:00 p.m., how many hours was he in the air?
8. Sharon leaves Little Rock at 6:00 p.m. and arrives in Seattle at 8:00 p.m. How many hours was she on the plane?
9. In what general direction would you fly from Miami to Boise?
10. Christina leaves Boise at 9:30 a.m. and arrives in Atlanta at 3:30 p.m. How long was she on the plane?

CHAPTER 19 REVIEW

A.   Define the following names, terms, and events:

map	compass rose	latitude	legend
globe	intermediate directions	longitude	
cardinal directions	grid	map scale	

B.   On your own paper, write your response to each of the following:

1.   What are the best methods for measuring the distance between two points?
2.   What are the main features of a physical map?
3.   Describe the features of a political map.
4.   What is the purpose of an economic map?
5.   What are the benefits of a historical map?
6.   What is a time zone map?
7.   What is the purpose of a time zone map?

C.   Additional Activity

     In a group or on your own, choose a state or country you would like to visit. This place should be 1000 or more miles from where you live. Find a good map of this place in a book or on the Internet. Make a copy of the map. Then answer the following questions.

1.   In which direction is this place from your home?
2.   Determine the nearest degrees of latitude and longitude of this place.
3.   Find the round trip distance from your home to this place in miles and kilometers.
4.   What land features would you expect to find?
5.   What is the capital? What states or countries border it?
6.   What are the main resources and products of this place?
7.   Identify two important events in history of this place.
8.   In which time zone is this place located?
9.   If you were traveling from your home to this place on an airplane, how long would the flight take?

CHAPTER 20
INFORMATION PROCESSING SKILLS

MAIN IDEAS IN MULTIPLE SOURCES

The ability to identify the **main idea** is an important skill on the **Social Studies Graduation Test**. You will be asked about the main idea in historical documents, newspapers, maps, graphs, and other publications. **The main idea is the central point or controlling idea of a document**. Many times it is stated directly in a title, the beginning, or at the end of a passage. Sometimes the main idea may only be implied rather than stated directly. **Now read the following paragraph and underline the main idea.**

Winston Churchill

One of the most famous prime ministers in British history was Sir Winston Churchill. Narrowly escaping death, he served very capably in the military in India and Africa. As a British prime minister during World War II, his moving speeches and strong leadership inspired his people to continue fighting against Germany despite the challenges.

If you underlined the first sentence of the paragraph, you are correct. The main idea is stated directly in the first sentence of this passage. The passage focuses on Sir Winston Churchill's role of prime minister.

Now underline the main idea in each of the following passages.

1. We need to remember as well as to celebrate the end of World War I. We need to remember the dead and the wounded, the widows and orphans, the destroyed and broken homes, farms, and businesses. We need to remember these casualties of war. We must prevent another such war from happening. — from a newspaper editorial about World War I

2. My family came to America in 1985. No one spoke a word of English. In school, I was in an English as a Second Language class with other foreign-born children. My class was so overcrowded that it was impossible for the teacher to teach English properly. I dreaded going to school each morning because of the fear of not understanding what people were saying and the fear of being laughed at My experiences as an ESL student from an immigrant family posed a serious challenge for me.. — Yu-Lan (Mary) Ying, an eyewitness account about learning English

3. Columbus' own successful voyage in 1492 prompted a papal bull dividing the globe between rivals Spain and Portugal. But the Portuguese protested that the pope's line left them too little Atlantic sea room for their voyages to India. The line was shifted 270 leagues westward in 1494 by the Treaty of Tordesillas. Thus, wittingly or not, the Portuguese gained Brazil and gave their language to more than half the people of South America.
    — "Portugal's Sea Road to the East." *National Geographic*, November 1992

UNDERSTANDING PRIMARY AND SECONDARY SOURCES

A **primary source** is firsthand information about people or events of the past. This first-hand account is usually written or created by a person who was directly involved in the event. Examples of primary sources are letters, diaries, paintings, photographs, videos, government documents, or eyewitness accounts.

A **secondary source** is writing or evidence about an event written by others. It is **not** a firsthand account. When you do research for a speech or report, you will often use a secondary source. Examples of secondary sources are biographies, newspaper editorials, magazine articles, or history textbooks.

Now review the primary and secondary sources on page 237. Yu-Lan (Mary) Ying's eyewitness account about learning English (**Passage 2**) is an example of a primary source. The World War I newspaper editorial (**Passage 1**) and the creation of Brazil (**Passage 3**) are examples of secondary sources.

For practice, read the following primary and secondary sources. Then answer the questions that follow.

Document A

On the night of March 5, 1770, colonists gathered outside the Boston customs house. They began shouting insults at the redcoated British soldiers guarding the building. They felt that the constant presence of the soldiers was a way of bullying them into paying unjust taxes to the King of England. Suddenly, someone shouted "Fire." The soldiers started firing their muskets into the crowd. When the smoke cleared, five people lay dead or dying. Newspapers across the colonies called this the **Boston Massacre**. Anger against the British government grew and spread among the people. – from a student report on the American Revolution

Document B

Then a general attack was made on the soldiers by a great number of heavy clubs, and snowballs being thrown at them, by which all of our lives were in imminent danger, some persons at the same time from behind calling out, "Damn your bloods! Why don't you fire?" Instantly, three or four of the soldiers fired. . . . On my asking the soldiers why they fired without orders, they said they heard the word "fire" and supposed it came from me. This might be the case as many of the mob called out "Fire! Fire!" but I assured the men that I gave no such order; that my words were, "Don't fire! Stop your firing!". . . – testimony of Captain Thomas Preston, commanding officer of the British soldiers at the Boston Massacre

1. Which document is a primary source? Why?
2. Which document is a secondary source? Why?
3. List the sequence of events in Document A and the sequence of events in Document B.
4. Explain how the documents differ on the events leading to the Boston Massacre.
5. According to Document A, what caused the soldiers to fire on the crowd?
6. According to Document B, what caused the soldiers to fire on the crowd?
7. **Bonus Question:** After the Boston Massacre, Captain Thomas Preston and several of his soldiers were brought to trial. Find out whether they were declared innocent or guilty.

FACT AND OPINION

Some questions on the **Graduation Test in Social Studies** will ask you to distinguish a fact from an opinion. A **fact** is a true statement that can be proven by observation, statistics, or research. An **opinion** is a judgment or viewpoint about a person, place, event, or idea. An opinion may not really be true, even though the author may want you to believe it is. Now, let's look at some examples of fact and opinion.

Fact: The Apaches were a nomadic people, subsisting on game, roots, and berries.
Opinion: Apache raiding parties were the most dangerous foes the United States Army ever encountered.
Fact: President Jimmy Carter, former governor of Georgia, was the 39th president of the United States.
Opinion: President Jimmy Carter was the greatest president of the United States.

Tips for Identifying Facts and Opinions

1. **Facts state information based on observation, statistics, or research.**
2. **Opinions express a personal viewpoint or belief about a person, place, event, or idea.**

Hint 1: Opinions contain adjectives like **best, worst, favorite, dishonest, etc.**
Hint 2: Opinions sometimes include phrases such as **I feel, I think, my view, my opinion, etc.**

For the following statements, write **F** next to facts and **O** next to opinions. Be able to support your answers.

1._____ South Carolina joined the Confederate States of America on December 20, 1860.
2._____ Africa is mainly jungles populated by wild animals.
3._____ Sudan is the largest country in Africa.
3._____ Colin Powell would make an outstanding president of the United States.
4._____ The Vietnam War lasted from 1963 to 1973.
5._____ The United States had no business fighting a war in Vietnam.
6._____ I believe the United States should have fought the war in Vietnam to stop communism.
7._____ North and South Vietnam were united in 1975.

In the following paragraph, write an **F** in front of statements that are facts and an **O** in front of statements that are opinions. Be able to defend your answers.

Frontier Adventure

1) In the evening, we pitched our tent near Miry Creek. 2) Our hunters killed a large doe and two bears. 3) No one loves bear better than men of the woods. 4) I don't think this is a proper diet for us because we may get sick. 5) However, we have subsisted plentifully on the bounty of this land. 6) We arrived at Coggins Point about four in the afternoon and then went on to Westover. 7) My happiness was complete when I learned my family prospered in my absence. – adapted from the *Diaries of William Byrd*

1._____   2._____   3._____   4._____   5._____   6._____   7._____

240

SEQUENCE OF EVENTS

Questions dealing with a **sequence of events or directions** will require you to make connections between events or instructions in a passage. The subject of these passages may be a historical event, a story, or a news report. The passage will generally follow a **chronological or time order,** starting with the first event, then the second event, third event, and so on. Sequence questions usually contain **key words** that will help you locate the answers in a passage. These **key words** are listed below:

first	before	next	second	after	earlier
third	then	later	finally	when	last

For practice with sequence of events, read the following passage, and answer the questions.

On Sunday, December 7, 1941, the Japanese attacked **Pearl Harbor**, in Hawaii, by surprise. President Roosevelt called it the day **"which will live in infamy."** He was right. The next day Congress declared war on Japan. Germany and Italy declared war on the United States a few days later. Since the Soviet Union had joined the Allies earlier in 1941, the Allied camp now had three strong powers: Great Britain, the United States and the Soviet Union.

1. What event happened first in the passage?
2. What event occurred last in the passage?
3. When did the United States declare war on Japan?
4. Make a timeline of the dates and events in the passage.
5. Underline the key words that guide the sequence of events in the passage.

CAUSE-EFFECT RELATIONSHIPS

Authors sometimes explain a topic by including the **causes** or reasons for an event and the **effects** or results of an event. Passages about **cause-effect relationships** may center on a story, a historical event, or a news event. Test questions will require you to identify causes or effects discussed in the passage.

Cause-effect questions often contain **key words** that will guide you in scanning the passage to find the answers. Key words for causes include the following: **why, reason, because, source, basis, due to**. Key words for effects include the following: **affect, result, consequence, outcome, product, aftermath.**

Read the following passage. Then circle the causes and underline the effects.

Many Americans are unaware of how pesticides affect our food supplies. Health risks are the inevitable result. Pesticides can run off into groundwater and run off into nearby streams, where they are carried from their original dispersal site. This is how pesticides end up in drinking water, fish, and game. And because of wind, rain, and evaporation, residues routinely show up in animals in the remotest parts of the world. For example, if grain fields or rough lands are sprayed with pesticides, residues can show up in poultry, eggs, milk, and butter. The end result is that every food we eat carries pesticides as the inevitable consequence of spraying crops with these poisons. And human exposure doesn't even end there; residues are transferred from mother to child through the placenta and mother's milk.

— *Citizen Action News*, Summer 1995

UNITED STATES HISTORY

| 1492 Columbus reaches America | 1513 Balboa reaches Pacific Ocean | 1535 Cartier explores St. Lawrence Seaway | 1539 Hernando de Soto explores the Southeast | 1565 Spanish settle St. Augustine | 1587 "Lost Colony" established by English at Roanoke |

| 1607 Jamestown settled | 1620 Pilgrims settle Plymouth | 1634 Maryland founded | 1675 King Philip's War | 1682 LaSalle reaches mouth of Mississippi |

1700 1730

1733 Georgia founded

1754-63 French and Indian War

1765 Stamp Act

1770 Boston Massacre

1776 Declaration of Independence

1781 Articles of Confederation adopted

1783 Treaty of Paris ends Revolutionary War

1788 Constitution ratified

1789 Washington 1st President

1794 Whiskey Rebellion

1800 Jefferson elected President

1820 Missouri Compromise

1822 Americans settle Texas

1825 Erie Canal completed

1838 Cherokee "Trail of Tears"

1846-48 War with Mexico

1848 Seneca Falls Convention

1861-65 Civil War

1865 Lee surrenders; Lincoln assassinated

1869 First Transcontinental Railroad completed

1898 Spanish-American war

1914-18 World War I

1929 Stock market crash; Great Depression begins

1941-45 U.S. in World War II

1945 United Nations organized

1950-53 Korean War

1964 Civil Rights Act

1964 Vietnam War escalates

1969 First man on the moon

1973 American forces leave Vietnam

1983 American forces invade Granada

1991 Breakup of Soviet Union

1991 Gulf War

READING A TIMELINE

A **timeline** is a line or series of lines that show the order in which historical events happened. Marks on the line record the significant person or event and the year of the occurrence. A timeline is a way of reviewing important historical events. It can also provide an introduction or overview of a historical period.

Study the timeline on page 242 of this book. Then answer the following questions.

1. What is the subject of the timeline?
2. What is the beginning and ending date of this timeline?
3. Read the timeline from left to right. What happened in 1770? What happened in 1969?
4. When did de Soto explore the Southeast?
5. When was the war with Mexico?
6. Read the following events. Then number them in the order in which they happened.
   _____ Missouri Compromise   _____ Breakup of Soviet Union
   _____ Georgia founded   _____ Pilgrims settle Plymouth
   _____ Balboa reaches Pacific   _____ Lincoln assassinated
7. What happened from 1941-45?
8. When did Washington become the first president?
9. Write down four important dates and events that you would add to the timeline. Insert them in the timeline.
10. Create a timeline of your own from the important events in Chapter 3.
11. Create a timeline for the life of a famous person in history.
12. Create a timeline of the years you have been in school. Include at least one important event you remember from each year.

INDEX

Book Index - an alphabetical list of topics in a book with page numbers. The index generally contains every topic mentioned in a book and tells you which pages discuss the topic.

> **SAMPLE INDEX**
>
> Namibia, diamonds 22, *map* 316   New Zealand, geysers 12
> Naples 13   waterfalls 44
> neap tide 21   nickel 11
> Nepal 54, *map* 348   Nile River 18-19, 43
>   mountains 56   Nigeria 42, *map* 44
>   *See* Mt. Everest *in this index*   nomad 37
> New Guinea, area 42   North Africa, deserts 37, 44

On what page(s) are each of the following located?

1. deserts
2. Nepal
3. diamonds
4. map of Namibia
5. New Zealand's geysers
6. the life of nomads
7. major city in Italy
8. Nile River
9. nickel

10. What kind of a book is the sample index taken from?

TABLE OF CONTENTS

A **Table of Contents** is a listing of chapters and topics. A table of contents appears in the front of a book and provides an overview of the content and organization of a book.

In which chapters would you find the following topics?

1. Courts
2. Constitution
3. Committee system
4. What kind of book does this Table of Contents come from?
5. In which chapter would you find the process for making a law?

GLOSSARY

Glossary - an alphabetical list of specialized words with their definitions. The glossary is placed at the end of a book. Glossaries are found in science, social studies, literature, math books, and many others as well.

Sample Glossary Page

monogamy - marriage to one person at a time.
monopoly - one company dominating a particular market such as cars or telephones.
monotheism - belief in one God.
mores - standards of conduct that are held by a particular culture.

multiculturalism - respecting and accepting many cultures.
nationalism - one nation having more rights that another nation.
nuclear family - a group consisting of two parents and their children.
occupation - a job for pay.

1. What is belief in one god called?
2. True or False. Arriving at school on time is an example of a more.
3. True or False. Racism is part of multiculturalism.
4. What is being married to one person called?
5. True or False. Nationalism occurs when everyone in the world is treated equally.

BIBLIOGRAPHY

Bibliography - a list of writings about a particular author or topic. The writings consist of books or periodicals in alphabetical order by author's last name. A periodical is a magazine such as **Newsweek** or **People**. If the source is a magazine, the title of the article is not italicized, but the name of the magazine is italicized. If the source is a book, the title of the book is italicized.

---

* SAMPLE BIBLIOGRAPHY

Adler, T. (1989). Causes and effects of world war II. *APA Monitor*, 20, 24.

Axelrod, S., & Apsche, J. (1983). *Germany's goals in the first world war.* New York: Academic Press.

Cattell, R.B. (1973). *The industrial revolution.* San Francisco: Jossey-Bass.

Dahlstrom, W.G. (1993). America's past: a look at the evidence. *American Historical Digest,* 48-64.

Erdelyi, M.H. (1985). *The politics of early America.* New York: Freeman.

Gallagher, J.J., & Ramey, C.T. (1987). *The scientific revolution and its effects.* Baltimore: Paul H. Brooks.

Gilligan, C. (1982). *The poor of the 18th century.* Cambridge, MA: Harvard Press.

Govoni, L.E. & Hayes, J.E. (1988). *Political and social change* (6th ed.). Norwalk, CT: Appleton & Lange.

---

1. Which listing in the bibliography was published first?
2. Who wrote the book about World War I?
3. Where was the book about the scientific revolution published?
4. How many magazine articles are listed above?
5. Who published the book about political and social change?

* **APA (American Psychological Association) style.**

READING TABLES

A **table** is a concise way to organize a lot of information using rows and columns. **Carefully read the table below and then answer the questions below.**

Average Life Expectancy		
Country	Male	Female
Bolivia	45	51
United Kingdom	72	77
India	46	43
Japan	74	81
Peru	52	55
Sweden	73	80
USA	71	78

1. Where do males live longer than females?
2. Where do women live the longest?
3. How much longer do men in the USA live than the men in Peru?
4. Where do people live the longest?
5. How much longer does a female in Sweden live than a male in Bolivia?
6. In which country can a female expect to live a shorter life than a male?

BAR GRAPHS

Bar graphs can be either vertical or horizontal. It is important to read the title of the graph as well as the labels for the horizontal and vertical axes in order to completely understand the information presented. **Carefully read the graphs below and then answer the questions.**

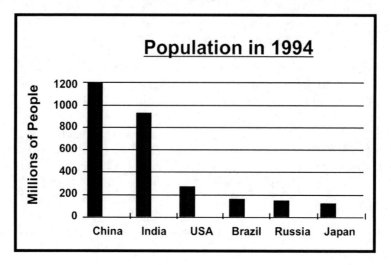

1.   Which country has over 1 billion people?
2.   How many countries have less than 200,000,000 people?
3.   How many more people does India have than Japan?
4.   What are the two least populated countries?

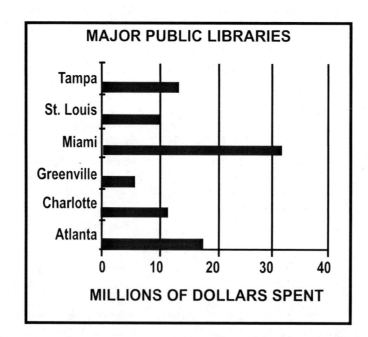

5.   How much did St. Louis spend on libraries?
6.   About how much did Atlanta spend on libraries?
7.   About how much did Greenville spend?
8.   About how much more did Miami spend on their libraries than Charlotte?
9.   About how much more did Atlanta spend on libraries than Greenville?

LINE GRAPHS

Line graphs are another way to present a large quantity of data in a small space. It would often take several paragraphs to explain in words the same information that one graph could do.

On the graph below, there are three lines. **Carefully read the key to understand the meaning of each line, and then answer the questions to the left of the graph.**

1. In which year did we import 3 billion more pounds of fish than we caught domestically?

2. How many billion pounds of fish were imported in 1986?

3. In 1984, what was the total weight of fishery products used?

4. How many billion pounds of fish were imported in 1988?

5. How many pounds of fish products were used in the United States in 1994?

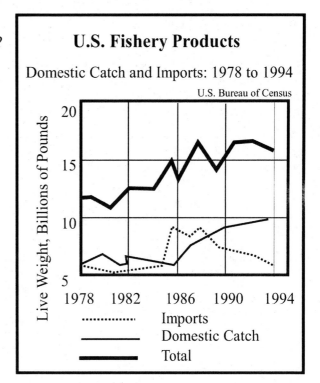

CIRCLE GRAPHS

Circle graphs always represent data expressed in percentages of a total. The parts in a circle graph should always add up to 100%. **Now answer the questions from the graph.**

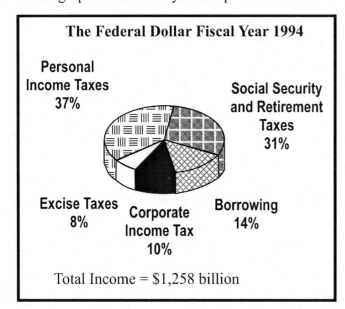

1. What was the largest source of income for the United States government in 1994?

2. What percentage of income came from borrowed money?

3. In this circle graph, $1,258 billion dollars represent what percent of the total income for the United States federal government?

4. How many total dollars came from corporate income tax?

247

CHAPTER 20 REVIEW

Suggested Activities
Work individually or in small groups.

1. Select 5-10 paragraphs from previous chapters in this book. Paragraphs should be no less than 50 words in length. Underline the main idea in each paragraph, or summarize it in your own words.

2. Locate a primary source and a secondary source on an event or person mentioned in this book. Bring this information to class. How do the two accounts differ? Are there any similarities? Which account seems to be more accurate? Why? Share your findings with other students.

3. Find 5-10 statements of fact and 5-10 statements of opinion in a newspaper, magazine, or book. Be able to defend your choices.

4. Skim through previous chapters of this book, and find 4-5 examples of sequence of events and 4-5 examples of cause-effect explanations about an event. Discuss your choices.

5. Locate 2-3 tables, graphs, or charts in other chapters in this book. Develop 4-6 questions about them with the answers, but keep the answers separate. Exchange the charts or graphs and the questions with other students. Then answer the questions, and check your choices against the answer keys. Discuss your findings.

6. Find tables, charts, or graphs in the newspaper, magazines, or a book. Discuss what you learned by reading these graphic aids.

SOCIAL STUDIES PRACTICE TEST 1

1. Marie Antoinette, the queen of France, once asked a court official why the people of Paris were so angry. The official replied, "Because they have no bread." The queen responded, "Then let them eat cake."

   This legendary story reflects which of the following causes of the French Revolution?

   A. the monarchy's extravagant spending practices
   B. inequality in the system of taxation
   C. government interference in the private lives of citizens
   D. all of the above

2. During the 15th and 16th centuries, the rise of nation-states led to economic competition in Europe, as seen in the theory of mercantilism. This competition spurred European exploration and colonization around the world. The significant economic changes in Europe during this time can be called a Commercial Revolution. Which of the following is **not** a characteristic of the Commercial Revolution?

   A. Large amounts of silver and gold from Americas caused inflation in Europe.
   B. Governments decreased their control over national economies.
   C. Capital investment began as investors took risks on explorers and new colonies.
   D. There was a movement from local to national and global economy.

Use the timeline below to answer question 3.

| 1914-18 A | 1929 Stock Market Crash | 1941-45 U.S. in World War II | 1945 United Nations organized | 1950-53 B | 1964 Civil Rights Act | 1964 Vietnam War escalates | 1969 C | 1973 American forces leave Vietnam | 1983 American forces invade Granada | 1991 Breakup of Soviet Union | 1991 D |

3. On the timeline above, what is the correct position of the Korean War?

   A. A   C. C
   B. B   D. D

4. How was the House of Burgesses in Jamestown significant to the formation of the United States?

   A. It granted land to proprietors for future settlements.
   B. It negotiated treaties with Native Americans so that England could settle land in Virginia.
   C. It was an example for how to create a democratic government.
   D. It was where Thomas Jefferson wrote the Declaration of Independence.

5. During World War I, battles between the armies of Europe produced no clear winners. The European nations then developed a new strategy for battle called total war. This strategy was fully implemented in World War II. Total war involves which of the following?

   A. There are no limitations in the course of battle.
   B. The war involves whole societies, not just armies.
   C. The end of the war comes only with complete defeat of the enemy.
   D. All of the above

6. Name the members of the Triple Alliance during World War I.

   A. France, Russia, and Great Britain
   B. Italy, Great Britain, and France
   C. Germany, Austria-Hungary, and Italy
   D. Russia, Germany, and Italy

7. After competing manufacturers copied his idea for the cotton gin, Eli Whitney turned to the manufacture of muskets. His method of production introduced an important concept (later used in industries all over the world) called

   A. specialization of labor.
   B. factory system.
   C. assembly line.
   D. interchangeable parts.

8. In February 1946, George F. Kennan sent a telegram to the United States from Moscow which included his recommendations for a foreign policy regarding the Soviet Union. The telegram described the Soviets as not wanting to start wars, but desiring control by undermining Western governments. He recommended that the United States strategically oppose Soviet expansion through economic and political pressure. This policy became known as

   A. containment.
   B. appeasement.
   C. the iron curtain.
   D. the cold war.

9. Economic systems differ regarding property ownership, income distribution, economic incentives, and the level of government control. One type of economic system relies heavily on government control of wages, production goals, prices, and ownership of resources. This economic system is called a

   A. traditional economy.
   B. command economy.
   C. free market economy.
   D. mixed economy.

10. Some people become citizens by being born in the United States. People who are not born in the United States, but who wish to become citizens, must fulfill which of the following requirements?

    A. live in the United States for five years
    B. pass a citizenship test
    C. take the oath of allegiance
    D. all of the above

11. What situation is causing the problem of worldwide hunger and malnutrition?

   A. There is not enough food to feed the world's population.
   B. There is an uneven distribution of the world's food supply.
   C. Rapid deforestation is diminishing the food supply.
   D. The food available in the world is of poorer nutritional quality.

12. Which of the following procedures describes the proper sequence of the way a bill becomes a law in the United States government?

   A. Congress passes the bill, the President signs it into law, and the states ratify it.
   B. Committees discuss the bill, Congress passes the bill, and the President signs it into law.
   C. Congress passes the bill, the states ratify it, the Supreme Court declares it constitutional.
   D. the President introduces a bill, the Congress passes it, and the Supreme Court declares it constitutional.

13. On the Great Plains of the United States, Native Americans created teepees out of buffalo hide. The hides were stretched and sewn together. Long wooden poles supported the hides and created a portable home. Why did Native Americans choose to live in teepees?

   A. Teepees best served the needs of a population on the move in search of buffalo.
   B. Trees were not available to build log cabins, so teepees were the best alternative.
   C. Teepees were made of the best material for keeping out rain.
   D. Teepees could be easily rebuilt after tornadoes.

14. Brazil is a nation with a small amount of economic and military might in comparison with the United States, yet the United States is very concerned with Brazil's natural resources. What makes Brazil so important to the United States?

   A. Brazil has very profitable gold mines.
   B. Brazil's fishing industry is competing with the United States.
   C. Brazil's rain forests supply half of the oxygen in the world.
   D. Brazil is a major supplier of food during famines in the United States.

15. Georgia is divided into three general regions: coastal plain, Piedmont, and mountains. Why do these regions allow for a more diversified economy?

   A. Different cultural groups separate themselves by geographic regions.
   B. Different economies develop in each geographic region.
   C. A wide variety of agricultural and business activities can be conducted in geographic regions.
   D. People speaking a variety of languages live in these geographic regions.

16. Because of the flat, dry, continuous terrain of the Southwest, people acquired large areas of land. As a result, this land was used for

   A. cash crop farming.   C. subsistence farming.
   B. cattle ranches.   D. manufacturing.

17. In what part of the United States did the Iroquois tribes live?

A. the Southwest
B. the Central Plains
C. the Eastern Woodlands
D. the Pacific Northwest

18. Which of the following was the first successful English colony?

A. Roanoke
B. Jamestown
C. New Netherlands
D. Philadelphia

19. By 1700, three European nations laid claim to land in North America. What were those three nations?

A. France, Austria, and Italy
B. England, France, and Spain
C. Portugal, Spain, and England
D. Russia, Spain, and the Ottoman Empire

20. Why did the Boston Tea Party (1773) occur?

A. British and American citizens met in Boston to celebrate the end of the Revolutionary War (1776-1783).
B. American colonists were forced to drink tea instead of their favorite beverage, coffee.
C. By dumping a tea shipment into the Boston harbor, American colonists were protesting the quartering of troops..
D. The laws of English Parliament limited trade and self-government in the American colonies.

21. In his farewell address, President George Washington advised that

A. the Constitution should be interpreted strictly.
B. the United States should make permanent allies with its neighbors.
C. political parties should be avoided.
D. both A and B

22. In 1856, a more efficient and inexpensive way of refining molten iron into steel was invented that paved the way for the growth of the steel industry. This invention is called

A. vulcanizing.
B. the Bessemer process.
C. the shotcrete method.
D. hydraulicing.

23. What role does the Solicitor General play in the federal government?

A. proposes legislation for raising funds for the government
B. oversees government operations to make things run more efficiently
C. defends the government in Supreme Court cases
D. enforces civilian control over the military

24.	Why were Northerners upset when Kansas was made into a slave state?

I.	Kansas had many resources and would provide a base of power for the South.
II.	Kansas would become the railroad center for the growing nation.
III.	Pro-slavery forces not living in Kansas illegally voted and changed the results.
IV.	Kansas lay above the parallel where slavery was permitted in the Missouri Compromise.

A.	I and II
B.	II and III
C.	I and IV
D.	III and IV

Read the following passage, and answer question 25 below.

After Reconstruction, African Americans faced a plight similar to what existed before the Civil War. The South remained primarily agricultural. African Americans were not permitted to own land, so they had to rent the land as sharecroppers from the wealthy white landowners. They lived on a bare subsistence level. In addition, they lost their voting rights through the use of poll taxes and literacy tests. White mobs frequently terrorized those who chose to exercise their rights.

25.	Based on the passage, which of the following problems existed in the Post-Reconstruction South?

A.	individual rights
B.	national identity
C.	law enforcement
D.	low taxation

26.	In 1803, the United States nearly doubled in size due to the Louisiana Purchase. Why was Napoleon willing to sell such a huge tract of land?

A.	The people of the region were organizing a rebellion from France.
B.	He considered the land of no industrial use.
C.	The Native Americans petitioned Napoleon to sell the land to the United States.
D.	Because of a revolt in Haiti, he feared he would soon lose political control of the region.

27.	For nine years after it declared its independence from Mexico, Texas remained an independent country. Why was there such a delay in admitting Texas to the United States of America?

A.	Its population consisted mostly of Mexicans.
B.	The United States feared another attack on the Alamo.
C.	The land was considered dry, barren, and undesirable.
D.	It would upset the balance of slave and free state representation in the Senate.

28.	The administration of President Andrew Jackson included which of the following?

A.	rewarding friends and supporters with government posts
B.	preventing people who do not own property from voting
C.	strengthening the civil rights of Native Americans
D.	ensuring that opposing views were heard at all levels of government

29. The California Gold Rush of 1849 expanded the California population from an initial population of 15,000 to a population of 93,000 when the Gold Rush ended in 1850. Soon after, California became a state.

The gold rush contributed to the completion of which of the following?

A. the election of Abraham Lincoln
B. Manifest Destiny
C. new immigration laws regarding people from Asia
D. the ending of the Civil War

30. In 1837, this reformer of the educational system was appointed head of the first state board of education in Massachusetts. This reformer became known nationwide as an initiator of school reforms such as increasing teachers' salaries and creating schools where teachers can learn to teach.

Who was this famous reformer?

A. Frederick Douglass   C. Horace Mann
B. Susan B. Anthony   D. G. Stanley Hall

31. Desiring to protect its own markets, the United States raised tariffs on imported goods in the mid 1800s. Upset over these tariffs, a senator from South Carolina claimed that a state is not required to enforce a federal law if the law is harmful to that state, and if H of the states agree, the law is unconstitutional. The senator described

A. the Spoils System.   C. the Secession Plan.
B. the Doctrine of Nullification. D. judicial review.

32. The First Amendment to the Constitution states:

"Congress shall make no law respecting an establishment of religion, or prohibiting the free exercise thereof; or abridging the freedom of speech, or of the press, or the right of the people peaceably to assemble, and to petition the government for a redress of grievances."

Which of the following is **not** a freedom protected by the First Amendment?

A. A citizen can publish a pamphlet criticizing the government.
B. A citizen can preach on a street corner about his/her religion.
C. Citizens can peaceably assemble to promote racism.
D. A citizen can shout "Fire!" in a crowded movie theater.

33. In the late 1800s, farmers faced various hardships. Which of the following were hardships faced by farmers in the late 1800s?

A. New agricultural machines were very costly.
B. Farmers couldn't produce enough food for the global demand.
C. Railroads were not available to transport their crops.
D. both A and C

34. From the 1880s to the civil rights movement of the 1950s and 1960s, Jim Crow laws were in effect in the South. These laws demanded the segregation of blacks and whites and the treatment of blacks as second class citizens. Which of the following examples would **not** be considered a Jim Crow law?

   A. All public schools must now be integrated.
   B. Blacks must now pass a special literacy test before they can vote.
   C. Separate drinking fountains and bathrooms must be built for the different races.
   D. Separate housing districts must be established for the different races.

Use the political cartoon below to answer question 35.

Abraham Lincoln   George B. McClellen   Jefferson Davis

THE TRUE ISSUE OF "THAT'S WHAT'S THE MATTER".

35. The cartoon above implies which of the following?

   A. Abraham Lincoln and Jefferson Davis are acting like stubborn children.
   B. As a Democratic nominee, General George McClellan will win the 1854 Presidential election against Lincoln.
   C. Like a torn map, the division of the country may be irreparable if the war continues.
   D. The true issue of the war is slavery.

36. "One feels his two-ness – an American, a Negro, two souls, two thoughts, two unreconciled strivings, two warring ideals in one dark body."

   The writer of this quote was a co-founder of the N.A.A.C.P. He wanted African-Americans to strive for social and political equality, so that their "two-ness" might be reconciled. Who is this person?

   A. W. E. B. Du Bois   C. Booker T. Washington
   B. George Washington Carver   D. Frederick Douglass

37. Which of the following is a policy or action **not** initiated by President Theodore Roosevelt?

    A. Pure Food and Drug Act (1906)
    B. National Park System
    C. New Freedom legislation
    D. breaking up trusts like the Northern Securities Trust

Use the political cartoon below to answer question 38.

38. The artist who drew this political cartoon was probably trying to convey which of the following ideas?

    A. After defeating Spain, the United States had become a world power by gaining control of Cuba and the Philippines.
    B. The Republicans (symbolized by the elephant) are draining the United States economy with their policies.
    C. The possession of the Philippine islands is proving to be a burden for the United States.
    D. The United States should stop importing elephants from the Phillipines.

39. For decades prior to the First World War, the stage was being set for conflict between the nations of Europe. Which of the following factors was **not** a contributing factor to the outbreak of World War I?

    A. a buildup of national military forces
    B. the break up of the Austro-Hungarian empire into smaller competing nations
    C. Darwin's ideas of "survival of the fittest" being applied to nations
    D. competition between colonial powers

40. When a rebellion broke out in Cuba in 1906, the United States established a temporary government in Cuba with the support of 5,000 United States troops. More than two years later, the Americans left. This action illustrates which foreign policy?

    A. the Open Door Policy   C. Roosevelt's Corollary
    B. the Monroe Doctrine   D. Isolationism

41. Using personal experience, the author of *The Great Gatsby* captured the spirit of materialism and decadent wealth prevalent in the 1920s. Who is the author?

    A. Zelda Fitzgerald   C. Ernest Hemingway
    B. F. Scott Fitzgerald   D. Muriel Hemingway

42. Which of the following was true of the Ku Klux Klan during the 1920s?

    A. It gained a huge following, claiming millions of members.
    B. It caused fear in many people but had no political power.
    C. It targeted only black people, leaving others alone.
    D. Its members burned crosses, sent hate letters, and burned houses, but they never tried to kill people.

43. Which of the following was **not** a role played by the Tennessee Valley Authority (TVA) in the Southeast during the Depression?

    A. The TVA provided jobs for thousands of the unemployed, thus stimulating the economy.
    B. The TVA provided needed electricity to Tennessee and other southern states.
    C. The TVA built dams which helped reduce flooding in the Tennessee area.
    D. The TVA discouraged business in Tennessee.

44. Which of the following is **not** an outcome of the Allied victory in North Africa?

    A. The Mediterranean Sea was opened to Allied shipping.
    B. The Allies could invade southern Europe.
    C. The Allies were more optimistic about the war's outcome.
    D. The Allies decided to focus their attack on Japan.

45. What policy did France and Great Britain follow by allowing Hitler to annex the Sudetenland of Czechoslovakia in 1938?

    A. Open Door Policy   C. blitzkrieg
    B. aggression   D. appeasement

46. Approximately how many Japanese Americans did the United States government keep in relocation camps during World War II?

    A. 500,000   C. 4,000
    B. 100,000   D. 1,000,000

47. During World War II, which of the following were **all** Axis powers?

    A. Britain, Italy, and Russia
    B. Spain, Switzerland, and Germany
    C. Italy, Germany, and Japan
    D. the United States, Britain, and France

Use the timeline below to answer question 48.

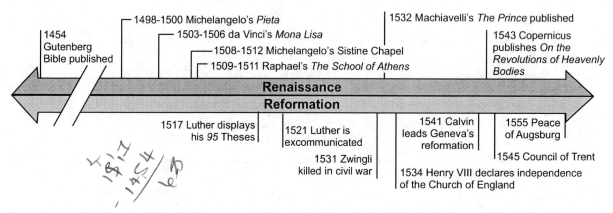

48. When Johannes Gutenberg published the first Bible printed with moveable type, he placed the Bible in the hands of people other than church officials. This event encouraged people to question certain practices of the Catholic Church. How many years passed between the publishing of the Gutenberg Bible and Luther displaying his 95 theses?

    A. 63 years   C. 80 years
    B. 91 years   D. 100 years

49. In the case of *Miranda vs. Arizona* (1966), the Supreme Court decided that when the police arrest a person they must inform that person of his or her 5th Amendment rights. Otherwise, verbal evidence from the accused cannot be used in a court of law. What was the significance of this decision?

    A. People arrested by the police were given more rights.
    B. People do not have the right to speak once they are arrested.
    C. All arrested people must have their constitutional rights read to them.
    D. All arrested people have the right to say anything, but their words cannot be used against them in court.

50. Which of the following is **not** a responsibility of the president of the United States?

    A. to negotiate treaties with other countries
    B. to command the military in times of war
    C. to enforce federal laws
    D. to raise money for the government

51. According to the Bill of Rights, why can't police officers enter a citizen's residence at random and search the house for contraband materials?

    A.   This action violates the 1st Amendment right of freedom of speech.
    B.   Citizens enjoy the right to trial by jury under the 6th Amendment.
    C.   Under the 4th Amendment, citizens cannot have their property searched without probable cause.
    D.   Under the 5th Amendment, citizens cannot be forced to present verbal evidence against themselves.

52. Judy lives in Albany, Georgia. She stays informed on political issues. She votes in all elections and referendums, attends town meetings, and volunteers her time to tutor underprivileged children. What assumption can be made about Judy?

    A.   Judy wants to use her rights responsibly to benefit the community.
    B.   Judy believes everyone should use their rights as she does.
    C.   Judy believes she should use her rights to get ahead in life.
    D.   Judy wants to run for a political office.

53. Which of Montesquieu's ideas from his *The Spirit of Laws* (1748) was incorporated into the United States Constitution?

    A.   The government should be elected by the people.
    B.   The government must protect individual rights such as freedom of speech.
    C.   The government is responsible for the economic welfare of its citizens.
    D.   The government should have separate branches and be balanced to protect the rights of the individual.

54. Why are third-party candidates usually unsuccessful in being elected to the presidency?

    A.   They lack the financial and political broad base of support to run a campaign successfully.
    B.   Voters are unfamiliar with third party issues.
    C.   Voters prefer having two candidates to choose from, not three.
    D.   They always lack political experience and so are undesirable.

55. Which of the following was a cause of the Great Depression in the United States during the 1930s?

    I.   strict government control
    II.   great difference in wealth between industry owners and workers
    III. low wages despite rise in cost of living
    IV.   conservative investing in the stock market

    A.   I, II, and III   C.   II and III
    B.   III and IV   D.   I, II, and IV

56. Eddie Blasedail is arrested for smoking marijuana on a sidewalk. He is released on bail and returns on his court date one month later with a court appointed lawyer. At the trial, he is found guilty of possession and is given the punishment mandated by the state.

Which of the following rights apply in this situation?

    I.   rights of search and seizure
    II.   rights of accused persons
    III.   right to a speedy trial
    IV.   rights concerning bail, fines and punishments

    A.   II, III, and IV
    B.   I, II, and III
    C.   II and IV
    D.   I and III

57. Which of the following is **not** a test that cases before the Supreme Court must pass in order to be heard?

    A.   the test of ripeness   C.   the mootness standard
    B.   the standing of the case   D.   the applicability rule

58. The description of New York City as located in a protected harbor on the eastern seaboard of the United States provides which of the following?

    A.   absolute location   C.   approximate location
    B.   relative location   D.   exact location

59. Colonists in Massachusetts fought British soldiers in Lexington and Concord in April 1775. The Declaration of Independence was not endorsed by the Continental Congress until more than a year later. What encouraged the Congress to declare independence from Britain?

    A.   The Congress hoped to gain foreign support from Britain's enemies.
    B.   George Washington's army continued to win military battles.
    C.   King George III's efforts to make peace showed Britain's weakness.
    D.   Benjamin Franklin proposed the Albany Plan.

60. According to the graph on the right, which industry provides the largest part of the gross product of Arkansas?

    A.   government
    B.   manufacturing
    C.   other
    D.   wholesale and retail trade

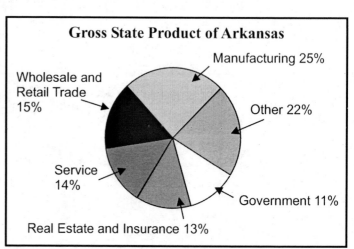

Gross State Product of Arkansas

Manufacturing 25%
Wholesale and Retail Trade 15%
Other 22%
Service 14%
Government 11%
Real Estate and Insurance 13%

61. Given the Cold War conflict between the Soviet Union and the so-called Western nations, what information shown on the map to the right has the greatest potential for dispute?

A. The city of Berlin, though under international control, is located within the Soviet zone.
B. France has control over the smallest region of Germany.
C. The Soviet Union and Great Britain share the longest border.
D. Great Britain and the Soviet Union control coastlines while the United States and France do not.

The Occupation of Germany after World War II

Use the chart below to answer question 62.

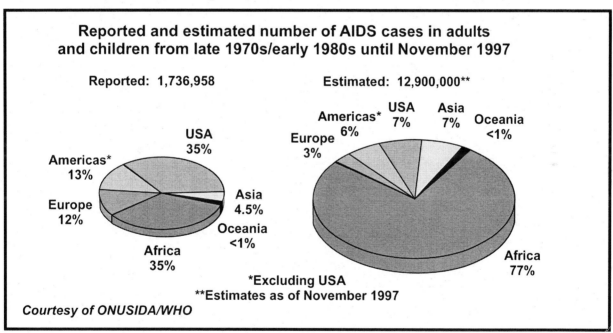

Reported and estimated number of AIDS cases in adults and children from late 1970s/early 1980s until November 1997

Reported: 1,736,958

Estimated: 12,900,000**

*Excluding USA
**Estimates as of November 1997
Courtesy of ONUSIDA/WHO

62. Which of the following conclusions can be drawn from the graph above?

A. The problem of AIDS in the United States isn't really as bad as is estimated.
B. There are a substantial number of unreported cases of AIDS, especially in Africa.
C. The experts who estimate the number of cases of AIDS are not well- informed.
D. In countries other than Africa, the number of cases of AIDS has decreased.

UNITED STATES MAP

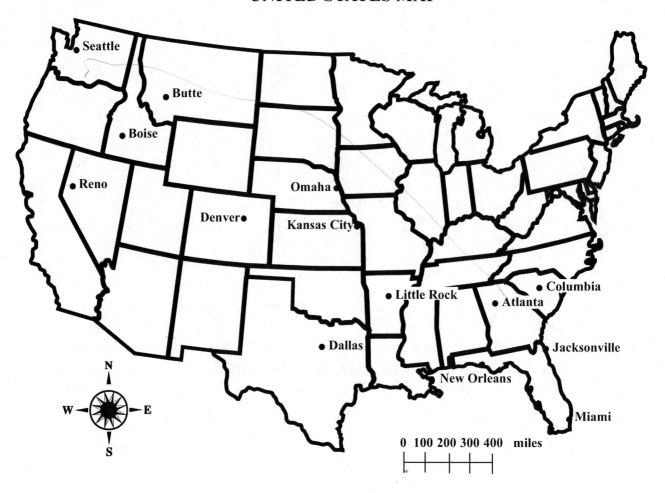

63. According to the map above, how many miles are between Denver and Dallas?

    A. 450 miles
    B. 500 miles
    C. 650 miles
    D. 800 miles

64. According to the map above, if Kris Jenson decided to fly from Seattle, Washington, to Atlanta, Georgia, in what direction would she fly?

    A. southwest
    B. south
    C. east
    D. southeast

65. Why did General Sherman's "March to the Sea" during the Civil War in the United States mark a turning point in the history of modern warfare?

    A. No general had ever won so great a victory.
    B. It set a precedent for how to resolve civil wars in other countries.
    C. Where wars had usually only involved soldiers, Sherman's soldiers destroyed cities and civilians.
    D. It was the longest military march in history.

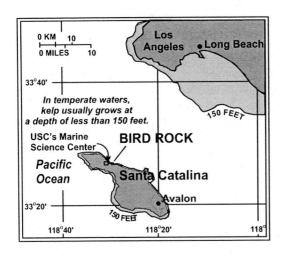

66. Based on the grid map to the left, where is the city of Avalon?

A. 33°40'N, 118°20'W
B. 33°40'N, 118°W
C. 33°21'N, 118°20'W
D. 33°27'N, 118°30'W

67. Based on the grid map to the left, what is located at 33°27'N, 118°30'W?

A. Avalon
B. USC's Marine Science Center
C. Long Beach
D. Los Angeles

68. The map to the right would be most useful to a

A. pilot flying from Argentina to Peru.
B. person sailing to the Arctic Ocean.
C. pilot flying from South America to Europe.
D. person traveling in Africa.

69. Longitude on the map to the right is represented by

A. vertical lines.
B. horizontal lines.
C. straight lines.
D. curved lines.

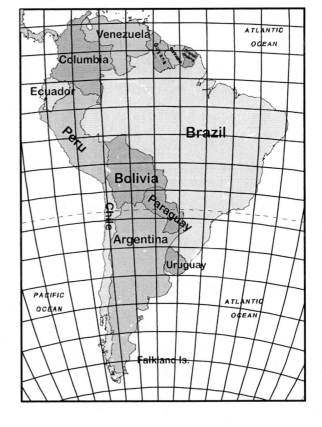

70. Look at the map to the left. Which world region is shown here?

A. Sub-Saharan Africa
B. Southeast Asia
C. Europe
D. Middle East

71. The shaded area on the map above shows the countries involved in which of the following international agreements or organizations?

A. OAS
B. OPEC
C. NAFTA
D. EU

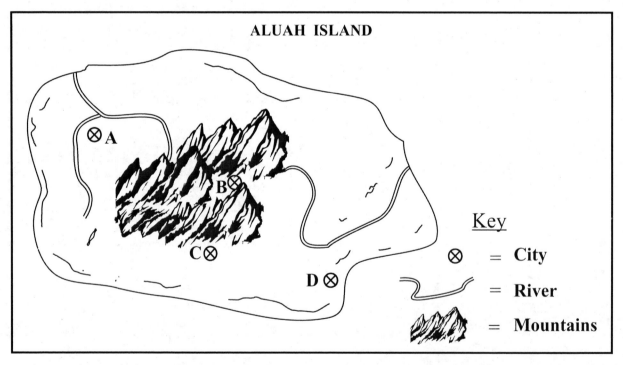

ALUAH ISLAND

Key
⊗ = City
〰 = River
🏔 = Mountains

72. Where would you probably find the most fertile farmland on the island shown in the map above?

A. City A
B. City B
C. City C
D. City D

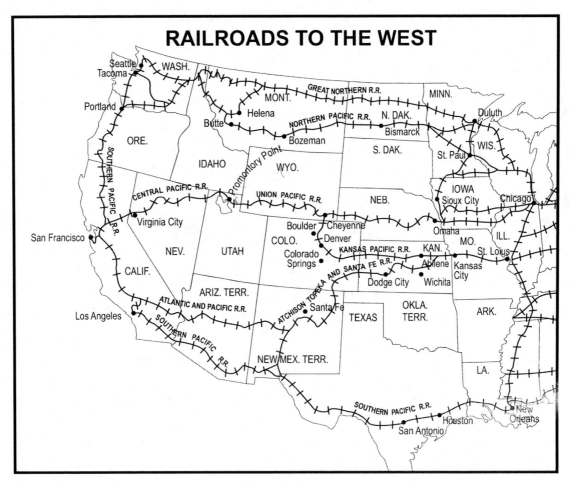

RAILROADS TO THE WEST

73. According to the map above, the Union Pacific Railroad and the Central Pacific Railroad connect at which of the following cities?

   A.   Cheyenne, Wyoming   C.   Chicago, Illinois
   B.   San Francisco, California   D.   Promontory Point, Utah

74. According to the map above, which railroad lines provide the most direct route from Los Angeles to Kansas City?

   A.   Southern Pacific - Atchinson, Topeka, and Santa Fe - Kansas Pacific
   B.   Atlantic and Pacific - Atchinson, Topeka, and Santa Fe - Kansas Pacific
   C.   Southern Pacific - Central Pacific - Union Pacific - Kansas Pacific
   D.   Southern Pacific - Northern Pacific - Union Pacific - Kansas Pacific

75. Based on the graph to the right, how many people received Social Security checks in 1970?

   A.   27,000,000
   B.   35,000,000
   C.   27,000
   D.   14,000

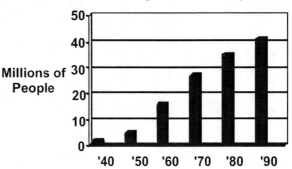

People Receiving Social Security Checks

Millions of People

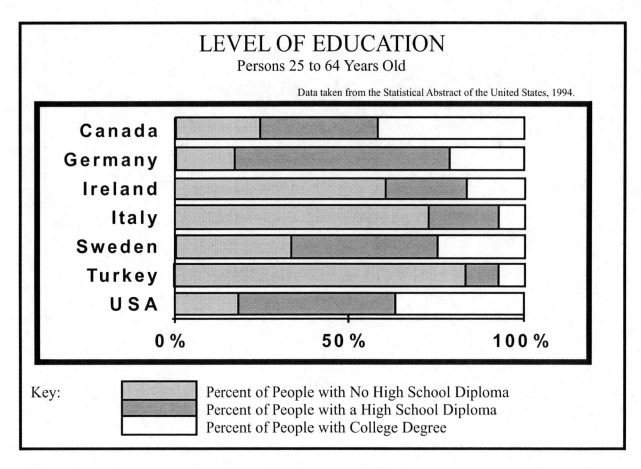

LEVEL OF EDUCATION
Persons 25 to 64 Years Old

Data taken from the Statistical Abstract of the United States, 1994.

Key:
Percent of People with No High School Diploma
Percent of People with a High School Diploma
Percent of People with College Degree

76. According to the graph above, what country has the highest percentage of people with a college degree?

    A. USA   C. Canada
    B. Turkey   D. Sweden

Study the following time line. Then answer questions 77 and 78.

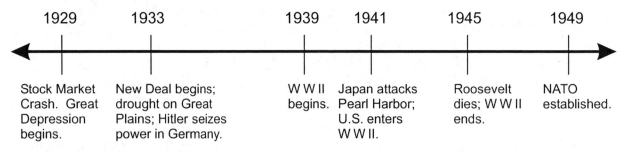

1929	1933	1939	1941	1945	1949
Stock Market Crash. Great Depression begins.	New Deal begins; drought on Great Plains; Hitler seizes power in Germany.	W W II begins.	Japan attacks Pearl Harbor; U.S. enters W W II.	Roosevelt dies; W W II ends.	NATO established.

77. How long did World War II last?

    A. Six years   C. Twenty years
    B. Four years   D. Five years

78. When did Hitler come to power in Germany?

    A. 1939   C. 1929
    B. 1933   D. 1930

266

Use the map below to answer question 79.

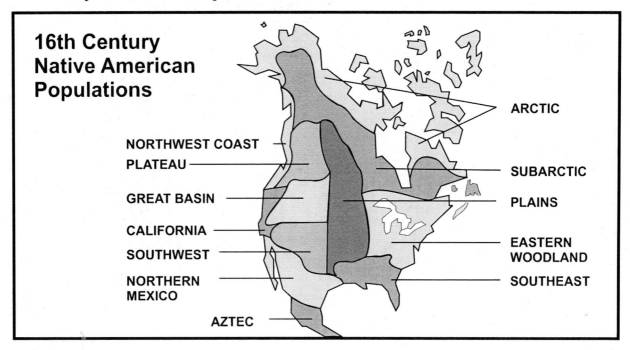

16th Century Native American Populations

NORTHWEST COAST
PLATEAU
GREAT BASIN
CALIFORNIA
SOUTHWEST
NORTHERN MEXICO
AZTEC

ARCTIC
SUBARCTIC
PLAINS
EASTERN WOODLAND
SOUTHEAST

79. The political boundaries of the present-day United States include which of the following Native American groups shown on the map?

   A. Arctic
   B. Aztec
   C. Plains
   D. Subarctic

80. In 1865, the 13th Amendment to the Constitution abolished slavery. Three years later, the Congress and the states found it necessary to endorse the 14th Amendment which stated that "all persons born or naturalized in the United States . . . are citizens." Why was the 14th Amendment necessary?

   A. Despite the abolition of slavery, blacks were not receiving equal treatment as citizens.
   B. Because of a large influx of immigrants in mid-nineteenth century, Congress wanted to limit citizenship to those born in the United States.
   C. The government couldn't process all the former slaves who wanted to be citizens, so it made them citizens by birth.
   D. The 14th Amendment allowed all the Southerners who had seceded from the United States to become citizens again.

81. In 1830, Congress passed the Indian Removal Act to move Native Americans out of the Southeast. Native Americans challenged the law, and the Supreme Court declared it unconstitutional. Even still, President Jackson enforced the law by ordering federal troops to force Native Americans from their land. This situation reveals which of the following weaknesses in the federal government's system of checks and balances?

   A. the will of the majority rules
   B. there are no limitations on presidential powers
   C. the Supreme Court has no power to enforce its decisions
   D. civilian control of the military

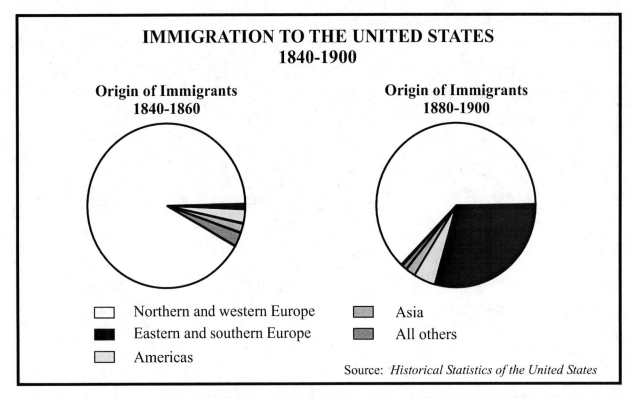

IMMIGRATION TO THE UNITED STATES
1840-1900

**Origin of Immigrants
1840-1860**

**Origin of Immigrants
1880-1900**

☐ Northern and western Europe ◼ Asia

◼ Eastern and southern Europe ◼ All others

☐ Americas

Source: *Historical Statistics of the United States*

82. According to the graph above, what is the most dramatic change in immigration rates between 1840-1860 and 1880-1900?

 A. The total number of immigrants increased.
 B. The total number of immigrants from northern and western Europe decreased.
 C. The percentage of immigrants from the Americas increased.
 D. The percentage of immigrants from eastern and southern Europe increased.

Read the following passages from the diary of Civil War veteran Colonel Marcus Spiegel and then answer question 83.

January, 1863 – "I am sick of the war. . . . I do not want to fight for Lincoln's Negro proclamation any longer." – Colonel Marcus Spiegel after hearing of the Emancipation Proclamation.

January, 1864 – "since I [came] here I have learned and seen more of what the horrors of Slavery was than I ever knew before. . . . I am [in] favor of doing away with the…accursed institution. . . . I am [now] a strong abolitionist." – Colonel Marcus Spiegel after fighting in Louisiana.

83. Based on these two statements from Colonel Marcus Spiegel's diary, which of the following is a valid conclusion?

 A. Colonel Spiegel was indifferent to slavery because he was tired of the war.
 B. Colonel Spiegel always believed that slavery was wrong before he heard the Emancipation Proclamation.
 C. Colonel Spiegel never believed in slavery but was willing to fight in Louisiana.
 D. Colonel Spiegel disliked the war, but he soon realized that slavery must be abolished.

84. The land shown in the photograph has been altered mainly to

    A. increase the beauty of the landscape.
    B. increase the availability of land that can be used for farming.
    C. divide land belonging to different people.
    D. enable residents to climb the slopes more easily.

Read the chart below, and then answer questions 85 and 86.

United States Patents Issued 1861-1900	
Five-Year Periods	**Number of Patents**
1861-1865	20,725
1866-1870	58,734
1871-1875	60,976
1876-1880	64,462
1881-1885	97,156
1886-1890	110,358
1891-1895	108,420
1896-1900	112,188

85. Inventors filed for patents so their ideas could not be used by other people. According to the chart, which five year period showed the greatest increase in the number of patents issued as compared to the previous five year period?

    A. 1861-1865   C. 1876-1880
    B. 1866-1870   D. 1896-1900

86. Which five year period showed a decline in the number of patents as compared to the previous five year period?

    A. 1861-1865   C. 1891-1895
    B. 1876-1880   D. 1896-1900

Read the two excerpts below and answer questions 87 and 88.

Document A

. . . the rights of the Cherokees are . . . plain, . . . and the duty of the government to secure those rights is as binding as ever . . .If the white man must oppress us-if he must . . . throw us penniless upon the wild world, and if our cries [mean] nothing at the door of those who have promised to be our guardians and protectors, let it be so. –Elias Boudinot, editor *Cherokee Phoenix* [1831]

Document B

During the 1830s, settlers seeking more land began to pressure the United States government to remove the Cherokee nation from Georgia. As Cherokees began to know of their opposition, they split into two camps. One, led by Elias Boudinot, advocated leaving the Cherokee lands in Georgia peaceably before they either went to war with the United States or were forced to leave. The other camp, composed of the majority of the Cherokee, chose to stay on their native lands. Boudinot's group peaceably left three years prior to the United States' forced march of the remaining Cherokee to Oklahoma –*The Trail of Tears*, AJS

87. Jeff wants to write a report on The Trail of Tears using primary and secondary sources. Which of the following is a primary source and why?

    A. Document A, because it was written a few years before The Trail of Tears.
    B. Document B, because it discusses both groups of Cherokee.
    C. Document A, because the language used is uncommon.
    D. Document B, because the passage is longer and not broken up.

88. Which is the best explanation for how the two writings differ in their presentation of Cherokee views of forced migration?

    A. Document A presents the opinion of Elias Boudinot. Document B does not.
    B. Document B was written to white settlers. Document A was written to Cherokees.
    C. Document A presents the opinion of Elias Boudinot. Document B presents both Boudinot's and the other Cherokees' decisions.
    D. In Document A, Boudinot likes the idea of moving off the Cherokee land. In Document B, the Cherokee people are against leaving their land.

Use the map at the right to answer questions 89 and 90.

89. On what kind of landform is Bombay located?

   A. archipelago
   B. isthmus
   C. island
   D. penninsula

90. Why are the railroads constructed on built-up areas?

   A. Railroads are cheaper to construct on built-up lands.
   B. The railroads are surrounded by wetlands.
   C. Railroads should be built next to roads.
   D. Built-up areas offer more scenic views.

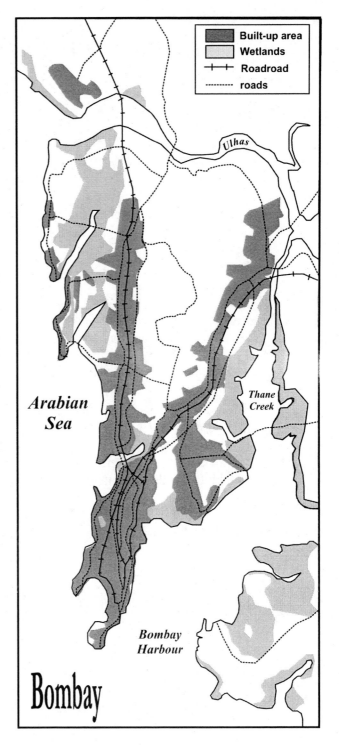

SOCIAL STUDIES PRACTICE TEST 2

1. While fighting the Crusades in the Middle East, European merchants made many profitable trading contacts with the Orient. Why did this lead to the discovery of the New World?

    A. European nobles were looking for huge lands to control, so they sent explorers everywhere looking for land.
    B. Trading with the Orient required land travel, which was very costly and took great amounts of time. Explorers began looking for a sea route to the Orient.
    C. The Pope urged crusaders to search the world over for more conversions to Catholicism.
    D. European merchants learned during the crusades that great mountains of gold were to be found across the ocean.

2. The League of Nations was an international peacekeeping organization, existing from 1920 to 1946. The League was ineffective in preventing World War II. The main reason for its ineffectiveness was that the United States never joined. What caused the United States to refuse to join the League of Nations?

    A. The United States House of Representatives refused to pass President Wilson's bill to join the League of Nations.
    B. President Wilson chose to follow a policy of isolationism in world affairs.
    C. Public opinion was neutral about joining the League of Nations.
    D. The United States Senate refused to pass President Wilson's bill to join the League of Nations.

3. Which of the following are ecological concerns of the global community?

    I.   women's rights
    II. global warming
    III. destruction of rain forests
    IV. industrial emission outputs

    A. I, II, and III   C. II and IV
    B. II and III   D. II, III, and IV

4. In 1972, the Supreme Court ruled that punishing criminals by execution was "cruel and unusual punishment" and, therefore, was unconstitutional. In 1976, the Court reversed its decision. What caused this reversal?

    A. The states rewrote their laws to make capital punishment constitutional.
    B. The President had overruled the Court's decision.
    C. Congress made an amendment to the Constitution legalizing capital punishment.
    D. The states had ignored the 1972 decision and continued to execute criminals.

272   Copyright © American Book Company

5. After 1900, the nations of Europe were in a constant state of tension due to conflicts concerning their overseas colonial possessions. Seeking security, these nations entered into military agreements of cooperation with other nations. Why did these agreements increase the likelihood of world war?

    A. These agreements were seen as threatening to nations not in an alliance.
    B. The European nations had to spend large amounts of money to become part of a military alliance.
    C. These nations wanted war so that the stronger alliance would receive more overseas colonies.
    D. Because of the opposing systems of alliances, an isolated conflict between two European nations could become a world war.

6. In which of the following ways can a bill be introduced to the legislative process?

    A. a special interest group can propose a bill to the Senate
    B. a Congressional committee sends a bill to the President
    C. the people vote on a referendum to introduce a bill
    D. the President sends a bill to Congress

7. Leonardo da Vinci is an excellent example of the Renaissance because

    A. he left many artistic works unfinished.
    B. he made great contributions to developments in music.
    C. he showed interest and skill in various arts and sciences.
    D. he designed the dome structure that influenced architecture throughout the Western world.

8. In 1687, Sir Isaac Newton published *Philosophiae Naturalis Principia Mathematica*. In this book, he proposed a unique theory about gravity. His law of universal gravitation explained the way in which the force of gravity affects the movement of all objects. This new theory greatly impacted European thoughts and attitudes in which of the following ways?

    A. This was the first scientific theory based on the mathematical system of calculus.
    B. The theory proposed that the earth revolved around the sun.
    C. The theory appeared to unveil the mysteries of the universe through human reason.
    D. The theory contradicted teachings of the Catholic Church.

9. Through French domination of much of Europe, Napoleon spread the democratic ideals of the French Revolution. In the New World, however, he wanted to make France rich by re-establishing slavery on the island colony of present-day Haiti. Which of the following events prevented Napoleon from reviving the French presence in the Western Hemisphere?

    A. The followers of Toussaint L'Ouverture defeated the French Army.
    B. The United States purchased the Louisiana territory.
    C. The Spanish tried to take over the island colony.
    D. The French Army suffered defeat in Russia.

10. The ideas of fascism and communism are different in many ways. One belief that the two political theories share is

    A.   promotion of nationalism.   C.   racism.
    B.   strict government control of society.   D.   abolition of religion.

11. Why didn't the Soviet Union prevent the United Nations forces from entering the conflict in Korea?

    A.   The Soviet Union was suffering its own internal difficulties.
    B.   By agreeing with the United Nations, the Soviet Union hoped to gain concessions on other issues it considered important.
    C.   The Soviets did not know the North Korean Communists were going to invade South Korea.
    D.   The Soviets were boycotting the Security Council in order to protest the United Nations' refusal to recognize Communist China.

12. The population of Shefelon comes from three basic ancestries. The people are either African, Native American, or Northern European.

Which statement is most likely true?

    A.   Shefelon can be divided into three political groups.
    B.   Shefelon can be divided into three cultural groups.
    C.   Shefelon can be divided into three economic groups.
    D.   Shefelon can be divided into three physical groups.

13. On the Arabian peninsula, there is a surplus of oil reserves. At the same time, there is a scarcity of freshwater. Most of the land is barren desert. Economically, one could conclude that

    A.   Arabian nations sell their oil to other nations for food.
    B.   the Arab nations are self-sufficient and do not need foreign trade.
    C.   Arab nations often trade oil supplies with each other.
    D.   tourism is the main industry of the Arab region.

14. Many bills that are brought to Congress never become law. In which of the following ways can a bill be stopped from becoming a law?

    A.   The Senate can refuse to confirm a bill signed into law by the President.
    B.   A two-thirds majority of both houses of Congress can stop the President from signing a bill into law.
    C.   A Congressional committee can prevent Congress from ever voting on a bill.
    D.   The Supreme Court can declare a bill unconstitutional before it becomes law.

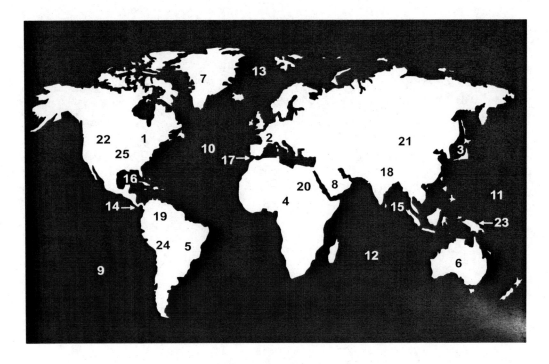

15. The number twelve refers to which ocean?

    A. Indian   C. Atlantic
    B. Pacific   D. Arctic

16. One way to encourage trade with another country is to

    A. create agreements eliminating tariffs between nations.
    B. devaluate the United States dollar.
    C. impose import quotas.
    D. deregulate the stock exchange.

17. Native Americans contributed greatly to the success of European colonies by

    A. practicing human and animal sacrifice.
    B. providing charts and maps of the New World.
    C. creating a vast network of trails and trade routes that established transportation and
        communication in the colonies.
    D. establishing factories in the Northeast and farms in the Midwest.

18. In 1999, thousands of refugees from Kosovo came to the United States. Which of the
    following describes their potential status as citizens of the United States?

    A. They can never become citizens because they weren't born in the United States.
    B. If parents become citizens, their children under 18 will also become citizens.
    C. They must live in the United States for five years before they can become citizens.
    D. both B and C

19. At the Constitutional Convention (1787), the Great Compromise resulted in

    A. slaves not being represented in the northern states.
    B. each state electing representatives in proportion to its population.
    C. the President having the power to veto.
    D. Congress having the power to declare war.

20. In the 1740s, evangelical preachers, using the example of the emotional preacher George Whitefield, held camp meetings and gave sermons that stirred the emotions of people in the English colonies of North America. This shared experience developed a feeling of unity among colonists and is known as

    A. the Great Awakening.   C. Woodstock.
    B. the Great Revival.   D. the Inner Light.

Use the political cartoon below to answer question 21.

21. What is the artist trying to communicate about the original thirteen colonies of the United States?

    A. The colonies are part of a great serpent and deserve to be cut up.
    B. Each colony wants to be separate but equal.
    C. The colonists feel that Great Britain has chopped them into small pieces.
    D. The colonies must unite, or they will lose the war with Great Britain.

22. Which leader of the Revolution gave a passionate speech about human rights, saying, "Give me liberty or give me death!" in the House of Burgesses prior to the start of the Revolutionary War?

    A. Thomas Paine   C. Samuel Adams
    B. Patrick Henry   D. John Locke

23. From 1804-1806, Lewis and Clark, with the aid of their guide, Sacajawea, explored which regions of the nation?

    I.   Oregon Territory
    II.   Mexican Cession
    III. Northwest Ordinance
    IV.   Louisiana Purchase

    A. I and IV   C. II and III
    B. I and III   D. II and IV

24. In 1845, the United States entered into a war with Mexico over a dispute concerning the boundary of the Texas Republic. The United States was victorious, and Mexican territory from the Río Grande to the coast of California was annexed to the United States. Which of the following ideals contributed to the fighting of this war?

    A. Emancipation Proclamation   C. Imperialism
    B. Sectionalism   D. Manifest Destiny

25. Which one of the following people traveled the Western frontier and classified the 58 language families of the Native Americans in the United States and Canada?

    A. John W. Powell   C. Franklin D. Roosevelt
    B. William Gilpin   D. Sacajawea

26. In what part of the British colonies did George Rogers Clark fight during the Revolutionary War?

    A. New England   C. Northwest Territory
    B. Georgia   D. Middle Colonies

27. The Whiskey Rebellion of 1794 challenged the power of the executive branch of the federal government. The citizens of western Pennsylvania began revolting against the government because their means of livelihood, distilling whiskey, had a large sales tax imposed on it. In order to stop the rebellion, President Washington had to mobilize and command the state militia.

    Which principle of government does this event illustrate?

    A. isolationism   C. world history
    B. immigration policy   D. national security/defense

28. In 1823, a policy was announced that would determine United States involvement in Latin America to the present day. The policy stated that no European power could establish colonies in newly independent states of Latin America.

    What was the name of this policy?

    A. the American System   C. the New World Order
    B. the Non-Intervention Treaty   D. the Monroe Doctrine

29. Why was the Union victory at Vicksburg, Mississippi, seen as an important turning point in the Civil War?

    A. This victory effectively split the Western portion of the Confederacy because the Union now controlled the entire Mississippi River.
    B. This victory enabled the Union to end the Southern offensive into Northern territory.
    C. This victory destroyed the vital railroad lines of the Confederacy, disrupting military supplies.
    D. This victory destroyed the manufacturing center of the Confederacy.

30. During the founding of the English colonies, labor was in short supply. To remedy this problem, indentured servants were brought to the colonies from England. What is an indentured servant?

   A. A person who is obligated to work for someone without pay for the rest of his or her life in exchange for free passage to the colonies.
   B. A person who works for someone without pay for a number of years in return for free passage to the New World.
   C. A person who works for a wealthy aristocrat in Europe and comes with the employer to the New World.
   D. A person who agrees to work for someone else in return for a free house.

31. In 1819, the United States and Spain made an agreement called the Adams-Onís Treaty. Which of the following were components of the treaty?

   I.   Spain agreed to relinquish its claim to the Oregon region on the western side of the Louisiana purchase.
   II. Spain agreed to cede part of present-day Texas to the United States.
   III. The United States agreed to pay Spain up to five million dollars.
   IV. Spain agreed to relinquish its claim to East and West Florida.

   A. I and II   C. II, III, and IV
   B. II and IV   D. I, III, and IV

32. Which of the following is **not** an effect of the growth of railroads in the 1800s?

   A. prevented growth of the automobile industry
   B. major cities grew around railroad junctions
   C. increased ability to travel
   D. allowed farmers to ship products to cities

33. Each of the following movements sought to reform society in some way. Which of the following was seeking primarily to support the rights of farmers in the Mid-West?

   A. the Temperance Movement   C. the Progressive Movement
   B. the Niagara Movement   D. the Populist movement

34. In a speech in 1906, President Theodore Roosevelt referred to the man with the *muck rake* in John Bunyan's *Pilgrim's Progress* (1678, 1684). The term "muckraker" was used in the early 20th century to refer to which of the following groups?

   A. authors who publicized the corruption of big business
   B. farmers who fertilized with moist manure called "muck"
   C. politicians who, out of self-interest, wanted to protect large companies
   D. those who swept dirty factory floors

Read the two passages about the working girls of Lowell. Then answer question 35.

"We are not aware, until within a few days, of the *modus operandi* of the factory powers in this village of forcing girls from their quiet homes to become tools and, like the Southern slaves, to give up their life and liberty to the heartless tyrants and taskmasters..."

– H.R. Warfel

"Few American fortunes will support a woman who is above the calls of her family; and a man of sense, in choosing a companion to jog with him through all the up-hills and down-hills of life, would sooner choose one who *had* to work for a living, than one who thought it beneath her to soil her pretty hands with manual labor in the home, although she possessed her thousands of dollars."

– C.B.

35. Based on these two passages, what can you conclude was the authors' opinion about women working outside the home?

     A. Women should work outside the home to gain their freedom.
     B. Women should stay at home and be homemakers.
     C. Women should strike against unfair working practices.
     D. Women should earn thousands of dollars and amass a fortune before marriage.

36. Members of the Progressive Movement in the early part of the 20th century did **not** support which of the following?

     A. increased opportunities for public education
     B. voting rights for women
     C. tax breaks for big business to stimulate economic growth
     D. political reform to ensure power was not in the hands of only a few people

37. From 1899-1900, United States Secretary of State John Hay tried to negotiate an Open Door Policy with several other nations in order to

     A. secure trade opportunities with China for the United States.
     B. open markets in South America for European trade.
     C. provide for limited spheres of influence in certain global markets.
     D. increase the labor force in the United States by allowing more immigration.

38. On Feb 1, 1917, Germany began using submarines to destroy all shipping to and from Great Britain. By April 6, 1917, the United States entered the war against Germany. Why did this submarine warfare anger the citizens of the United States?

     A. Americans had a distaste for submarine warfare.
     B. German U-boats attacked the United States' base at Pearl Harbor.
     C. The United States felt that Great Britain was the "underdog" in this situation.
     D. Germany used U-boats to sink American merchant ships trading with Great Britain.

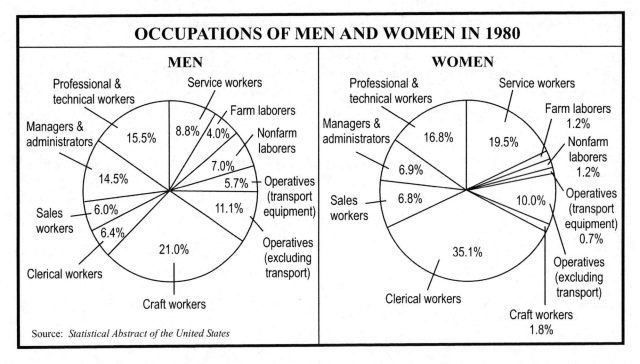

OCCUPATIONS OF MEN AND WOMEN IN 1980

MEN

- Professional & technical workers 15.5%
- Service workers 8.8%
- Farm laborers 4.0%
- Managers & administrators 14.5%
- Nonfarm laborers 7.0%
- Operatives (transport equipment) 5.7%
- Sales workers 6.0%
- Operatives (excluding transport) 11.1%
- Clerical workers 6.4%
- Craft workers 21.0%

WOMEN

- Professional & technical workers 16.8%
- Service workers 19.5%
- Farm laborers 1.2%
- Managers & administrators 6.9%
- Nonfarm laborers 1.2%
- Sales workers 6.8%
- Operatives (transport equipment) 0.7%
- Clerical workers 35.1%
- Operatives (excluding transport) 10.0%
- Craft workers 1.8%

Source: *Statistical Abstract of the United States*

39. Compare the two circle graphs above showing the kinds of work done by men and women in 1980. Which of the following conclusions can be drawn from the information provided by the graphs?

    A. Women earn less money than men in the same jobs.
    B. Women are more likely than men to work in service and clerical jobs.
    C. The number of women in professional and managerial jobs increased during the 1970s.
    D. Sales workers are more often men than women.

40. In 1893, one group revolted against the rule of Queen Liliuokalani of the Hawaiian Islands. Which group revolted?

    A. student protesters who called for democracy
    B. white plantation owners from the United States
    C. United States military forces
    D. Japanese citizens who wanted control of the island of Maui

41. The following excerpts were taken from articles describing the *U.S.S. Maine* explosion on Feb. 15, 1898. Which of the following would **not** be an example of yellow journalism?

    A. "Patriotic citizens advocate resorting to arms to wreak vengeance upon Spain for the cruel and cowardly destruction of the *Maine*." – *The Examiner*
    B. "The serious catastrophe which took place near Havana on Tuesday…calls for a most searching scrutiny on the part of the American govt." – *The Washington D.C. Bee*
    C. "…No foreign power can sympathize with Spain in its base and cowardly treachery." – *The Gazette,* Cleveland, Ohio
    D. "How patriotic Americans would like to hear the cannon's reverberation on this 12th of April to avenge the slaughter of the boys in blue on board the *Maine* in Havana's harbor two months ago." – *Humboldt Times*

42. The American economy gained strength after World War I, leading to the era known as the "Roaring 20s." There was a downside to this era, however. Which of the following were hardships of the 1920s?

    I.   Blacks and immigrants refused to work for low wages causing increased unemployment.
    II.   Autoworkers were laid off due to the growth of the railroad industry.
    III.   Farmers produced so much food that prices fell.
    IV.   The coal industry was weakened by growth in oil production.

A.   III and IV   C.   II and IV
B.   I and III   D.   II only

43. After World War I, there was a growing fear of foreigners in the United States. Which of the following is an indication of that fear?

    I.   growth of the Ku Klux Klan
    II.   immigration laws passed at this time
    III.   the Red Scare
    IV.   the Scopes Trial

A.   I and III   C.   II and IV
B.   I, II, and III   D.   III only

44. To prevent banks from collapsing, Congress enacted the Federal Deposit Insurance Corporation (FDIC) in 1933. What power did the FDIC exercise?

A.   The FDIC loaned money for electrification projects in rural areas.
B.   The FDIC let the government decide which banks could reopen.
C.   The FDIC insured savings accounts up to $100,000.00 in case of bank failure.
D.   The FDIC provided money to start new banks.

45. Which of the following names an economic period of higher unemployment, lower wages, and reduced demand for products?

A.   inflation   C.   deflation
B.   deficit spending   D.   recession

46. The growth of the counterculture during the 1950s and 1960s was a response to which of the following characteristics of United States society?

    I.   growth of the consumer culture
    II.   lack of educational opportunities
    III.   strictly defined social roles
    IV.   economic recession

A.   IV only
B.   I, II, III, and IV
C.   I and III
D.   I and II

47. Following World War II, the European colonies of Africa and Asia gained independence. These technologically and economically underdeveloped nations came to be called the Third World. The United States and the Union of Soviet Socialist Republics tried to gain influence in these newly independent countries in which of the following ways?

    A. threatening to use nuclear weapons
    B. forcing the United Nations to give them control
    C. providing economic aid to the countries
    D. sending in troops to take over the country

48. At town meetings in New England, all male residents could speak, and most could vote directly on matters of town government. These meetings were early examples of which of the following foundational principles of the United States government?

    A. popular sovereignty   C. separation of powers
    B. equality before the law   D. federalism

Use the graph below to answer questions 49 and 50.

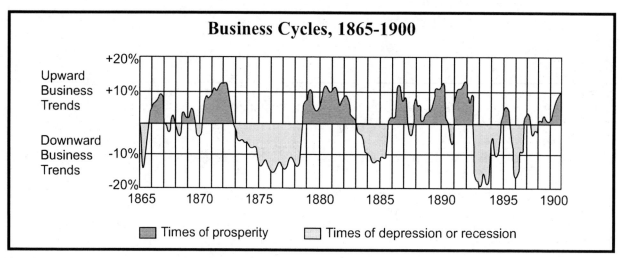

49. In the decades following the Civil War, the United States economy struggled through a series of ups and downs. According to the graph above, the longest sustained period of prosperity (without a downward trend) lasted for how many years?

    A. 7 years   C. 41 years
    B. 61 years   D. 5 years

50. According to the graph above, the most severe depression occurred in which year?

    A. 1865   C. 1893
    B. 1876   D. 1895

51. Each of the following movements sought to reform society in some way. Which of the following was seeking primarily equal rights and status for people, regardless of color?

    A   the Temperance Movement   C. the Progressive Movement
    B. the Niagara Movement   D. the Populist movement

282

52. The political campaign in Susan's district has been very confusing. The challenger, Mack Crumby, has claimed that the incumbent, Jessie Jones, has been absent during important votes concerning the district's future. Mr. Jones has adamantly denied this charge.

What resource should Susan use to discover whether the charges are true?

A. recent newspaper ads about the campaign
B. the encyclopedia
C. her close friends
D. the Congressional Record

53. A suspect was arrested and charged with murder. The case was brought to the State Superior Court and the suspect was found guilty of the crime. One month later, new DNA evidence points to the suspect's innocence.

If the decision of the State Superior Court is appealed, what is the correct process of appeals in this case?

A. United States Court of Appeals to United States Supreme Court
B. Lower Court to Superior Court
C. State Appellate Court to State Supreme Court
D. State Supreme Court to United States Supreme Court

54. Why are Central America and South America often grouped together and considered as one region?

A. the land area is small enough to easily group them together.
B. both regions share significant cultural and economic similarities.
C. the nations in the area share a similar government under the Organization of American States (OAS).
D. the climate and geography of both regions are nearly the same.

55. John and Susan Myers are United States citizens working in Mexico. Susan gives birth to a child while in Mexico. Under current United States laws of immigration, the child will

A   have seven years to be naturalized.   C.   be an illegal alien.
B. be a legal alien.   D.   be a United States citizen.

56. The Tenth Amendment to the Constitution states "The powers not delegated to the United States by the Constitution, nor prohibited by it to the States, are reserved to the States respectively, or to the people."

According to this amendment, which of the following is **not** true?

A. United States citizens can peaceably assemble whenever they wish.
B. Powers not belonging to the federal government cannot belong to the states.
C. Powers not belonging to the federal government belong to the states or to the people.
D. Rights that are not listed in the Constitution can be restricted.

57. At the Potsdam Conference during World War II, President Harry S Truman informed the other Allied leaders of a "new weapon of unusually destructive force." When the other leaders agreed to allow its use, President Truman authorized the dropping of atomic bombs on Japan. In this instance, which two roles did Truman exercise as President?

    A.   Chief Executive and Chief Diplomat
    B.   Chief of State and Commander in Chief
    C.   Commander in Chief and Chief Diplomat
    D.   Chief Diplomat and Chief Legislator

58. In *Gibbons vs. Ogden* (1824), the Supreme Court ruled that the federal government has ultimate control over all navigable waterways that lie within more than one state.

    This decision had which of the following consequences?

    A.   States could now place tolls on their waterways to create revenue.
    B.   Private citizens could purchase navigable bodies of water.
    C.   Roads and canals could be built without interference from state governments.
    D.   States could control the amount of commerce entering and leaving the state.

59. The United States has a federal government. What makes the government "federal?"

    A.   The government's power is divided between state governments and the national government.
    B.   The government has three branches with different powers.
    C.   The government is elected by the people.
    D.   The government is bound by the Constitution.

60. According to the map on the right, what is the location of Rosport, Luxembourg in degrees and minutes?

    A. $49^0 30'N, 60^0 25'E$
    B. $49^0 41'N, 6^0 25'E$
    C. $6^0 25'N, 49^0 50'E$
    D. $49^0 50'N, 6^0 30'E$

61. According to the map on the right, how many latitude minutes separate the capital of Luxembourg from Bettendorf?

    A.   10'   C.   35'
    B.   20'   D.   45'

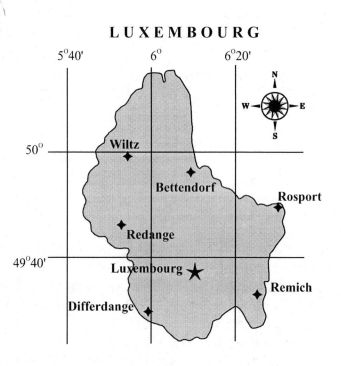

LUXEMBOURG

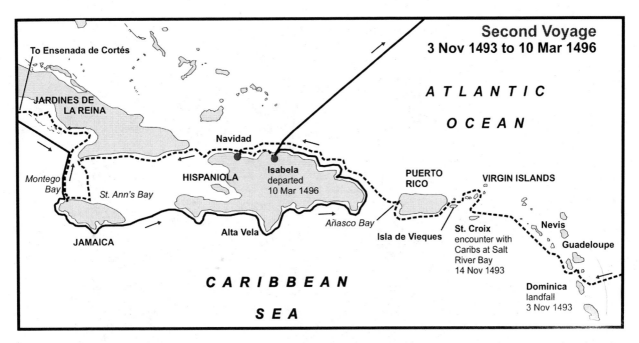

62. Based on the map above of Columbus' second voyage, how many months was Columbus in the Caribbean?

A. 34
B. 28

C. 24
D. 16

63. Which of the following climate descriptions would most accurately describe region A, shown on the map to the right?

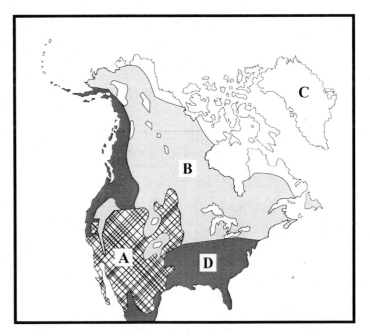

A. continuously warm with abundant moisture and dense vegetation
B. mild temperatures, humid with mixed forests and grasslands
C. hot summers, cold winters, moderately dry with grass and some desert shrubs
D. long, cold winters and short, cool summers with sparse vegetation

Use the following map to answer questions 64 and 65.

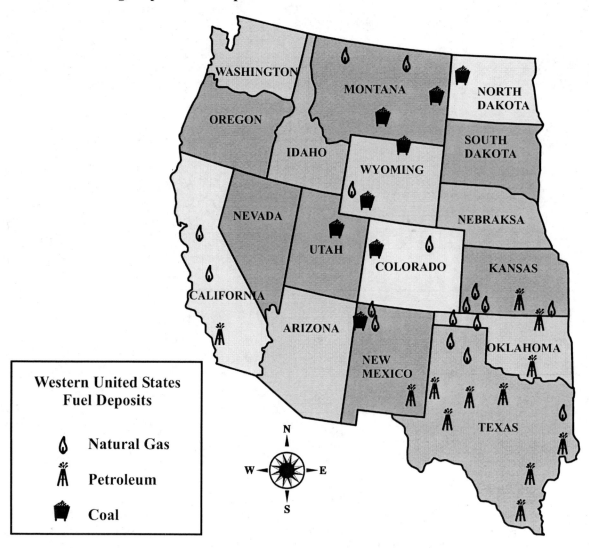

64. What state is located in the northwest corner of this map?

   A. California   C. Montana
   B. Nebraska   D. Washington

65. According to the map, which state has the most oil reserves?

   A. Texas   C. Nevada
   B. California   D. Oklahoma

66. Farming today is very different from 100 years ago. Even in the last 20 years the amount of food producing capacity has increased substantially. What is one reason for that increase?

   A. More people have become interested in agriculture and become farmers.
   B. By clearing forests, the amount of a land that can be farmed has increased.
   C. There have been significant developments in farming technology and plant breeding.
   D. Organic farming methods have become more popular.

286

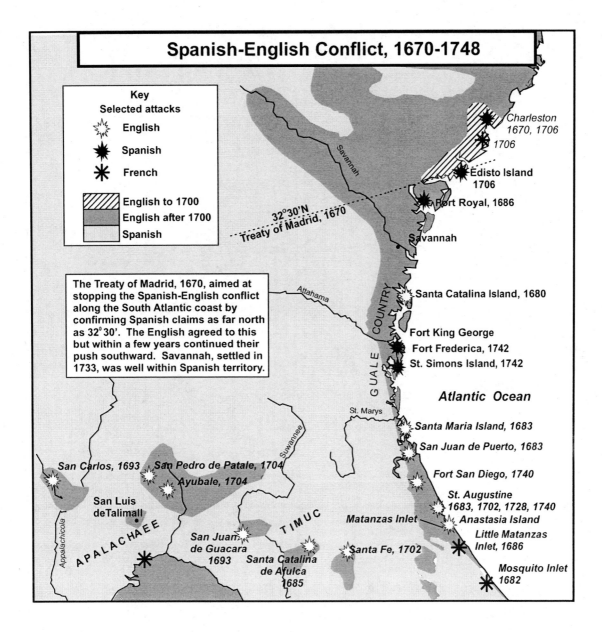

Spanish-English Conflict, 1670-1748

Key
Selected attacks
- English
- Spanish
- French

English to 1700
English after 1700
Spanish

32°30'N
Treaty of Madrid, 1670

The Treaty of Madrid, 1670, aimed at stopping the Spanish-English conflict along the South Atlantic coast by confirming Spanish claims as far north as 32°30'. The English agreed to this but within a few years continued their push southward. Savannah, settled in 1733, was well within Spanish territory.

Charleston 1670, 1706
1706
Edisto Island 1706
Fort Royal, 1686
Savannah
Santa Catalina Island, 1680
Fort King George
Fort Frederica, 1742
St. Simons Island, 1742
GUALE COUNTRY
Atlantic Ocean
St. Marys
Santa Maria Island, 1683
San Juan de Puerto, 1683
Fort San Diego, 1740
St. Augustine 1683, 1702, 1728, 1740
Anastasia Island
Little Matanzas Inlet, 1686
Matanzas Inlet
Mosquito Inlet 1682
Santa Fe, 1702
San Carlos, 1693
San Pedro de Patale, 1704
Ayubale, 1704
San Luis deTalimall
APALACHAEE
Appalachicola
San Juan de Guacara 1693
Santa Catalina de Afulca 1685
TIMUC
Suwannee
Attahama
Savannah

67. Based on the map above, how many times did the French attack the region?

A. one
B. two
C. three
D. four

68. Based on the map above, which nation was fighting the most offensive war to gain more territory?

A. the United States
B. France
C. Spain
D. England

69. Based on the map above, who made the first attack?

A. the French
B. the English
C. the Spanish
D. the Indians

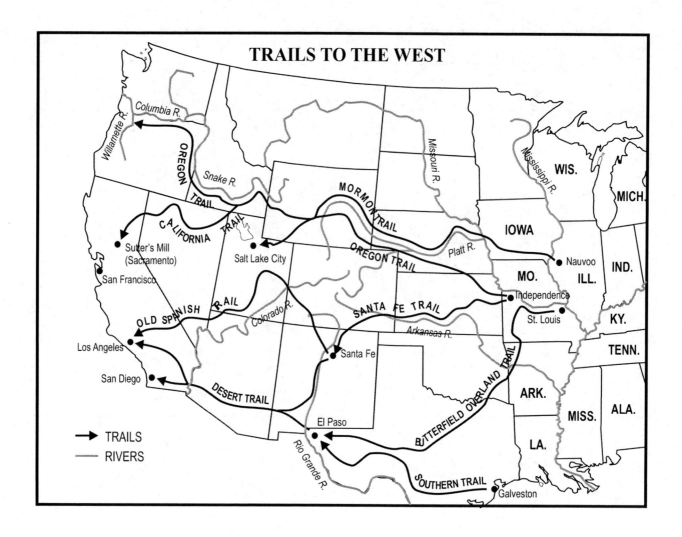

TRAILS TO THE WEST

70. Which of the following cities was a meeting place for three major trails to the West?

   A.   Independence   C.   Galveston
   B.   Los Angeles   D.   Santa Fe

71. If a settler were traveling west from Santa Fe to Los Angeles, by way of the Old Spanish Trail, the wheels of the settler's wagon would touch the soil of how many present-day states?

   A.   4   C.   6
   B.   5   D.   7

72. If a family were traveling from Independence to Sutter's Mill, which trail(s) would the family use?

   A.   the California Trail
   B.   the Mormon Trail
   C.   the Mormon Trail and the Oregon Trail
   D.   the Oregon Trail and the California Trail

288

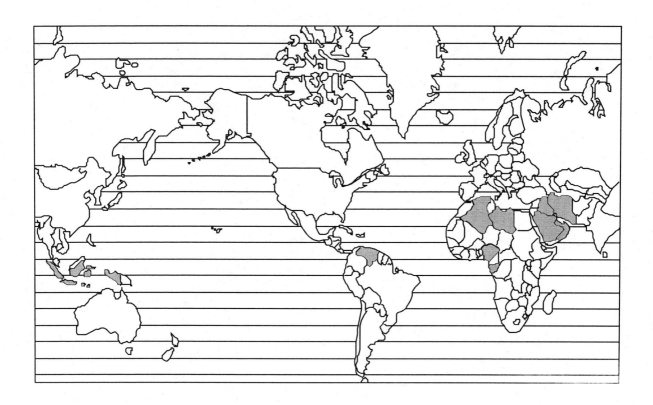

73. On the map above, the shaded countries represent the membership of

A. OPEC   C. ASEAN

B. NAFTA   D. WTO

74. According to the graph on the right, which of the following processes emits the smallest amount of methane?

A. manure management
B. enteric fermentation
C. rice cultivation
D. agricultural waste burning

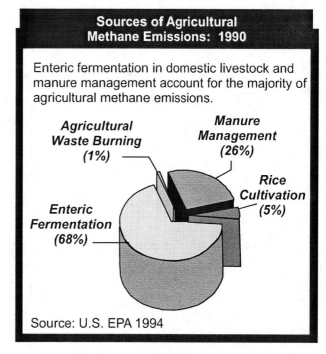

Sources of Agricultural Methane Emissions: 1990

Enteric fermentation in domestic livestock and manure management account for the majority of agricultural methane emissions.

Agricultural Waste Burning (1%)

Manure Management (26%)

Rice Cultivation (5%)

Enteric Fermentation (68%)

Source: U.S. EPA 1994

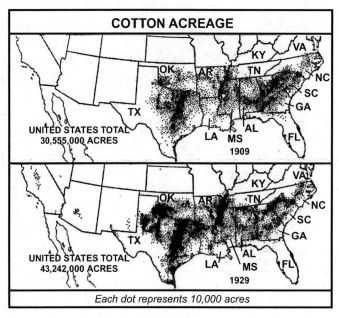

COTTON ACREAGE

UNITED STATES TOTAL
30,555,000 ACRES
1909

UNITED STATES TOTAL
43,242,000 ACRES
1929

Each dot represents 10,000 acres

75. Look carefully at the maps above. Which state has the greatest number of acres under cotton cultivation in 1929?

A. Louisiana   C. Arkansas
B. Texas   D. South Carolina

76. Compare the two maps above. Which state experienced the least increase in cotton cultivation acreage from 1909-1929?

A. Tennessee   C. Texas
B. Arkansas   D. Oklahoma

77. According to the chart on the right, which sector of the United States creates the most carbon dioxide emissions from petroleum?

A. utilities
B. transportation
C. residential
D. commercial

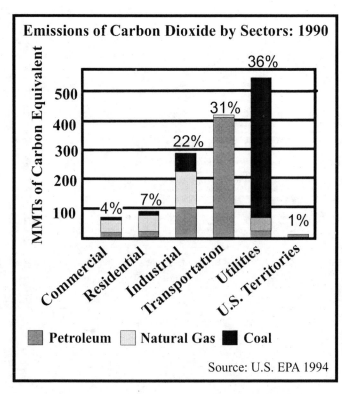

Emissions of Carbon Dioxide by Sectors: 1990

Source: U.S. EPA 1994

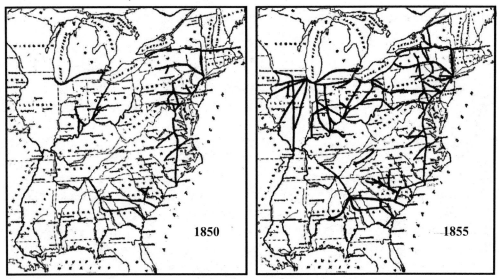

RAILWAYS IN UNITED STATES, 1850 AND 1855.

78. Compare the two maps above. Which region gained the most railroad lines over the course of these five years?

A. the Midwest
B. New England
C. the Southeast
D. the Southwest

Read the following passage. Then answer the questions 79 and 80.

During the 1830s, fur trading reached its golden age in the unsettled West. However, it was a time of great danger. Competing fur companies, potentially hostile Native Americans, and the dangers of nature awaited "mountain men" at every turn. One of the legends from that time tells of Scott, a fur trapper, who got sick on a company expedition. While two of his comrades were carrying him, they became separated from the main group. The main group had established a meeting point in case of separation. When the three arrived there, the company had already left. Since Scott could not walk, his friends left him. They were out of supplies and had no weapons for food or protection. They overtook the main group after several days of fast traveling on foot. Scott was found dead when the company returned the following year.

79. Which of the following is the most logical solution to prevent similar occurrences later?

A. avoid the hostile Native American tribes in the area
B. establish forts or outposts within a day's journey of each other
C. ban all fur trapping in wilderness areas
D. create animal farms where the animals can be raised for fur

80. Based on the above story, which of the following actions would have most likely prevented Scott from dying in the wilderness?

A. Scott's friends provide him with a gun for protection before they leave.
B. Scott brings abundant food supplies with him.
C. Scott's friends make sure they don't get separated from the main group.
D. Scott and his friends meet the company at a different location.

Read the following passage and then answer questions 81 and 82.

After the Blast

At first glance, the beach at Bikini Atoll, a small island in the Pacific Ocean, looks like a tropical paradise. But in truth the land and water share a poisoned past, from the era when 23 atomic tests were conducted at Bikini Atoll.

In 1946, all 167 Bikini residents were relocated. Then 42,000 people and 90 vessels used the island for target practice. This was to be the first peace-time testing of nuclear weapons.

Testing continued until November 1958. The most damaging explosion came on March 1, 1954, when a 15 megaton hydrogen bomb, code-named Bravo, was exploded on the island. This bomb was the most powerful ever exploded by the United States. It was a thousand times more powerful than the bomb dropped on Hiroshima. Not only did it open a mile-wide crater on Bikini Atoll, but it also vaporized one small island and part of another.

To this day, the soil on Bikini contains too much radioactive cesium to permit the Bikinians, now numbering 2,025, to return from their exile.

81. Why was an atomic bomb exploded on Bikini Island in 1954?

    A. Few people lived on the island, so they were easily moved to a new location.
    B. Nuclear bombs were being tested for use as weapons.
    C. The soil was already radioactive from earlier blasts.
    D. The United States was preparing to drop a bomb on Hiroshima.

82. Which of the following groups of citizens would have most strongly objected to this testing in 1954?

    A.   sailors on Bikini
    B.   Bikini residents
    C.   environmentalists
    D.   farmers in the Midwest part of the United States

83. Which of the following is a reason why the two-party system prevails in the United States?

    A.   The checks and balances of the Constitution make cooperation between the legislative and executive branches of government necessary.
    B.   A two-party system allows people with differing views to join together and express their beliefs.
    C.   There are only two possible different approaches to government.
    D.   There are not enough people to allow another party to compete.

84. A group of citizens gathers together in a state park to attend a wedding officiated by an Episcopal priest. Which two freedoms apply in this situation?

    A.   the freedom of the press and freedom of religion
    B.   the freedom of assembly and freedom of religion
    C.   the right to bear arms and freedom of assembly
    D.   the right to a speedy trial and the right to bear arms.

Use the political cartoon below to answer question 85.

MRS. NORTH AND HER ATTORNEY.

MRS. NORTH. "YOU SEE, MR. LINCOLN, WE HAVE FAILED UTTERLY IN OUR COURSE OF ACTION; I WANT PEACE, AND SO, IF YOU CANNOT EFFECT AN AMICABLE ARRANGEMENT, I MUST PUT THE CASE INTO OTHER HANDS."

85. The cartoon above implies which of the following?

  A. Abraham Lincoln's health is failing, so he will probably leave the White House and return to his law practice.
  B. Mrs. North is a friend of Lincoln's, and she needs his legal advice regarding the death of a family member.
  C. People in the North are demanding victory in the Civil War at any cost.
  D. Lincoln's candidacy for a second term as president is weak because people are tired of war and Lincoln's policies.

86. The Supreme Court interprets the law as written in the Constitution. What can Congress do if it disagrees with a Supreme Court Decision?

  A. Congress can dismiss the Supreme Court justices.
  B. Congress can propose an amendment to the Constitution to be ratified by the states.
  C. Congress can reduce the powers of the Supreme Court.
  D. Congress can create new laws which supersede the Constitution.

87. Under the United States Constitution, which branch of the government makes the laws?

  A. Executive   C. Military
  B. Legislative   D. Judicial

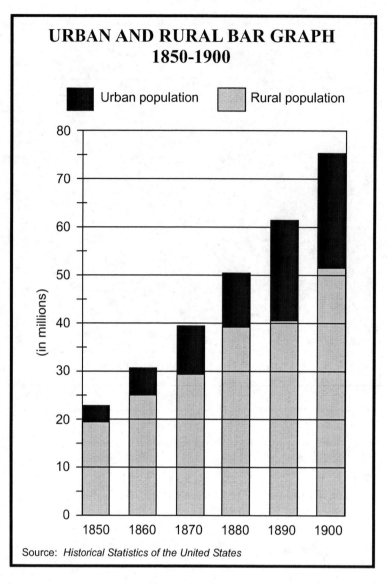

**URBAN AND RURAL BAR GRAPH
1850-1900**

■ Urban population   ▨ Rural population

(in millions)

Source: *Historical Statistics of the United States*

88. In 1900, about how many people lived in cities?

    A. 30 million   C. 23 million
    B. 75 million   D. 52 million

89. About how much did the urban population grow from 1880 to 1890?

    A. 10 million   C. 50 million
    B. 20 million   D. 60 million

90. About how many more people lived in rural areas in 1900 as compared to 1890?

    A. 75 million   C. 11 million
    B. 4 million   D. 62 million

INDEX

Bloody Mary-18
Bloody Sunday-187
blue collar-122
Blues (music)-135
Board of Education of Topeka, Kansas-184
bodies of water-218,223,*map* 220
Boleyn, Anne-17
Bolívar, Simón-56,57
boll weevil-112
Bologna Academy of Sciences-51
Bolshevik(s)-131,137, 151,153
    Party-151
bombers-156
Bonaparte, Napoleon-55-56,67, 128
Bonhomme Richard-45
booms-144
Booth, John Wilkes-99
bootleggers-138
Borromeo, Charles-18
Bosnia-128
Boston (Massachusetts)-37,39,40, 44,79,116
Boston
    Customs House-40
    Harbor-40
    Massacre-40,43,45, 239, *timeline* 242
    Tea Party-40,43
Boxer Rebellion-126
boycott(s)-39,40,185, 174,182,184,189,190
Boyle, Robert-51
Brazil-29,201,238
Breckinridge, John-90
bribery-120
bridges-25
Britain-(*also see* Great Britain) 38,41,55,56,64,74,75,80,82, 130,138,155,157,162,169,173,17 7,184,221
British-31,183
    colonies-184
    government-239
    North American colonies-30
    oil industry-178
    Parliament-39,40
    rule-183
brokers-139
Brooke, Edward W.-191
Brooklyn, New York-191
Brown vs. Board of Education of Topeka-184-185,213
Brown, John-89
Brown, Linda-184
Bryan, William Jennings-112
Buddhism-217
Buffalo-107-109
Buffalo, New York-70

Buffalo Soldiers-108
buildings-223
Bulgaria-175
bull market-139
Bull Run-91
bullets-129
Bunche, Ralph J.-190
bureaucracy-125
burgess(es)-34,40
Burgoyne, British General-44
Burma-183
Butler, Senator Andrew-88
Byzantine emperors-170

C

Cabinet-208
Cabot, John-23
calculus-51
Calhoun, John C.-68,73, 74
California-25,76,77,87,107,190
Calvert, George (Lord Baltimore)-35
Calvin, John-16,17
Cambodia-183
Cambridge-41
Canada-23,38,39,45,79,80,106, 108,11,138, 163,173,200,216
    British-68
Canal Zone-126
canal(s)-69-72,86,113,126,216
Canary Islands-22
Candidate-map 130
cape-218
Cape of Good Hope-22, 27
Capitalism-149-151,154, 194
capitalist(s)-149,152,154
capitol-16
Capone, Al-138
caravel-22
cardinal directions-227
Caribbean-30,56,124-127,138,200
    islands-37,38
    Sea-218
Carmichael, Stokley-188
Carnegie, Andrew-114, 116
Carolinas-95
carpetbaggers-101
Carranza-127
cars-192
Carter, President Jimmy-240
Cartier-*timeline* 242
Carver, George Washington-122
Carver's Hybrid-122
cash and carry-156
cash crops-36
Castro, Fidel-179
casualties-164
catechism-18
Catherine of Aragon-17
Catholic Church-(also see Roman

Catholic Church) 23,217
Catholic(s)-17,35,116,137,206,216
cattle-86,107,112
    driving-107
Caucasian-153
cause-effect relationship-241
causes-241
Cavaliers-19
Celtic Sea-*map* 130
censorship-194
censured-177
Centers for Disease Control and Prevention-203
century(ies)
    13th-14
    14th-13,14,15
    15th-14,22,50
    16th-13,15,16,26,50,149
    17th-13,26,30,149
    18th-26,52,69
    19th-56,79,81,106, 114,120,128
    20th-124,184,191
Centurion-map 130
Ceylon-183
Chamberlain, Neville-155,156
chancellor-153
Chancellorsville (Battle)-94
Charles I (King of England)-18,19
Charles II (King of England)-19,35
Charleston (South Carolina)-37
charter-29
Chattanooga (Battle)-95
Chavez, Ceasar-189
checks and balances-208
chemistry-51
Cherokee-25,68,74,*map* 109, *timeline* 242
    Nation-211
Cheyenne (Native American tribe)-108
Chiang Kai-shek-174-176
Chicago (Illinois)-106, 137,186, 188
Chickamauga-95
Chickasaw(s) (Native American tribe)-25,74,*map* 109
chief-150
Chief Joseph-108
Chief Justice-65
children-136,140,141, 149
Chile-56,202
China-22,23,31,124,126,155,157, 168,174,175,177,198,202,218, 221

Chinese-117,155

62
constitutionalism-62,207
consul-55
Consulate-54
consumable goods-146
consumers-143
consumption-150
containment-171,172
continent(s)-110,136,218
Convention-55
    of 1818-72,76
Cooper, James Fenimore-82
Copernican theory-51
Copernicus, Nicolas-14
copper-27,112
CORE-*see Congress of Racial Equality*
corn-28
Cornwallis, General-45,46
corruption-102,120
Cortez, Hernando-27
cosmetics-112
cotton-27,69,70,86,98, 112
    gin-70
    mill-69
Council of Trent-17,51
counterculture-192-194
    movement-194
cowboys-107
creationists-138
credit-146
Cree-25
Creek(s)-25,68,74
    map 109
crime-190
Cromwell, Oliver-19
Crosby, Bing-193
Crow-25
crude oil-222
Cuba-38,125,179,218
Cuban Missile Crisis-179
cultural
    diffusion-28
    features-216
    geography-216
    resources-223
culture area-24
Cumberland-70
Cunard-*map* 130
Custer, General-108
Cyprus-183
czar-151
Czechoslovakia-132,155,156,162,
    172,175

D

da Gama, Vasco-22, *map* 23
da Verrazano, Givovani-30
da Vinci, Leonardo-15,16
Dakota(s)-107,108,140

Daladier, Edouard-155
dams-216,223
    hydroelectric-141
Dark Ages-13
Darwin-114,128,138
Daughters of Liberty-39
David-15
Davis, Benjamin O., Sr.-190
Davis, Jefferson-90,101
Dawes Act-108
D-Day-161
de Cervantes Saavedra, Miguel-15
de Champlain, Samuel-30
de facto-116
de Klerk, F. W.-184
de la Salle, Robert-30,*timeline* 242
de Lafayette, Marquis-46
de Soto, Hernando-*timeline* 242
death camps-164
debt(s)-146,151
Declaration of Independence-42-
    44,46,59,63,80,206,*timeline* 242
Declaration of the Rights of Man
    and of the Citizen-53
Deep South-191
Deere, John-110
Defender of the Faith-17
deficit spending-145
Deism-52
Delaware River-44
Delaware-36
democracies-155
democracy-34-36,45,57,79,88,95,
    128,131,137,150,152,153,157,
    188
Democrat(s)-74,87,90,89,100,103,
    209
    Eastern-112
    Southern-99,112
    Western-112
democratic-16,18,20,46,52,54,55,
    73,131,151-153,161,189
    national convention-90,189
    Party-90,112,140,209
    republic-206
demonstrations-194
Denmark-156,173
Denver (Colorado)-106
Department of Justice-213
department store-114
depot, train-107
depression-60,102,112,140,154
    Great-139-143,145,150,152,
    153,156,158,189,192,*timeline*
    242
Descartes, René-51
desegregation-159,184-186
    (military)-184
desert-25,217,219
deserters-67

Detroit-159,190
Dewey, Commodore-125
Diaries of William Byrd-240
Dias, Bartolomeu-22
Dickenson, Emily-82
dictator-152,153
directions-241
discount rate-144
discrimination-137,159,160,165,
    186,190,191
disease(s)-28,51,126
    sexually transmitted-194
    world-203
disenfranchisement-122
Disney, Walt-142
dissections-15
    animal-14
    human-14
distance-231
distribution-150
Divine Comedy-14
divine right of kings-52
Dix, Dorthea-79
Doctrine of Nullification-73,87
Dollar Diplomacy-127
domino theory-175
Don Quixote-15
double burden-192
Douglas, Stephen A.-87,89,90
Douglass, Frederick-80
"doves"-194
draft-132,153
drafted-96
Drake, Sir Francis-30,31,*map* 23
Dred Scott Decision-88,89
drug(s)-190,193,194
Du Bois, W. E. B.-122
due process-212
Duma-131
durable goods-146
Dust Bowl-140
Dutch East India Company-29
Dutch-30,37,183
    Parliament-29
    Reformed Church-36
Dylan, Bob-194

E

Eagle Forum-191
Earl of Lathom-*map* 130
Earth-14,51
Earth Day-198
East Asia-197,200
East Coast-68
East-22,23,106,107,110,113
Easter-216
Eastern Front (WWI)-131

economic

Limited Test Band Treaty-198

Lincoln, Abraham-89,90
  President-94,96,97,99
  timeline 242
Lincoln Memorial-186
line graphs-247
Line of Demarcation-23
Lippmann, Walter-171
literacy test-187
literature-14,15,16,82
  humanist-14
  Renaissance-14
Little Richard-193
Little Rock Central High School-185
Little, Malcolm-188 (*also see* Malcolm X)
Livingston, Robert-42
Locke, John-19,42,206
Lockerbie, Scotland-201
locomotive-70
London-157
Lonely Crowd, The-193
longitude-229,230
Lookout Mountain-95
Lord Baltimore-35
lord(s)-149,150
Los Angeles (California)-160,187
Lost Colony-30,*timeline* 242
Lost Generation-135
lottery-79
Louis XIV-30
Louis XVI, King-53,55
Louisiana Purchase-67,72
Louisiana-30,38,56,67,72,90,103
lower courts-213
Loyalist(s)-43,44,46
Ludlow Amendment-156
Lusitania-130,*map* 130
Luther, Martin-16-18
Lutheran(s)-16,17,35
Luxembourg-173,190
lynching(s)-102,122,137

M
MacArthur, General Douglas-140,163,173
Machiavelli, Niccoló-14
machine guns-129,140
machine(s)-69,70
Madison, James-62,63,68,206
Magellan, Ferdinand -23,*map* 23
Magna Carta-206
Mahan, Admiral Alfred-124
main idea-238
Maine, battleship-125
Maine-87
Major League Baseball-190
majority vote-208,210

malaria-126
Malaysia-183,201
Malcolm X-188,189
malnutrition-140
Manchuria-132,153,155,163
Mandan-25
Mandela, Nelson-184
Manhattan Project-163,164
Manhattan-30
manifest destiny-76,77,170
Manila-125
Mann, Horace-79,120
manufacturing-69,149
Mao Tse-tung-(*See* Mao Zedong)
Mao Zedong-174,176,177
map-227,230
  key-233
  scale-231
marble-112
Marbury vs. Madison-65,213
March on Washington-186
marches-191,194
Marconi, Guglielmo-113
Marines (US)-127,159,163
market economy-150
market price-143
Marlowe, Christopher-15
Marshall Plan-172,176
Marshall, Chief Justice John-64
Marshall, George C.-160,172,174
Marshall, James W.-77
Marshall, Thurgood-191
marshals, United States-186
martial law-96,102
Marx, Karl-149,151,154
Mary I (Queen of England)-18
Mary (mother of Jesus)-15
Maryland-35,36,70,80,90,94,96,206,*timeline* 242
Massachusetts-30,34-36,40-42,44,46,60,74,79,99,138,206
Massachusetts Board of Education-120
Massacio-15
materialism-193
materialist-154
materialistic-135
mathematics-51
Matthew-23
Maya(s)-25-27
Mayflower Compact-34,36
Mayflower-34
McCarthy Era-176
McCarthy, Joseph R.-177
McCarthyism-177
McClellan, General George B.-94
McKinley, William-112
McVeigh, Timothy-201
measles-28
Mecca, Saudi Arabia-188

mechanization-111
medicine-51
medieval-13
meditation-193
Mediterranean-13,161,162,219
  Sea-160,179,183,218
Memphis, Tennessee-100,188
Mennonites-43
mercantilism-26,27,50
mercenaries-41,44
merchants-22,37,38,68,75
Mercury Capsule-178
mergers-106
Mexican Americans-160,189
Mexican Cession-*map* 78
Mexican War-76,77,79,131
Mexico City-77
Mexico-28,75-77,87,108,127,130,131,139,200,216
Michelangelo-15,16
Michigan-86
microscope-51
Middle Ages-13,149
Middle Colonies-36
Middle East-124,178,179,200,201,216,217,222
Middle Passage-34
Midway-163
Midwest-110,111
militarism-194
  German-162
militaristic-152
military dictatorships-169
military-129,150,153,155,211
  French-54
  United States-127
militia-41
militiamen-41
militias-39
Million Man March-190
millionaires-114
mineral resources-179,223
minimum wage-141
Minnesota Territory-*map* 88
Minnesota-86
minority(ies)-102,137,189,210
minutemen-41,44,45
minutes
  latitude-230
  longitude-230
Miry Creek-240
missionaries-75
missionary diplomacy-127
Mississippi River-45,70,91,94,110,*map* 220
Mississippi riverboat-70
Mississippi-30,38,72,90,94,101,103,135,186,*timeline* 242

Missouri Compromise-87,89,

planets-14
plantation(s)-36,56,125
  system-86
plants-216,223
Plateaus-218
Plato-16,50
Pledge of Allegiance to the Flag-192
Plessy vs. Ferguson-122,185
PLO-(*see* Palestine Liberation Organization)
plow, steel-110
Plymouth-*timeline* 242
  Colony-30,35
Poe, Edgar Allen-82
poison gas-129
Poland-132,156,161,162,175
political
  map-233
  party(ies)-64,209
politics-14,18,192
Polk, James K.-76
poll tax-187
pollution-197,198
Polo, Marco-22
polyphony-15
Ponce de Leon, Juan-28
Poor People's Campaign-188
pop art-193
Pope-16,17,23
  Leo X-16
  Paul III-17
popular sovereignty-87,89,90,206
population
  growth-203,*map* 115
  size-223
Populist Party-112
porcelain-22,31
Portugal-22,23,27-29,31,173,238
Portuguese-22,238
  (language)-216
post office-59,60
post-war-165
potatoes-28
Potomac River-140
Potsdam Conference-163
Potsdam Declaration-163
poverty-136,150,152,187
Powell, John Wesley-106
prayer-16
preamble (Constitution)-208,214
prejudice-117
premier, French-155
Presbyterian church-17
Presbyterians-35
President

(of the United States)-62,63,65,
73,99,101,102,207,208,210,211,
212
(of the Confederacy)-101
presidential cabinet-211
Presley, Elvis-193
Preston, Thomas (Captain)-239
priests, Catholic-36
primary source-239
prime meridian-229
Prime Minister
  British-155,156,160,162
  (of Iran)-178
  (of Japan)-157,163
Prince, The-14
Princeton-36,44
printing press-14
prisoners of war-164
private enterprise-151
privateers-68
Proclamation of 1763-39
Proclamation of Neutrality-63
producers-143
production-150
Progressive Movement-120
progressive tax-145
progressive-121
Progressives-120
Progressivism-120
Prohibition-121,138
Prohibitory Act-41
Promontory, Utah-106
propaganda-129,131
proprietors-35
pro-slavery-81,87,88
prostitutes-163
protectionism-146
Protestant(s)-16-18,27,35,53,81,
116,137,138,154
  Reformation-16,17
Protestantism-17
protests-189
Prussia-53,128
public education-120
Pueblo (Native American tribe)-25,
map 109
Puerto Rico-125
Punitive Force Acts of 1870 and
1871-102
Pure Food and Drug Act-121
Puritans-19,30,34-36,206
pyramids-25

Q

Quaker(s)-35,36,43,80
Quebec-30

R

racial
  inequality-189
  segregation-185,213
racism-117,159
racist(s)-153,187
radar-157
radiation-163
Radical Reconstruction-102
Radicals-99,101,102
radio-113,136,143
railroad(s)-72,98,102,106,107,
110,111,113,116,120,121,127,
136,150,161
railways-86
Raleigh, North Carolina-185
Raleigh, Sir Walter-30
rallies-191
ranchers-107
ranching, cattle-107
Raphael-16
ratification-208
ratified-59,62
rationing-159
"Raven, The"-82
raw materials-
27,34,37,69,70,124,164
Reagan administration-199
reality-14
rebellion-60
recession(s)-97,129,144
reconnaissance-129
Reconstruction Act-100,101
Reconstruction-99-103,106,122,
191
Red Army-162,170,176
Red Cross-159
Red Scare, The-137
Red Sea-179,218
reforms-186
refrigeration-110
region-216
Reign of Terror-54,55
religion-14,18,154,190,192
Renaissance,14-16
reparation(s)-151,162
representation-60
reprieve- (*See* pardon)
republic-19,53,55,79,82
Republic of South Africa-184
Republic of Texas-75
Republican(s)-73,88,89,98-100,
101,103,107,120,121,140,191,
209
Republican Party-73,87,90,121,209
reservations-67,108,109,142
reserve requirement-144
resources-222,223
Restoration-19
Revels, Hiram R.-101
Revere, Paul-41,44

Revolution(s)-19,47,72,137,151,
182,188
    American-52,53,170
    commercial-50
    French-52,53,55,56,63
    industrial-55,69,113
    scientific-50
revolutionaries-182

Revolutionary War (US)-46,54,
69,81,91,*timeline* 242
Rhineland-155
Rhode Island-36,45,61,69
rice-36,217
Richmond-90
Riesman, David-193
rifles-70
right to vote-102
rights-214
Río Grande River-75,76,127
Río Treaty-172
rioting-160,186,187
riots-139,183,186-188
    (race)-187
ripeness test-213
river-219
Roanoke Island-30
Roanoke-*timeline* 242
Roaring Twenties-135
robber barons-114,116
Robespierre, Maximillien-54
Robinson, Jackie-190
rock and roll-193
rock music-193,194
Rockefeller, John D.-114,116,137
Rocket-70
rockets, Soviet-199
rocks-216
Rocky Mountain(s) -72,106,107,
216,*map* 220
Roe vs. Wade-192
Roman Catechism-18
Roman(s)-13,14,152
    Catholic(s)-16,17,19,23,27,87
    Catholic Church-13,14,16-18,152
    Empire-217
Rome, Italy-15
Rome-16,17,160
Rome-Berlin-Tokyo Axis-155
Rommel, General-160
Rookie of the Year-190
Roosevelt (President Franklin D.)-
140-143,157,158,160,162,164,
241
Roosevelt, Eleanor-142
Roosevelt, Theodore
    Lieutenant Colonel -124-126
    President-121
Roosevelt's Corollary-126
Rosenberg, Julius and Ethel-176

Rosie the Riveter-159
Rough Riders-125
Roundheads-19
Rousseau, Jacques-52,206
Royal Air Force-157
rubber-159
rule of birth-214
rule of law-212
rule of soil-214
rum-37
Russell, Bill-191
Russia-55,126,128,129,131,137,
150,151,153,154
Russian Communist Party-151
Russians-151,217

S

Sacajawea-67
Sacco and Vanzetti Trial-138
Sacco, Nicola-138
Sacramento-77
Saint-Domingue-30
Saipan-163
Salerno-160
Salish (Native American tribe)-25
SALT-(*see* Strategic Arms
    Limitation Talks)
Sampson, Deborah-46
San Antonio (Texas)-75
San Francisco (California)-
162,168,193
San Juan Hill (Battle of)-125
San Martín, José de-56
sanctions-155,202
sans-culottes-54
Santa Anna, General Antonio-75,77
Santa Maria-22
Saratoga, Battle of-44,46
Sardinia-128
Savannah (Georgia)-44,95
savannas -218
scalawags-101
scapegoating-153
Scarlet Letter, The-82
Schlafly, Phyllis-191
scholars-182
School of Athens, The-16
School of the Americas (SOA)-202
science(s)-13-15,51,52
scientific method-50
SCLC-(*see* Southern Christian
    Leadership Conference)
Scopes Trial-138
Scopes, John-138
Scotland-17,19,201
Scott, Dred-88
Scott, General Winfield-77
scrap metal-157
Scriptures-14
sculpture, classical-15

Sea of Japan-218,*map* 220
sea-217,218
seafood-221
SEATO-(*see* South East Asia
    Treaty Organization)
secede-73,91
seceded-90,99
seceding-69
secession-87,90,99
Second Bank of the United States-
69
Second Continental Congress-41,
47,59
Second Great Awakening-78
Second World War-168
Second World-182
secondary source-239
Secretary of
    Agriculture-211
    Commerce-211
    Defense-211
    Education-211
    Energy-211
    Health and Human Resources-
211
    Housing and Urban
    Development-211
    Labor-211
    State-63,72,126,211
    Interior-211
    Veterans Affairs-211
    War-101
secular-15
Security Council (of the United
    Nations)-168,174
segregated-159
segregation(s)-116,122,184-186,
189,190
self-determination-128,182
self-preservation-14
self-reliance-190
self-sufficient-149
self-sufficiency-152,188
Selma, Alabama-187
seminaries-18
Seminole(s)(Native American
    tribe)-25,74
semi-tropical-25
Senate-61,62,75,76,87-89,101,102,
140,191,208-210
senator-69,101,191
Seneca Falls Convention-80,
    timeline 242
Separation of Powers-207
sequence of events-241
Serapis-45
Serbia-128,132
serf-149
Servicemen's Readjustment Act of
1944-165

settlements-222
Seven Years' War-53
Shah of Iran-178
Shakespeare, William-15,18,194
sharecroppers-98
Shawnee (Native American tribe)-25
Shays, Daniel-60
Shays' Rebellion-60
Shepard, Alan B.-178
Sherman Antitrust Act-120,121
Sherman Silver Purchase Act-111
Sherman, General-94,95,97
Sherman, Roger-42
Sherman's March-*map* 95
Shiloh-94
Shoshone (Native American tribe)-25,67,*map* 109
Showa-153
shuttle program-199
Sicily-160
Sierra Club-197
    Legal Defense Fund-197
silk-22,31
silver-26,27,29,31,50,74,111,112
Sinatra, Frank-193
Sinclair, Upton-120
Sioux (Native American tribe)-108,109,*map* 109
Sioux Wars, The-108
Sistine Chapel-15
sit-ins-185,189,194
Sitting Bull-109
Sitzkrieg-156
skyscrapers-110,114
Slater, Samuel-69
slave(s)-31,34,36,37,45,56,61,77,80,81,87-89,96-98,101,103,122
    state(s)-75,76,87
    trade-46
slavery-45,46,73,77,79,80,86,87,89,90,97-99,*map* 88
Slavs-163
Slidell, John-76
small pox-28
Smith, Adam-149
Smoot-Hawley Tariff-152
SNCC-(see Student Nonviolent Coordinating Committee)
Snow White and The Seven Dwarfs-142
SOA-(*see* School of the Americas)
soap-112
Social Contract Theory-206
Social Contract, The-52
social criticism-193
Social Darwinism-114,128
social protest-184
Social Security Act (SSA)-141
Social Studies Graduation Test-

238,240
Society of Friends-35
society-150
soil-216
Solicitor General-213
songs-15
sonnets-14
Sons of Liberty-39,40,45
South-44,45,56,68-70,73,74,79,86,87,89-91,95-99,100-103,106,111-113,122,137,141,142,159,185-187,191,193
South Africa-184,202,217
South America-23,24,111,200,218,221,238
    map 220,227
South American-56,57,72
South Asia-216,217
South Carolina-36,46,68,73,74,87,90,102,103
South China Sea-218
South Dakota-189
South East Asia Treaty Organization (SEATO)-175,176
South Korea-174-176
South Vietnam-183
southeast (SE)-227
Southeast Asia-175,217
Southern Christian Leadership Conference (SCLC)-185,187,190
Southern Democrats-99,112
Southern Farmers' Alliance-111
Southern Hemisphere-229
Southern Pacific Roadroad-77
Southerners-81,86,89,98,99,101-103
southwest (SW)-227
Southwest-87,160
sovereignty-60
Soviet(s)-162-164,177
Soviet nuclear missiles -179
Soviet Policy of Peaceful Coexistence-177
Soviet Union-161,163,164,168-179,182,198,199,202,241
    timeline 242
soybeans-122
space
    exploration-199
    program-178
    race-177,178
    technology-199
Spain-15,17,18,22,23,27-29,31,38,46,56,60,68,72,125,238
Spanish
    Armada-18,29
    Inquisition-17
    (language)-216
Spanish-American War-125,*timeline* 242

speakeasies-138
special interest groups-210
species loss-197
speculation-50,102
speculators-60
Spenser, Edmund-15
spices-22
Spirit of Laws, The-206
spoils system-73,120
Spokane-25,*map* 109
Springfield-60
Sputnik-178,199
    I-177,178
    II-177
Square Deal, The-121
Sri Lanka-183
St. Augustine-28,*timeline* 242
St. Clair, Sally-46
St. Lawrence Seaway-*timeline* 242
St. Louis-67,106
    East-137
St. Peter's Basilica-15,16
St. Petersburg-151
Stalin, Joseph-153,154,157,160-164,171,177
Stamp Act-39,43,46,*timeline* 242
Standard Oil Company-116
Stanton, Elizabeth Cady-80,81
Stanton, Secretary of War-96
Star Spangled Banner, The-68
Star Wars-199
starvation-150
state branch (court system)-212
State Courts-213
State Department-177
steam engine-70
steel-110,116,120
Steinam, Gloria-191
Stephenson, George-70
steppe-219
Stevens, Thaddeus-102
Stevens, Uriah-119
stock market-112,139
    crash-139,146,*timeline* 242
stock(s)-139,145,146
stockholders-34,145
Stokes, Carl B.-191
Stop ERA-191
Stowe, Harriet Beecher-80
Strait of Gibraltar-219,*map* 220
Strait of Suez-219
strait-219
Strategic Arms Limitation Talks (SALT)-199
Strategic Defense Initiative-199
strike(s)-119,182,184
Strong, Josiah-124
Stuart monarchs-18
Student Nonviolent Coordinating Committee (SNCC)-109,185,